Introducing Tibetan Buddh

'Geoffrey Samuel provides a welcome introduction to Tibetan Buddhism and the religious history of Tibet. Concise, lucid, and authoritative, this is one of the best and most useful introductions available to date. It will no doubt become an indispensable reference for students.'

Bryan J. Cuevas, *Florida State University, USA*

'This book highlights the practical dimensions of the religious culture of Tibet. Samuel provides a current and accessible guide to the roles Buddhism plays in the lives of Tibetan people, as identities of place and religion continue to be negotiated as Tibetan Buddhism is defined in the contemporary world.'

Douglas S. Duckworth, *East Tennessee State University, USA*

This lively introduction is the ideal starting point for students wishing to undertake a comprehensive study of Tibetan religion. It covers the development and influence of Tibetan Buddhism and the key schools and traditions, including Bon. Geoffrey Samuel helps students get to grips with a complex set of beliefs and practices and provides a clear sense of the historical, cultural and textual background. Important contemporary issues such as gender, national identity and Tibetan Buddhism in the world today are also addressed. Illustrated throughout, the book includes a chronology, glossary, pronunciation guide, summaries, discussion questions and suggestions for further reading that will aid understanding and revision.

Geoffrey Samuel is a Professor based in the School of History, Archaeology and Religion at Cardiff University, UK, and an experienced teacher of Tibetan religion.

W[illegible]

Edit[illegible] Damien[illegible]harles S. Prebish

This exciting series introduces students to the major world religious traditions. Each religion is explored in a lively and clear fashion by experienced teachers and leading scholars in the field of world religions. Up-to-date scholarship is presented in a student-friendly fashion, covering history, core beliefs, sacred texts, key figures, religious practice and culture, and key contemporary issues. To aid learning and revision, each text includes illustrations, summaries, explanations of key terms, and further reading.

Introducing Buddhism, second edition
Damien Keown and Charles S. Prebish

Introducing American Religion
Charles Lippy

Introducing Chinese Religions
Mario Poceski

Introducing Islam
William Shepard

Introducing Daoism
Livia Kohn

Introducing Judaism
Eliezer Segal

Introducing Christianity
James R. Adair

Introducing Japanese Religions
Robert Ellwood

Introducing Hinduism
Hillary Rodrigues

Introducing Tibetan Buddhism
Geoffrey Samuel

Introducing Tibetan Buddhism

Geoffrey Samuel

First published 2012
by Routledge
2 Park Square, Milton Park, Abingdon, Oxon OX14 4RN

Simultaneously published in the USA and Canada
by Routledge
711 Third Avenue, New York, NY 10017

Routledge is an imprint of the Taylor & Francis Group, an informa business

British Library Cataloguing in Publication Data
A catalogue record for this book is available from the British Library

Library of Congress Cataloging in Publication Data
Samuel, Geoffrey.
Introducing Tibetan Buddhism / Geoffrey Samuel.
p. cm. – (World religions series)
1. Buddhism–China–Tibet Autonomous Region. 2. Bon (Tibetan religion)
I. Title.
BQ7604.S27 2012 294.3'923–dc23
2011041256

ISBN: 978–0–415–45664–7 (hbk)
ISBN: 978–0–415–45665–4 (pbk)

Typeset in Jenson Pro and Tahoma
by Bookcraft Ltd, Stroud, Gloucestershire

Contents

List of Illustrations

List of Figures

List of Tables

Chronology

c.1900 BCE	Legendary visit of the Bonpo founding figure, Tönpa Shenrab, to Tibet.
c.400 BCE	Approximate date of the *parinirvāṇa* (death) of the historical Buddha Śākyamuni.
c.250 BCE	Buddhism receives state patronage by the Mauryan emperor Aśoka and is established throughout much of present-day India, Pakistan and Bangladesh.
5th century CE	Approximate date of semi-legendary king Lhato Tori of the Yarlung dynasty in whose time Buddhist scriptures, including the Kārandavyūha Sūtra, are said to have first reached Tibet.
c.629–649 CE	Reign of Songtsen Gampo, king of the Yarlung dynasty, the first of the three 'Dharma Kings', becomes first ruler over a united Tibet. He is said to have introduced Buddhism to Tibet, to have married princesses from the then Buddhist countries of Nepal and China, to have established the capital at Lhasa and to have established the Jokang and Ramoche temples there. These events began the *Chidar* or 'earlier propagation' of Buddhism in Tibet. Shangshung may have been incorporated into the Tibetan empire during his reign, or in that of Trisong Detsen.
c.755–c.797/804 CE	Reign of Trisong Detsen, the second of the three 'Dharma Kings'. He is said to have invited Padmasambhava, Śāntaraksita, Vimalamitra and other Buddhist teachers to Tibet, to have established the first Tibetan monastery at Samye in Central Tibet, to have become a disciple of Padmasambhava, and to have decided at a Council at Samye or Lhasa for the Indian rather than the Chinese version of Buddhism to be practised in Tibet.
c.775–779 CE	Approximate date for the establishment of Samye, first Tibetan monastery, by Padmasambhava and Śāntaraksita under the patronage of Trisong Detsen.
c.815–c.838 CE	Reign of Ralpachen (Tritsuk Detsen), the third of the three 'Dharma Kings'.
c.838–c.841 CE	Reign of Langdarma. Buddhist tradition describes him as a supporter of the Bon religion and persecutor of Buddhism. He is said to have been killed by the monk Lhalung Pelgi Dorjé, bringing the Tibetan empire and the *Chidar* to an end.
Late 9th and early 10th centuries	Contact with Buddhism in India and Nepal was largely lost during this period, and Buddhism continued primarily as a tradition of hereditary village lamas and Tantric ritualists.
Late 10th century	Reign of Yeshe Ö, king of Guge and Purang in Western Tibet. He criticized the practices of Tibetan Buddhists of his time, and patronized the translator Rinchen Sangpo and other Tibetan scholars who re-established contact with India, beginning the *Ngadar* or 'later propagation' of Buddhism in Tibet.

c.1037–c.1057	Reign of Changchub Ö, king of Guge and Purang. He further patronized Buddhist scholarship, and invited the Indian scholar Atiśa (Dīpaṁkaraśrījñāna) to Tibet.
1042	Atiśa came to Tibet and founded the monastery of Nyetang near Lhasa with the support of his wealthy lay follower Dromtön. This was the origin of the Kadampa tradition of Tibetan Buddhism. Atiśa died in 1054.
11th century	Drokmi (993–1077), Marpa (?1012–1093), and other Tibetan scholars visited India to acquire Tantric and other teachings and bring them to Tibet. This led to the establishment of the 'New Tantra' (Sarmapa) traditions in Tibet.
1073	Foundation of the monastery of Sakya in West-Central Tibet by Kön Konchok Gyelpo of the hereditary lama family of Kön. His successors acquired the Tantric practices of Virūpa from Drokmi; these became the basis of the Sakyapa tradition of Tibetan Buddhism.
12th century	Marpa's student Milarepa (1040–1123) established the tradition of Nāropa in Tibet; the students of his disciple Gampopa (1079–1153) founded the monastic centres (Densa Til 1158; Drigung 1179; Ralung 1180; Tsurpu 1189) from which the Kagyüdpa traditions developed.
11th–12th centuries	Reconstruction of the surviving lineages of hereditary lamas with the aid of terma revelations, leading to the Nyingmapa and (Yungdrung) Bon traditions.
13th century	Development of the system of recognizing reincarnate lamas, initially in the Kagyüdpa traditions
13th–early 14th century	Sakya Paṇḍita (1182–1251), Putön Rinchen Drubpa (1290–1364) and others re-established the monastic and scholarly aspects of Indian Buddhism in Tibet.
1247	Sakya Paṇḍita met with the Mongol ruler Godan, negotiating Tibetan acceptance of Mongol rule as a so-called 'priest–patron' relationship.
1276	Sakya Paṇḍita's nephew Pakpa became ruler of Tibet under the Mongol overlordship.
1354	Collapse of Mongol rule over Tibet; Changchub Gyantsen, a Tibetan administrator under the Mongols and supporter of the Kagyüdpas, becomes ruler of Central Tibet, with his capital at Neudong in East-Central Tibet.
14th century	Longchen Rabjampa (1308–1363) ordered the Nyingmapa teachings into a consistent system, bringing them into relation with the 'New Tantra' traditions.
1405	Founding of Menri monastery by the great Bonpo scholar Nyame Sherab Gyaltsen (1356–1415)
Early 15th century	Tsongkapa (1357–1419), created a new synthesis based on Kadampa, Kagyüdpa and Sakyapa teachings. His monastery of Ganden (founded 1409) near Lhasa became the centre of this 'New Kadampa' or Gelukpa tradition. Tsongkapa's disciples founded other great monastic teaching centres, including Drepung (1416), Sera (1419) and Tashilhunpo (1447). Gedün Drup (1391–1474), the founder of Tashilhunpo, was to become the first of the reincarnate lamas series now known as the Dalai Lamas.
1577	Sonam Gyatso (1543–1588), the second rebirth of Gedün Drup, established a 'priest–patron' relationship with the Tumed Mongol prince Altan Khan, who gave him the title 'Dalai Lama'.
1590s	Following the death of Sonam Gyatso, the grandson of Altan Khan's successor was recognized as his rebirth, thus becoming the 4th Dalai Lama (1589–1617)

1590s	Following the death of the Fourth Gyalwang Drukchen, Pema Karpo, head of the Drukpa Kagyüdpa, there was a conflict between supporters of two candidates, leading to one candidate, Shabdrung Ngawang Namgyel (1594–1651), fleeing to Bhutan in 1616 and becoming the head of a new Bhutanese state.
15th to early 17th centuries	Ongoing political conflicts in Central Tibet, brought to an end by the establishment of Gelukpa rule over Central Tibet, as well as large parts of Eastern and Western Tibet, by Gushri Khan, a Khoshut Mongol chieftain and supporter of the Fifth Dalai Lama, Ngawang Lobsang Gyatso (1617–1682)
1697	The death of the Fifth Dalai Lama, which had been concealed by the Regent, Desi Sangye Gyatso, was revealed, and the Sixth Dalai Lama enthroned.
1706	The Sixth Dalai Lama was deposed by the Khoshut Mongol chieftain Lhasang Khan, with the encouragement of the Manchu ruler of China. Lhasang Khan was subsequently killed by a force led by the Dzungar Mongol chieftain Tsewang Rabten, leading to further political conflict. The Manchu rulers of China intervened in Tibet, removing the Dzungars and recognizing one of two competing candidates as Seventh Dalai Lama. Effective power was re-established by the Tibetan noble Pholané in 1728, but a Chinese garrison and two Manchu officials (the Ambans) remained at Lhasa until 1911.
1788–1792	A war with the Gurkha regime in Nepal led to a further Manchu intervention and the Qianlong Emperor's imposition of control over the recognition of senior reincarnations, which continued to the early 19th century.
19th century	During the 19th century, the Ninth to Twelfth Dalai Lamas all died young, and effective power in Central Tibet was exercised by a succession of regents, mostly selected from four major Lhasa monasteries.
1903–04	A British army under the leadership of Sir Francis Younghusband invaded Central Tibet, imposing a trade agreement on the Lhasa government.
1910–11	Attempts by the Chinese rulers of Qinghai to impose control over Eastern Tibet culminated in an invasion of Central Tibet and the flight to India of the Thirteenth Dalai Lama (Tupten Gyatso, 1876–1933). He returned after the fall of the Manchu regime in 1911. The Simla convention of 1914 recognized the autonomy of 'Outer Tibet' (i.e. the area under the Lhasa government) under Chinese 'suzerainty'. It was not signed by China, but the Lhasa government was *de facto* independent until 1949. Fighting continued intermittently during the 1920s and 1930s in East Tibet.
1920s	The Lhasa government, under the Thirteenth Dalai Lama, attempted to modernize and centralize the Tibetan state. This led to conflict with the Panchen Lama, who fled to China.
1933 onwards	The Dalai Lama's death and the removal of the regent Reting Rinpoche brought the movement to modernization to an end, with conservative monastic rule re-established under the regent Taktra Rinpoche.
1949–1951	Following the Communist takeover in China, the Fourteenth Dalai Lama (b.1935) took over as head of the Tibetan government in 1950. The Chinese government asserted direct control over 'Inner Tibet' (the Tibetan areas of Qinghai, Gansu, Sichuan and Yunnan), now renamed the 'Tibet Autonomous Region', and imposed the '17 Point Agreement' on the Lhasa government.
1956–59	Increasing conflicts resulting from Chinese government policy led to an unsuccessful revolt against Chinese rule and the flight of numerous refugees, including the Fourteenth Dalai Lama, to India and Nepal.
1959–62	Famine in Tibet as result of Chinese agricultural policy.

1966–76	Cultural Revolution led to further widespread suppression of Buddhist practice and destruction of Buddhist institutions throughout Tibet
1980 onwards	A degree of liberalization and reform following Party Secretary Hu Yaobang's visit to Tibet, but more repressive policies were gradually reintroduced. Further demonstrations against Chinese rule have taken place periodically from 1987 onwards, and been forcibly suppressed.

Language and pronunciation guide

The vocabulary of Buddhism is most familiar to English-speaking readers in Sanskrit and Pāli form; thus words like *Buddha, Bodhisattva* and *nirvāṇa* are likely to be recognizable to many readers. In Tibet, Buddhism was translated into the Tibetan language, and rather than borrowing words from Indian languages the Tibetan translators preferred to create Tibetan equivalents for their terminology, using words and roots already present in the Tibetan language. I have gone for a somewhat eclectic mix of Sanskrit and Tibetan here, since to use Tibetan alone would make it difficult for readers to make connections with material on other Buddhist traditions. The Glossary at the end provides equivalents and further assistance where that seemed useful.

I use the standard transcription for Sanskrit, and some brief notes about pronunciation are given below. The situation for Tibet is more complicated. Tibetan spelling conventions are systematic but complex, with numerous prefixes and suffixes included in the written forms which are not pronounced. Thus the Tibetan equivalents for *Buddha, Bodhisattva,* and *nirvān·a,* in a literal transcription of the Tibetan spelling, would be *sangs rgyas, byang chub sems dpa'* and *mya ngan 'das.* These are pronounced something like *sangyé, changchub sempa* and *nyangendé* in contemporary Lhasa Tibetan. Other Tibetan spellings are even more forbidding to the non-Tibetanist; a well-known Tibetan religious tradition is spelled *bka' brgyud pa* and pronounced 'Kagyüpa' or 'Kajüpa' depending on dialect. Rather than adding another idiosyncratic phonetic transcription to the many that already exist, I have adopted the simplified spelling of the Tibetan and Himalayan Library's 'Simplified Phonetic Transcription of Standard Tibetan'. Details of this system can be found on the web (at http://www.thlib.org/reference/transliteration/#essay=/thl/phonetics/). In a few cases, however, where names are familiar under different forms, I have retained those more familiar forms (so Dzogchen rather than Dzokchen, Bon rather than bön).

How to pronounce Sanskrit

Sanskrit spelling in the standard conventions is phonetic but may be challenging at first, particularly to English speakers. While Sanskrit vowels are reasonably close to those of many European languages, the Sanskrit consonant system is somewhat different and more complex than that of English and most European languages. Readers who want to learn how to pronounce Sanskrit consonants accurately will need to look elsewhere, but it is worth noting the following:

> 'h' marks aspiration (a brief puff of air after the consonant), so that ph, th are similar to English p and t in 'pack' and 'tack' (Sanskrit p and t are by contrast softer and unaspirated, more like the initial consonants in English 'pick' and 'tick').
>
> ṣ and ś are both pronounced something like English sh
>
> c is pronounced similarly to English ch
>
> ṛ is pronounced close to ri
>
> a is pronounced close to u in 'but'; in modern languages it is often omitted when final (so dharma in Hindi is 'dharm'); ā is similar to English a in 'bar'
>
> i as in 'hit', ī as in 'eat'
>
> u as in 'but', ū as in 'boot'
>
> ai as in 'rise', o as in 'boat', au as in 'bout'
>
> t and ṭ, th and ṭh, d and ḍ, dh and ḍh are distinct sounds in Sanskrit

How to pronounce Tibetan

The Tibetan and Himalayan Library's 'Simplified Phonetic Transcription of Standard Tibetan' used in this book is intended to be pronounced more or less as in English. Note that 'ng' is a single consonant.

1 *Background*

In this chapter

This introduction sketches the historical, cultural and geographical background to the formation of Tibetan Buddhism, both in India and in Tibet itself, with emphasis on the environment and society within which Tibetan Buddhism developed and which helps to understand many of its characteristic features. The major schools and traditions of Tibetan Buddhism are introduced. The main bodies of textual material (such as the Kangyur, Tengyur, Nyingmé Gyudbum, *terma* collections and the writings of major lamas) are also briefly introduced.

Main topics covered

- Buddhism, Tibetan Buddhism and Tibetan society
- Environment and society in Tibet
- The growth of Buddhism in Tibet
- The evolution of the four main traditions
- Tibetan religious literature

Buddhism, Tibetan Buddhism and Tibetan society

Tibetan Buddhism is a form of Buddhism, and as we will see in the course of this book it shares much with forms of Buddhism that have developed in other regions. Tibetan Buddhism also has many specifically Tibetan features. To understand why it has developed in the way that it has, and why it has its own specific features, we need to consider the specific environment of the Tibetan plateau, the peoples who have lived there and the society which they have constructed in this difficult and challenging location. Buddhism in Tibet has become an integral part of Tibetan identity and the Tibetan way of life. Along with the Bon religion (see below, and Chapter 11), which in its modern forms is essentially a variant form of Tibetan Buddhism, Buddhism has totally dominated the religious life of the Tibetan people, the only

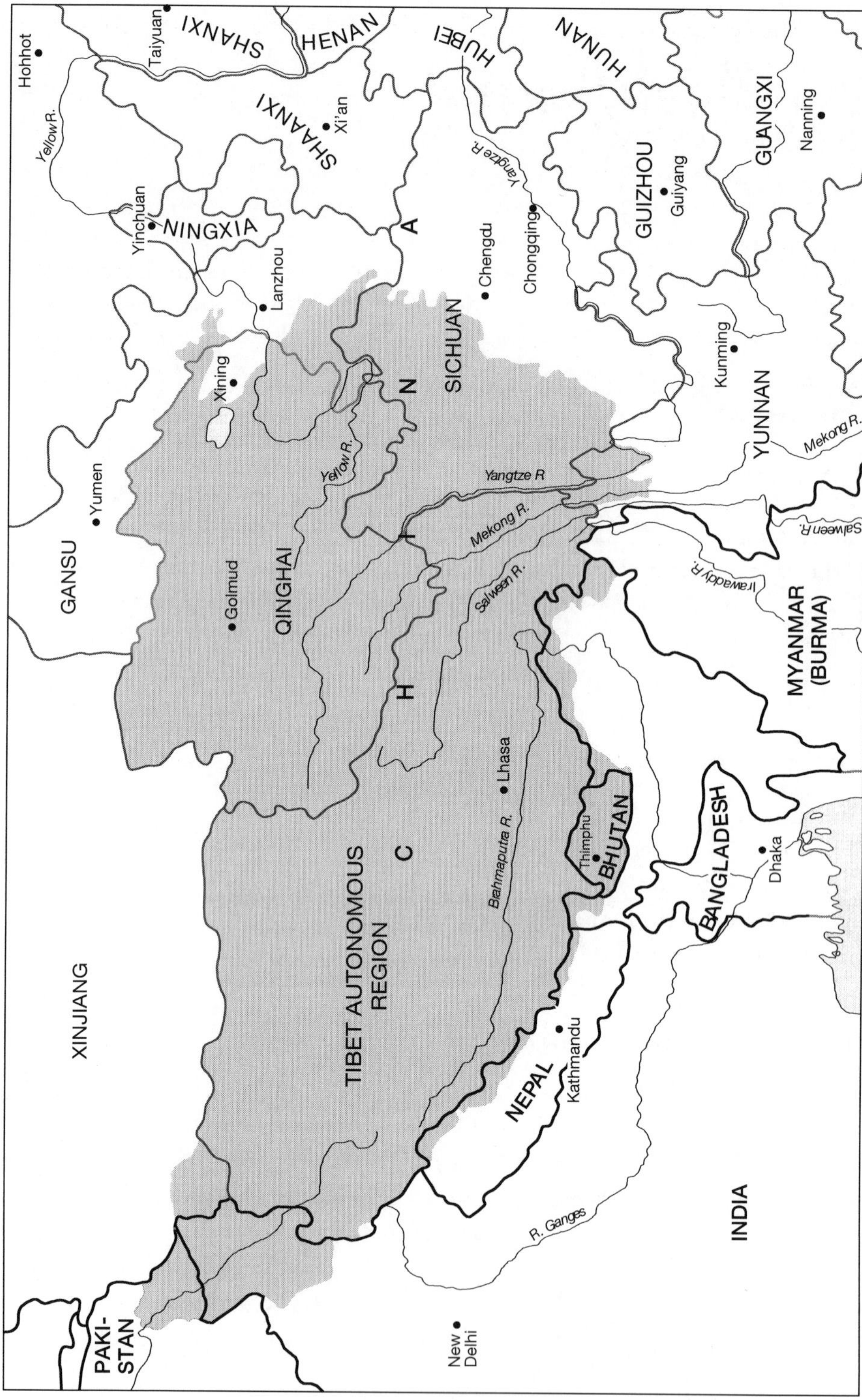

Figure 1.1 Map showing Tibetan regions of China and adjoining countries (2011)

exception being some conversion to Islam in the far western areas of Ladakh and Baltistan. Before looking in more detail at the various features of Tibetan Buddhism, we should spend some time looking at Tibetan society and its history, and consider how Buddhism came to be established there.

Tibetan society in this book includes communities in several different modern nation states. Most Tibetans today (around five million) live in Tibetan regions of the People's Republic of China (PRC). Historically, these regions were effectively independent until 1949–50, although subject to temporary and intermittent control by Mongol and Manchu rulers of China. In 1949, Tibetan regions of Qinghai, Gansu, Sichuan and Yunnan, made up of a number of small states and self-governing regions, were effectively incorporated into the respective Chinese provinces. Shortly after, the areas to the west, formerly an independent state under the Dalai Lama's government at Lhasa, were formed into the Tibet Autonomous Region. This too was fully incorporated into the Chinese state after the flight of the Dalai Lama, the Lhasa government and many other senior lamas to India in 1959. Tibetan religion was initially tolerated, then forcibly suppressed during the Cultural Revolution period (1966–late 1970s), then gradually allowed to re-emerge under strict government control after 1980.

Other regions of Tibetan society and culture in northern India and northern Nepal were progressively integrated into those modern states, as was the small multi-ethnic Himalayan kingdom of Sikkim (formerly a British and then Indian protectorate, but incorporated into India in 1975). Another small multi-ethnic Himalayan state, Bhutan, like Sikkim a region of Tibetan Buddhist religion and culture, remains independent. In all these areas, Tibetan religion has continued to be freely practised, and the settlement of numerous refugee lamas and monks in these areas and elsewhere in India and Nepal has led to a religious revival. Many new monasteries have been built and individual religious traditions have been re-established in the new situation.

Tibetan Buddhism was also adopted in subsequent centuries by the Mongolian people and by a number of smaller ethnic groups to the east and north of Tibet. There continue to be religious connections with these regions, but their histories and cultures are largely distinct from those of Tibetan societies, and will not be dealt with explicitly in this book.

The Chinese takeover from 1949 onwards was a dramatic (and in many ways traumatic) break with the past for a large part of the Tibetan population, both those who remained and those who left as refugees. Tibet before 1949 was far from static, and there had been considerable modernization, particularly in the 1920s and 1930s, but change was progressive and largely generated from within. After 1949, Tibetan societies had to come to terms with a powerful state imposing a largely alien system of government and administration, while Tibetan religion within the PRC went through a period of widespread destruction, followed by partial reconstruction in the context of a largely hostile regime. This creates problems for any straightforward generalizations about 'Tibetan religion', since the post-1949 situation differs so extensively from the earlier state of affairs. There are also considerable differences between the three major contexts of the PRC, the traditionally culturally Tibetan Himalayan regions, and the Tibetan diaspora. Within this book, the emphasis is primarily on Tibetan Buddhism as it developed in the pre-1949 period, and continued in culturally Tibetan regions of India, Nepal and Bhutan. Chapter 12 gives a brief description of the state of Tibetan Buddhism today, including its recent expansion into a global religion with many non-Tibetan followers.

Environment and society in Tibet

Tibetan society throughout its recorded history has had two major components, farmers (agriculturalists) and nomadic herdsmen (pastoralists). These may well have separate origins, and they have remained distinct into modern times, although they have in common the Tibetan Buddhist religion, the Tibetan spoken and written language and many other cultural features. Particular communities remain clearly distinguishable as either farmers or pastoralists, although some farming communities, particularly in more remote areas, also carry out a limited amount of pastoralism.

Figure 1.2 Tibetan pastoral settlement, Amdo (Northeast Tibet). Photo by author (2010).

Tibetan pastoralists (*drokpa* in Tibetan) lived, and continue to live today, on the high plateaux, mainly in the north and northeast of Tibet, where they herd flocks of cattle (including the famous Tibetan yaks), sheep and goats. Until recently they lived mostly in tents, travelling on horseback with their herds between regular grazing grounds in a seasonal cycle. Pastoralist society was divided into tribes and sub-tribes, with membership defined primarily by descent from the father's side, and a strong sense of independence and self-reliance, often expressing itself in the past in fighting and feuding. Under Chinese rule, much of the pastoralist population has been settled in more permanent housing.

Tibetan agriculturalists or farming people (*shingpa* – 'field people', also called *rongpa* 'valley people') live mostly along the river valleys and other lower areas where there is land suitable for farming. The main high-altitude crop is barley, though millets, rice, potatoes and maize are grown in lower valleys. These farming communities depend on high levels of cooperation, particularly in areas such as West Tibet and Ladakh where rainfall is low and elaborate irrigation systems are needed to make agriculture possible. Tibetan farmers live in villages, often built closely together for protection against the harsh Tibetan climate, and there is a strong ethic of collective responsibility towards the village community, which is made up of a number of households around which village duties and obligations, including religious duties, rotate in a regular cycle.

Figure 1.3 Village in Yarlung Valley, in Central Tibet. Photo by the author (1987).

The larger households in agricultural regions often arranged their marriages on a polyandrous pattern, with several brothers married to the same woman, a tradition that was explicitly seen as a way of keeping the household and its property together over generations. It also provided flexibility and stability if one or more brothers went on long-distance trading journeys, or wished to spend time as religious practitioners.

It may well be that the agriculturalist side of Tibet is older, and the pastoralists are a later arrival, sharing as they do much of their pastoral technology with Turkic and Mongol pastoral peoples to the north and northeast of Tibet. If so, however, most of them have long been integrated into a specifically Tibetan version of pastoralism, which has become an integral part of the Tibetan cultural and ecological adaptation.

Two of the three basic ingredients of the Tibetan diet, butter and tsampa (roasted barley-flour), derive respectively from the pastoralist and agriculturalist components of Tibetan society. The third, tea, is traded from China. Trade is a vital part of the Tibetan cultural adaptation in its own right, and the viability of life on the high plateaux was probably always linked with the long-distance trade routes between China, India, Kashmir and Iran. The small towns that were the largest population centres on the plateau until the mid-twentieth century, such as Lhasa, Shigatse, Gyantse, Leh, Chamdo and Dartsemdo, were all primarily trading centres, either on the edge of the Tibetan plateau or on the main trading routes across it. Most

Figure 1.4 Tibetan trading community (Gyantse). Photo by author (1987).

had a mixed population of Tibetans living alongside non-Tibetans from a variety of backgrounds: Han Chinese, Chinese Muslims, Newars from Nepal, and Kashmiris.

For the most part this was a fairly decentralized society, a state of affairs dictated to a large degree by the environment. Even the farming communities are restricted for the most part to relatively small areas in the river valleys, and travel from one valley to the next often involved a laborious journey over a high mountain pass. Travel from one end of Tibet to the other in pre-modern times took several months, and traders often journeyed in large caravans for protection against bandits.

The adoption of the military technology of the Turkic and Mongolian nomadic peoples in the first few centuries of the common era led to the growth of an expansionist empire centred at Lhasa in Central Tibet, based initially on a loose association between the leading families of different regions, linked through marriage and ritual ties to the *tsenpo* or emperor. Songtsen Gampo, the *tsenpo* who led the initial expansion of this early Tibetan empire, remains an important figure for Tibetans, and his marriages with Chinese and Nepalese princesses are a significant reference-point for Tibetan political self-understanding.

In the course of the seventh and eighth centuries CE, this empire defeated and incorporated the neighbouring state of Shangshung to the west, fought with and against a variety of Turkic, Arabic and Mongol peoples, took control of virtually the entire area of present-day Tibetan settlement, and briefly occupied the then capital of the Chinese empire, Chang'an (in 763). It was during the period of this empire, which gradually adopted features of Chinese bureaucratic state organization, that the first major transmission of Buddhism to Tibet took place, although Tibetan chronicles refer to some earlier contacts. Traditionally, both Chinese and Indian forms of Buddhism came to Tibet, and the Tibetan rulers decided at a perhaps mainly legendary debate to adopt the Indian form.

This early Tibetan empire collapsed, however, probably in the 840s. Some of the descendants of the old ruling families continued to hold on to regional kingdoms, and many of the more remote areas remained effectively out of state control. More extensive political units grew up in later centuries, but were mostly dependent on some kind of alliance with non-Tibetan military powers, initially Mongol and later Manchu. These alliances led to temporary association with the Chinese empire, which was itself under Mongol (and later Manchu) rule for long periods. The regions of Tibetan population, however, remained linguistically, culturally and to a large degree also politically distinct from China.

This Tibetan society was divided into a variety of political units. The largest of these by the early twentieth century was under the administration of the Dalai Lama's government at Lhasa, but there were many others, including independent kingdoms such as Derge, Nangchen, Powo, Sikkim and Bhutan, largely autonomous sub-units of the Lhasa state such as Shigatse and Sakya, as well as areas that were effectively self-governing peasant or pastoral communities.

Even the most effective of Tibetan states before the twentieth century did not have the kind of detailed day-to-day control over life that was characteristic of much of the Chinese empire itself. In many areas, aristocratic families, or local representatives of the Lhasa state or other regimes, had some presence and authority. The relationship of individuals, families and communities to these authorities, however, was primarily one of fulfilling tax obligations, which might also include contributing free labour for the authorities and, in the case of villages, the provision of young men to serve as monks in local monasteries. Provided that these obligations were met, there was little direct interference in daily life. Disputes were settled mostly by mediation. Village and pastoralist communities for the most part looked after their own affairs, with village politics dominated by locally-important big men, and pastoralist groups directed by hereditary tribal chieftains.

Tibetan society has been described as 'feudal', but this is misleading both in formal terms (the relationship between local aristocracy and central government was quite different from that in European feudalism) and also in the picture it tends to convey of a harsh and oppressive regime. The tax-paying peasant farmers who dominated Tibetan village society were often wealthy people with large landholdings, solid, comfortable houses and substantial possessions, which might be passed down through many generations. Tibetan society was stratified, however, with a lower class with little or no landholdings, and there was little security except to the extent that it was supplied by household or by village community.

The growth of Buddhism in Tibet

Tibet's dual society, with its basis in farming villages and pastoral tribes, and its lack of large urban centres, has a significant bearing on the development of Tibetan religion. Buddhism in India all along had its main strength in the urban centres, with its support coming initially from merchants, artisans and others of the city-dwelling populations of the fifth and fourth centuries BCE onwards, and later from the pro-Buddhist rulers of the new large-scale states that developed in South Asia from that time onwards. While there were certainly rural monasteries, retreat centres and pilgrimage sites, village religion in most of India never really seems to have been Buddhist, and once state and urban patronage disappeared, Buddhism progressively vanished from rural India.

Buddhism in Tibet began in much the same way, if the traditional accounts can be accepted, during the early Tibetan empire. Initially it was a religion supported and promoted by the emperor and his family, and other members of the nobility. The early Buddhist temples, at Lhasa, and elsewhere, were royal foundations, as was the first monastery at Samyé.

With the collapse of the Tibetan empire in the mid to late ninth century, probably assisted by the economic decline of the trade routes to China at around the same time, these institutions lost their economic base. However, Buddhism did not disappear from Tibet. Instead, it became transformed into a local-level religion among farmers and pastoralists. Over time, Buddhist temples and Buddhist monasteries became essential components of Tibetan villages, and vital institutions within Tibetan pastoral regions. Local rulers played a part, where they existed, but Buddhism became something which was owned by the Tibetan people as a whole, and which they came to see as necessary for their wellbeing.

From a traditional Tibetan point of view (see Chapter 9), this transformation was understood in terms of the salvific activity of Buddhist deities, above all the Bodhisattva of Compassion, Avalokiteśvara (Chenresik in Tibetan), who took birth as the monkey-ancestor of the Tibetan people, introduced them to agriculture, and was reborn again and again, along with fellow-deities, to guide them towards the Buddhist teachings. From a less explicitly Buddhist perspective, there were perhaps a number of factors that aided the survival of Buddhism in the difficult period after the collapse of

Figure 1.5 Avalokiteśvara. Sangdog Pelri Gompa, Kalimpong. Photo by author (2009).

the Tibetan empire, including the support of traders and surviving royal lineages, and the availability of Buddhist teachers from India seeking new sources of patronage or simply escape from the increasingly inhospitable environment south of the Himalayas.

The key development in Buddhism's eventual survival however was that Tantric (Vajrayāna) Buddhism came to provide the principal set of techniques by which Tibetans dealt with the dangerous powers of the spirit world. This is not to dismiss Buddhism as a path to the attainment of Enlightenment, which undoubtedly became a matter of real meaning and urgency for the relatively small number of Tibetans who became dedicated practitioners. For the society as a whole, though, what was more significant was that Buddhism, in the form of Vajrayāna ritual, provided a critical set of techniques for dealing with everyday life. Tibetans came to see these techniques as vital for their survival and prosperity in this life. This is why the performance of Tantric ritual and the preservation of the Tantric teaching lineages, and the support of the institutions that allowed for these things, became sufficiently important for virtually every village to acquire (in time) its own *gompa* (temple or monastery), and substantial numbers of Tibetans to become monks, nuns or lay practitioners.

Figure 1.6
Padmasambhava. Jangsa Gompa, Kalimpong. Photo by author (2007).

The key figure here was Guru Padmasambhava (also called Pema Jungné or Guru Rinpoche, see Chapters 2, 4 and 7), the semi-legendary Tantric guru who visited Tibet in the eighth century, subdued and tamed the powerful gods and spirits of the Tibetan landscape and established the commitments and relationships by which future generations of Tibetan Buddhist ritualists would be able to control the Tibetan spirit world. People in many parts of the world have understood their relationship to their environment in terms of interaction with a world of spirits. For Tibetans, such matters have been particularly significant. Tibet from the beginning must have been a marginal and risky environment. While it seems the climate may once have been milder in western Tibet than it is today, Tibetans have always lived with the daily possibility of natural disasters, from snowstorms and avalanches, dangerous wild animals, and the risk of epidemics, crop failure or animal disease among herding populations. Long-distance trading, too, must always have been a risky business, with returns unpredictable and the possibility of loss through bandit attack or bad weather a constant reality.

The basic Tibetan model for understanding such matters is that it is essential to stay on good terms with the gods of the environment, above all with the local and

Figure 1.7 Painting of local deities, local deity temple, Rebkong (Northeast Tibet). Photo by author (2010).

regional spirits (*sadak* or 'soil-lords', *shipdak* or 'lords of place'). These are the supernatural counterpart to the big men from noble or locally dominant families who dominate local life. *Sadak* and *shipdak* are mostly male mountain gods, portrayed as warriors mounted on horses or on wild animals such as the *drong* or wild yak, and often married to goddesses associated with lakes, although some of the most important of the mountain deities are themselves goddesses. They have a close relationship to the human populations of their region. Lay Tibetans make regular offerings of aromatic herbs and woods (*sang*) to the local gods, and village communities and monasteries also make such offerings. Aristocratic families often have legends of descent from the gods, and all families have inherited links to specific regional gods. It seems likely that at an earlier stage the link was even closer, with a sense that mountains, lakes and other significant places were not simply the home of a regional god but a kind of external location and source of an individual or community's vitality, personal power and good fortune (see Chapter 9).

The mountain gods can extend their protection to the people who live in their region or who have family connections to them, but they can also turn against them, often because of unintentional acts of disrespect or offence. Spirit-mediums (*lhawa*, *pawo*, etc.) provide channels of communication with these gods, and allow them to communicate when they have been offended and to state their requirements for reparation. The gods rule over and control a host of lesser spirits and deities, many of them explicitly hostile and malevolent towards human beings. Consequently,

Figure 1.8 Mountain deity in Rebkong. Photo by author (2010).

human beings are reliant on the assistance of the regional gods to keep these lesser harmful spirits under control. Other gods, though not necessarily hostile, can also be offended and cause illness. The *lu* or water-spirits associated with rivers and other water sources can cause skin disease or leprosy if offended, particularly through the water source or river being polluted. These *lu* were equated by the early Buddhists to the *nāgas* of Indian thought.

Throughout Tibet, as elsewhere in Asia, the environment was seen as full of spirit life, and human existence as closely dependent on the maintenance of a good relationship with this spirit life. Undoubtedly, pre-Buddhist Tibet had its own means of dealing with this vital relationship. What Tantric Buddhism was able to do in Tibet was to establish itself as the standard set of techniques for handling the relationship with the environment and its dangers. Buddhism did not remove the mountain gods and their spirit-mediums, nor for the most part (as in Japan) did pre-Buddhist mountain gods become redefined as specifically Buddhist deities. What happened instead was that the Buddhist ritual specialists (*lamas* – the element *la* in this word is probably linked with *la* in the sense of 'soul' or 'spirit force') became the primary experts in handling the spirit world.

The mountain gods were thought of as having been converted to Buddhism, above all by the great Tantric culture hero Padmasambhava. The selection, training and supervision of spirit-mediums increasingly became a matter for the lamas. Above all, the Tantric rituals of the lamas were seen as essential ways of maintaining a proper relationship with the local spirit world.

The term *lama* (see Chapter 7) thus acquired a range of meanings considerably wider than that of the Indian term *guru*, which it is used to translate, and significantly different from that of the *bhikṣu* (Tib. *gelong*) or fully-ordained monk, the main leadership role in most other Buddhist societies. The lama is indeed a teacher, particularly of Tantric practice, but he (very occasionally she) is also a performer and director of ritual. A lama's reputation is linked to how effective he and his community are believed to be as ritual performers. The lama is also a human representative of Buddhahood, and a focus of devotion for his students and disciples, who will visualize him in the form of a Tantric deity. This does not mean that Tibetan people are unrealistic about the human failings of lamas; they are generally less naïve about such matters than Western Buddhists. The fact that the lama 'stands for' the Buddha in many senses nevertheless says something important about the role of the lama in Tibetan society. Fully-ordained monks are certainly respected by Tibetans, but lamas may nor may not be monks, since the critical issue is their ability to exercise the power of Tantric ritual, and in some circumstances being a celibate monk can be an obstacle to ritual power.

The Tibetan *gompa* (see Chapter 7) also became something rather different from the modern Western picture of a monastery, or in all probability from what the monastic centres of large Indian states had been like in the eighth to tenth centuries. In some cases a Tibetan *gompa* is little more than a temple (*lhakang*) where villagers with some ritual training would come to perform ritual on behalf of the community. More often, there would be a resident lama, and there might or might not be buildings nearby belonging to households in the associated villages, where members of those households might live if they were adopting a monastic lifestyle. This normally involved celibacy, but did not necessarily involve taking monastic vows. The idea of a substantial community of celibate ordained monks or nuns grew up relatively slowly, and the very large monasteries of Tibet in the twentieth century were a fairly late development.

As time went on, the Indian monastic tradition of scholarship became increasingly established, partly through services to the various local regimes that supported the larger urban monasteries. These monasteries provided education, and competent scholars with skills in literacy and correspondence were essential for the emerging centres of political authority. At the same time the scholarly curriculum of Indian Buddhism, including philosophical study, debating, medicine and a wide range of ritual arts, was gradually established, finding a new home where it could survive and prosper despite its disappearance in India itself (see Chapter 5).

Buddhism as an ethical ideal also became progressively established among the Tibetan population, along with ideas of karma and of past and future lives, and the need for virtuous action to secure a good rebirth (Chapter 6). So too did the fundamental and central goal of the achievement of Buddhahood or Enlightenment, both as a basic horizon for the understanding of the human situation, and as a meaningful personal goal for an increasing number of Buddhist practitioners (Chapters 3 and 4). The baseline throughout, however, remained the ability of Tibetan Buddhist clergy to offer mediation with the spirit world, and so to provide help with the practical, day-to-day issues of life in Tibet. The skills that Tibetan yogic practitioners were held to acquire on the path to Buddhahood, primarily through Tantric practice, were basic to this mediating function, and so to the whole presence of Buddhism in Tibet, so that the maintenance and preservation of the training and practice lineages of Tantric yoga (Chapter 4) also became a key concern for Tibetans.

The evolution of the four main traditions

Contemporary Tibetan Buddhists often speak of four main religious traditions, schools or religious orders. These are the Nyingmapa, Sakyapa, Kagyüdpa and Gelukpa. Often the last three (Sakyapa, Kagyüdpa and Gelukpa) are referred to as Sarmapa (New Schools), dating back to the renewed contact with Indian Buddhism in the eleventh century onwards, as opposed to the Nyingmapa (Old School), which claims its origins in the period of the early empire. The differences between these four schools are often subtle, and there are informal divisions within each, so the four schools do not act as distinct organizational entities within Tibetan religion. Frequently, the Bon religious tradition is counted as a fifth school.

The Tibetan government-in-exile at Dharamsala has appointed heads of the four schools or traditions, which has given them a certain institutional reality that they did not necessarily have in Tibet. The names of these traditions will recur frequently in later chapters, and is worth some discussion of what they meant in Tibetan history, since it is often assumed that they have a stronger institutional or sectarian character than they in fact possessed. Certainly, they varied greatly in the degree to which they functioned as organizational units or had real corporate identity.

While there was often intense competition for power and influence within Tibetan Buddhism, this did not take place between the four schools as such but between monasteries associated with them or, even more specifically, between the households (ladrang) of senior lamas within monasteries. Over time, these could become extremely powerful units, with extensive landholdings, possessions and a network of subsidiary monasteries. Thus the government of the Dalai Lama at Lhasa, which was known as the Ganden Podrang, originated in the personal household of the Dalai Lama at Drepung monastery one of the three large Gelukpa monasteries near Lhasa, and remained formally separate from the Gelukpa order within which the Dalai Lama was unquestionably the senior lama. The official head of the Gelukpa order was the successor of Tsongkapa, the founder of the Gelukpa order, at Tsongkapa's own monastery of Ganden. Other major lamas and monasteries within the Gelukpa tradition also had considerable autonomy. Thus the Panchen Lama's monastic estate, based at Tashilhunpo, near Shigatse, was a major rival to the Dalai Lama's government for political influence and power in Central Tibet. This was despite its close historical and spiritual links to the Dalai Lama. The big Gelukpa monasteries in Northeast Tibet, such as Kumbum and Labrang Tashikyil, also had a high level of autonomy while retaining links to Central Tibet.

Similarly, the Kagyüdpa tradition traces its origins to a specific set of teaching lineages, in particular the lineage claimed to have been transmitted from the Indian teacher Nāropa to his Tibetan student Marpa and on to Marpa's student, the poet-saint Milarepa. The competing units within the Kagyüdpa (Karma Kagyüd, Drukpa Kagyüd, Drikung Kagyüd, Taklung Kagyüd, etc.) were based on a series of monasteries founded by the disciples of Milarepa's own student, Gampopa, in the late twelfth century, and the differences between them had little philosophical basis, since they all essentially shared the same core teachings. Over time these Kagyüdpa 'sub-orders' rose and declined in importance, while a split over the leadership succession of the Drukpa Kagyüd led to the development of two separate Drukpa traditions based in Tibet and Bhutan. The Sakyapas originated in a single monastery, Sakya in West-Central Tibet, but two subsidiary monasteries later became the centres of autonomous sub-orders (Ngorpa and Tselpa).

The Nyingmapa tradition was considerably less structured again than the various Sarmapa traditions, since it was largely based on relatively small-scale hereditary lama households and monasteries, and thus remained largely outside the political infighting between the major Sarmapa monasteries. The numerous *terma* lineages also easily became the basis of distinct local or regional traditions. Over time, six main teaching centres evolved (Dorjedrak and Mindrolling in Central Tibet; Katok, Peyül, Dzogchen and Shechen in the East), and took on a similar role to the major Kagyüd and Sakya monastic centres. The Bon tradition (see Chapter 11) is somewhat similar, with a number of important hereditary lineages and two major teaching monasteries.

In the mutual competition between these various monastic units, occasionally reaching the level of violence and armed conflict, sectarian allegiance was rarely a significant or primary issue. In any case this was rarely a straightforward issue, since monasteries and lamas often had more than one 'identity' in terms of schools and traditions. Particularly outside the Gelukpa order it was common for lama households to acquire and transmit several sets of practices belonging to different 'schools', including for example both Nyingmapa and Kagyüdpa teaching and practice lineages. The Dalai Lamas themselves, although their primary identification was Gelukpa, own and continue to transmit a series of Nyingmapa and Dzogchen practices going back to personal revelations received by the Fifth Dalai Lama.

Thus, while the Dalai Lama's government was undoubtedly closely linked with the Gelukpa tradition, and it was associated in the sixteenth and seventeenth century with the takeover and suppression of monasteries of other traditions, this was less a question of sectarian conflict than the establishment of an effective power base and the removal of potential rivals, such as the Kagyüdpa monasteries associated with the Kings of Tsang who had been the principal competitors of the Gelukpa in the fifteenth and early sixteenth centuries. In other words, the conflicts between monasteries belonging to the four 'schools' had little to do with differences in philosophy or practice, although such differences certainly existed. The connections between the Nyingmapa, Kagyüdpa and Sakyapa in particular have often been very close, particularly since the development of the 'non-sectarian' (*Rimé*) movement among these religious traditions from the late eighteenth century onwards.

The division into four schools is also misleading in that not all of the religious traditions of Tibetan Buddhism had or have a distinct monastic base. When the great nineteenth-century Rimé lama Jamgön Kongtrul compiled his 'Treasury of Teachings' (*Damngag Dzöd*), only ten of the nineteen volumes comprised teachings directly associated with the 'Four Main Schools' (two each for the Nyingmapa, Kadampa-Gelukpa, and Sakyapa, and four for the Kagyüdpa). Others include volumes on the teachings of the Jonangpa, an important early order suppressed by the Gelukpa but surviving in Eastern Tibet and revived by the Rimé teachers, and the Shangpa Kagyüdpa, a parallel Kagyüdpa tradition to the main (Marpa) Kagyüdpa that was passed down by the Jonangpa lama Tāranātha. Further volumes include the Shichepa teachings associated with the Indian guru Padampa Sangyé, and the Chöd teachings originated by his Tibetan disciple, the important woman teacher

Machik Labdrön. These, Chöd in particular, are practised by all Tibetan schools. Other volumes include yogic lineages associated with the Kālacakra Tantra, and a variety of minor teachings and lineages, many of them associated with teachers and schools that no longer have a significant monastic base, such as the Bodongpa.

In part, this reflects the interest of Kongtrül and the Rimé lamas in maintaining and reviving what had become minor and obscure lineages of teaching and practice, but it also helps to make the point that seeing Tibetan Buddhism in terms of the 'Four Main Schools' can be misleading. The really important links in Tibetan Buddhism are between lamas and their communities of students, and what goes along with this is that Buddhism is above all a tradition of practice. Knowledge is there not for its own sake (although undoubtedly there is great respect for knowledge and its possessors, and a desire to pass it on to the future) but because it can be used. It is important to transmit a practice lineage as purely and accurately as possible, but it is also good to have access to a wide range of practices, and the question of whether their philosophical bases are all compatible with each other is not an especially significant one.

Particularly outside the major monasteries, Tibetans were often much more interested in a lama's powers than his knowledge or his specific tradition. What went along with this was an elaboration of theatre and display; elaborate forms of chant and music, dramatic and impressive rituals, spectacular forms of ritual dance and theatre. These need to be seen in the pre-modern context of Tibet. There was no cinema and no professional theatre in Tibet before the 1950s, with the exception of small theatre troupes that performed traditional dance-dramas on religious themes (the *aché lhamo* plays). The monastic dances (*cham*) and festivals were by far the most elaborate, colourful and important cultural productions of the Tibetan people, and must have created a spectacular and impressive effect on people whose daily lives had very little of the constant entertainment and stimulation of the contemporary world (see Chapter 8).

The 'Four Main Schools', with Bon as a fifth, are nevertheless an important part of how Tibetans today understand their religion, and they will recur repeatedly in the course of this book. The contrasts between them are also significant and it may be useful to tabulate these (see Table 1.1).

The contrast in the second column derives from that presented in more detail in my earlier book *Civilized Shamans* (published in 1993). As noted there, there is a broad contrast across the schools in terms of the emphasis they give to yogic practice and to the visionary dimension of Buddhism, as compared to textual and philosophical study and the celibate monastic life, with the Nyingmapa at one end and the Gelukpa at the other. In *Civilized Shamans*, I referred to this as a contrast between 'shamanic' and 'clerical' modalities, with the Nyingmapa at the shamanic end, and the Gelukpa at the clerical. As also noted in that book, this is not at all an absolute contrast. Yogic and visionary practice are important for all Tibetan Buddhist traditions, as is scholarship and celibate monasticism. The difference is one of emphasis, and considerable

Table 1.1 The Four Main Schools

<table>
<tr><td>Nyingmapa</td><td>Strongest emphasis on yogic-visionary-'shamanic' dimension (but also includes scholarly-celibate-clerical dimension); many married lamas</td><td>Origins traced to 'early propagation of Dharma' at time of early empire (7th to 9th centuries) and 'Old' (Nyingma) Tantra transmission</td><td rowspan="3">Teachers from all these traditions were involved in the 'Rimé' (eclectic, universalist) approach which developed in the 19th and 20th century; emphasis on multiplicity of approaches and teachings</td></tr>
<tr><td>Kagyüdpa</td><td rowspan="2">Intermediate</td><td rowspan="3">Origins traced to 'later propagation of Dharma' in 11–12th centuries and 'New' (Sarma) Tantra transmission</td></tr>
<tr><td>Sakyapa</td></tr>
<tr><td>Gelukpa</td><td>Strongest emphasis on scholarly-celibate-clerical dimension (but also includes yogic-visionary-'shamanic' dimension); lamas normally celibate</td><td>Little involvement in 'Rimé' approach; emphasis on single unified approach to teachings</td></tr>
</table>

variety can be found within all of the four Schools. The Bonpo are not included in the above table, but in most respects resemble the Nyingmapa School (see Chapter 11).

More will be said about yogic practice and about the scholarly dimension of Tibetan Buddhism in later chapters, but some comments on Tibetan religious literature will be useful here, since it again provides basic information that will be referred back to in many subsequent chapters.

Tibetan religious literature

Tibet has had a strong tradition of scholarship and textual production, focused originally on the translation of Buddhist texts, mostly from Sanskrit and Indian vernaculars, into Tibetan, but increasingly as time went on involving the production of original works by Tibetan scholars. This last section of the chapter gives a brief sketch of this body of literature.

Book production was aided by the introduction of woodblock printing from around the fourteenth century onwards. This technology enabled any medium- to large-sized monastery to build up a stock of carved woodblocks from which books could be run off on demand. The books themselves take the form of a pile of sheets of paper in the form of long rectangles, printed on both sides and usually kept in cloth covers.

The initial process of translation of Buddhist texts, carried out in a relatively *ad hoc* way by individual groups of Indian and Tibetan scholars, was followed towards the end of the imperial period (late eighth century) by the compilation of a glossary of standard Tibetan equivalents of Sanskrit terms and the progressive revision of earlier translations to attain a high degree of accuracy and consistency. Many of these texts no longer survive in Sanskrit versions, but those that do bear witness to the learning and scholarly precision of the translation teams, and the care with which the texts have been preserved by later editors. The accurate and systematic nature of the translations has also been a major boon to Western scholars of Indian Buddhism, both in giving access to texts no longer extant in Sanskrit or other Indian languages, and in providing an independent check on sources that survive in the original, often in late and inaccurate copies.

The body of translated material was compiled under the editorship of the great thirteenth-century scholar Butön Rinchendrup into two major collections: the Kangyur, which contains translations of the Sūtra and Tantra material, and which is held to represent the actual word of the Buddha; and the Tengyur which consists of commentarial material and individual treatises by Indian scholars. These collections were initially copied in manuscript versions, but later produced in a number of woodblock versions. The Kangyur is generally compiled in 108 volumes. The Tengyur editions vary but are generally around 250 to 260 volumes. The precise

Figure 1.9 Tibetan books, Tirpai Gompa, Kalimpong. Photo by author (2007).

works included vary a little from edition to edition, though the differences are minor for the most part.

Some editions of the Kangyur include a selection of the Nyingma Tantras, the early Tantric texts associated with the Nyingmapa school, while others omit these. A more extensive collection of Nyingma Tantras, the Nyingmé Gyudbum, was assembled by the *tertön* lama Ratna Lingpa in the fifteenth century and revised by Jigmé Lingpa. This too exists in a number of variant versions.

For the Tibetans themselves, the material in the Sūtras and Tantras is often more significant for its spiritual value than its literal content. Many of the treatises and commentarial works in the Tengyur have however been extensively read and commented upon by Tibetan scholars. These treatises provided the Tibetans with the foundations on which their own quite substantial scholarly tradition developed in later centuries. This later development of Tibetan scholarly literature is discussed in subsequent chapters, particularly Chapters 3–5.

The Bonpo tradition has two canonical collections similar to the Buddhist Kangyur and Tengyur. Since there are only a few fragments of original texts held to have been translated from the Shangshung language (see Chapter 11), these collections consist almost entirely of *terma* texts and of commentarial and independent works by Bonpo scholars.

Most leading Tibetan scholars throughout the centuries have had their works produced in collected editions (*sungbum*), of which there must be several hundred at least, containing tens of thousands of individual texts. Many more individual texts of all kinds were produced in the pre-modern period, including thousands of volumes of ritual texts, philosophical texts for study in the various monastic colleges, texts on medicine, astronomy and other bodies of knowledge, histories, pilgrimage guides, literary works, and so on.

The nineteenth-century Rimé lamas, under the direction of Jamgön Kongtrül and Jamyang Khyentsé, compiled a series of major collections of works as part of their project of bringing together the large number of Tibetan lineages of practice and teaching that were still available at that period. These collections include the *Rinchen Terdzöd,* a massive collection of *terma* texts whose empowerments are often given collectively over a period of several months, the already-mentioned *Damngag Dzöd,* a collection of methods and instructions for practice from the various different schools and traditions of Tibetan Buddhism, and the *Drubtap Küntü,* a collection of practice texts for different deities from the various Sarmapa traditions. A number of other similar encyclopaedic projects have been carried out by various lamas of different periods, so that the total bulk of Tibetan religious literature is quite large.

Despite the widespread destruction of Tibetan religious literature during the Cultural Revolution, much of this book production has survived within or outside the areas of Chinese control, and much has been reprinted or reproduced in book or digital form in recent times, so that a very wide range of Tibetan literary material is now easily available. A growing proportion of this material has also now been translated into English and other Western languages, both by academic scholars and within the growing number of Dharma centres devoted to propagating Buddhism throughout the world. Tibetans produced one of the world's most substantial bodies of pre-modern literature, much of which has survived to the present day, and it is only gradually becoming known by and accessible to the outside world.

Tibetan Buddhism, however, is above all a tradition of practice. Tibetan lamas would see its central achievement not in terms of the production of literature as such but in terms of what that literature derives from and is intended to support: the high level of spiritual practice cultivated within the numerous ongoing lineages of Tantric yoga. We will see more of this in later chapters. In Chapter 2, however, we look at how Buddhism developed in Tibet, beginning with an examination of the later period of Indian Buddhism from which it mainly derived.

Key points you need to know

- Tibetan Buddhism is one of a number of forms of Buddhism. While it shares the central concerns and many features common to other Buddhist traditions, it also has many specific features and aspects of its own.
- Tibet's environment and society, with its farming villages, pastoralist communities, and trading centres, form an essential background for understanding Tibetan Buddhism.
- Tibetan Buddhism was originally introduced to Tibet under court patronage during the imperial period (seventh to ninth century). It survived after the collapse of the early empire by becoming an integral part of village and pastoral society, especially by providing the techniques through which Tibetan communities dealt with the world of spirits through which they understood their relationship to their often dangerous and threatening natural environment.
- Tibetan Buddhism developed in the form of a number of separate but related traditions, often grouped into four main schools, the Nyingmapa, Kagyüdpa, Sakyapa and Gelukpa. The Bon religion, which claims pre-Buddhist but non-Tibetan origins, has close similarities to Buddhism and is in some respects a fifth school.
- Tibet has a very large body of religious literature, much of which has survived and been reproduced in recent years, and substantial parts of which are now available in translation. Tibetan religion is, however, centrally a tradition of practice, and its most important feature for the Tibetans is the ongoing practice tradition of Tantric yoga.

Discussion questions

1 How was Buddhism established in Tibet?
2 How did the specific nature of the Tibetan environment and Tibetan society affect Tibetan Buddhism?
3 What are the main schools and traditions that have developed within Tibetan Buddhism?
4 What is the role of books and texts in Tibetan Buddhism?

Further reading

Beckwith, Christopher I. *The Tibetan Empire in Central Asia: A History of the Struggle for Great Power among Tibetans, Turks, Arabs and Chinese during the Early Middle Ages.* Princeton, NJ: Princeton University Press, 1987.

Cabezón, José Ignacio and Jackson, Roger R. (eds). *Tibetan Literature: Studies in Genre: Essays in Honor of Geshe Lhundup Sopa.* Ithaca, NY: Snow Lion, 1996.

Davidson, Ronald M. *Indian Esoteric Buddhism: A Social History of the Tantric Movement.* New York: Columbia University Press, 2002.

Dollfus, Pascale. *Lieu de Neige et de Genévriers: Organisation Sociale et Religieuse des Communautés Bouddhistes du Ladakh.* Paris: Éditions du CNRS, 1989.

Ekvall, Robert B. *Tibetan Skylines.* New York: Farrar, Straus and Young, 1952.

Ekvall, Robert B. *Tents Against the Sky.* London: Victor Gollancz, 1954.

Fürer-Haimendorf, Christoph von. *Himalayan Traders: Life in Highland Nepal.* London: John Murray, 1975.

Goldstein, Melvyn C. *A History of Modern Tibet, 1913–1951: The Demise of the Lamaist State.* Berkeley, CA: University of California Press, 1989.

Goldstein, Melvyn C. *A History of Modern Tibet: Vol. 2: The Calm Before the Storm, 1951–55.* Berkeley, CA: University of California Press, 2007.

Goldstein, Melvyn C. and Cynthia M. Beall. *Nomads of Western Tibet: The Survival of a Way of Life.* London: Serindia, 1990.

Kapstein, Matthew T. *The Tibetans.* Oxford and Malden, MA: Blackwell Publishing, 2006.

Karmay, Samten G. and Jeff Watt (eds). *Bon The Magic Word: The Indigenous Religion of Tibet.* New York: Rubin Museum of Art; London: Philip Wilson Publishers, 2007.

King, Richard. *Orientalism and Religion: Postcolonial Theory, India and 'The Mystic East'.* London and New York: Routledge, 1999.

Lopez Jr., Donald S. (ed.). *Curators of the Buddha: The Study of Buddhism under Colonialism.* Chicago: University of Chicago Press, 1995.

Lopez Jr., Donald S. *Prisoners of Shangri-La: Tibetan Buddhism and the West.* Chicago and London: University of Chicago Press, 1998.

Ramble, Charles. *The Navel of the Demoness: Tibetan Buddhism and Civil Religion in Highland Nepal.* New York and Oxford: Oxford University Press, 2008.

Samuel, Geoffrey. *Civilized Shamans: Buddhism in Tibetan Societies.* Washington, DC: Smithsonian Institution Press, 1993.

Samuel, Geoffrey. *The Origins of Yoga and Tantra: Indic Religions to the Thirteenth Century.* London and New York: Cambridge University Press, 2008.
Shakabpa, W.D. *Tibet: A Political History.* New Haven, CT and London: Yale University Press, 1967.
Shakya, Tsering, *The Dragon in the Land of Snows: A History of Modern Tibet since 1947.* New York: Columbia University Press, 1999.
Stein, Rolf A. *Tibetan Civilization.* London: Faber, 1972.
Stein, Rolf A. *Tibeta Antiqua. With Additional Materials.* Translated and edited by Arthur P. McKeown. Leiden: Brill, 2010.
Walter, Michael L. *Buddhism and Empire: The Political and Religious Culture of Early Tibet.* Leiden: Brill, 2009.

2 The development of Buddhism in Tibet

In this chapter

This chapter describes the development of Tibetan Buddhism in more detail, beginning with a description of the later Indian Buddhist tradition from which it mostly derived. It presents the major contemporary schools (Nyingmapa, Kagyüdpa, Sakyapa, Gelukpa) in their historical context, with emphasis on the development of fundamental patterns of Tibetan religion in the ninth to thirteenth centuries, the growth of Gelukpa dominance from the sixteenth century onwards and the effects of the Rimé movement in the nineteenth and twentieth centuries.

Main topics covered

- The later development of Buddhism in India
- The 'early diffusion' of the Dharma in Tibet
- The 'later diffusion' and the establishment of the Sarmapa schools
- The reshaping of the Nyingmapa tradition: *kama* and *terma*
- A note on the Bon tradition
- The Gelukpa school and later developments
- The twentieth century onwards

The later development of Buddhism in India

As Chapter 1 explained, Buddhism in Tibet derived primarily from India. In Tibet, it adapted to a new situation of local rather than state patronage, becoming an intrinsic part of Tibetan communal life, above all as a key way of dealing with the everyday problems of promoting health and prosperity and avoiding misfortune. What was it, though, about Indian Buddhism that allowed it to develop in this way in Tibet? This book does not have space for a detailed history of the development of Buddhism in India, but some discussion may be useful. The descriptions in many older books can be misleading, particularly when it comes to the relationship between Buddhism and Hinduism, and the parts played by each in Indian society in the early period.

It is worth remembering that the religious geography of South Asia in the seventh to twelfth centuries was very different from what it is in the twenty-first century. We think of South Asia today as Hindu territory, with the religion of villages, courts and urban centres being recognizably 'Hindu'. Hinduism as we know it today, however, as a religious tradition based on Vedic and Brahmanical material and distributed through all levels of society, was a fairly late development in much of India. This was particularly true in relation to the religious life of Indian villages. Buddhism and Jainism had been patronized by the Mauryan regime (c.320 – c.185BCE) and the Indo-Greek, Kushan and other regimes that dominated during the subsequent few centuries tended to be equally tolerant to the various religious traditions of their subject peoples. While the Gupta and Vākāt-aka regimes in the third to fifth centuries mainly patronized the new Brahmanical deities, Buddhism and Jainism continued to flourish under their rule. During all this period, it is likely that Vedic-Brahmanical ritual had still only penetrated to a limited degree to the village level, especially in areas away from the Vedic-Brahmanical heartland in the northwest. Local religion had little to do with Buddhism, Jainism or Hinduism as we know them today. It was mainly concerned with local gods and spirits who only gradually became assimilated to the major Brahmanical deities.

From the seventh to twelfth centuries, the most significant period for the transmission of Buddhism to Tibet, the Vedic-Brahmanical religious traditions that we now know as 'Hinduism' were taking on an increasingly expansionary character. They were adopted to varying degrees by elites in south and central India and in Southeast Asia, replacing the Buddhism which had been the dominant state-supported cult in many areas. Towards the later part of this period, the main area where Buddhism was still patronized on the subcontinent was in the Pāla empire in East India. This empire included an area corresponding roughly to present-day Bihar, Bengal and Orissa. This was the location of the great monastic universities that were major sources of the Buddhist scholarly tradition for the Tibetans.

Buddhism is often divided into Hīnayāna or 'Lesser Vehicle' schools, primarily represented in the contemporary world by the Theravāda Buddhism dominant in Sri Lanka and Southeast Asia, Mahāyāna or 'Great Vehicle' schools, represented today throughout the rest of the Buddhist world, including China and East Asia as well as Tibet, and Vajrayāna or Tantric Buddhism, represented primarily in Tibet but also in Nepal, Japan and Indonesia. This division will be discussed further in Chapters 3 and 4.

In the nineteenth and early twentieth century, scholars often saw these three schools as representing a historical decline from an initially rational and scientific doctrine, represented by the Theravāda, through the growth of irrational belief and mystification in the Mahāyāna, followed by a descent into outright corruption, decadence and sexual

Figure 2.1 Remains of the Central Shrine at Somapura Vihara (Paharpur, Bangladesh), one of the monastic universities of mediaeval India. Photo by author (2003).

immorality in the case of Tantra. Versions of this story can still be found in popular books, but the whole picture is distorted and misleading, beginning with the presentation of early Buddhism as a set of primarily rational or scientific teachings. Decadence and corruption are doubtless problems for all religious traditions, but the negative views of the later Indian and Tibetan Buddhist developments bear little relationship to reality.

In part this story of decline is modelled on older Protestant polemics against Catholicism, in which the Catholic Church was presented as a decadent and superstition-ridden development from the supposedly pure early Christianity of the New Testament. In part, this picture of original Buddhism as a set of primarily rational teachings also grew out of an understandable desire of Buddhists to present their tradition as modern and scientific. From the late nineteenth century onwards, initially in Sri Lanka and later through much of the Buddhist world, Buddhism has been involved in an often conflict-ridden encounter with both Christian missionaries and scientific rationalism. Contemporary presentations of Buddhism often reflect this history, portraying Buddhism as a rational and scientific teaching compatible with Western science. There are certainly aspects of Buddhist teachings that provide some basis for doing this, but to treat them as central or primary involves a drastic impoverishment of a tradition that is by no means simply rational and scientific.

Whether the historical Buddha himself was a scientist, a shaman or both is impossible to know for certain, since our sources all date from well after his lifetime. We certainly have no reason to assume that he disbelieved in the spirit world, since the Buddhist Sūtras, including those with good claim to be relatively early, have

Figure 2.2
Śākyamuni. Modern Tibetan painting in author's possession. Photo by author.

numerous accounts of dialogues between him and various gods and spirits. What is undoubtedly true is that the Buddhist tradition, from the earliest stages of which we have knowledge, included both rational and mystical or visionary elements, and that these cannot really be separated from each other.

The terms mystical and visionary remind us that the central insights of Buddhist knowledge were not thought of as being immediately available to ordinary, unaided human reason. Those central insights were always regarded as difficult to attain, and accessible only after a long period of inner purification, except perhaps for a fortunate few who had prepared themselves through experience and training in previous lives as well as their present existence, and who encountered a teacher who were able to lead them to a direct experience of Enlightenment. A key issue here is that Buddhahood is not just a question of 'knowledge' in an intellectual or cognitive sense. It is thought of as grounded in a total transformation of the mind-body of the practitioner. One has to be a Buddha in order to see and understand the world as the Buddha does, and that involves achieving a radical transformation of the emotional and physical basis of one's existence.

While Buddhism, like other religious traditions based on a radical transformation of ordinary understandings of the world, developed a complex and sophisticated body of philosophical approaches to the true nature of reality as experienced by an enlightened Buddha, the real core of the tradition was concerned with technique, with how to get there, rather than with philosophical understanding. The techniques developed and were refined over time. In the case of Vajrayāna or Tantric Buddhism in particular, they evolved into complex and subtle manipulations of the cognitive, emotional and psychophysical basis of human existence, guided by detailed visualizations, exercises and liturgical procedures. The methods by which Tantric practitioners in Tibet are held to contact and control the Tibetan spirit-world and provide other practical services to the Tibetan population, such as the strengthening of life-energies in longevity practice, are from the Tibetan perspective by-products, if in practice important by-products, of these techniques for the attainment of Buddhahood.

The techniques of Tantric Buddhism began as the progressive development of visionary methods already found in the Mahāyāna Sūtras from the first or second centuries CE onwards. These Mahāyāna Sūtras presented teachings which were said to have been given by the Buddha but not revealed to human audiences during his earthly career. It seems likely that these texts were themselves the result of visionary processes of some kind. In any case, they teach a variety of meditational practices that involve building up a sense of the imagined presence of the Buddhas and other deities, interacting with them and making real and/or visualized offerings to them. The deities involved are for the most part peaceful, although there are fierce guardian spirits of various kinds, some of them versions of deities mentioned in the earliest Buddhist Sūtras, such as the Four Great Yakṣa Kings. It seems that these early Tantric techniques became basic components of Buddhist monastic ritual. They provided a Buddhist equivalent to the evolving procedures of Brahmanical temple ritual. This Brahmanical ritual was centred around the new universal deities such as Śiva or Viṣṇu who were coming to importance at the same time, and who would in time provide a central component of modern Hinduism. The idea of a *maṇḍala* of deities, which again has parallels in the non-Buddhist traditions of India, developed in the Mahāyāna Sūtras by the fourth or fifth centuries CE. The *maṇḍala* in this sense is a structure in which a central deity is surrounded by a number of subsidiary figures, typically in the four or eight directions, which are understood as manifestations or projections of the central figure. Forms of meditation in which the practitioners imagined themselves as being a form of the Buddha, or receiving purifying nectars or rays of light from a Buddha above or within their bodies, also developed. These too had probably been around for a long time and were progressively synthesizedwith the *maṇḍala* visualizations.

Each of the various forms of the Buddha and of male and female *bodhisattvas* which appeared in these texts served as a focus – *iṣṭadevatā* in Sanskrit, *yidam* in Tibetan – for personal devotion and spiritual practice for Buddhist practitioners.

The *iṣṭadevatā* might be visualized or brought to imaginative existence in isolation, but the deity could also be imagined as at the centre of an array or *maṇḍala* of secondary deities. This became a standard process for early Tantric practice. In later Tibetan tradition (see Chapter 4), all these practices are classified as Kriyā or Caryā Tantra, to use the Sanskrit terms by which they are usually referred to in English. These deities were also represented as paintings and sculptured images, providing the basis for an increasingly elaborate body of imagery.

This developing body of Buddhist practices provided ways of invoking and appealing to Buddhist deities, understood as forms of the universal Buddha, for support in the pursuit of Buddhahood, and also for practical assistance and support for the state authorities or other donors who were funding the monastery or paying for the specific ritual.

As time went on, a further set of practices developed. This was known as Yoga Tantra. Initially the contrast seems to have been that in Yoga Tantra, as opposed to Kriyā and Caryā, the emphasis was primarily on performing the practice through inner visualization rather than external worship. The usage of these terms (Kriyā, Caryā, Yoga) seem to vary between early scholars, however. The Tibetan tendency to group Tantras exclusively into one class or another (see Chapter 4) developed at a considerably later date and only reached its final form in Tibet.

While protective rituals involving warrior deities such as the Four Great Deva Kings and other *yakṣa* lords go back to the earliest stages of Buddhism as we know it, and were doubtless widespread in the general religious background of pre-Buddhist North India, the central figures in these early Tantras were positive and benevolent in nature; more aggressive deities were limited to the role of subsidiary guardians. The evolution of the fierce deity practices that are characteristic of much Tibetan ritual seems to have taken place considerably later, in conjunction with the development of similar practices in the Śaivite religion, which was one of the main components of the evolving body of practices that was to become Hinduism.

The Śaivas, like the Buddhists and Jains, were ascetics competing for state patronage, and there were evidently elements of both competition and mutual borrowing. The dominant fierce deity form in the Śaiva tradition was Bhairava, a deity in the form of a charnel-ground-living, ash-covered ascetic, and master of the *yoginīs* or *ḍākiṇīs*, fearsome female spirits also associated with charnel grounds and similar scary places. Bhairava was adopted by the Buddhists as the Tantric deity Vajrabhairava and also as Mahākāla, while specifically Buddhist deities such as the *yakṣa* Vajrapaṇi also developed features and attributes similar to Bhairava. This development seems to have been well under way within Buddhism by the seventh century CE. On the Śaiva side it may have begun with traditions of state-sponsored sorcery and military magic, and Buddhist monasteries and colleges of Tantric practitioners were undoubtedly called upon to perform similar services on behalf of their employers. The fierce deities were however also interpreted in terms of the internal processes of Buddhist practice, as ways of transforming and overcoming internal obstacles to practice, such as destructive emotional or motivational states. Tantric ritual techniques for achieving more positive forms of ritual action were also developed, including rituals for healing, longevity and prosperity. Versions of all of this material would in time be transmitted to Tibet.

At around the same time, the Buddhist Tantras began to incorporate a body of internal yogic practices that was again shared with Śaiva practitioners. These are the various 'subtle body' practices involving flows of subtle substances, particularly *prāṇa* or (subtle) breath, along internal channels (Skt. *nāḍī*) meeting at a series of circles or centres (*cakra*), of which the best known are those located along the spinal column. The flows are closely associated both with breathing and with sexual practices, and may well have been influenced by similar Chinese practices that had been in existence for many centuries.

A series of new Buddhist Tantric cycles involving these practices developed from the eighth century onwards, beginning with the Guhyasamāja and Guhyagarbha Tantras and developing through other major Tantric cycles such as the Hevajra, Cakrasamvara and Kālacakra, all of them to be of great importance for the Tibetan tradition. The names of these cycles are also in most cases the names of the central deities of their increasingly complex *maṇḍala* structures. These central deities, again serving as *yidam* deities with which the practitioner can identify, generally have the form of male–female couples in sexual union, and move progressively away from the peaceful Buddha figures of earlier times.

All these practices were generally regarded as forming a later stage of the Yoga Tantras, and were initially referred to by a variety of names, including Yoga, Mahāyoga, and Atiyoga, as well as a term generally (though probably incorrectly) referred to by Western scholars as Anuttarayoga ('Supreme Yoga'). The last and most complex of these new Tantric systems, the Kālacakra (Wheel of Time) Tantra, appeared in north India in the early eleventh century. The main text of the Kālacakra Tantra shows strong signs of the increasingly militaristic and threatened state of Northern India at the time, and includes both reference to Islam and a detailed account of military technology. Vesna Wallace has described its inclusive approach to Brahmanical society as an attempt to form a common front against what was clearly seen by many at the time as a coming catastrophe.

It was particularly these later Tantric practices with their more violent and aggressive imagery that came in useful in Tibet in relation to the spirit world. They provided a basic set of techniques for 'taming' the powers of the landscape and converting them into protectors of Buddhism and so of the Tibetan population, now seen as Buddhist practitioners whom these oath-bound deities were committed to guard and assist.

The precise context of these practices in India is not always easy to reconstruct. The Tibetan annals speak of two main sources from which they obtained teachings. One was the great monastic universities of Nālandā, Vikramaśīla, Somapura and others. The other was the Tantric *siddhas*, who are portrayed in Tibetan accounts as independent practitioners, often former monks at one or another of the universities, who had broken away to practise the new Anuttarayoga cults in a non-monastic context. The stories of the *siddhas* are for a large part the stuff of legend and story, however, and it seems likely that by the eleventh and twelfth centuries these two contexts were becoming closer to each other. *Siddhas* such as Nāropā had established teaching centres and were patronized by local rulers, while monks at the monastic universities were increasingly also skilled in the new advanced Tantric techniques.

However it is clear from all this that the coming of Buddhism from India to Tibet was not the export of a single unproblematic, state-endorsed version of Buddhism from one society to another. It was a much more complex and varied business that took place over a considerable period of time, in which Tibetans travelled to India as individuals or in small groups, occasionally sponsored by local rulers, to bring back Buddhist teachings, and Indians travelled to Tibet, again as individuals or in small groups, to look for patronage and support on the high plateau. In either case, there might be any of a wide range of different kinds of practice and teaching, Tantric or non-Tantric, involved in the transmission process.

The 'early diffusion' of the Dharma

Tibetan historians traditionally speak of two periods of diffusion or propagation of the Buddhist teachings, the *ngadar* (early diffusion), up to the collapse of the Tibetan empire in the ninth century, and the *chidar* (later or general diffusion), which began with the translation activity promoted by the rulers of Guge in the late tenth century and extended until the Muslim invasions of North India in the early thirteenth century, which cut the Tibetans off from their main source of Buddhist teachers and texts in northeast India. From the early thirteenth century, while contact with the outside world, including the Buddhist centres of Nepal and China, was never completely cut off, Tibetan Buddhism essentially developed on its own terms on the basis of the material, traditions, and teaching lineages which were transmitted during these two periods.

The early and later diffusion correspond to two main groups of teachings and traditions mentioned in Chapter 1, the Nyingmapa and the Sarmapa, followers of the older and newer tradition respectively (*nyingma* = old, *sarma* = new). The Nyingmapa claimed to continue the Buddhist teachings that came to Tibet during the time of the Tibetan empire, though it appears now that what survived from the early days was extensively reshaped and developed in the ninth to thirteenth centuries. Its origins nevertheless go back to the imperial period.

The first Tibetan monks, traditionally a group of seven men from the aristocracy chosen for the purpose, took on their vocation at the time of the early Tibetan empire, in the late eighth century, and provided the initial personnel for the first

Tibetan monastery, at Samye in East-Central Tibet. As well as Sūtra material, much Tantric material was transmitted during this period, including Yoga Tantra texts from the Guhyasamāja and Guhyagarbha cycles. According to Nyingmapa tradition, Padmasambhava, who tamed the local deities and thus made it possible for the first monastery to be built, had twenty-five main Tibetan disciples, including the then king, Trisong Detsen, and the princess Yeshe Tsogyel, and these disciples played a key role in the establishment of Tantric Buddhism in Tibet.

The Nyingmapa also claimed to have a continuing lineage of monastic ordination transmitted from the imperial times, but for many centuries most Nyingmapa were non-monastic practitioners, often belonging to hereditary lama families, and they continue in modern times to provide many of the local Tantric ritualists (*ngagpa*, mantra specialists) in Tibetan communities at the village level. The Nyingmapa gradually developed their own scholarly and monastic tradition, which has continued until modern times. The Nyingmapa, along with the Bon religion, with which they have some similarities, came to be the most creative and flexible component of Tibetan Buddhism, and they were at the centre of a major spiritual renaissance in East Tibet in the nineteenth and twentieth centuries, the so-called Rimé or 'non-sectarian' movement.

The 'later diffusion' and the establishment of the Sarmapa *schools*

The Sarmapa or 'New Schools' derived from a somewhat later stage of Indian Buddhism, and they introduced many new texts and teaching lineages that did not form part of the Nyingmapa heritage, particularly the late Indian 'Anuttarayoga' Tantric cycles such as Cakrasamvara, Hevajra and Kālacakra. These became the basis of a strong yogic and meditative tradition. A variety of Sarmapa traditions grew up from the eleventh and twelfth centuries onwards. These included the Kadampa, which was a tradition strongly associated with monastic asceticism, the Sakyapa, Jonangpa, Shalupa, and others, mostly named after their main teaching monasteries, and the various Kagyüdpa yogic traditions, which were mainly transmitted through a series of further teaching monasteries.

The Sarmapa schools included a number of major scholars, such as Sakya Paṇḍita, Butön Rinchendrub and Dolpopa Sherab Gyantsen, and the new Sarmapa centres provided the context within which the scholarly tradition of the Indian monastic universities was transplanted to Tibet. The Sarmapa centres, particularly the Kadampa, also placed a renewed importance on monasticism, and it was at this time that monastic practice became firmly established as part of the Tibetan version of Buddhism. Many, though by no means all, of the Sarmapa lamas were celibate monks, and most monastic ordination lineages in Tibet are traced back to the re-introduction of the monastic ordination at this time.

The new monasteries were however centred on Tantric practice at least as much as scholarly study or monastic discipline. While broadly resembling each other, each of these traditions had its specific property of Tantric teaching lineages, associated with specific cycles of deities, transmitted within its main teaching centres, and forming the basis of its ritual practice. Each also built up a network of branch or daughter monasteries, following the tradition of the main centre.

Thus the Sakyapa, who were directed by a lineage of hereditary lamas who claimed to go back to the imperial period, had a body of teachings (the *lamdré*) focused around the Hevajra cycle. They also preserved a transmission of the Vajrakīlaya practice from the *ngadar* period that was held to be especially powerful. The Kagyüdpa, founded by the disciples of the Tibetan teacher Marpa and his student Milarepa, emphasized the practice of Cakrasamvara.

This latter cycle of Tantric teachings was associated with a series of subtle body practices (the so-called 'Six Teachings of Nāropa') that included the conscious guiding of the reincarnating consciousness (*namshé*) through the process of dying, the intermediate state and rebirth. A number of early teachers in the Kagyüdpa schools claimed to be rebirths of earlier lamas who had achieved control over this practice and so been able to take conscious rebirth with some memory of their previous lives. In the course of the thirteenth and fourteenth centuries, this became the basis of the system of *trulku* or reincarnating lamas, in which a rebirth would be found for the head lama of a monastery or other senior lama and trained to take over the position of his former incarnation (see Chapter 7). This process first became systematized among the Gyalwa Karmapa lamas, who were held to be successive rebirths of Düsum Kyenpa, the founder of the Karma Kagyüdpa school, and his successor Karma Pakshi, and gradually spread among other schools. By modern times, there were at least a thousand of these reincarnating lamas in Tibet and Mongolia, among all Buddhist schools. The term *trulku* derives from the well-known Mahāyāna idea of the 'three bodies of the Buddha', and corresponds to the third of these, the *nirmāṇakāya* or material body (literally 'magically-produced' or 'illusory' body), so there is also an implication that the reincarnated lama represents the physical presence of the Buddha.

The reshaping of the Nyingmapa tradition: kama *and* terma

The Nyingmapa tradition was also reshaped during this period, and this involved a second major cultural innovation that was in time to be as significant as the *trulku* or reincarnate lama. This was the principle of *terma* or 'rediscovered' texts and objects. Like the *trulku*, it was built on an Indian Buddhist idea, but developed it further in a way that grew out of specifically Tibetan conditions and circumstances. Thus the Mahāyāna Sūtras were regarded in Indian Buddhism as having been taught by the historical Buddha but not propagated during his physical existence on earth.

They were guarded by *nāgas* or other spirit-beings to await the time at which they should be revealed to later human followers of the Buddhist tradition. Similarly the Tantras were taught by cosmic or transcendental forms of the Buddha and revealed at a specific time to human disciples. As suggested above, one can assume that these revelations were at least in part visionary processes, such as have formed a part of many religious traditions.

The *terma* were produced by a similar revelatory process, with the origin of the teachings and practices traced back to Padmasambhava (Guru Rinpoche, the 'Precious Guru'), who by the time of the *chidar* had come to be seen as the central figure in the transmission of Tantric Buddhism to Tibet during the *ngadar* or imperial period. The main body of ritual that the Nyingmapa continued from the *ngadar* period was a series of eight ritual cycles, the *kagyé*, which were held to have been passed down as a lineal transmission (*kama*) from the time of Padmasambhava, and to have been originally transmitted from India by him or other gurus of the time. From the eleventh century onwards, a whole series of new ritual practices and other teachings gradually appeared. These *terma*, 'treasure' or 'rediscovered' teachings, were also held to have been taught by Padmasambhava to his inner circle of twenty-five disciples, but not revealed publicly during the *ngadar* period. Instead they were written down by Yeshe Tsogyal, Padmasambhava's Tibetan Tantric consort, and concealed, along with ritual objects, images and other materials, to await the time at which they should be revealed to a wider body of practitioners. Specific lamas, the *tertön* or 'treasure-finders', were able to discover and reveal these teachings at the appropriate time, and were regarded as rebirths of one or other of Padmasambhava's twenty-five disciples.

It is possible that at least some early *terma* were actual, physical texts that had been hidden during the imperial period and later rediscovered. The theory of *terma*, however, rapidly expanded to included other, less material forms of discovery. The physical text might not exist at all in material form, or consist of a few cryptic words in the script of the *ḍākiṇī*, which the *tertön* might expand into many volumes of teachings and practices, often with the help of other lamas. Since each *tertön* was a rebirth of an actual disciple of Padmasambhava, the *tertön* was thought to have been present at the time of the original transmission of the practice by Padmasambhava. The revelation of the *terma* was thus a recovery or remembering of something that was already present within the mental continuum of the *tertön*.

The *terma* concept allowed for a process of regular introduction of new practices and concepts within the Nyingmapa tradition. It was adopted to a lesser degree within the other traditions too, along with other forms of visionary techniques such as the *daknang* or pure vision in which a lama had visionary contact with a Tantric deity, who revealed teachings to him directly. Specifically for the Nyingmapa, the *terma* concept allowed for the compilation and legitimation of a whole body of teachings, in part no doubt based on fragmentary or incomplete material surviving from the *ngadar*, in other cases representing creative innovations, which enabled them to compete with the new materials and techniques transmitted by the Sarmapa schools.

One issue here was that the Sarmapa scholars, such as Sakya Pandita and Butön, had gradually established the principle of the authority of Indian texts and lineages. A practice or teaching was only regarded as legitimate by these lamas if it could be convincingly demonstrated that it had an authentic Indian lineage. This was generally a question of the existence of a Sanskrit text or of material reliably known to be translated from Sanskrit. Much of the Nyingma material, including many of the Tantras transmitted from the *ngadar*, did not fall into this category. In some cases, these texts probably were authentic translations of Indian texts, since their names occur in known lists of Indian Tantric material. In other cases their Indian origin is less certain, and they may have been Tibetan adaptations of Indian ideas.

The amount of material passed down from the early period was in any case evidently quite limited. The *terma* process provided an answer to this difficulty. The *terma* concept did not necessarily convince hard-line Sarmapa scholars of the validity of the Nyingmapa tradition, but it did provide a channel through which the Nyingmapa could build up a substantial body of systematic material for practice and teaching, with a claim to legitimacy in its own terms. In particular, the *terma* process allowed for the development and elaboration of the Dzogchen teachings, which became a particular property of the Nyingmapa lineages, and was seen as a parallel and alternative path to the Sarmapa Tantras for the attainment of Enlightenment (see Chapter 4). A series of major Nyingmapa scholars, of whom the best known is the fourteenth-century lama Longchen Rabjampa, worked to systematize these *terma* teachings, and a series of six teaching monasteries were gradually set up in Central and East Tibet, specialising in particular *terma* cycles.

A note on the Bon tradition

The *terma* process and the Dzogchen teachings were shared by the Bon religion, which claimed to continue a religious tradition existing in Tibet before the arrival of Buddhism (see Chapter 11). The *terma* concept may in fact have originated with them, since the first known Bonpo *terma* seem to have been revealed somewhat earlier than the first Nyingma *terma*. There are indications too of some collaboration between early Bonpo and Nyingma *tertöns* in finding *terma*, though these may have been exaggerated by later writers for polemical purposes. At any rate, this is a suitable place to say something about the Bon tradition.

To start with, it should be noted that we are speaking here of Bon as a living Tibetan religious tradition with continuities from the ninth and tenth centuries through to modern times. The term 'Bon', which is used as the name of this tradition, has been used in a variety of different ways by both Tibetan and Western scholars, and this has the potential to create some confusion. In particular, Bon has been used by Western scholars as a label for an imagined indigenous pre-Buddhist Tibetan religion, thought of variously as shamanic or animistic, and it has been used by Buddhist scholars in Tibet as a label for village sorcery and other despised practices, seen as a kind of negative inversion of Buddhist practice. What we are talking about here is quite different from either of those.

The pre-Buddhist religious scene in Tibet was evidently complex. If the later Bon religion continues elements of it, which is not certain, it clearly only continues some specific elements, presumably a court religious tradition associated with the *bon* and *shen* ritual specialists mentioned in some early texts. The later Bon religious tradition is also quite explicit that its origins are not indigenous to Tibet, but come from elsewhere, from the realm of Olmo Lungring or Tazik, to the west of Tibet, and that they were transmitted through the kingdom of Shangshung, in present-day Western Tibet, which was incorporated into the Tibetan empire in the mid-seventh century. The locations of Olmo Lungring and Tazik are uncertain – Olmo Lungring might be the upper Indus valley, or somewhere further west, and Tazik is an ethnonym for Iranian populations – but the claims of external origins are entirely plausible, though the traditional Bonpo chronology, which places these events many tens of thousands of years in the past, is more problematic.

The Bonpo regard the main teacher of their tradition, Shenrab Mibo, as himself a form of the Buddha. He grew up in Olmo Lungring, where he is said to have practised and taught the equivalent of the Buddhist Sūtra and Tantra teachings, and passed these on to his disciples. Among these was a version of the Dzogchen tradition, the Shangshung Nyengyüd or 'oral tradition of Shangshung', which the Bonpo today regard as their one directly-transmitted practice, corresponding to the Nyingmapa *kama* category. Almost all other practices of the contemporary Bonpo derive from *terma* revelations, and the set of ideas concerning these closely resembles that found among the Nyingmapa Buddhists. The Bonpo tradition has hereditary and reincarnate lama lineages, monasteries and Sūtra and Tantra practices, in many ways similar to those of the Nyingmapa. With some exceptions such as the shared Dzogchen and Phurba (Vajrakīlaya) traditions, however, the names and details of deities and practices differ.

At any rate, whatever the extent of continuity with the Indian or Tibetan past, it seems that much of the work of construction of the Nyingmapa and Bon traditions as we know them took place in the same period, the late tenth to twelfth centuries, when the New Tantra material was being imported from India. It seems that Nyingmapa and Bon derive from two different styles or strategies by which the surviving lineages of Tantric-style practitioners in Tibet reconstructed their practices to meet the demands of the new period. One strategy, the Nyingmapa, stressed Indian origins, and worked in terms of a paradigm of Buddhist teachings concealed during the time of Padmasambhava, and later rediscovered through the activities of visionary lamas. The other, the Bon, worked in terms of pre-Buddhist and more 'indigenous' origins, building in more connections with pre-Buddhist or folk religion practices. It presented its teachings as deriving from pre-Buddhist lineages of teaching forced to go underground as a result of Buddhist persecution, and again rediscovered through the activities of visionary lamas, only this time Bon rather than Buddhist lamas.

The Gelukpa school and later developments

By the end of the *chidar* period, in the early thirteenth century, most of the ingredients of Tibetan religion as we know it in recent times were in place, including the monasteries and monks, the hereditary and reincarnate lamas, the scholarly traditions derived from Indian Buddhism, and the traditions of yogic practice, also of Indian origin though developed and augmented by Tibetan practitioners. Versions of all but one of the major schools of modern Tibetan Buddhism were also in existence, and monasteries were beginning to build up significant political power and influence in their own right. This process developed much further during the period of Mongol overlordship in Tibet, during which Karma Kagyüdpa, Sakyapa and other lamas went to the Mongol court, and the Sakya lamas became in effect viceroys for Mongol rule in Tibet.

Figure 2.3
Tsongkapa. Tirpai Gompa, Kalimpong. Photo by author (2007).

The one major component of Tibetan Buddhism as we know it today which did not yet exist was the Gelukpa tradition. This was to become both numerically the most important Buddhist tradition in Tibet, and its lamas, including the Dalai Lama, were eventually to achieve political control over large parts of Tibet. The Gelukpa tradition was founded by the lama Tsongkapa and his students, who included the lama Gedündrup who was later recognized as the first Dalai Lama. The Gelukpa tradition combined the ascetic and monastic emphasis of the Kadampa school with elements of philosophical teaching and Tantric practice from the Sakyapa and Kagyüdpa tradition, built into a new synthesis which progressively established itself as a dominant presence within Tibetan society. The Gelukpa tradition placed great importance on celibate monkhood, and it was this tradition within which the great monastic universities of Central Tibet, Ganden, Sera and Drepung, the largest with more then 10,000 monks in modern times, developed. It was also the form of Tibetan Buddhism which was supported by the Manchu emperors of China and which almost entirely dominated Mongolian Buddhism.

While the Gelukpa became the largest single tradition in Tibet, and was closely associated with the Lhasa government, it was never totally dominant within ethically Tibetan regions. As mentioned earlier, for most of their history Tibetan Buddhists have lived in a variety of different states and stateless areas, and communications around the country have been slow and often difficult. While there have also been unifying factors – the long-distance trade routes, the common written language, pilgrimage centres, the widespread respect for the Dalai Lama – the persistence of local regimes with varying interests have militated against suppression of religious difference or the development of a unified, centralized religious style. The Nyingmapa tradition, which for much of its history has been small in scale and close to the concerns of ordinary lay Tibetans, has developed a whole tradition of 'hidden valleys' (*béyül*) where people can go for refuge in times of conflict or for the peaceful pursuit of religious practice. The former kingdom of Sikkim, now incorporated within India, originated as a *béyül* of this type, and there are a number of other such valleys in the Himalayas. One of the functions of *tertöns* was to discover and open such valleys.

The political dominance of the Gelukpa order over much of Tibet, however, which was originally established in the 1640s through a military alliance between the Fifth Dalai Lama and the Mongol chieftain Gushri Khan, nevertheless led to a reaction among the other traditions. In the nineteenth century, a group of lamas from the Nyingmapa, Kagyüdpa and Sakyapa traditions developed a 'non-sectarian' (*rimé*) approach, based on the principle that the wide variety of Tibetan teachings and practice lineages represented alternative and equally valid approaches to the attainment of Buddhahood, any of which might be of value for a particular practitioner. A dominant influence was the late eighteenth-century Nyingmapa lama Jigmé Lingpa, who created a highly influential new cycle of *terma* teachings, the Longchen Nyingtig, linked to the Dzogchen tradition. The main founding figures of the Rimé movement itself were Jamyang Khyentsé, who came from the Sakyapa tradition, Jamgön Kongtrül, a Kagyüdpa lama from a Bonpo background, and the Nyingma *tertön* Chokgyur Lingpa. These lamas worked under the patronage of the rulers of the small Eastern Tibetan state of Derge to preserve and bring together as many as possible of the variety of different teachings, lineages and traditions still existing within Tibet. This movement remained centred in East Tibet (Kham), and lamas and students in these three traditions in that region frequently studied at each other's centres, took teachings from each other, and worked together to preserve and transmit the whole range of Tibetan Buddhist practice traditions available in their time. Their students, and the collections of texts and practices that they compiled, have been enormously influential among the non-Gelukpa traditions since the late nineteenth century, and have provided an alternative focus to the increasingly conservative Gelukpa tradition.

The twentieth century onwards

The degree of isolation of Tibetans from the outside world before the twentieth century can be overstated. Tibetans were traders. Many of them travelled outside Tibet, and information about the countries between which they traded was a useful commodity for a trading people. As texts such as the early nineteenth-century *Dzamling Gyéshé* ('Description of the World') witness, Tibetans had quite detailed knowledge of neighbouring countries, and their picture of far-distant Europe, if sketchy, was probably more accurate than the European picture of Tibet. However, Tibetans until the end of the nineteenth century interacted with the rest of the world largely on their own terms, and foreign powers had little direct effect on day-to-day living on the high plateau. Even the authority of the Manchu emperor, as mediated through his representatives at Lhasa (the *ambans*) from the late eighteenth century onwards, was intermittent and had little influence on Tibetan society. The Qianlong emperor's decree of the 1793 regulating the selection of the Dalai Lama and other high reincarnations, a matter of direct relevance to the Chinese government in Beijing, had in effect become a dead letter by the early nineteenth century.

Matters were not much different in Eastern Tibet (Kham), where the heads of the small states of Kham were generally recognized by the Manchu regime as *tusi* or local indigenous chieftains and left to run their own affairs, or in Northeast Tibet (Amdo), where pastoral tribes maintained a high degree of independence. Northeast Tibet was an ethnically diverse region, with a substantial Han Chinese population, as well as Chinese Muslims (Hui), Mongols, Tu (Monguor), Salar and other minority groups, but Chinese rule was mainly significant in the areas of substantial Chinese settlement down in the valleys, particularly around the Chinese administrative centre of Xining. It was only in the far west, in Ladakh and Baltistan, after the Dogra conquest in the early nineteenth century, that a Tibetan Buddhist society experienced some degree of incorporation into a modern bureaucratic state.

Things began to change substantially in the early twentieth century, with the 1903–4 British military expedition to Central Tibet and the new and more interventionist Manchu government policy that followed. This involved imposing more direct Chinese rule over East Tibet, and led to a general uprising and a Chinese military invasion of Central Tibet. The Dalai Lama and much of the Tibetan government fled to India. The Manchu government fell in the following year, and further fighting led to a peace treaty negotiated by the British in 1918. This restored the local rulers in the area east of the Yangtse (Dri Chu) river ('Inner Tibet'), who were now regarded as ruling under Chinese sovereignty. The area to the west of the Dri River ('Outer Tibet') along with some other territories was recognized as under the control of the government of the Dalai Lama at Lhasa, under the name of the Tibet Autonomous Region. In practice, Chinese control remained very limited until 1949, when the new Communist regime began to integrate 'Inner Tibet' directly into the Chinese provinces of Gansu, Qinghai, Sichuan and Yunnan.

Meanwhile, the Lhasa government under the Thirteenth Dalai Lama had been working towards modernizing the Lhasa state. This process included the introduction of a basic public health system and elements of Western-style schooling, as well as the creation of a standing army and the forcible takeover of the areas of Shigatse and Powo, under the rule of the Panchen Lama at Tashilhunpo and the Kanam Depa in Southern Tibet. Attempts at modernization halted after the death of the Dalai Lama in 1933. In 1950–51 the Chinese army invaded Central Tibet and imposed the so-called Seventeen-Point Agreement on the Lhasa government. This allowed in theory for some degree of political autonomy, but in reality Chinese rule became increasingly oppressive. Resistance to the Chinese regime led to large-scale revolt and the escape of the Dalai Lama and many other lamas, monks, members of the Tibetan administration and ordinary Tibetans to India and Nepal in and after 1959.

Since that time, the regions of Tibetan population within the Chinese state, though nominally given the status of autonomous provinces and regions, have been fully incorporated under Chinese control. The Cultural Revolution in Tibet, commencing in 1965, involved the large-scale destruction of Tibetan monasteries and the persecution of lamas, monks and other religious practitioners. A period of liberalization and relative tolerance followed after the visit of the Chinese party secretary, Hu Yaobang, to Tibet in 1980, but an uprising in Lhasa in 1987 led to further violent suppression, and the Chinese state has maintained tight control over life in the Tibetan regions since that time. Many monasteries have been rebuilt, often with overseas funding, but religious activities remain rigorously controlled, particularly in the Tibet Autonomous Region. Attempts at political protests, such as those during the period running up to the Beijing Olympics in 2008, continue to be subject to violent suppression.

Consequently, most Tibetans since the 1950s and 1960s have grown up within the structures of a modern Chinese state, including the Chinese health and educational system and the introduction of roads, railways and other aspects of modernity on the Chinese pattern. The effects of these events on Tibetan Buddhism, and of the re-establishment of Buddhist institutions in areas of Tibetan population outside Chinese rule and throughout the rest of the world, will be considered in more detail in Chapter 12.

After this brief historical survey, we turn in Chapter 3 to the path to Buddhahood as cultivated within the Tibetan religious tradition.

Key points you need to know

- The techniques and practices of Tibetan Buddhism derived from late Indian Buddhism, and incorporated material from all stages of the development of Buddhism in India.
- Tantric Buddhism was developed much further in Tibet. The lama was a specialist in Tantric ritual and so important not only as a spiritual guide but also as an expert in handling Tantric power on behalf of the wider community.
- A major source of innovation within Tibetan Buddhism was provided by the revelations known as *terma*, revealed by a class of visionary lamas known as *tertön*.
- Tibetan Buddhism developed in the form of a number of separate but related traditions, often grouped into four main schools, the Nyingmapa, Kagyüdpa, Sakyapa and Gelukpa. The Bon religion, which claims pre-Buddhist but non-Tibetan origins, has close similarities to Buddhism and is in some respects a fifth school.

While not isolated from the outside world, Tibetan religion and Tibetan society developed largely on their own terms until the early twentieth century. The incorporation of most areas of Tibetan population into the Chinese state in 1949–59 began a new period in which Tibetan religion has struggled to survive in the context of an unsympathetic and often violently hostile Chinese state. During this period, Tibetan Buddhism has been re-established in areas outside Chinese control and has increasingly been taught through many parts of the world by refugee lamas and non-Tibetan converts.

Discussion questions

1 Discuss the role of Buddhism and Hinduism in Indian village society, and compare it with the place that Buddhism eventually occupied in Tibetan village society.

2 How did the complex imagery of later Indian and Tibetan Buddhism develop?
3 Discuss the interaction between Śaivas and Buddhists in the evolution of the fierce deities of later Tantric traditions.
4 Explain the difference between Nyingmapa and Sarmapa traditions in Tibet.
5 What are *terma* and what part did they play in the growth of the Nyingmapa and Bon traditions?
6 How did the development of the system of recognizing reincarnations of lamas contribute to the onwards development of Tibetan Buddhism?
7 What aspects of Tibetan society assisted the maintenance of a large number of local traditions?
8 How and when did Tibet become incorporated into the People's Republic of China?

Further reading

Blondeau, Anne-Marie and Katia Buffetrille. *Authenticating Tibet: Answers to China's 100 Questions*. Berkeley, Los Angeles and London: University of California Press, 2008.

Davidson, Ronald M. *Indian Esoteric Buddhism: A Social History of the Tantric Movement*. New York: Columbia University Press, 2002.

Davidson, Ronald M. *Tibetan Renaissance: Tantric Buddhism in the Rebirth of Tibetan Culture*. New York: Columbia University Press, 2004.

DeCaroli, Robert. *Haunting the Buddha: Indian Popular Religions and the Formation of Buddhism*. New York: Oxford University Press, 2004.

Dollfus, Pascale. *Lieu de Neige et de Genévriers: Organisation Sociale et Religieuse des Communautés Bouddhistes du Ladakh*. Paris, Éditions du CNRS, 1989.

Goldstein, Melvyn C. *A History of Modern Tibet, 1913–1951: The Demise of the Lamaist State*. Berkeley, CA: University of California Press, 1989.

Goldstein, Melvyn C. and Matthew T. Kapstein. (eds). *Buddhism in Contemporary Tibet: Religious Revival and Cultural Identity*. University of California Press, 1998.

Huber, Toni (ed.). *Sacred Spaces and Powerful Places in Tibetan Culture*. Dharamsala: Library of Tibetan Works and Archives, 1999.

Kapstein, Matthew T. *The Tibetan Assimilation of Buddhism: Conversion, Contestation, and Memory*. Oxford: Oxford University Press, 2000.

Kapstein, Matthew T. *The Tibetans*. Oxford and Malden, MA: Blackwell Publishing, 2006.

Karmay, Samten G. and Jeff Watt (eds). *Bon The Magic Word: The Indigenous Religion of Tibet*. New York: Rubin Museum of Art; London: Philip Wilson Publishers, 2007.

King, Richard. *Orientalism and Religion: Postcolonial Theory, India and 'The Mystic East'*. London and New York: Routledge, 1999.

Linrothe, Rob. *Ruthless Compassion: Wrathful Deities in Early Indo-Tibetan Esoteric Buddhist Art*. London: Serindia, 1999.

Linrothe, Rob (ed.). *Holy Madness: Portraits of Tantric Siddhas*. New York: Rubin Museum of Art, 2006.

Lopez Jr., Donald S. (ed.). *Curators of the Buddha: The Study of Buddhism under Colonialism*. Chicago: University of Chicago Press, 1995.

Lopez Jr., Donald S. *Prisoners of Shangri-La: Tibetan Buddhism and the West*. Chicago and London: University of Chicago Press, 1998.

Ramble, Charles. *The Navel of the Demoness: Tibetan Buddhism and Civil Religion in Highland Nepal*. New York and Oxford: Oxford University Press, 2007.

Samuel, Geoffrey. *Civilized Shamans: Buddhism in Tibetan Societies*. Washington, DC: Smithsonian Institution Press, 1993.

Samuel, Geoffrey. *The Origins of Yoga and Tantra: Indic Religions to the Thirteenth Century*. London and New York: Cambridge University Press, 2008.

Shakabpa, W.D. *Tibet: A Political History*. New Haven, CT and London: Yale University Press, 1967.

Shakya, Tsering. *The Dragon in the Land of Snows: A History of Modern Tibet since 1947*. New York: Columbia University Press, 1999.

Smith, E. Gene. *Among Tibetan Texts: History and Literature of the Himalayan Plateau*. Boston: Wisdom Publications, 2001.

Snellgrove, David L. *Indo-Tibetan Buddhism: Indian Buddhists and Their Tibetan Successors*. 2 vols. Boston: Shambhala, 1987.

Snellgrove, David L. and Hugh E. Richardson. *A Cultural History of Tibet*. London: Weidenfeld & Nicolson, 1968.

Stein, Rolf A. *Tibetan Civilization*. London: Faber, 1972.

Tucci, Giuseppe. *The Religions of Tibet*. London: Routledge & Kegan Paul; Berkeley: University of California Press, 1980.

Wallace, Vesna A. *The Inner Kālacakratantra: A Buddhist Tantric View of the Individual*. New York and Oxford: Oxford University Press, 2001.

3 *Tibetan Buddhism as a path to liberation I*

Sūtra teachings

In this chapter

This is the first of two chapters discussing Buddhahood or Enlightenment, the central goal of the Buddhist tradition in Tibet, and the techniques and approaches through which Tibetan Buddhists are encouraged to pursue it. We examine what the Tibetans meant by the distinctions between Hīnayāna and Mahāyāna, and between Sūtra and Tantra teachings. We also examine the concept of the Three Bodies of the Buddha (*trikāya*) and the idea of the 'gradual path' (*lam rim*).

Main topics covered

- The path to liberation
- Theravāda, Hīnayāna, Mahāyāna
- Sūtra and Tantra (Vajrayāna)
- Regional varieties of Buddhism in the contemporary world
- Buddhist deities and the Three Bodies of the Buddha (*trikāya*)
- Emptiness (*śūnyatā*)
- The 'gradual path'
- Refuge and *bodhicitta*
- The path of the *bodhisattva*

The path to liberation

Any religious tradition that has been followed by millions of people over centuries has to have the ability to be understood and appreciated at a variety of levels by people of different backgrounds and orientations. It also has to have a good central story that makes intellectual and emotional sense to its followers. This chapter is the first of two that deal with the aspect of Tibetan Buddhism that is probably most familiar to the majority of English-speaking readers: Tibetan Buddhism as a path to liberation from the suffering of life in the everyday world.

This central story of Tibetan Buddhism is straightforward, though it can be understood at various levels and in different ways. It begins with the standard Buddhist idea of rebirth, which is indeed shared by most Indian religious traditions. All ordinary 'sentient beings' (a class which includes animals and various classes of spirit-beings as well as humans) experience themselves as living, dying and being reborn over and again in the eternal cyclical process known as *saṃsāra* (in Sanskrit; *korwa* in Tibetan). For Buddhists, our involvement in this process is the fundamental problem of human existence. *Saṃsāra* is characterized by suffering, which is caused in its turn by desire, hatred and delusion (*rāga, dveṣa, moha* in Sanskrit), the 'three roots' of *saṃsāra*. Sometimes this suffering is intense and immediate, at other times less so, but it is always there, a universal undertow to the ordinary condition of sentient beings.

However, it is possible to attain to an altogether different state or condition of being, that of Buddhahood (Sanskrit *bodhi*, Tibetan *changchub*). *Bodhi* is often translated into English as 'Enlightenment'; though the meaning is closer to 'awakening', a reminder that this is not only a state of intellectual realization but a transformation of the entire mind–body continuum, including the totality of one's emotions and ways of relating to the world. This is the condition which was attained by the historical Buddha (Buddha is a Sanskrit word, the Tibetan is *sangyé*) but it has equally been achieved, according to the Tibetans, by many great beings in the past, and remains open to achievement in the past and the future.

In this respect the Tibetans are more positive about the possibility of human access to Buddhahood than some other Buddhist traditions. Thus the historical Buddha, Siddhartha Gautama, usually known to the Tibetans as Shakya Tubpa (Sanskrit Śākyamuni, the 'sage of the Śākya people'), is only one example of a state of being that is ultimately available to all. For ordinary lay people, and indeed for most Buddhist practitioners, it might be distant as a personal goal, glimpsed as a possibility at the end of a long series of future lives, but the historical Buddha and the many others who had attained Buddhahood served as proof that it could be attained.

The techniques for the attainment of Buddhahood were brought to Tibet by a succession of great spiritual masters, of whom the most famous and significant was the Indian teacher Padmasambhava ('Lotus-born'), known in Tibetan as Pema Jungné or Guru Rinpoche ('Precious Teacher'). Padmasambhava was probably a historical figure who visited Tibet in the late eighth century. For Tibetans, however, he is a second Buddha, whose visit to Tibet involved the taming and conversion of the spirits of the land, and was crucial for the establishment of the Buddhist tradition within Tibet. Tibet itself produced a long series of further great masters, who passed on the teachings and practices from generation to generation. Here it is important always to remember that Tibetan Buddhism is a matter of practice as well as of formal teaching, and it is the practice that is most important, not the verbal presentation. For the Tibetans, the central issue is always the effective passing on of the tradition of practice. Intellectual understanding without practice and personal realization has little value.

What is Buddhahood or Enlightenment and what purpose does it serve? Here Tibetan tradition insists that Buddhahood is fundamentally characterized by love and compassion, a love and compassion that is energized by an awareness of the sufferings inherent to life in *saṃsāra*. One can only attain Buddhahood through the development within oneself of the strong and intense motivation to free all beings from their suffering. This state or condition (*bodhicitta* in Sanskrit, *changchub sem* in Tibetan) is a vital stepping-stone towards Buddhahood. The idea of *bodhicitta* is very important and we will return later to its significance and to the techniques and approaches used to develop it. *Bodhicitta* is sometimes translated in English as the 'thought of Enlightenment', but as we will discover it too is understood within Tibetan Buddhism as being much more than a merely cognitive process; it is something that engages and entrains the entire human being, including both emotions and physiology. Once *bodhicitta* has been awakened or aroused within an individual, that person is on the path to Buddhahood. This idea of a path is another important image: Buddhahood is the endpoint of a pathway along which individual human beings can and should travel.

The condition of Buddhahood itself is characterized by omniscience and by virtual omnipotence. A Buddha knows everything and can intervene in life in numerous forms and guises in order to help human beings and relieve their sufferings. Thus the state or condition of Buddhahood represents a source of enormous potential for assistance in daily life, and also for those travelling themselves along the path to achieving *bodhi*. Lamas, yogins and monks can access these powers in various ways for the benefit of their followers. Here it is important to be aware, as described in Chapter 1, that pre-modern Tibetans lived in a world of spirits and powers which pervaded everything from the individual to the mountains, lakes and skies. Within this world, all things were understood to be causally connected and to affect each other. There was a constant need for assistance in influencing these processes of causal connection so as to defend individuals and communities against malevolent forces, and to bring about healing and prosperity.

Thus Tibetan Buddhism offers a strong central story of the historical Buddha and the path to the attainment of Buddhahood, and a variety of ways in which individuals could engage with that story, from seeking to attain Buddhahood oneself to asking the magical assistance of those already 'on the path'. In practice, there was and is a kind of implicit deal or exchange between ordinary people and 'serious' practitioners, whether the latter are lamas, monks or lay yogins. Those actively engaged on the path, the lamas, monks and yogins, are supported by the population as a whole in return for their ritual and magical services as well as for their teaching.

The story of Tibetan Buddhism also has sub-narratives. There are stories of lamas or yogins who used their powers for good or in some cases for evil. Lamas became progressively involved in the realm of politics, and this involvement may be seen by Tibetans (including the lamas themselves) either as appropriate and justified in terms of the spiritual realization of great lamas or as mistaken or irrelevant, on the grounds that 'true' Enlightenment has nothing to do with hierarchy and protocol of the wealthy lama's court. We will see some of these complexities as we proceed. For the present, we are concerned with the central story.

How, though, does the Tibetan version of the path to Enlightenment differ from the versions taught by other Buddhist traditions? Here there are a number of issues to consider. These include the distinction between *nirvāṇa* and Buddhahood, and the implication of the idea of Buddhahood as a universal potentiality. Underlying both of these however is a third issue; the idea of the Buddha's skill in means, and so of the range of different Buddhist teachings.

The fundamental idea here is that the primary concern of the Buddha, and ultimately of any Buddhist teacher, is to lead his or her disciples or followers to Buddhahood. Buddhahood itself is a state of being, and so inexpressible in words. It can only be fully understood by attaining it through one's personal spiritual development. Consequently, any specific teaching is incomplete and inadequate; it can only express a relative or conventional truth (*kundzob denpa*, Skt. *saṃvṛti-satya*), valuable as a guide for people at a certain level of spiritual development. Part of the Buddha's skill in means, and that of a competent lama, is to give the teaching or behave in the way that is appropriate to a disciple at a particular stage of development. As we will see, this concept of 'skill in means' (*upāya-kauśalya* in Sanskrit) is a highly developed idea in Tibetan religion, and the idea of different 'levels' of meaning and of practice (often three, 'outer', 'inner' and 'secret') is firmly embedded in the culture and the language. *Upāya*, 'means' (*tap* in Tibetan), is the essential complement of the wisdom or penetrating insight (*prajñā* in Sanskrit, *sherap* in Tibetan); they are conceptualized in terms of the duality of male and female, they are seen as elements present within all human beings, and they are seen as the two wings that the bird of Buddhahood needs in order to take flight.

Theravāda, Hīnayāna, Mahāyāna

A corollary, though, is that the various teachings of the Buddha do not necessarily form a single consistent body of material. Here the Tibetans are representative of one of the two main contrasting directions in which Indian Buddhism developed. It seems that relatively early on in the history of Buddhism, certainly by around 100 BCE, perhaps three centuries after the death of the historical Buddha, it was becoming clear that the various texts, initially orally transmitted but now increasingly committed to writing, that represented the teaching of the historical Buddha were not necessarily in agreement with each other. Over the following centuries, two approaches grew up in response to this problem. One was to work out a single consistent body of material, and regard other texts as inauthentic or unimportant. This was by and large the orientation of the early schools (the so-called Nikāya Buddhism). The Nikāyas were primarily traditions of ordination, in other words one belonged to a Nikāya because one was ordained by members of that Nikāya, but they gradually developed distinctive doctrinal positions over time. These positions each aimed to define a canon of valid texts and develop a systematic understanding of the teachings on that basis. Only one of these traditions, the Theravāda ('Teaching of the Elders'), has survived into modern times as a live tradition, though the Theravāda as we know it represents later developments, and is perhaps better understood as the result of an attempt, about a millennium after the time of the Buddha, to recreate an authentic early Buddhism. This was the work of Buddhaghosa and his contemporaries, who worked in Sri Lanka in the fifth century CE, and the Pali Canon, the canonical collection of texts for most Southeast Asian and Sri Lankan Buddhists today, derives largely from their activity. For the Theravādins, and for the early schools as a whole, the central goal was not Buddhahood itself but the condition known as *nirvāṇa* in Sanskrit (*nibbāna* in Pali, *nyangendé* in Tibetan) or withdrawal from *saṃsāra*, the cycle of rebirth.

By the time of Buddhaghosa, an alternative approach, the so-called 'Mahāyāna' ('Great Vehicle'), had become widely established in many parts of India and the Buddhist world. The term 'Mahāyāna' is somewhat problematic, particularly if it is taken to define a distinct movement with an institutional presence. The Mahāyāna was more a growing tendency and way of thinking and practising their religion among Buddhist monks and lay practitioners who for the most part remained (in ordination terms) part of the early Nikāyas. Certainly this is true of the Tibetans today, who continue this tendency in Indian Buddhism; the Tibetans belong to the Sarvāstivādin Nikāya, which was one of the early Nikāyas, not to any specifically 'Mahāyāna' tradition of ordination. The same is true of almost all East Asian Buddhists.

The term Mahāyāna means 'Great Vehicle', and the followers of the new tendency referred to the earlier tradition as 'Hīnayāna' or 'Lesser Vehicle'. The image here is of the various teachings (as in a famous story in the *Saddharmapuṇḍarīka* or 'Lotus Sūtra', one of the most influential of early Mahāyāna texts) being seen as 'vehicles' by means of which the Buddhist could travel along the path to Enlightenment or Buddhahood. For the Mahāyāna followers, Buddhahood was the only true goal, and the lesser goal of *nirvāṇa* or liberation from suffering promized by the 'lesser vehicle' (Hīnayāna) was simply there to attract people along the path until they had progressed far enough to see beyond it to the more advanced goal of Buddhahood. In Tibetan and Mahāyāna tradition, this 'lesser vehicle' is also often known as the teachings of the 'Śrāvakas and Pratyekabuddhas'. The Śrāvakas and Pratyekabuddhas here are a generic term for realized beings who are held to have achieved awakening from *saṃsāra*, but, according to the later traditions, are unable to reach the level of full Buddhahood because of their failure to practise the higher and more profound teachings of the Mahāyāna.

More generally, the supporters of the new tendency held that there were many different expressions of the Buddhist teachings. Each of them had been taught in some sense by the Buddha, either in the form of the historical Buddha Śākyamuni or in various visionary forms; some had been taught by Śākyamuni but concealed in order to be revealed at a later period for which they were appropriate. These various teachings were not necessarily logically consistent with each other, but each was valid in its own terms and was potentially useful to people of a particular kind at a particular stage in their progress along the path to Buddhahood. This idea of the multiplicity of teachings is a corollary of the concept mentioned earlier of the Buddha's skill in means, by which he is able to teach appropriately for each student. This perspective made it possible to accept the whole series of new approaches and techniques that gradually emerged over the centuries from around 100 BCE onwards.

These new approaches were presented in texts that had the general form of conventional Buddhist Sūtras. In other words, they present a narrative of an occasion on which the historical Buddha had given the teaching in question to a specific, named audience, and read as if they are giving a literal description of that occasion by an eye-witness. The idea, initially at least, was that these were indeed descriptions of teachings given by the historical Buddha but that had not been made public at the time of the Buddha, since his audiences at that time were not ready for them. Instead they had been preserved by non-human agencies such as the *nāga* spirits until such a time as it was appropriate for them to be revealed. These texts included the so-called 'Mahāyāna Sūtras' and, at a later period, the Buddhist Tantras or Vajrayāna teachings. As we have seen, these new texts described *nirvāṇa* as a temporary and partial goal, a stepping-stone on the path to Buddhahood that was taught only for those who were not as yet ready for the message of Buddhahood itself.

By the seventh century CE, when we have accounts from the Chinese monk-pilgrims who visited India, the distinction was clearly well developed. These pilgrims described monasteries around South Asia in terms of whether their monks were Mahāyāna, Hīnayāna or (as was often the case) mixed. The 'Mahāyāna Sūtras' are however themselves far from a single consistent body of teachings and concepts. In time, a number of classificatory schemes grew up to provide some logic to the variety of different teachings contained in what became a very large and heterogeneous body of material, much of which has still received little detailed attention from Western scholars.

In one influential scheme, the 'Three Turnings of the Wheel of the Dharma', the Mahāyāna is further subdivided into two general categories of teachings: Cittamātra (Tib. *semtsampa*, literally 'mind only') (also known as Vijñānavāda, 'consciousness tradition' or Yogācāra, through its association with the practice of yoga), which gave primacy to the nature of consciousness, and the Mādhyamika (Tib. *umapa*) teachings, which gave primacy to insight into the voidness or emptiness of phenomena. In this scheme the 'First Turning' took place when the historical Buddha taught the 'Hīnayāna' (here understood to be Sarvāstivāda) teachings at Sarnath, the second when he expounded the Mādhyamika teachings, and the third when he preached the Yogācāra teachings. The distinctions between Sarvāstivāda, Yogācāra and Mādhyamika refer essentially to differences between philosophical positions (*siddhānta; drupta* in Tibetan), rather than practical methods for attaining Enlightenment. In terms of methods for practice, the Mahāyāna developed a great number of techniques, particularly involving visualisation of the Buddhas and *bodhisattvas* and imaginative transformation of the world into their realms. These in their turn formed the basis of the later development of the Tantras.

Sūtra and Tantra (Vajrayāna)

Originally, no doubt, the Hīnayāna–Mahāyāna distinction was, as much as anything, a polemical strategy to validate the approach of the new Mahāyāna tendency as against those of their competitors. However it had the potential to become something else, the basis of a progressive scheme of teachings: one begins with the teachings of the Hīnayāna Sūtras, and then moves on to the various levels of teaching in the Mahāyāna Sūtras. What became known as the Tantric teachings, were originally seen as part of the Mahāyāna, but gradually came to be seen as a third stage to follow after the Mahāyāna Sūtras: the Vajrayāna or '*vajra* vehicle'. *Vajra*, originally the name of the thunderbolt-sceptre of the Vedic god Indra, is a complex term combining ideas of intense strength, power and toughness.

The Tantric teachings were mentioned in Chapter 2, and more will be said about them in Chapter 4. Vajrayāna teachings were not seen as implying a new goal as such, since they too are aimed at the attainment of Enlightenment or Buddhahood. Nor were they necessarily seen as proposing a new philosophical perspective (*siddhānta*). They were seen however as 'difficult' and advanced teachings, fraught with danger and to be undertaken only by advanced practitioners who had already established a solid basis through other practices, so it made sense for them to be seen as a third stage after Hīnayāna and non-Tantric Mahāyāna. This was, in Tibet, part of a kind of compromise reached between the local rulers of Guge in Western Tibet, a key location for the establishment and systematization of Buddhism in the tenth and eleventh centuries, and Tantric teachers such as Atiśa. The kings of Guge were suspicious of much that was happening under the label of 'Tantra'. They wished to control the practice of Tantra and to emphasize the practice of Buddhism by celibate monastic practitioners. Similar movements in other Buddhist countries, such as Burma and Sri Lanka, were largely successful. Types of Buddhist practice derivative from and analogous to Tantra were marginalized, and 'professional' Buddhist practice became primarily a matter for fully-ordained monks. In Tibet, however, this never happened, in part perhaps because of the lack of centralization mentioned in Chapter 1, in part because the ritual services provided by lay Tantric practitioners (*ngakpa*) became so much part of how Tibetan communities managed their affairs, and were so highly valued.

Regional varieties of Buddhism in the contemporary world

The long, complex and varied historical relationship between Buddhism and politics, and the differences between how it worked out in one or another region of Asia, is a major factor behind the contrasts between the various contemporary forms of Buddhism. Another is the tendency of Buddhism to become indigenized and adapted to local needs and requirements in the various societies where it has continued to be practised. It may be useful to give a brief description of these regions.

Roughly speaking, one can divide the Buddhist regions of Asia today into three main areas. These are often labelled Theravāda, Mahāyāna and Vajrayāna, but this is an incorrect and misleading use of these terms, none of which was really intended to designate a regional variety of Buddhism. Here I shall follow Peter Harvey's suggestion and refer to them simply as Southern, Eastern and Northern. In the Southern region, which includes the Southeast Asian Buddhist traditions (Myanmar, Thailand, Laos, Cambodia) and the Buddhists of Sri Lanka, Mahāyāna and Tantric practices were progressively marginalized or even prohibited, although they continued to have a strong influence on popular and esoteric versions of Buddhist practice in many of these countries. Official Buddhism today in the Southern Buddhist countries belongs to the Theravāda school, and claims to represent an 'original' (pre-Mahāyāna and pre-Tantric) version of the Buddhist teachings. The Buddhist texts here are taught and practised in the Pali language, an ancient Indian language closely related to Sanskrit. Buddhism has largely vanished from India, Pakistan and Bangladesh themselves, although at one period these were all regions where Buddhism flourished, as it has from Afghanistan, Iran and the various regions along the old Silk Route. The small remaining community of Buddhists in Bangladesh are now followers of Theravāda Buddhism, while several million Indians from Dalit ('untouchable') communities, particularly in Northwest India, have been converted to a modernist form of Buddhism, initially under the influence of the great Dalit leader Bhimrao Ramji Ambedkar (1891–1956).

The Eastern region of the contemporary Buddhist world consists of China and the other regions that have formed part of the Chinese cultural world, including Taiwan, Korea, Vietnam, and Japan. Buddhism here was transmitted through the Chinese language, and eventually onwards into other regional languages. In the process it became deeply engaged with East Asian spiritual traditions, including Confucianism and particularly Daoism. Both Mahāyāna and Tantra were transmitted to East Asia, but for the most part this consisted only of the earlier stages of Tantra (Kriyā, Caryā, some early Yoga Tantra). Tantric practice still persists, particularly in Japan, but is relatively marginal to East Asian Buddhism, which developed a strong Chinese cultural flavour. In recent years, though, Tibetan Buddhism, which was influential

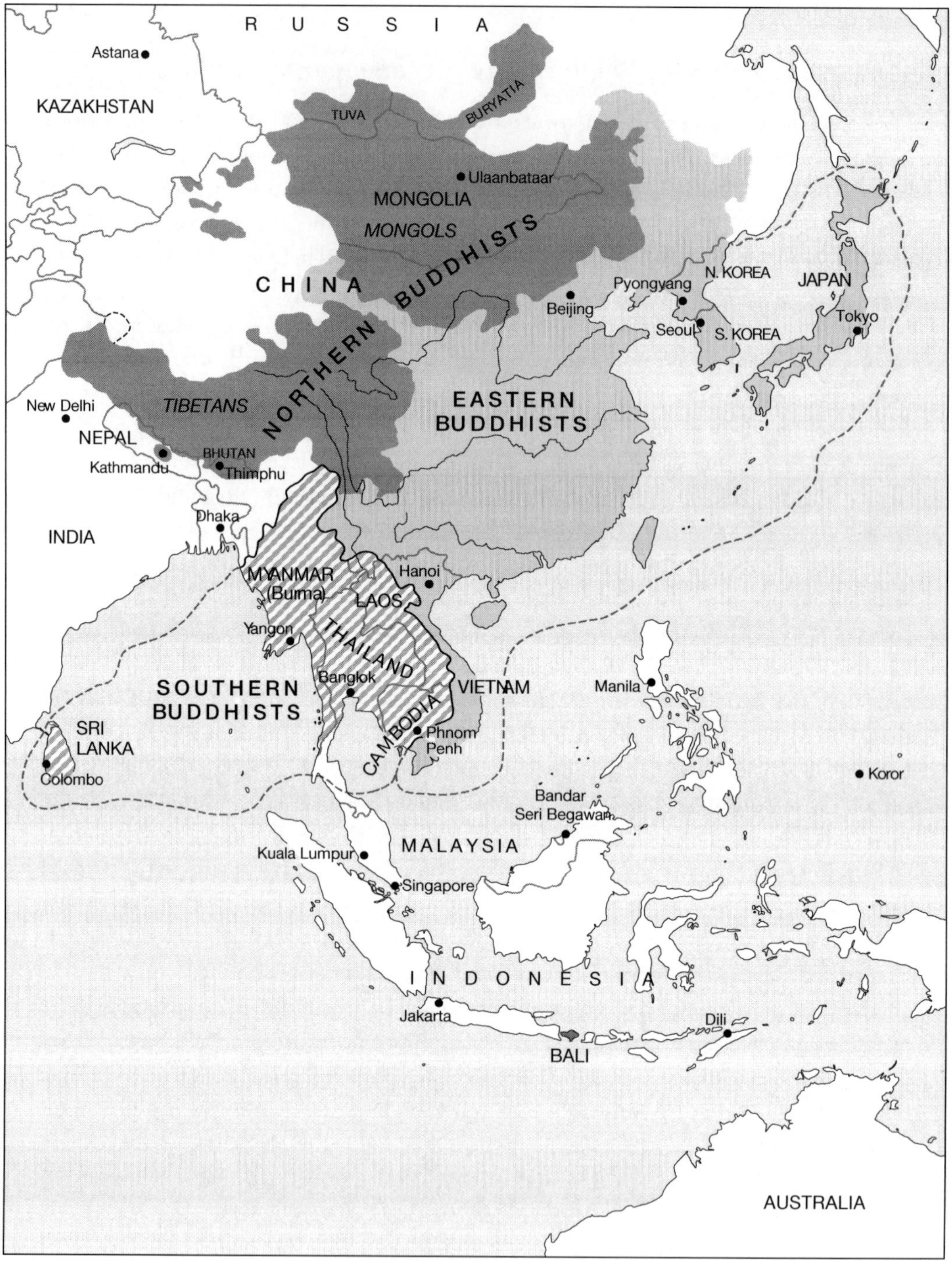

Figure 3.1 Map of regional varieties of Buddhism

during the Manchu dynasty, has again become a significant presence within both mainland and overseas Chinese communities.

The full range of Mahāyāna and Tantric teachings and practices survived primarily in the Northern region. This includes the Tibetan regions of China, India and Nepal, along with Bhutan and a number of Central Asian regions (Mongolia, including both independent Mongolia and the Mongolian regions of the People's Republic of China, as well as Tuva and Buryatia) that received Buddhism from the Tibetans. Here Buddhism was translated into Tibetan, and later on into Mongolian, languages, and went through a process of indigenization which has already been sketched in Chapter 2, in which it was reworked in terms of the local needs and requirements of the Tibetan population. Other forms of the Indian Mahāyāna–Tantric synthesis have survived on a smaller scale among the Newar people of the Kathmandu Valley and on the island of Bali in Indonesia.

This brief sketch may help to situate the Buddhism discussed in this book in relation to other Buddhist traditions. These various traditions have now spread around the world, so that when one encounters 'Buddhism' in contemporary Europe, North American or Australia it can belong to any of these regional varieties, or their many sub-varieties.

Buddhist deities and the Three Bodies of the Buddha (trikāya)

One feature of the Mahāyāna material was the appearance of a wide variety of Buddhist deities. Deities from the common Indian pantheon of local and regional spirits, such as the *yakṣa* Vajrapāṇi and the four great *deva* kings of the four directions, all of whom became special protectors of the Buddha and his teachings, are already extensively present in the early Buddhist texts. The Brahmanical deities such as Brahmā and Indra are also described as acclaiming and supporting the Buddha. By the first century BCE however there are signs of the early Buddhists developing a specific pantheon of their own. A major part was played in this by divine forms of the Buddha himself, particularly a set of four Buddhas associated with the four directions who came to have an important role in meditational practices.

The idea of the *bodhisattvas* (Tib. *changchub sempa*), heroic beings who have irreversibly created within themselves the Enlightenment-motivation mentioned earlier (*bodhicitta*), also provided the basis for a kind of deity. This development was already underway in Buddhist iconography from the Gandhāran period, with figures such as Maitreya (Tib. *Jampa*), Avalokiteśvara (Tib. *Chenresik*), and Mañjuśrī (Tib. *Jambeyang*) taking on a quasi-divine status. Maitreya is the future Buddha predicted in the early texts, while Avalokiteśvara and Mañjuśrī act as representations of the Buddha's compassion and his wisdom respectively. A range of further deities evolved, including a number of female figures, of whom Tārā (Tib. *Drölma*) is the most prominent. All of these have become of great significance for the Tibetans, since the ritual

Figure 3.2
Maitreya (Jampa). Image in Sera Monastery. Photo by author (1991).

practices that evolved around them was part of the body of material that formed the basis for the Buddhist Tantras.

Another important classificatory scheme served as a way of making sense of the place of these various deities in relation to the ultimate nature of Buddhahood on one side and the human beings who attain Buddhahood on the other. This is the so-called *trikāya* (Tib. *kusum*) or 'three body' scheme. This works in terms of three 'bodies' or levels of manifestation of Buddhahood, often depicted in later Tibetan Buddhist art as a process of downwards emanation. At the highest level is the Dharmakāya (Tib. *chöku*) or 'Dharma-body'. Then follows the levels of the Tantric deities, including the directional Buddhas, *bodhisattvas* and goddesses. This is called the Saṃbhogakāya (Tib. *longchödku*) or 'enjoyment body'. Finally comes the level of human manifestations (*nirmāṇakāya*, Tib. *trulku*) of the Buddha, which included the historical Buddha Śākyamuni and other human beings thought to have attained Buddhahood.

This concept allowed for a flexible and sophisticated understanding of the relationship between Buddhahood and individual human beings (or more exactly sentient beings, Tib. *semchen*, which include gods, animals and other living beings as well as humans). It should be remembered that for Buddhists our sense of our personal individuality and separateness from the world is ultimately an illusion to be transcended. This also applies to the apparent dichotomy between the idea of the Buddha as a historical person who attained a particular state of spiritual development and the idea that Buddhahood exists as some kind of universal quasi-divine power (*dharmakāya*) that manifests in many different ways, so that the historical Buddha Śākyamuni and other human beings thought to have attained Buddhahood can be seen as projections or emanations (*nirmāṇakāya*) of that power.

One can certainly find both kinds of language used in the ways that Tibetans talk about Buddhahood, but the conflict between them is more apparent than real. Within Tibetan Buddhist thought, human beings are not ultimately separate from the world around them, including their fellow human beings in the past, present and future. One can imagine Buddhahood as something like a universal possibility available to humans and also to all other living beings. From one point of view, Buddhahood is a state, characterized by universal love, compassion and altruistic activity, that can be 'tuned into' and realized by those prepared or able to make the effort. From another, it is a fundamental modality of the universe, which is expressed in varying degrees through countless different human and non-human manifestations.

Emptiness (śūnyatā)

A significant issue here is the concept of emptiness or voidness (Skt. *śūnyatā*, Tib. *tongpanyid*) that is one of the key attributes of the Buddhist Enlightenment for Mahāyāna Buddhists. *Śūnyatā* is at one level a further development of the universal Buddhist assertion of selflessness. All Buddhist traditions assert that the self is illusory and impermanent. The Mahāyāna goes further, in claiming that the same is true of all phenomena. Mahāyāna Buddhism holds that there cannot be an ultimately valid and accurate language in which the universe can be fully and definitively described. Some of the eighteen early schools probably also came close to asserting or implying the same thing, but for the developing Mahāyāna tendency it became a central idea, represented by the term *śūnyatā* or 'emptiness'. Phenomenal reality is 'empty' or 'void' in the sense that our understandings of it are empty and illusory; the ultimate reality that lies beyond it is also 'empty' in that emptiness is all that can be positively asserted about it.

In fact, from some points of view, the *dharmakāya*, the ultimate nature of Buddhahood and of the universe, is emptiness. It is evident, though, that 'emptiness' is not quite the same as there being nothing there. The universe is not a void in the sense of an absence of anything real, in some ways quite the opposite. It is rather void or empty in the sense of the absence of any specific thing, concept, feeling or state that human processes of consciousness may assume is there. Here Buddhism comes quite close to certain kinds of contemporary Western thought, both the relativistic mode of thinking underlying much of modern physics, and the deconstructionist tendencies significant in modern philosophy and philosophy of science. As Tibetan teachings often say, however, one can take *śūnyatā* too far, in which case it becomes a kind of nihilism.

It can be equally somewhat problematic to describe Buddhahood in its ultimate form, the *dharmakāya*, in positive language, as a state of infinite potentiality or the like, since this can easily lead to a kind of reification or concretization of Buddhahood as a 'thing' of some kind. The exact balance between these different languages is one of the key issues of Buddhist philosophy in Tibet, emerging in particular in the contrast between so-called *rangtong* ('empty of own nature') approaches, which stress the 'emptiness' side, and *shentong* ('empty of other nature') approaches, which stress the side of positive potentiality. This is not just a philosophical dispute, since *rangtong* and *shentong* can be seen as leading to different ideas about the relationship between the Buddhist path and society, and so to different social and political arrangements.

This assertion of emptiness as the true nature of reality, whatever the specific details, does not mean that particular Tibetans may not think of themselves on an everyday basis as separate individuals pursuing personal goals in their lives. Thinking of oneself in such a way is probably a universal aspect of human biology, and Tibetans are as liable to it as anyone else. However, a central feature of Tibetan Buddhism is that it aims to undercut this tendency, it regards it as a basic human problem, and it sees the ultimate answer to that problem for each living being as their eventually attaining the transpersonal goal of Buddhahood. Thus *bodhicitta*, the key motivational state that directs and drives living beings towards the attainment of Buddhahood, is described in words as the desire to attain full and complete Enlightenment or Buddhahood so as to be able to relieve all living beings from their suffering.

Śūnyatā is generally presented in philosophical terms, but it is important to recognize, as with *bodhicitta* and *bodhi* themselves, that these words are intended to refer to emotional, felt concepts as much as to formal doctrines. Thus *śūnyatā* also refers to the human experience of the superficiality and meaninglessness of things, the 'emptiness' or everyday existence, as something that needs to be transcended by the awareness of a deeper and more significant meaning to human life.

The 'gradual path'

The path to Buddhahood thus involves a progressive purification or transformation of the entire human mind–body complex (referred to by the Tibetans as 'body, speech and mind' – *ku sung tuk*). The Tibetans developed a whole series of progressive schemes of training aimed at this goal, using the large range of material which they received from India and to some extent also from other Buddhist countries (China, perhaps Buddhist Central Asia). We will come across a number of these in the course of this book, but here we begin with one that was especially influential: the 'stages of the path' (*lam rim*) scheme which goes back to the important Indian teacher Atiśa who worked in Tibet in the mid-eleventh century.

Atiśa's short text begins with a division clearly derivative from the Hīnayāna–Mahāyāna distinction, but now developed into three levels (see the box below).

The three kinds of practitioners according to Atiśa

In his *Lamp for the Stages of the Path*, Atiśa divides Buddhist practitioners into three types. Different teachings are appropriate to each type, and these form a progressive series of three stages, from lowest to highest.

The lowest and least spiritually advanced kind of person still seeks the pleasures of *saṃsāra* and is concerned only for himself or herself. Such a person is at best motivated by the desire to avoid suffering in a future life.

The middle type of person has rejected *saṃsāra*, but is still selfishly motivated. This, in other words, is the 'Hīnayāna' practitioner, who has not gone beyond seeking an end to his or her own suffering.

The highest type of person, who is the Mahāyāna practitioner, is driven by the need to end the suffering of all beings.

The rest of Atiśa's text is mostly concerned with explaining the path for the highest type of person, who is taught to take the Three Refuges (Buddha, Dharma and Saṅgha), develop the *bodhicitta* motivation or 'thought of Enlightenment', and follow the classical Buddhist triple training of discipline (*śīla*), meditation (*samādhi*) and wisdom or insight into reality (*prajñā*), ideally as a monk. It concludes with a brief discussion of Tantric practice. Atiśa himself did not expound in further detail the teachings for the 'Lowest' and 'Middle' person, but these were supplied by later scholars, most notably by Tsongkapa in his *lam rim* texts.

The box below gives a summary of the scheme of Tsongkapa's *lam rim* teachings, which were presented by him and later writers in many different versions of various lengths and degrees of detail.

The teachings for the three types of person according to Tsongkapa's *lam rim* scheme

Lowest type of person

- Devotion to a spiritual guide
- The importance and difficulty of attaining birth as a human being with the ability to practise the Dharma
- The certainty of death and the uncertainty of when it will come, so the importance of making as good a use as possible of the unique opportunity provided by our having been born as human beings while we are still alive, since when we die only the Dharma can be of any help

- The sufferings of the lower realms of rebirth (beings in the various hell realms, *preta* or hungry ghosts, animals)
- Taking refuge
- Cause and effect (karma) and its inevitability, and the need to abandon non-virtuous actions with negative karmic consequences.

Middle type of person

- The sufferings of the higher realms of rebirth (human beings, *asura* or demigods, gods in the various heavens)
- The suffering of existence in *saṃsāra* in general
- The consequent need to become purified from grasping at the self and develop the triple training (*śīla, samādhi* and *prajñā*) in order to escape from *saṃsāra.*

Highest type of person

- Methods for the development of *bodhicitta* (e.g. cultivating love and compassion, the need to repay the kindness of other beings, exchanging self and others) and the conduct of a *bodhisattva*
- The six *pāramitā* or 'perfections': *dāna* (generosity), *śīla* (discipline, self-control), *kṣānti* (patience), *vīrya* (energy, perseverance), *dhyāna* (meditative concentration), *prajñā* (wisdom)
- *Śamatha* (calming meditation to develop *dhyāna*)
- *Vipaśyanā* (insight meditation to develop *prajñā*)

The *lam rim* scheme concludes with the need to undertake Tantric practice in order to progress further.

In Tsongkapa's scheme (see the box), the teachings for the first two levels are largely structured around a widely-used set of 'preliminary practices', the 'four thoughts that turn the mind towards the Dharma'. These 'four thoughts' are the importance of having attained human rebirth, the inevitability and uncertainty of death, the inescapable law of cause and effect (karma) and the pervasiveness of suffering in *saṃsāra*. We will come across these four thoughts again in Chapter 4, where they appear as part of the preliminaries to Tantric practice.

These four contemplations are based on what might be regarded as the standard Buddhist attitude of the process of *saṃsāra* in terms of the effects of karma or action. All deliberate and willed action by beings caught within the bounds of *saṃsāra* imply consequences in future lives. These affect both the overall nature of rebirth (in other words, whether one is born as a human, animal, as a god or demi-god, *preta* spirit or hell-being) and the detailed character of one's life; who one's parents might be, whether one is poor or wealthy, healthy or not, whether one is born in a country such as Tibet where the Buddhist teachings are available, and so on. We will see more of this karma-theory in Chapter 6 in relation to Buddhist ethics.

Refuge and bodhicitta

The three sets of teachings that make up the *lam rim* scheme also include material on the two important ritual steps that are the almost invariable introduction to all significant Tibetan religious activities: 'going for refuge' and 'arousing or developing *bodhicitta*'.

'Going for refuge' (*kyabdro* in Tibetan) is a universal Buddhist act in all Buddhist traditions and in fact is often regarded as the defining characteristic of a Buddhist. A Buddhist, in other words, is someone who has formally 'gone for refuge' to the Buddha, the Dharma (i.e. the teachings of the Buddha) and the Saṅgha (the Buddhist community). Here 'going for refuge' has the sense of relying on for protection and guidance in one's life. In contemporary Theravāda Buddhism, the standard form for going for refuge is a formula which involves a triple repetition of the words, 'I go for refuge to the Buddha, I go for refuge to the Dharma, I go for refuge to the Saṅgha', with the Saṅgha implicitly understood as the community of ordained Buddhist practitioners, particularly the fully-ordained monks (*bhikṣu*).

Tibetan Buddhist refuge (*kyabdro*) formulae are omnipresent, and as mentioned above almost all Tibetan ritual sequences involve one near the beginning. Their wording often varies from the Theravāda formula, in particular when they assume a Tantric context of practice. Here the lama (Skt. *guru*) takes precedence in a sense over the Buddha, Dharma, and Saṅgha, since the lama is the means of access to Buddha, Dharma, and Saṅgha. In fact the refuge is generally made in Tantric ritual contexts before a refuge field (*tsokshing*) imaginatively created in the space before the practitioner, with the lama at the centre transformed into a specific Tantric *yidam* or Tantric patron deity such as Padmasambhava, and the male and female deities of the *yidam*'s *maṇḍala* surrounding the central figure, along with other deities, Tibetan and Indian Buddhist teachers, volumes of the teachings, and so on. In reciting the refuge formula, practitioners are encouraged to imagine all living beings taking refuge along with them.

The specific wording of the refuge formula varies from practice to practice but often the guru (lama) is added to the triad of Buddha, Dharma, and Saṅgha, or they are supplemented or replaced by the triad Guru, Deva, Ḍākinī (guru, meditational deity and female guardian spirit). Here as an example is the well-known *Ma Namka* refuge formula:

> I along with all mother sentient beings equal in number to the whole of space go for refuge to the precious lama Buddha;

> I along with all mother sentient beings equal in number to the whole of space go for refuge in Buddha, Dharma and Saṅgha;
>
> I along with all mother sentient beings equal in number to the whole of space go for refuge in Guru, Deva and Ḍākinī;
>
> I along with all mother sentient beings equal in number to the whole of space go for refuge in consciousness itself, empty and luminous, the Dharmakāya.

Here the reference to 'mother sentient beings' alludes to one of the standard Tibetan contemplations for the arousal of *bodhicitta*, the altruistic motivation that is the basis for the attainment of Buddhahood. Since there is no beginning to time, all sentient beings have at some time been our mother, and so all are owed the love and compassion we would show to our own mother. Thus we should be energized to release them from their sufferings, just as we would for our own mother, and so to strive to achieve Buddhahood for the sake of freeing all sentient beings from their suffering. These *semkyé* (arousal of *bodhicitta*) practices are a recapitulation of the vow of the *bodhisattva*, which Tibetan practitioners will have undertaken in ritual contexts, including that of Tantric initiations, just as the refuge verses are a recapitulation of the initial taking of refuge before a lama which Tibetans will also have undertaken at some stage.

In fact Atiśa and Tsongkapa's 'highest type' of person is the *bodhisattva*, or at least someone who is aspiring to be a *bodhisattva* (and so to possess the precious motivational state of *bodhicitta* that drives the pursuit for Buddhahood). There is of course a difference between repeating the vow, and actually creating the motivation of *bodhicitta* within oneself, as is recognized by the Tibetans, but the *bodhicitta* formula nevertheless is one of the leitmotifs of Tibetan Buddhist teaching and practice, constantly repeated in all kinds of context, and re-asserting the logical connection between the suffering of living beings and the attainment of Buddhahood.

Often refuge and *Bodhicitta* verses are combined, as in one of the simplest and most common of Tibetan formulae of this kind:

> I take refuge in Buddha, Dharma and the Supreme Assembly,
> Until I achieve awakening.
> May I through generosity and the other [*pāramitā*]
> Achieve Buddhahood for the sake of all beings.

The refuge and *Bodhicitta* formulae are complemented by the closing formulae of Tibetan rituals, which generally involve a dedication of merit (*ngowa*) in which the merit or positive karma created by the practice is dedicated – typically for the attainment of liberation from suffering by all sentient beings, the continuation of the Dharma, and the practitioner's own attainment of Buddhahood – and by other auspicious verses, including prayers for the long life of one's own guru and the lamas of his tradition. All this points to a key feature of Tibetan Buddhist practice: in a world where everything has karmic consequences, any practice that one undertakes is not just a means for self-improvement but a virtuous act in its own right with positive consequences for the future, and these consequences can be directed and guarded by correct intention and dedication. This kind of process of mutual reinforcement is characteristic of Tibetan practice. It is as if one is constantly being reminded that any good action is precious, and one should make the most of it.

The path of the bodhisattva

The main source for the teachings on the six perfections in Tibetan tradition is Śāntideva's revered work, the *Bodhicaryāvatāra* ('Entering the path of Enlightenment'), much of which consists of a detailed description of each of the six *pāramitā* or perfections, attributes to be developed or cultivated by the aspirant *bodhisattva*. The last two of the perfections, *dhyāna* (meditative concentration) and *prajñā* (wisdom), correspond to the two basic dimensions of Buddhist meditational practices in the Sūtra tradition, *śamatha* (Tibetan *shiné*, corresponding to Pali *samatha*) meditation, which is concerned with calming, centring and controlling the mind–body complex, and *vipaśyanā* (Pali *vipassanā*, Tibetan *lhaktong*), which is concerned with directing the calmed and centred mind to achieve insight into the true nature of reality. Tsongkhapa's presentation of *vipaśyanā*, characteristically of the Gelukpa tradition that grew out of his teaching and activity, focuses on using the calmed mind to understand the intellectual arguments for Buddhahood. These intellectual arguments, which were developed very extensively by the Gelukpa using elaborate techniques of formal debating, and to a lesser degree were practised by other traditions as well, are of considerable importance within Tibetan monastic culture, but Tsongkapa and the Gelukpa tradition were also committed to Tantric practice, and the *lam rim* teachings conclude with a presentation of the arguments to proceed to Tantric practice.

Even for the Gelukpas, the path for the 'highest type' of beings is expected to be the Vajrayāna (*dorjé tegpa*), the path of Tantric Buddhism, since this is the way in which the mind, body, consciousness and personality can most rapidly and effectively be reshaped towards the achievement of Buddhahood. At the same time, the Tibetan tradition constantly asserts that Tantric practice is dangerous, and that it is a path to be undertaken only by those who are truly dedicated and committed.

The complexity and ambivalence surrounding Tantric practice is already marked in the Indian Buddhist context and comes from a variety of sources. As we have already seen in Chapter 2, Tantra is a complex term and does not designate a single undifferentiated body of practices. What is really at issue here is not so much the deity worship of the so-called 'lower Tantras' as the radical self-transformation that constitutes the goal of the highest class of Tantra, the so-called Anuttarayoga Tantras.

Figure 3.3 Monks debating at Sera Monastery near Lhasa. Photo by author (1987).

These practices involve working directly and intensively with strong emotional states, including the experiences of sexuality, aggression and death. Monastic practitioners would not normally undertake sexual practices with an actual partner, since this would contravene their vows of celibacy, but all Tantric practitioners, including celibate monastics, are involved in stirring up deep and powerful human motivations, and it is recognized that the process can go wrong, particularly in such contexts as extended solitary retreat. This is one reason for the strong emphasis on the role of the guru (lama) or spiritual guide in Tibetan Tantric practice. Tantra is a large and central topic in Tibetan Buddhism and Chapter 4 is devoted to a discussion of it.

Key points you need to know

- The 'central story' of Tibetan Buddhism is that Buddhism is a path to liberation from the suffering of life in the everyday world (*saṃsāra*), through the attainment of a superior state or condition of being that was attained and taught by the historical Buddha. This state (Buddhahood) may be difficult to attain, but in principle it is accessible to everyone. It is fundamentally characterized by love and compassion, and its achievement comes about through *bodhicitta*, the intense desire to relieve all beings from their suffering.

- The teachings on the attainment of Buddhahood are transmitted from lama (guru) to student, so creating teaching lineages that continue through the ages. They were brought to Tibet by a series of great teachers, including Padmasambhava who is thought of as taming the spirits of the land and creating a reservoir of spiritual power that can still be accessed. Those actively engaged on the path to Buddhahood, the lamas, monks and yogins, are supported by the lay population in return for their ritual and magical services as well as for their teaching.
- Different Buddhist traditions both within and outside Tibet emphasize different aspects of the teachings, and also vary in whether they favour unity and consistency, or breadth and variety. Labels such as Theravāda, Hīnayāna and Mahāyāna derive from internal polemics between schools and can be misleading. Tibetan Buddhism is however notable for its breadth and variety; the multiplicity of teachings, schools and lamas is valued, since different paths may be appropriate for different people.
- The distinction between Sūtra and Tantra teachings developed in India and is important for the Tibetans. The Vajrayāna (Buddhist Tantric) teachings are seen as difficult practices that are suitable for advanced practitioners, and that also enable them to assist lay people in practical and this-worldly matters. Lamas are expected to have mastered these teachings.
- The three *kāyas* or 'bodies' of the Buddha distinguish between different aspects or levels of Buddhahood. Buddhist deities, including *bodhisattvas* such as Tārā or Avalokiteśvara, may be treated by lay people as external deities, but are also understood to be manifestations of a universal Buddha-nature present within all beings and all experience.
- The overcoming of dualistic thought, particularly the division between self and others, and between self and the external world, is a key issue in Tibetan Buddhism. Apparent phenomena, including the self, are really 'empty' or 'void' of independent existence. This 'emptiness' (*śūnyatā*) can be described both in negative and positive terms.
- The Sūtra teachings provide the basic foundation necessary before one can practise Tantra properly and safely. They are generally presented in schemes of progressive teachings, and each of the main Buddhist traditions has its own versions of these.

Discussion questions

1 How does Buddhism in Tibet as a system of ideas and teaching compare with or differ from Buddhism in other Buddhist societies?

2 What are the three bodies of the Buddha? How do they relate to the existence of Buddhist deities?
3 What is involved in the overcoming of dualistic thought?
4 Discuss the difference between positive and negative understandings of *śūnyatā*.

Further reading

Collins, Steven. 'On the very idea of the Pali Canon.' *J. Pali Text Society*, 15: 89–126.

Dalai Lama I (Gendun Drub). *Bridging the Sutras and Tantras*. Compiled and translated by Glenn H. Mullin. Ithaca, NY: Gabriel/Snow Lion, 1982.

Dalai Lama II. *Selected Works*. Compiled, edited and translated by Glenn H. Mullin. Ithaca, NY: Snow Lion, 1985.

Dalai Lama VII. *Songs of Spiritual Change*. Translated by Glenn H. Mullin. Ithaca, NY: Gabriel/Snow Lion, 1982.

Dudjom Rinpoche, H.H. *The Nyingma School of Tibetan Buddhism: Its Fundamentals and History*. 2 vols. Translated and edited by Gyurme Dorje and Matthew Kapstein. Boston, MA: Wisdom Publications, 1991.

Guenther, Herbert V. (trans.). *The Jewel Ornament of Liberation*. Boston: Shambhala Publications, 2001.

Lessing, Ferdinand D. and Alex Wayman (trans.) *Mkhas grub rje's Fundamentals of the Buddhist Tantras*. The Hague and Paris: Mouton, 1968.

Ngorchen Konchog Lhundrub. *The Beautiful Ornament of the Three Visions*. Singapore: Golden Vase, 1987.

Obermiller, E. *History of Buddhism (Chos-ḥbyung by Bu-ston)*. 2 vols. Heidelberg: In Kommission bei Otto Harrassowitz, Leipzig, 1932–33.

Pabongka Rinpoche. *Liberation in the Palm of your Hand: A Concise Discourse on the Path to Enlightenment*. Boston: Wisdom Publications, 2006.

Patrul Rinpoche. *The Words of My Perfect Teacher*. Revised ed. Boston: Shambhala, 1998.

Prebish, Charles S. *Buddhist Monastic Discipline: The Sanskrit Prātimokṣa Sūtras of the Mahāsāṃghikas and Mūlasarvāstivādins*. University Park, PA: Pennsylvania State University Press, 1975.

Śāntarakṣita, *Bodhicaryāvatāra*. Translated by Kate Crosby and Andrew Skilton. Oxford: Oxford University Press, 2008.

Sherburne, Richard. (trans.). *A Lamp for the Path and Commentary by Atiśa*. London: Allen and Unwin, 1983. [Includes translation of *Bodhipathapradīpa*.]

Sopa, Geshe Lhundub and Jeffrey Hopkins. *Practice and Theory of Tibetan Buddhism*. London: Rider, 1976.

Tsong-kha-pa. *The Great Treatise on the Stages of the Path to Enlightenment: The Lamrim Chenmo by Tsong-kha-pa*, 3 vols. Translated by the Lamrim Chenmo Translation Committee, Joshua Cutler, Editor in Chief. Ithaca, NY: Snow Lion, 2001–2.

Wangyal, Geshe. *The Door of Liberation*. New York: Maurice Girodias, 1973.

4 *Tibetan Buddhism as a path to liberation II*

Tantric teachings

In this chapter

This is the second of two chapters discussing the techniques and approaches within Tibetan Buddhism for attaining Buddhahood or Enlightenment, the central goal of the Buddhist tradition. This chapter discusses the Tantric teachings. In it we look at the ideal of the Tantric teacher as a component of the role of the lama, consider the various subdivisions of the Tantras in the Sarma and Nyingma traditions, and consider the questions of Tantric empowerment and preliminary practice. There is also a discussion of the non-Tantric teachings of Dzogchen, which form the highest teaching within the Nyingmapa tradition and were a central influence on the nineteenth-century Rimé movement.

Main topics covered

- Tantric practice and the lama
- Retreat and the training of the subtle body
- Tantra and sexuality
- Tantric deities
- Classes of Sarma Tantra and Nyingma Tantra
- Empowerment and preliminary practice (*ngöndro*)
- Dzogchen

Tantric practice and the lama

Tantra in the last chapter (Chapter 3) was introduced as part of a developing series of techniques for personal spiritual cultivation as part of the path to Buddhahood. While the Sūtra teachings are fairly similar across the various Buddhist traditions, Tantric practices are more varied. The basic principles are the same throughout, but Tantra is passed down through individual lineages of practice, and there are many differences in detail between different Tantric practices. Each of the main Tantra

Figure 4.1 Lama Kunzang Dorjee performing Tantric ritual, Jangsa Gompa, Kalimpong. Photo by author (2009).

systems practised by the Tibetans for the achievement of Enlightenment (principally Guhyasamāja, Cakrasaṁvara, Hevajra and Kālacakra for the New Tantra or *sarma* traditions, plus the various *kama* and *terma* traditions of the Nyingmapa) are themselves syntheses of elements from different Indian lineages of practice. There are also non-Tantric meditational systems (Sūtra Mahāmudrā and Dzogchen) that are often regarded as alternative paths to Buddhahood, though themselves strongly influenced in practical terms by Tantric modes of thought.

While Tantra is generally presented by Tibetan lamas and scholars in terms of personal spiritual cultivation, and Tantra is often practised in retreat conditions for spiritual development, much other Tantric practice is only secondarily oriented towards this end. Tantric practice, whether undertaken by an individual practitioner, or by a lama with the assistance of a small or large team of other practitioners, is often performed either in response to a specific commission by a patron, or as part of the ongoing ritual practice of a monastery.

Such rituals can be quite elaborate, with complex sequences of offerings and ritual movements, lengthy liturgical texts with many hundreds of lines of verses, chants with elaborate musical structures and a small orchestra of monastic instruments, including drum, cymbals, shawms (*gyaling*), conches (*dungkar*), short and long trumpets (*kangling, radung*), and even costumed sequences of ritual dance within the temple and in the monastery courtyard. Particularly when performed by a large monastic establishment with practitioners of a wide range of ages and experiences, the level of participation or understanding may be quite varied, with many of the younger or less skilled monks doing little more than reciting the text; the point here is less that everyone is carrying out the inner visualizations and processes with great accuracy, but that the performance is carried off properly as a whole.

Nevertheless it is also thought to be critical for the effective performance of these rituals that the central performers, and above all the lama who is conducting the ritual, do in fact have the training and ability to perform the inner visualizations and practices correctly. What guarantees this is that the lama is somebody who has had appropriate training and above all has carried out lengthy retreats in which he or she has acquired the relevant skills under the supervision of a skilled teacher and Tantric practitioner. In this, Tibetan ritual differs from the position often attributed to the Roman Catholic Church, in which the sacraments are valid even if performed by an incompetent, morally corrupt or otherwise inadequate priest. The effectiveness of Tibetan ritual is dependent on the competence and spiritual development of the lama. This is only partly a matter of technical skill, since in a large monastic ritual most of the technical details are left to the lama's ritual assistants. These include the *umdzé* or chant leader and one or more *kyorpön* who assist with making offerings, bringing ritual implements to the lama, and performing other necessary tasks. The key issue for ritual efficacy is really the depth of the lama's spiritual realization. The more effectively he is able to invoke the deities at an inner level, the greater efficacy of the ritual as a whole.

This role of Tantric teacher is in fact the primary meaning of the word *lama*, which translates Sanskrit *guru*, though the term lama has come to have a wider range of meanings in Tibetan society, which will be discussed in more detail in Chapter 7.

Retreat and the training of the subtle body

Retreat (*tsam*) is thus a key component of Tantric practice and, particularly in the non-Gelukpa traditions, the expectation is that becoming an effective lama involves at least one retreat of the traditional period of three years, three months and three days. 'Becoming an effective lama' in this context really means acquiring the level of control over one's own mind–body processes (*tsalung*, see below) that enables the effective invocation of the deities for Tantric ritual purposes. This is a matter of practising meditation (*gom*, corresponding to Sanskrit *bhāvana*) or yoga (*neljor*, which translates Sanskrit *yoga*), terms that in the Tibetan context generally imply training in the visualizations, liturgy, mind–body cultivation and other aspects of Tantric practice, ideally in retreat conditions.

Typically, while extended retreats of this kind involve large amounts of solitary practice, they are undertaken in a group with a number of fellow practitioners under the supervision of an experienced meditation teacher. It is in this context that Tibetans acquire the skills that enable them to function afterwards as lamas. Each lineage of Tantric practice, centred on one or more major deities, has its own specific technique and practising it involves being given formal empowerment, ritual permission and detailed teachings (*wang lung tri* or *wang lung menngak*). The basic principles are much the same for most of these practices, however, so that once one has learned to do a range of key practices in a particular tradition, the skills acquired can easily be adapted to other Tantric deities and lineages. This is true also for the various ancillary skills, such as learning the hand-gestures (*chakgya*, *mudrā* in Sanskrit) that accompany the practices, learning how to make the *torma*, often very elaborate offering-cakes of barley-flour and butter that form an important part of Tantric ritual, and acquiring the ability to play the drums, bells, cymbals and other musical instruments used in ritual contexts.

Tantra is above all a performative tradition. Tantric training is much more about learning how to do things than learning the theory behind them, though many Tantric traditions also include extensive explanatory texts and teachings. Tantric visualization and liturgical practices are often complemented by physical exercises (*trulkor*) aimed at conditioning the 'subtle body' (*tsalung*) of channels along which the inner winds (Tib. *lung* = Skt. *prāṇa*) travel. Thus while Tibetan yoga can include physical practices related to those familiar in Western postural yoga, these are essentially secondary exercises, as indeed they generally also were in non-Buddhist contexts in India until the twentieth century.

This is not to say that the mind–body cultivation aspects of Tantric yoga are unimportant. In some respects, they are quite central to the achievement of Buddhahood. The process of the arousing of *bodhicitta*, of the development of the crucial motivational state of compassion for the sufferings of other beings, can also be seen in terms of *tsalung*, as a concentrating and directing of *prāṇa* along the central channel. Key elements here are the *tiklé* (Skt. *bindu*) that correspond to the male and female sexual substances and polarities, and to the corresponding forces of love and compassion within the individual (both men and women are understood to contain both polarities). These are often spoken of as forms of *bodhicitta* ('red *bodhicitta*', corresponding to menstrual blood and the female polarity, 'white *bodhicitta*' corresponding to semen and the male polarity) that have to be controlled and directed through the practice. In terms of contemporary Western scientific understandings, one could perhaps see this process as being a way of achieving mastery over the central nervous system and the internal hormonal flows of the body, which accompany and govern our moods and responses. It could also be understood as a way of controlling and harnessing for the path to Buddhahood the intense positive emotional affect towards another human being which can be entrained by sexual experience.

Tantra and sexuality

The sexual aspects of the Tantric inner yoga processes raise the question of the sexual aspects of Tantra as a whole in the Tibetan context. Sexual symbolism is undoubtedly important in the more 'advanced' Tantric teachings (Anuttarayoga, Mahāyoga, etc.). Beyond this, as we have seen, the inner yogic practices are based on an internal physiology (the 'subtle body') that understands the processes of the attainment of Buddhahood, of dreams, sexual intercourse, dying and death within essentially the

Figure 4.2
Guru Dewa Chenpo. Wall painting at Kardang Gompa, Lahul.
Photo by author (1989).

same framework. This framework of ideas can be and is put into operation in the form of meditational practices that involve sexual intercourse, but while such practices certainly exist in Tibet, they are not necessarily widely employed.

This is in part because most, though by no means all, Tibetan Buddhist practitioners are monks and have taken vows of celibacy. The proper performance of the sexual practices also requires high levels of control over internal physiological processes, which makes it difficult for them to be undertaken except by dedicated yogins who have undertaken the relevant training and are living in retreat-type conditions. At the same time not all lamas are monks, and the wives and female partners of non-celibate lamas are conventionally referred to as Tantric consorts (*sangyum*), this may or may not mean in reality that the relationship involves significant elements of Tantric sexual practice.

Tibetans understandably tend to regard such matters as private, particularly in the contemporary context where the likelihood of negative misinterpretation is high. Some well-publicized recent cases where Tibetan lamas appear to have used Tantric sexuality as an excuse for abusive and exploitative sexual relationships with Western disciples have also made this whole area highly charged and difficult to discuss openly. There seems little doubt that there were and are occasional elements of abuse, both in pre-modern Tibet and today. Equally, though, it seems likely that most *sangyum* relationships were either contexts of genuine spiritual practice, ordinary marital relationships, or a mixture of both.

Tantric deities

We touched on the topic of Tantric deities in Chapter 2. As described there, they are of many types, including both peaceful (*shiwa*) and fierce (*trowo*) principal deities, male and female forms, and often a substantial entourage of subsidiary deities – up

Figure 4.3
Amitayus (Chime Sogtik). Wall painting at Jangsa Gompa, Kalimpong. Photo by author (2007).

to several hundred in number – arrayed around a more or less elaborate *maṇḍala* structure, visualized or represented physically as a 'sand *maṇḍala*' constructed from stones, ground and appropriately coloured, as a painting or occasionally as a three-dimensional structure.

There are many hundreds of these deities, some deriving directly from India, others representing Tibetan developments or elaborations, and each tradition and sub-tradition has slightly different versions of the principal ones, as well as subsidiary protectors and guardian deities of its own. What I will do here, after some further explanation, is present some examples of different types and discuss one of the principal classificatory schemes that are used by Tibetans to organize these deities.

First though it is worth considering the ideas that underlie the employment of such deities. If we think in terms of the idea of Buddha-nature, one of the central Mahāyāna teachings, then the potentiality for Buddhahood is inherent in all beings and indeed in all of phenomenal reality. Thus Buddhahood can in a sense be awakened or accessed at any point and time by someone who has the appropriate skills. This is why the Tantric path is sometimes referred to as 'making the result (i.e. Buddhahood) into the path'. Doing this may be part of a process of self-cultivation in order to progress along the path to Buddhahood, or it may be a way of accessing the powers of the deity to bring about effects in the external world, such as healing, protection or good fortune.

If Buddhahood is a source of infinite potentiality accessible at any time, then the Tantric deities are in a sense partial aspects, refractions of that total potentiality. Visualizing one of these deities, or oneself identifying with one of them, is not, in Tibetan Tantric thought, a technique to worship an external entity. Rather, it is a way of accessing or tuning into something that is an intrinsic part of the structure of the universe – as of course is the practitioner him- or herself. This is represented in the invocation of the deity by a process in which the deity is invoked within oneself (what is called in Sanskrit the *samayasattva* – the Tibetan is *damtsik sempa*) and then the wisdom nature of the deity (*jñānasattva, yeshe sempa* in Tibetan) is invited into the visualized deity and the two merged together. This standard Tibetan ritual sequence is based on the idea that the practitioner's visualization can be as it were tuned in to the deity (as a genuine aspect of Buddhahood) and the two made non-dual. Part of the point here is that the separation between individual and universe (and so individual and deity) is at the ultimate level illusory.

Some of the Tantric deities are familiar figures from the general Mahāyāna pantheon of deities, including such figures as Avalokiteśvara (Chenrezik in Tibetan), Mañjuśrī (Jambeyang) or the goddess Tārā. Others are lamas from the past such as Padmasambhava, Tsongkapa or Milarepa, treated as deities. Since Tantric practice is always performed within a specific lineage of transmission that authorizes the practice, and in some sense goes back to a specific manifestation of the deity him- or herself, the practitioner is not invoking Avalokiteśvara in general but a specific form of Avalokiteśvara with whom he or she has established a bond through the empowerment ritual which is required in order to perform these practices. There are thus hundreds of different forms of Avalokiteśvara, each with its own specific iconography, with subtle or more dramatic differences existing between them. One of the best known of Avalokiteśvara practices is the short Tangtong Gyelpo practice known as *Kakyabma* ('Pervading All Space'), which is given in the box.

A simple Tantric practice of Avalokiteśvara

One of the most widely known of Tibetan Tantric practices is a short practice to Chenrezig (Avalokiteśvara) created from a vision by the fifteenth-century lama Tangtong Gyelpo and known as the *Kakyabma* ('Pervading All Space') practice. Though short, it contains the essential elements of a Tantric practice, including refuge, *bodhicitta*, visualization, transformation into deity, receiving of blessings, recitation of mantra, dissolution, and dedication of merit.

To begin, the practitioner recites a standard refuge and *bodhicitta* verse three times:

I take refuge until I attain Buddhahood in Buddha, Dharma and Saṅgha. Through the merit of my practice of generosity and the other perfections, may I attain Buddhahood for the sake of all sentient beings.

The practitioner then recites the description of the deity, imagining the visualization as he or she proceeds:

On the heads of all beings 'Pervading All Space', above a white lotus and moon throne, is a letter HRĪḤ which transforms into the deity Chenrezik, radiating clear light of the five colours. He gazes with smiling and compassionate eyes. He has four arms, the first two joined together at his heart, the lower two holding a crystal rosary and white lotus. He is adorned with silk and jewel ornaments, an antelope skin on his upper body, and Öpame (Amitābha) as a crown on his head. He sits with his two feet in vajra posture, a stainless moon at his back. He becomes the essence of all refuges.

Then repeat the following invocation three times, seven times, or as many times as possible, imagining that all beings are reciting along with one:

I bow to the Lord Chenrezik, whose white colour is unveiled by any stain, whose head is ornamented by the Perfected Buddha, and who looks upon all beings with compassionate gaze.

Then imagine the following:

Having thus prayed one-pointedly, light radiates from the Holy One's body, cleansing impure karmic appearances and illusory understandings. The external world becomes the Paradise of Dewachen (Sukhāvatī). The body, speech and mind of beings within it become the body, speech and mind of Chenrezik. Appearances, sounds and thoughts become empty and undifferentiated.

Meditating like this, recite the six-syllable mantra of Chenrezik, *Oṁ maṇi padme hūṁ*, as many times as possible.

Finally, let the mind remain absorbed in its own nature, without distinction between subject, object and action, and recite:

I and all others appear as the body of the Holy One. All sounds are the melody of the Six Syllables. All thoughts are the great expanse of Wisdom.

At the end, one dedicates the merit produced by having done the practice:

Through this merit, having quickly attained the state of Chenrezik, may I establish all beings without exception to the same level.

Figure 4.4
Contemporary image of Avalokiteśvara, Kathmandu. Photo by Daniel Palmer (2011).

The central process in this short Avalokiteśvara practice is the cleansing of impure karmic appearances and illusory understandings, which is an essential component of the progress to Buddhahood. The practice of major Tantric *yidam* deities, like Guhyasamāja, Cakrasamvara, Hevajra or Kālacakra, is also specifically connected with the path to Buddhahood, and involves a series of technical yogic processes which are understood as part of the path. Other deities however are invoked for more everyday purposes – the 'ordinary *siddhis*' (Tantric accomplishments): White Tārā, or the various forms of Amitāyus, for health and long life, Mañjuśrī for wisdom and to aid study, Dzambhala for prosperity, forms of Dorje Yudronma in relation to divination, Vajrapani, Vajrakīlaya and other fierce deities for protection. A developed Tantric practice for each of these deities will however generally allude in numerous ways to the pursuit of the 'ultimate' or 'supreme' *siddhi* (Buddhahood), as well as to the specific relative or ordinary *siddhi* that is the immediate point of the practice.

Invoking a Tantric deity is closely connected with the idea of *mantra*. Mantras are formulae, usually in Sanskrit and often fairly short, which are used to summon the deity's presence. They represent the commitment of the Tantric deity to take part in the ritual. Thus *oṁ maṇi padme hūṁ* (as in the inset practice) represents the essence of Avalokiteśvara, *oṁ tare tuttare ture svāhā* that of the Goddess Ṭārā, *oṁ arapacana dhīḥ* that of Mañjuśrī, *oṁ āḥ hūṁ vajra guru padma siddhi hūṁ* that of Guru Padmasambhava. In fact all of these deities have multiple mantras corresponding to different forms and functions; the ones quoted are the most familiar, and are very widely known in Tibet, as well as being inscribed on rocks, stones and walls all around Tibetan regions.

Focusing on and reciting the mantra is a way of bringing the deity into presence and so accessing the deity's powers. In the case of an enlightened Tantric deity, who is an aspect of the Buddha, and can be called on as a *yidam* or personal guardian or guide, this could be said to take place because the deity has vowed it to happen. Stories in the Sūtras and Tantras describe how deities such as Tārā, when *bodhisattvas* on the course to Buddhahood, vowed that after their attainment of Buddhahood they would assist all those who called upon them, and the deity's availability for the practitioner today is in a sense the fruit of a vow of this kind.

The same technique can be used with worldly, unenlightened, spirits and deities, and here the idea is rather different, since such gods are thought of as having yielded up their mantras when 'tamed' by the Tantric power of Padmasambhava or other great Tantric gurus. Thus the practitioner today can call on the vows made by the

Figure 4.5 The mantra *Oṁ maṇi padme hūṁ* inscribed on a rock by the roadside in Dalhousie, India. Photo by author (1996).

deity when he or she submitted to Padmasambhava, and indeed threaten the deity with the Tantric power used by Padmasambhava in that initial conquest. As the similarity in techniques suggests, the line between worldly, unenlightened deities and enlightened *yidam* is not absolute. Certain Tibetan worldly deities, are regarded as highly evolved beings, themselves well advanced on the path to Buddhahood. Deities such as the Four Guardian Kings have a somewhat intermediate position, well beyond the level of ordinary worldly deities but not normally regarded as aspects of Buddhahood in their own right. In addition, fully enlightened Tantric deities may also manifest and be invoked in the form of worldly deities in order to help tame and control them, which again helps to blur the line between the various kinds of deity (all of which can be referred to by the same Tibetan term, *lha*).

Thus Tantric deities can be experienced or thought of in different ways by practitioners at different levels and by ordinary lay people, and a sense of Tārā or Chenrezi (Avalokiteśvara) as an external entity who can be appealed to for assistance remains present alongside a body of theory that allows for a more subtle and less external reading. This is not really a contradiction, since the aim of Tibetan Buddhism is not so much logical consistency as practical efficacy. Being able to appeal to Tārā or Padmasambhava as an external deity allows for a directing of emotion and devotional feeling into the process of Tantric invocation that is undoubtedly an important part of how these ritual processes work and are effective.

An important underlying scheme for the Tantric deities is that of the five deities of the Vajradhātu Maṇḍala. This is a basic *maṇḍala* structure consisting of a central deity (in the original version, the Buddha Vairocana) surrounded by four other Buddha figures in the four directions. This is an old Buddhist visualization scheme that can be found in basic form as early as the *Suvarṇaprabhāsa Sūtra*, which dates back at least until the late fourth century CE, and was incorporated into early Yoga Tantra texts; versions of it are also found in Chinese and East Asian Buddhism. This set of Buddhas is often referred to in Western writings as the 'Five Dhyāni Buddhas' although this name does not appear to go back to any Sanskrit term. The five Buddhas of the centre and four directions have relatively standard associations, some of which are given in Table 4.1.

This pentadic structure underlies many Tantric *maṇḍalas*, which frequently involve sets of four deities in the four directions surrounding the main figure or couple in the centre. They often use the same colour symbolism, and are also divided into quarters of these four colours. In a sand or painted *maṇḍala*, such as the one shown in Figure 4.6, the deities may be represented by symbols or simply by dots, but such a *maṇḍala* is essentially a support for visualizing or bringing into imaginative existence a full-scale three-dimensional structure in which the deities are also full three-dimensional figures.

A particularly important aspect of the associations here is that to do with function or activity. Specific deities are thought of as belonging to one or another family

Table 4.1 Vajradhātu *Maṇḍala*, basic associations

	Vairocana	*Akṣobhya*	*Amoghasiddhi*	*Amitābha*	*Ratnasaṃbhava*
Direction	Centre	East	North	West	South
Family	Buddha	Vajra (thunderbolt sceptre)	Karma (action)	Padma (lotus)	Ratna (jewel)
Element	Space	Water	Air	Fire	Earth
Colour	White	Blue	Green	Red	Gold/yellow
Main activity	Turning wheel of Dharma	Protection, destruction	Pacifying	Magnetizing, subjugating	Increase
Obstacle	Ignorance	Hate	Envy	Selfishness	Pride, greed
Consort	Dharmadhatvisvari	Locanā	Tārā	Pandara	Mamaki
Bodhisattva	Samantabhadra	Vajrapāni	Viśvapāni	Avalokiteshvara	Ratnapani
Seed syllable	OM	HUM	AH	HRIH	TRAH

Figure 4.6 Chime Soktik Sand *Maṇḍala*, Jangsa Ganpa, Kalimpong. Photo by author (2009).

(e.g. Avalokiteśvara, Amitābha, Amitāyus and Padmasambhava all belong in the Lotus family) and this symbolism is developed in their visualizations and the ritual sequences for the deities. The detailed working out of this scheme is complex and specific to the particular practice, but the general structure is familiar and helps to provide a degree of order, coherence and familiarity throughout the various practices. There are also other standard sets of deities; eight *bodhisattvas*, sixteen offering goddesses, and so on, so that the apparent complexity and multiplicity of Tibetan practices becomes considerably more familiar when one gets to know a set of related practices in a particular tradition.

Classes of Sarma Tantra *and* Nyingma Tantra

A brief outline of the history of Buddhist Tantra in India was given in Chapter 2. What is now classed as Tantra encompasses a variety of developments in India which were also referred to by a variety of different names. These included both a series of new meditational procedures based around the visualization of Buddhas and related figures, and the meditator's imaginative identification with them; monastic ritual procedures directed towards peaceful and benevolent deities, often oriented towards practical and this-worldly results, perhaps in part derived from these meditational procedures; rituals of fierce deities, often directed towards aggressive and protective purposes; and forms of spiritual cultivation based around 'inner yogic' practices to do with 'energies' within the 'subtle body'.

In Tibet these became systematized and classified in two main ways within the Buddhist tradition. These were the Nine Vehicle Scheme of the Old Tantra (Nyingma) system, the scheme adopted by the Nyingmapas, and the Four Tantra Classes of the New Tantra (Sarma) system, which was adopted by the other Buddhist traditions. While there are parallels between these schemes, they are also rather different in function and meaning. More specifically, the Four Tantra Class scheme is primarily a classificatory device within which the various Tantric texts can be organized, while the Nyingmapa scheme, particularly in its more recent versions, is more of a progressive scheme of Tantric teachings leading towards the culminating non-Tantric teaching of Dzogchen. We look first at the Sarmapa (New Tantra) scheme (see the box, overleaf).

In present-day Sarmapa traditions, which are primarily those of the Sakyapa, Kagyüdpa and Gelukpa, the focus for the attainment of Buddhahood is very much on the fourth class, the Anuttarayogatantra practices, and the way in which these are practised is based on a systematic compilation of elements from the various Anuttarayogatantra traditions, particularly Guhyasamāja and Cakrasamvara for the Kagyüdpa and Gelukpa, and Hevajra for the Sakyapas. The first three classes (Kriyā, Caryā and Yoga Tantra) tend to be used primarily for practices aimed at this-worldly ends such as healing or prosperity, or for more basic and introductory stages of Tantric practice.

The Four Tantra Classes according to the Sarmapa (New Tantra) system

1 **Kriyā** Explained in terms of emphasis on purificatory ritual and external activities. Typical Tantras include the Mañjuśrīmūla, Padmajāla, Amoghapāśa-kalparājā
2 **Caryā** Balance between external activities and internal practices, e.g. Mahāvairocana-abhisaṃbodhi
3 **Yoga** Primarily concerned with internal practices, e.g. Tattvasamgraha
4 **Anuttarayoga**
   - *Father Tantras* Emphasis on illusory body and on completion stage, e.g. Guhyasamāja, Yamantaka
   - *Mother Tantras* Emphasis on pure mind (clear light) and development stage, e.g. Cakrasamvara, Hevajra
   - *Non-dual Tantras* Emphasis on both equally; Kālacakra

In particular, Anuttarayogatantra as practised in Tibet involves two successive but complementary stages. These are the 'generation phase' (*kyerim* in Tibetan) and the 'completion' or 'fulfilment phase' (*dzokrim*). The generation phase, which is largely based on material from the 'Mother Tantra' category, is based on the practice of 'deity yoga', in which one visualizes oneself as the Tantric deity at the centre of the *maṇḍala* and develops the sense of 'pure vision' in which this represents the valid and authentic view of the universe that replaces our ordinary perception. The completion phase focuses on the inner yoga practices derived from the 'Father Tantra' category, and is directed towards conforming the inner flows and currents of subtle 'energy' within the body into the appropriate form for the attainment of Buddhahood.

The Nyingma Nine Vehicle scheme (see box) contains many of the same elements, but put together in a somewhat different format and structure. It consists of nine stages that are seen as sequential, in that each is deeper and more profound than the next, but all are aimed towards the primary goal of Buddhahood.

Here the first three stages are Sūtra vehicles, the Śrāvakas and Pratyekabuddhas, corresponding to the 'Hīnayāna' level of the teachings, and the Bodhisattva vehicle, in other words the non-Tantric teachings of the Mahāyāna. They are followed by the first three ('Lower') Tantra vehicles, here called Kriyā, Ubhaya (sometimes Upa) and Yoga. These are explained and differentiated in various ways, but one simple and significant one is the question of the relation to the deity. In Kriyā the relationship with deity is regarded as analogous to that between master and servant, and one appeals to the deity as to one's lord and master. In Ubhaya, the relationship is like that between friends, whereas in Yoga Tantra one becomes the deity oneself.

The Nine Vehicles according to the Nyingmapa (Old Tantra) system

Three Sūtra vehicles

1 *Śrāvaka* Sūtra practices aimed at personal liberation from suffering
2 *Pratyekabuddha* second class of Sūtra practices aimed at personal liberation from suffering
3 *Bodhisattva* Sūtra practices aimed at cultivating *bodhicitta* and liberating all beings from suffering

Three Lower Tantra vehicles

4 *Kriyā* explained in terms of regarding the *yidam* deity as a superior being external to oneself
5 *Ubhaya* explained in terms of regarding the *yidam* deity as a friend external to oneself
6 *Yoga* explained in terms of regarding oneself as the *yidam* deity

Three Higher Tantra vehicles

7 *Mahāyoga* generation phase – transformation of ordinary reality through pure vision
8 *Anuyoga* – completion phase – *tsalung* practices
9 *Atiyoga (Dzogchen)* – spontaneous self-liberation, 'beyond' tantra

Mahāyoga and Anuyoga can be seen in generic terms to correspond to the generation phase and completion phase practices, in that Mahāyoga focuses on the relationship with the deity (including internal yogic practices, and also the practices of sexual yoga for those appropriately qualified) and Anuyoga on the internal 'subtle body' practices. This leaves the ninth and final stage, Dzogchen, which as previously mentioned is conceptually at least a non-Tantric form of meditation practice, but is also regarded as the highest point and culmination of the Nyingmapa version of the Buddhist path. We will consider Dzogchen again at the end of this chapter, but for the present we return to the more preliminary phases of the Tantric path.

Empowerment and preliminary practice (ngöndro)

An important initial step in Tantric practice is the initiation or empowerment (*abhiṣeka* in Sanskrit, *wangkur* or just *wang* in Tibetan). This constitutes both a giving of permission to perform the practice and a formal introduction to the deities of the *maṇḍala*, and also involves the making of a formal request and offering to the lama, who here is acting as Tantric guru, and taking of vows. If it is being done in elaborate form, a sand *maṇḍala* representation of the *maṇḍala* in question may be made, and destroyed at the end of the ritual.

These days it is not unusual for Tantric empowerments to be given for general audiences of lay people without extensive preliminaries, as a kind of blessing, a practice which is quite widespread among Tibetans as well as with Tibetan lamas in the West. Where an empowerment is being taken with the intention of a serious commitment to practice, however, a lama will normally require that the student undertakes preliminary practices before bestowing the empowerment. In the non-Gelukpa traditions, this generally takes the form of the Tantric *ngöndro* practices, so these practices in fact function as the first serious introduction to Tantra, at least in the non-Gelukpa traditions. Similar practices, if not necessarily under the same name, are also taught by Gelukpa lamas for students wanting to proceed to Tantric meditation.

Thus the first stage in Tantric practice for the serious practitioner is generally some form of *ngöndro* or 'preliminary practice'. In fact *ngöndro* is a general term for

Figure 4.7 Tibetans performing prostrations in front of the Jokang Temple, Lhasa. Photo by Ruth Rickard (2006).

introductory or preliminary practices, whether Tantric or non-Tantric, whether performed as the first part of a longer practice session or in stand-alone form, but the term used in a Tantric context without qualification, as here, generally refers to the preliminary practices which are normally required by a lama as the initial phase of Tantric training. These consist of a fairly standard set of practices each of which is performed 100,000 times (in practice the number may be rather more, such as 111,111). Typically performing the *ngöndro* takes some months, even if one devotes a substantial amount of time each day to the practice. It is also physically fairly demanding, because of the full prostrations that form one of the items to be repeated, so that one may need to build up to being able to undertake large numbers of these at a single session.

The box below presents a well-known set of Karma Kagyüd preliminary practices, the *Chariot for Travelling the Path to Freedom* by the Ninth Karmapa Wangchuk Dorjé (1556–1603). These give an initial sense of what undertaking Tantric meditation in the Tibetan context actually involves.

Karma Kagyüd Ngöndro (after Karmapa Wangchuk Dorjé's *Chariot for Travelling the Path to Freedom*)

Ordinary preliminaries

The *ngöndro* begins with the 'four ordinary preliminaries', which are the 'four thoughts that turn the mind to the Dharma' that we came across above. These involve the following contemplations:

- we have attained the extremely precious condition of birth as a human being with access to the Buddhist teachings;
- that condition is impermanent and we could die at any time;
- the results of karmic action are inevitable, so that our future rebirth depends critically on our actions in what remains of our present life;
- existence within *saṃsāra* is characterized by suffering, so it is essential that we reject it and seek liberation while we have the opportunity.

Main part

The main part of the *ngöndro* consists of a series of actions, each repeated 100,000 times.

***1 Refuge and* bodhicitta**

The first consists of the refuge and *bodhicitta* verses, which are carried out before a visualization of the appropriate refuge tree/field for the tradition. In the case of the Karma Kagyüd *ngöndro,* the refuge visualization is a tree that grows out of a lake in the centre of a flowering meadow. Its trunk divides into five branches, one in each direction and one going straight up at the centre. On a jewelled throne at the point where the branches separate is one's principal guru ('root lama', *tsawé lama* in Tibetan) in the form of Vajradhara, a deity who represents the Dharmakāya aspect of Buddhahood, with the gurus of the Karma Kagyüd Mahāmudrā tradition in a vertical line above his head, surrounded by the great saints and scholars of India and Tibet. On the remaining four branches of the tree are:

i the various *yidam* or Tantric deities;
ii the Buddha Śākyamuni surrounded by the Buddhas of the three times (past, present and future) and ten directions (eight compass points, up and down);
iii the books of the Buddhist teachings (the Dharma);
iv the countless *bodhisattvas* and disciples who make up the Saṅgha.

Beneath the refuge tree are countless other deities including the various worldly protector deities of the teachings. We are to imagine ourselves as facing this assembly, accompanied by one's father and mother and numerous other beings with whom one has had connection, including beings who have been hostile to one in this and previous lives. Facing this visualization, we recite the verses of refuge and *bodhicitta*. This practice, performed 100,000 times, and accompanied by 100,000 full-length prostrations, constitutes the first of the four components of the *ngöndro* proper.

2 Vajrasattva practice

The second practice consists of 100,000 repetitions of the 100-syllable purificatory mantra of the deity Vajrasattva. The deity is visualized above one's head, with nectar dripping down from his body through the crown of one's head to pervade one's body, purifying one's own negative karma and the obscurations which block one's progress towards Buddhahood.

3 Maṇḍala offering

The third practice consists of the offering of a *maṇḍala*, here meaning a physical offering of rice, often mixed with precious stones, which represents the entire universe of traditional Buddhist cosmology with Mount Meru at its centre.

4 Guru yoga

The fourth practice consists of 100,000 repetitions of the Guru yoga, in which one requests one's visualized root lama in the form of Vajradhāra to bless one to achieve Buddhahood, and receives blessings from him.

This is typical of *ngöndro* though as always the precise details vary somewhat from one tradition and practice to another. In practice, it takes several months at least to complete the *ngöndro*, so one does a certain amount on each day. *Ngöndro*, like many Tibetan practices, also acts as a kind of microcosm of the whole path; as the lamas say, while *ngöndro* is preliminary it is not minor or unimportant, since it is the foundation of the whole path. Its aim is to bring about the initial reorientation of the mind–body totality away from ordinary worldly life that is the basis for subsequent practice. As such, it is significant that it includes a central part for bodily and verbal actions as well as for mental or imaginative procedures.

Ngöndro would ideally be followed by an extended retreat, in the non-Gelukpa traditions normally for three years, three months and three days. This would involve receiving a series of empowerments for different practices, learning the technical skills (offerings, chants, gestures, etc.) involved in their performance, and doing these practices intensively until the student gains real familiarity with both the technique and the inner processes involved. As mentioned earlier, this constitutes the basic qualification for operating as a lama. The most respected Tantric lamas however would have done much more than this, over many decades, and there is an active network of gossip and reputation among Tibetans regarding the skills, power and abilities of different lamas.

Dzogchen

Dzogchen is thus the 'highest' of teachings within the Nyingmapa structure of teachings. While closely associated historically with the Nyingmapa tradition, it gained considerable importance for those Sarmapa lamas who became involved in the ninteteenth-century 'Rimé movement', in particular through the influence of the great late eighteenth-century Nyingmapa lama Jigmé Lingpa. Within the Rimé movement Dzogchen was often regarded as a non-conceptual level of illumination equivalent to *Mahāmudrā*, a term used in the Sarma Tantras for their own highest level of illumination. Dzogchen and Chakchen (the Tibetan for *Mahāmudrā*) could then be considered as parallel paths suitable for different students, and teachers such as the early twentieth-century lay lama Śākyaśrī explicitly maintained both traditions of training, choosing that most appropriate for each student.

Dzogchen is often described as a teaching of 'self-liberation', and sometimes compared with the Ch'an teachings of China (corresponding to Japanese Zen) as a practice of direct entry into the awakened state. There has been considerable discussion about the possibility of Ch'an influences on Dzogchen, and Ch'an teachings from China were certainly known in Tibet in the late imperial period, although later tradition regards them as having been rejected in favour of Indian Buddhist teachings. The Buddhist Dzogchen traditions themselves (there are also similar Bonpo Dzogchen teachings, which will be discussed briefly in Chapter 11) claim an Indian origin, through a probably largely mythological series of early teachers going back to a figure known in Tibetan as Garab Dorjé. Garab Dorjé (the name might be Prahevajra in Sanskrit) is said to have been born in Uḍḍiyāna, which is generally identified by scholars with the Swat Valley in present-day Pakistan, not long after the time of the historical Buddha, and to have received the Dzogchen teachings directly from the Buddhist deities. They were transmitted on through a series of teachers to Vimalamitra, Padmasambhava, and Vairocana, who brought them to Tibet. Dzogchen, as taught in the Buddhist tradition, however derives in practice from *terma* revelations, so claim their origin like other Buddhist *terma* in Padmasambhava's teachings in Tibet.

Garab Dorjé's own teaching is summed up in his famous 'three essential points':

- Direct introduction to one's true nature;
- Remaining without doubt;
- Continuing with confidence.

These three points refer to a central feature of Dzogchen, its stress on the attainment of direct awareness (*rikpa* in Tibetan) of the true nature of reality. *Rikpa* is the ordinary Tibetan term for knowledge, but it here has a specialized and different meaning.

The term Dzogchen itself also describes the primordial state of the Dzogchen practitioner, also known as *shi* (ground or base). This is a term close in meaning to such standard Mahāyāna terminology as Dharmakāya and *śūnyatā*. *Shi* as ground of being is however very much a source of positive potentiality, bringing Dzogchen closer in philosophical terms both to some of the Yogacāra formulations and to the more positive *shentong* interpretations of Mādhyamaka. It can further be described in terms of a set of three terms, *ngowo* or essence (described as both 'open' and 'innately pure'), *rangshin* or 'nature' (described as characterized by 'spontaneity' and 'luminosity') and *tukjé*. *Tukjé* is the standard Tibetan term for 'compassion' (Skt. *karuṇā*), but with a somewhat different emphasis. *Tukjé* here is energy or activity, the compassion-driven movement that leads to the arising of phenomena out of the 'ground' or *shi*. Through a process of wandering or obscuration, the pure intelligence of being becomes caught up in ignorance and dichotomizing thought, and this becomes the basis for ordinary reality. However the real nature of mind is intrinsically pure, and can be recognized at any time. The specific training of Dzogchen is directed towards this goal. The method can be described as simply letting the mind be or rest in its own place, but while in a sense very simple this is also far from easy for ordinary people, which is why Dzogchen is regarded as an advanced practice and generally taught within a framework of more conventional Tantric practice.

The ultimate goal of Dzogchen is Buddhahood, but the specific way in which this goal manifests in this world is also different from the Tantric paths and characteristic of the Dzogchen teachings, which emphasize visual manifestations and the dissolution of apparent reality into their underlying elemental aspects, which appear as coloured light. Accomplished Dzogchen masters are described as attaining *jalü*, the 'rainbow body', at the end of their lives. In standard descriptions of how this happens, the dying master instructs his disciples to sew up the door of his tent or seal the door to his room, and leave him for seven days. When they return and open the door, the master has disappeared, leaving behind only his hair and fingernails, parts of the body that are thought to be too material to be dissolved into the subtle energies of the *jalü*. In some cases, if the process is interrupted too soon, the body may still be present, but shrunk to a small fraction of its normal size. A number of recent lamas are said to have attained *jalü*, including the Bonpo Dzogchen master Shardza Tashi Gyaltsen, who died in around 1933. Several lamas are also described as having attained or partially attained *jalü* when imprisoned by the Chinese authorities during the Cultural Revolution.

Within much Nyingmapa Tantric practice, particularly in the Rimé lamas, and in the *tersar* or 'New *Terma*' traditions associated with nineteenth- and twentieth-century lamas such as Chokgyur Lingpa, Dudjom Lingpa and the latter's rebirth Dudjom Rinpoche, also appears within standard Tantric contexts as a possibility of deeper and more direct insight. This fits easily into a general Tibetan tendency to work in terms of progressive levels of more esoteric and secret meanings, often signalled by the triadic structure of 'outer inner and secret' (*chi nang sang*). Thus the Tantric *ngöndro* practices of Jigmé Lingpa, associated with his Longchen Nyingtik cycle of *terma* teachings, provides outer, inner and secret levels, with the secret level essentially presenting a Dzogchen interpretation, and the Chimé Soktik longevity practices elaborated by Dudjom Rinpoche on the basis of the *terma* revelations of one of his own teachers, Silnön Namkai Dorje, likewise constantly includes 'reminders' of the Dzogchen level of interpretation of each phase of the liturgical action.

This concludes what is inevitably, given its length, a brief and somewhat superficial survey of the large and complex body of traditions and practices that constitute the basis of Tibetan Buddhist practice. This account has necessarily focused mostly on the 'theory', though enough has been said about the practical side to make it clear that this is an elaborate and technical field of study, somewhere between an art and a science in Western terms. It takes many years to become a specialist in these technical procedures, and to learn how to carry them out accurately and fully.

We turn in Chapter 5 to Tibetan Buddhism as a system of knowledge. Lamas are not only Tantric teachers but scholars and educators. If Tibetan Buddhism can carry conviction for its followers, and in effect create a world within they can live and be enclosed and protected, that is in part because Tibetan Buddhism also offers a powerful explanatory model for understanding the world and one's place within it. We have seen some elements of this in the previous two chapters; the ideas of karma and rebirth, the view of history in terms of the salvific action of the Buddhas and

Bodhisattvas, the concept of voidness, and so on. In the following chapter we look at some of these issues in more detail.

Key points you need to know

- Tantric practices are varied and classified in different ways but are based on common principles.
- The Tantric deities around which they are structured can be seen as aspects of Buddha-nature and as ways of accessing the powers and insight of the Buddha. They are structured in complex geometrical arrays (*maṇḍala*) and form part of elaborate schemes of correspondences, and are invoked in rituals which can vary considerably in elaboration and complexity.
- Tantric practice can be performed by a single practitioner or by a large monastic team under the direction of a senior lama. In either case, the central performer or performers needs to have the expertise to carry out the inner visualizations and practices effectively.
- These skills, normally acquired in extended retreat, are what defines a lama. They involve both a range of ritual skills and learning control over relevant mind–body processes, typically in an extended retreat of three years, three months and three days. Acquiring these skills is the purpose of yoga and meditation.
- The internal processes are integrally linked with the development of the key emotional and motivational aspects of Buddhist practice, which can be expressed in terms of *tsalung* or the internal structure of channels and subtle breath. Tantric sexual practices, where performed, are also closely related to these internal processes.
- Tantric practices may be performed for this-worldly (practical) aims such as health and prosperity, but their ultimate goal is personal spiritual cultivation, leading eventually to the attainment of Buddhahood.

Discussion questions

1. What is Tantric practice? How does it relate to yoga and meditation?
2. How does the Tantric ritual performed in a large monastery temple connect with Tantric ritual as performed by a yogic practitioner in retreat conditions?
3. What is the role of mind–body cultivation in Tibetan Buddhist practice?
4. What are the Tantric deities? How do Tibetans understand them and relate to them?

Further reading

Beyer, Stephan. *The Cult of Tara: Magic and Ritual in Tibet*. Berkeley, CA: University of California Press, 1973.

Cozort, Daniel. *Highest Yoga Tantra: An Introduction to the Esoteric Buddhism of Tibet*. Ithaca, NY: Snow Lion, 1986.

Dalai Lama I (Gendun Drub). *Bridging the Sutras and Tantras*. Compiled and translated by Glenn H. Mullin. Ithaca, NY: Gabriel/Snow Lion, 1982.

Dalai Lama II. *Selected Works*. Compiled, ed. and transl. by Glenn H. Mullin. Ithaca, NY: Snow Lion, 1985.

Guenther, Herbert V. *Tibetan Buddhism in Western Perspective*. Emeryville, CA: Dharma Publishing, 1977.

Hopkins, Jeffrey. *Tantric Techniques*. Ithaca, NY: Snow Lion, 2008.

Huntington, John C. and Dina Bangdel. *The Circle of Bliss: Buddhist Meditational Art*. Columbus, OH: Columbus Museum of Art; London: Serindia, 2003.

Kongtrul, Jamgon. *The Torch of Certainty*. Translated by Judith Hanson. Boulder and London: Shambhala, 1977.

Kongtrul, Jamgon. *Jamgon Kongtrul's Retreat Manual*. Translated by Ngawang Zangpo. Ithaca, NY: Snow Lion, 1994.

Landaw, Jonathan and Andy Weber. *Images of Enlightenment: Tibetan Art in Practice*. Ithaca, NY: Snow Lion, 1993.

Lati Rinpoche and Jeffrey Hopkins. *Death, Intermediate State and Rebirth in Tibetan Buddhism*. Ithaca, NY: Snow Lion, 1985.

Lessing, Ferdinand D. and Alex Wayman (trans.). *Mkhas Grub Rje's Fundamentals of the Buddhist Tantras*. The Hague and Paris: Mouton, 1968.

Mullin, Glenn H. (trans. & ed.). *The Practice of the Six Yogas of Naropa*. Ithaca, NY and Boulder, CO: Snow Lion, 2006.

Mullin, Glenn H. *Death and Dying: The Tibetan Tradition*. London and New York: Arkana, 1986.

Reynolds, John Myrdhin. *The Golden Letters*. Ithaca, NY: Snow Lion, 1996.

Ringu Tulku. *The Ri-Me Philosophy of Jamgön Kongtrul the Great: A Study of the Buddhist Lineages of Tibet*. Boston and London: Shambhala, 2006.

Samuel, Geoffrey. *The Origins of Yoga and Tantra: Indic Religions to the Thirteenth Century*. Cambridge: Cambridge University Press, 2008.

Studstill, Randall. *The Unity of Mystical Traditions: The Transformation of Consciousness in Tibetan and German Mysticism*. Leiden: Brill, 2005.

Thondup Rinpoche, Tulku. *Buddha Mind: An Anthology of Longchen Rabjam's Writings on Dzogpa Chenpo*. Ithaca, NY: Snow Lion, 1989.

Yuthok, Lama Choedak T. (trans.). *The Triple Tantra by Panchen Ngawang Choedak*. Canberra: Gorum, 1997.

5 *Tibetan Buddhism as a system of knowledge*

In this chapter

Chapter 5 looks at the way in which Tibetan Buddhism in the past provided an overall and comprehensive system of knowledge for the people of Tibet. This body of knowledge, which was self-contained but not entirely closed to outside influences, appears to have largely satisfied the needs of Tibetan people for understanding the world around them and for making sense of their own lives and society. It also gave them ways to act when necessary in relation to that world. Much of the Tibetan body of scholarly knowledge came from India, and the chapter begins by looking at the ways in which Tibetans took over the scholarly tradition of first-millennium India. The Tibetans however also drew on other sources, including China and Central Asia, and developed their own understandings on an eclectic basis, particularly in areas such as medicine.

Main topics covered

- Introduction
- Basic understandings of the universe
- The Indian monastic universities, their curriculum and its adoption by the Tibetans
- Philosophy
- Other classical fields of Indian learning
- Non-Buddhist aspects of Tibetan knowledge
- Medicine

Introduction

For most citizens of the contemporary global world the claims of science to be the single true source of knowledge are overwhelming, and religious knowledge tends to be seen as a separate and largely unconnected realm of understanding. To appreciate the place of Buddhist knowledge in the Tibetan society of the past we have to realize that this was not the case. Buddhism was very much part of the wider set of understandings through which Tibetans made sense of the world around them. As we saw in Chapter 3, the starting points for the Buddhist path included the theory of karma and the associated cosmology of the six realms of rebirth, including the hell realms and heavens, familiar from its depiction at the entrance to many monasteries in the form of the *Sipé Korlo* or 'Wheel of Existence' (see below). Buddhist philosophy was closely involved with the general development of philosophical thought in India, with logic in particular being an area where Buddhist scholars made particular contributions.

For most pre-modern Tibetans, much of this knowledge would have had a strong sense of being 'Buddhist'. It was translated into Tibetan by lama-scholars working in a specifically Buddhist religious context, and was studied in monastic schools. To the extent that people were aware of its origin they would have associated it with India, a country strongly connected with Buddhism for Tibetans. In this chapter we will look at this body of knowledge and its various sources, and examine how Buddhism largely provided the context in which scholarship took place in Tibet.

For those living in Christian and post-Christian societies, it is natural perhaps to see this situation as similar to that of mediaeval Europe, where scholarship also largely took place under religious auspices, and the Church acted as an ultimate arbiter of what was permissible knowledge. The comparison has some truth in it but is misleading in other respects. While much of the Tibetan body of specialist knowledge developed in Buddhist contexts, its relationship to Buddhism as a religion was somewhat different from that between mediaeval Christianity and the European scholarship of its time.

Christianity historically developed as a religion that makes strong and categorical claims about the history and nature of the universe. Christian traditions and sects have often defined themselves in terms of theological statements, assertions about the true natures of God and of Jesus Christ, and expected their followers to support these statements, at least in public, even where the true nature of the dispute may have been more to do with political or economic factors. In this, however, Christianity is unusual among major pre-modern world religions. Even the differences between Sunni and Shi'a Islam and the later controversies about the status of the Shi'a Imams have a somewhat different character, since these are primarily about authority, not about theology.

There are, as I have said, some parallels between the history of Christianity and the situation in Buddhism. The early schools linked with the various Nikāyas became associated with differing ideas about the nature of reality, and indeed many of the Nikāyas are named after their key philosophical assertions, for example the Sarvāstivādins, whose name derives from their assertion that all dharmas, here meaning elemental components of experience, really exist (*sarva asti*). As we have seen in Chapter 3, however, the Nikāyas were primarily based around ordination lineages, and ideas of orthodoxy and heresy were no part of the way they functioned. Such linkages as there may have been between theory and monastic community seem to have largely broken down with the growth of the Mahāyāna. The new philosophical tendencies and modes of practice which are nowadays labelled as Mahāyāna grew up among members of several different Nikāyas, and the monks and lay followers who adopted the Mahāyāna approaches continued to remain members of their parent Nikāyas even though their philosophical positions might be very different from those officially associated with that Nikāya. Indeed, all ordained Tibetan Buddhists still formally belong to the Sarvāstivādin Nikāya, though Tibetan Buddhist philosophy consistently rejects the assertion that all dharmas really exist after which that Nikāya is named. The only real exception here was constituted by the Theravādins, and the ongoing development of the Theravādin school, initially mainly in South India and Sri Lanka, and later in Southeast Asia, had little relevance or salience for the mainstream of Mahāyāna scholarship, which very rarely refers to it. In any case, it is doubtful how far even Theravāda Buddhism can be understood in terms of orthodoxy, especially in pre-modern times.

Belonging to a monastery associated with a particular Nikāya thus did not necessarily imply subscribing to any particular beliefs about the nature of the universe beyond those which are in a sense intrinsic in the act of going for refuge to Buddha, Dharma and Saṅgha, in other words that the Buddha and his teaching (the Dharma) represent a genuine path to liberation and that the Saṅgha in some sense embody that teaching. The body of knowledge we are discussing in this chapter is thus 'Buddhist' in the sense that it was mostly taught by, written and transmitted by scholars who were Buddhist, rather than Buddhist in the sense of rigidly defining how Buddhism has to be understood as a path to liberation. While some Tibetan traditions, particularly the Gelukpa, developed a relatively sharply-defined description of the path to Buddhahood, others were more inclusive in their approach. In public at least, virtually all contemporary lamas and scholars would accept the validity, at some level, of the practices taught by all of the Buddhist traditions of Tibet.

Having said this, the philosophical understanding of the path to Buddhahood cannot be rigidly separated from the nature of the path itself, since insight into reality is itself an important part of the Buddhist goal. Consequently, polemical writing is quite common in the Tibetan context, and is generally devoted towards demonstrating the superiority of one's own school or sub-tradition. Thus Sakya Paṇḍita, one of the first great Tibetan masters of the Indian tradition of philosophical disputation, argues at length for the superiority of his understanding of Tantric practice over that of the Nyingmapa and Kagyüdpa lamas of his time. For all this, actual religious persecution was relatively uncommon in Tibet. The most notable examples are the closure of the Jonangpa monasteries and the suppression of their teachings by the Gelukpas in Central Tibet in the later seventeenth century, and the intermittent suppression and persecution of Bon teachings, again mainly by the Gelukpa regime.

In general, then, Buddhist philosophy or theology was not engaged in the levels of political conflict and religious wars associated with Christianity during periods of European history. The role of scholar and of source of knowledge was and still is nevertheless a very important part of the role and persona of Buddhist teachers in Tibet, and an account of Tibetan Buddhism would be incomplete which does not consider the body of knowledge which was transmitted by the Buddhist teachers, and which formed an essential background against which Buddhism unfolded its liberatory strategy.

Indeed, the boundaries between general scholarly knowledge and specifically Buddhist knowledge is not always easy to draw in the Tibetan context. I have chosen to discuss the five classical philosophical schools in this chapter, although they are closely associated with the Buddhist teachings, and have also included a number of other topics such as medicine. I have discussed the issue of karma however mostly in Chapter 6, because of its close links to ethics, and some of the body of Buddhist knowledge regarding the fate of living beings after death in Chapter 8, because while it has a theoretical component it is much more concerned with practice than with theoretical knowledge.

Basic understandings of the universe

We start off though with what might be called the basic parameters for understanding the universe: the nature of the world we live in, the nature of death and rebirth. Here the Tibetans took over the Buddhist form of the standard Indian models.

We might begin with the well-known diagram, the *Sipé Korlo* or 'Wheel of Existence', which is very commonly painted in the entrance hall to monasteries. It depicts the six worlds into which 'sentient beings' (*semchen*, living beings that have consciousness) may be reborn: the heavens of the gods, the realms of the *asuras* or demigods who are at constant war with the gods; the world of human beings; the realm of animals; the realm of the *yidak* (Skt. *preta*), spirits who are fated to perpetual thirst and hunger; and the hell-realms with the dreadful punishments of the cold and hot hells. This is a depiction of the process of *saṃsāra*, a point which is reinforced by the central ring, with the 'three roots' that drive the samsaric process, desire, hatred and delusion (*rāga*, *dveṣa*, *moha*), symbolized by the cock, snake and pig, and the small figures climbing up and down on either side in the next ring out.

The outermost ring, outside the six sectors for the six realms, contains twelve small drawings depicting the twelve links of the Buddhist formula of *pratītya-samutpāda* (*tendrel* in Tibetan), the process of dependent origination, of the arising of phenomena in mutual dependence. Each of the six sectors includes a Buddha figure, representing

Figure 5.1 *Sipé Korlo*. Wangdu Podrang, Bhutan. Photo by author (2009).

the teaching of Buddha to the beings of that realm. The whole structure is held within the jaws of Yama, the god who presides over death, judgement and the hell-realms.

These are familiar images in Tibet, and while not necessarily understood in detail by all viewers, the general message is clear enough: there is an ordered universe and while it contains positive and negative experiences there is nothing but the teaching of the Dharma that can prevent us from a blind succession of rebirths in one or another unsatisfactory condition. Even the bliss of the gods comes to an end, and is followed by rebirth into a lower realm, most likely one of intense pain, fear, hunger or thirst.

Closely linked to the wheel of rebirth is the classical Tibetan model of death and rebirth. Death involves the separation of consciousness (*namshé*) from the body. The experience of death is thought of as closely related to experiences such as sleep and orgasm, and can be modelled in terms of the subtle body theory, but this is relatively technical knowledge, certainly not accessible to most Tibetans without specialist Tantric training. While the *bardo tödröl* teachings (teachings from the so-called 'Tibetan Book of the Dead') are undoubtedly better known in the West than to most Tibetans, the general idea that death provides an opportunity for liberation or more plausibly rebirth in Dewachen, the Western Paradise of the Buddha Amitābha or some other celestial realm is familiar, and the *powa* practices that are intended to assist in achieving this are quite widely taught to lay people. The idea is also well known that if one fails to take advantage of this opportunity, one's consciousness will wander through a series of frightening experiences for a period of 49 days, following which one will be reborn into one's next life – as an animal, hell-being, or whatever else, depending on the karmic burden one has acquired in the present life or inherited from past lives.

Another component of the traditional model of the universe is the standard cosmology and geography inherited from the Indian texts. This involved a world centred on Mount Meru, continents and subcontinents in four directions, the heavens of the gods and demigods above, and the hells below (see Figure 5.2; the hell-realms are not shown here, but would be understood to be beneath the diagram).

Figure 5.2 Diagram showing the structure of the universe, with Mount Meru and heavens of the gods and the continents. Trongsa Dzong, Bhutan. Photo by author (2009).

As with much Tibetan traditional thought, one might wonder how literally much of this was and is believed. There were certainly elements of scepticism within premodern society, but on the whole much of the basic structure of ideas presented above formed a taken-for-granted background to Tibetan thought. There are two caveats that might be entered to that statement however. The first is that contemporary Western thought is characterized by the absolute dominance, at least in an ideological sense, of Western science. Modern Westerners may attend church services, consult alternative healers (who will do their best to present themselves as scientific), read the astrology columns in the newspaper, visit a tarot reader, and indulge in any of a variety of religious practices. Each of these, and many other human activities, involve structures of discourse and knowledge that are largely incompatible with scientific knowledge, but all of this and much else is done within a society where it is taken for granted that scientific knowledge in some sense has the last word. All of this, of course, has little to do with the actual level of understanding of science, or with the provisional, partial and hypothetical nature of scientific knowledge. Much of science is also formulated in technical languages such as that of mathematics, which only a small proportion of the contemporary Western population could begin to decipher. It is true too that the demand for logical consistency of our thought and for the ultimate solidity of scientific knowledge is actually more fantasy than reality. The hierarchy of knowledge is nevertheless clear and well understood by all except a small minority of adherents to fundamentalist Christianity and parallel variants of other religions.

The sources of Tibetan knowledge are equally incomprehensible and mysterious, no doubt, to most Tibetans, and equally traditional Tibetan knowledge contains a variety of different modes of discourse. There is a significant difference, though, in that none of these have the same absolute priority or authority that contemporary Western society concedes – at least in theory – to science. Discourses of rebirth in different realms, stories of the magical powers of great lamas, a variety of systems of astrology and divination, coexist with rational and straightforward modes of thinking, but they exist in parallel, rather than in a hierarchical structure. The truth of one does not invalidate the truth of another; each has its own place where it belongs and is taken seriously in its own terms.

In part this goes along with a perspective in which all of these modes of knowledge are in a sense provisional and partial attempts to grasp a reality which no one thinks of as totally comprehensible, at any rate by ordinary people. This is in its way both a central assumption of Mahāyāna and Tibetan Buddhism, in the form of the concept of *śūnyatā* or 'emptiness' of our assumptions about ourselves and the universe, and also a kind of everyday relativizing of knowledge.

A second and perhaps related point is that the classic Buddhist model of the universe, while taken seriously in its own way, does not negate the possibility of acquiring accurate empirical knowledge about the world. Thus a Tibetan scholar living in the early nineteenth century, Lama Tsenpo, produced a description of the world, the *Dzamling Gyéshé*, which included surprisingly accurate descriptions of the social and political arrangements of contemporary Britain – certainly more accurate than most of the knowledge possessed about Tibet by British scholars of that time. Equally, the esoteric anatomy of the subtle body did not stop Tibetan surgeons from dissecting dead bodies and trying to work their inner structures out for themselves.

A further point though points to another significant feature of the Tibetan worldview, which it shares perhaps with many 'religious' worldviews but not with the dominant perspective in contemporary Western society. This is the idea that everything that happens is significant, meaningful and connected with everything else. Nothing is a matter of accident or arbitrary coincidence. At one level, this is implied by the logic of karma and the concept of dependent origination (*pratītya-samūtpada*). However, the Tibetan implication is somewhat stronger than this, as is implied by the various usages of *tendrel*, the Tibetan term for *pratītya-samūtpada*. *Tendrel* is frequently used in the sense of 'omen' or 'sign' – some event is a *tendrel* of something that is going to happen at a later date. One can also perform an action in order to create a *tendrel*, so that one might, for example, ask a lama to give a short teaching or perform a short ritual in a particular context so as to create a *tendrel* for his future connection as a teacher to that place or that group of people. Specific rituals can be performed and texts recited so as to create positive (auspicious) *tendrel* – such as the *Tashi Gyepa* prayer of Mipam Rinpoche, which is often recited at the beginning of an undertaking to create auspicious circumstances. Other prayers are devoted to averting negative influences or obstacles (*barché* – an important term for Tibetans). One of the best-known of these is the *Barché Lamsel* prayer, a *terma* prayer to Padmasambhava discovered by the nineteenth-century *tertön* lama Chokgyur Lingpa (1829–1870).

These ideas about auspiciousness and connection are linked to the significance of astrology in Tibetan culture. The Tibetans derived astrological knowledge from both India and China, and popular almanacs are produced on the basis of the combined systems which provide information about whether each day is auspicious or inauspicious for particular undertakings. Thus (to quote from the *Bhutan Observer*, which has a regular astrological column giving the data for the current week), Friday April 29, 2011 was:

> Auspicious For: Making incense-offering and conducting purification rituals, and making daily offerings. Inauspicious For: Arranging marriage, celebrating wedding, starting education, starting construction of new house, moving house, handing and taking over anything, making and taking medicine, starting business, and calling upon superiors.

Predictions can likewise be made for whether particular days, months or years are auspicious or inauspicious for a particular person. If a particular year is inauspicious (in other words, if there are *barché*, obstacles, for that person in that particular year) then ritual activities and prayers may be undertaken to counter the obstacles. The system both provides a sense of different days having different characters and influences that might be positive or negative in general or for particular purposes and individuals, and a series of counter-measures that can be adopted to deal with negative influences and problems.

Thus Tibetans lived within a set of everyday assumptions about the world which might seem strange and exotic to citizens of contemporary Western societies but which nevertheless were both naturally accepted and less restrictive in practice than one might assume.

The Indian monastic universities, their curriculum and its adoption by the Tibetans

A key body of scholarly knowledge for the Tibetans originated in the monastic Buddhism of North India, including Nepal and Kashmir. A particularly important role was played by the so-called monastic universities of North India. There were several of these, all in present-day Bihar and Bengal. The oldest and most famous, Nālandā, dated back probably to the fifth century CE, when it was founded by one of the Gupta rulers of north India. The remaining four (Odantapuri, Vikramaśīla, Somapura and Jagaddala) were founded by rulers of the Pāla empire that emerged in the mid-eighth century and was based in Bihar and Bengal. These monastic universities were large establishments that taught an extensive curriculum. They appear to have served as educational institutions for the laity as well as providing religious training. They also, no doubt, provided ritual services on behalf of the Pāla state and its successors the Sena dynasty. All of these institutions were destroyed or brought to an effective end by the Muslim invasions in the early thirteenth century, but between the ninth and twelfth centuries they were thriving centres of study attended by students from many parts of the world, including Tibet.

The curriculum at these universities, according to the Tibetans, was divided into two stages, the five lesser fields of study (poetics, drama, astrology, and the linguistic sciences) which led to the degree of 'Lesser Paṇḍita', and the five greater fields of study (grammar, medicine, fine arts, logic and Buddhist philosophy) which led to the degree of 'Greater Paṇḍita' (*paṇchen* in Tibetan, the title later given to the Panchen Lamas in honour of the high scholastic abilities of the first of the series). Many of the standard texts in these areas were translated into Tibetan and included in the Tibetan canonical collection of Indian treatises and commentarial material, the Tengyur. The Tibetans themselves gradually acquired mastery over this material, aided by Indian scholars such as the Kashmiri Pandit Śākyaśrībhadra who came to India in the early thirteenth century. According to Tibetan accounts, it was Śākyaśrībhadra who acknowledged that the Sakya lama Kunga Gyaltsen (1182–1251) had achieved the status of a Paṇḍita (hence the name by which he is now referred to, Sakya Paṇḍita). Others, such as the great Buton Rinchendrub, who was responsible for cataloguing and codifying the Kangyur and Tengyur, and also wrote an important historical account of the origins of the Buddhist teachings in India, soon followed, and with the disappearance of the monastic universities from India, Tibet became the primary location in which much of this knowledge was preserved.

While Tibetan scholars from Sakya Paṇḍita onwards saw themselves primarily as preserving this tradition, they also added to it and developed it. In time they developed scholarly centres of their own that have in their turn been referred to as monastic universities, above all the great Gelukpa monasteries of Central Tibet, Ganden, Sera and Drepung. Each of these consisted of several colleges (*shedra*) with different buildings and curricula and numerous hostels for students from different parts of Tibet, along with the households (*labrang*) of the various reincarnate lamas who became in time associated with the monasteries. Similar institutions in Northeastern Tibet (Amdo), at Kumbum and Labrang Tashikyil, were attended extensively by Mongolian as well as Tibetan students and passed on the Indo-Tibetan scholarly tradition to Mongolia.

Of these ten areas of study, only one was intrinsically linked to Buddhism, the study of Buddhist philosophy, though the study of logic, which encompassed epistemology and the establishment of valid forms of argument (*pramāṇa*) was also almost exclusively concerned with the articulation of Buddhist philosophical positions. All ten fields however took on to a greater or lesser degree a specifically Buddhist form in Tibet, since their primary context of transmission was Buddhist. As in India, though, scholarship was of use to the secular authorities for administrative purposes, and the scholars trained in these various institutions were often employed by the various regional governments and authorities, secular or religious, as clerical and administrative officials.

The Indian monastic universities were enormously important in forming the Tibetan image of scholarship as well as in providing much of its ongoing content, but they were not the only sources of Tibetan knowledge. Tibet, as we have seen, had its own sense of indigenous forms of knowledge at the time of the arrival of Buddhism, but it also imported forms of knowledge from other parts of the world, which is hardly surprising considering the apparent involvement of Tibetans in long-distance trade from very early times. China and the general region of Iran and Central Asia both seem to have made significant contributions. China was a source especially for one of the major forms of Tibetan astrological and divinatory knowledge, and also for knowledge about government and how to run a state. It appears that the political structure of the Tibetan state, with its ranked officials, is indebted to Chinese structures of government. Architecture is also an area in which Chinese influences are noticeable. Another field in which knowledge from China was significant was medicine. Iran and Central Asia contributed to medicine and perhaps also to architecture.

Philosophy

The philosophical understandings associated with the Nikāya schools were similar to those of other Indian currents of thought at the time associated with ascetic practice, including the Sāṃkhya school of Brahmanical thought, and the philosophical approach of the Jainas. Like these, it was based on an analysis of existence into a number of elements (*dharma*) that were thought of as basic constituents of both consciousness and material reality. In the case of Buddhism, this analysis was directed towards assisting the Buddhist practitioner to detach from concepts of the self (*atman*) through the realization that such a concept could not be identified with any of these elements. This mode of analysis, the Abhidharma (*abhidhamma* in Pali), was developed in somewhat different forms in different early schools, including the Theravādins and Sarvāstivādins.

The Mahāyāna consisted of a wide variety of different developments, including new understandings of the goal of Buddhism, of the techniques to be used to approach it, and of the nature of the Buddha's activity in the world. It also included a range of new philosophical or theological approaches, which developed as attempts to systematize the various philosophical insights and assertions made in the Mahāyāna sūtras. These were frequently complex and lengthy works, often with a strong visionary component, and were not easily reducible to a single consistent body of ideas.

The first major Mahāyāna philosopher, Nāgārjuna, who probably lived in the second or third century CE, was particularly associated with the *Prajñāpāramitā* or 'Perfection of Wisdom' Sūtras that had appeared from around the first century BCE onwards, and which provided the initial presentation of the concept of *śūnyatā* or 'emptiness'. Nāgārjuna developed this in his central work, the *Mūlamadhyamakakārikā* or 'Fundamental Verses on the Middle Way', into a systematic process of refutation of all assertions that could be made about the nature of reality. His work was continued by other scholars, including Āryadeva, said to be his disciple, and Candrakīrti, who lived perhaps in the sixth century.

This approach became known as Mādhyamika or Mādhyamaka. In relation to the path to Buddhahood, the central idea here was to provide a technique for showing that any assumptions that were made about the nature of life and the universe were inadequate and inconsistent. Whatever reality was, it was beyond any kind of logical grasp or description. The point of philosophy, for these scholars, was to demonstrate that our ordinary ideas about the world were insufficient. This kind of 'deconstruction' (the comparisons with the 'deconstructive' work of late twentieth-century philosophers such as Jacques Derrida have been explored by a number of scholars), is intended to open the way to direct insight into the nature of reality. Nāgārjuna and Āryadeva are said to have been advanced yogins and meditators, and a large number of yogic and Tantric works in later centuries were also attributed to them. Nāgārjuna was also regarded as an expert on medicine, on erotic science, and on magical techniques, and to have attained the power (or *siddhi*) of endless life; legend describes him as voluntarily giving up his life after living for several centuries. It is unlikely that many of these texts and legends tell us much about the historical Nāgārjuna, but they help to remind us that philosophy here was very much at the service of a wider spiritual agenda.

The radical deconstruction of the Mādhyamika philosophers was much admired, and it was generally held by the Tibetans that in some sense this was the peak of philosophical achievement. There remained, however, a gap between the radical position of the Mādhyamika and more ordinary understandings of the world. Philosophical issues included such questions as how one could describe the processes by which the mistaken and illusory understandings of the world came about, and how one could make sense of the subtler perceptions and modes of consciousness that yogic practitioners uncovered in their meditative states. For the yogins themselves, there was a need for a more positive sense of the goal of spiritual practice, if only as a provisional guide along the way.

A number of further Mahāyāna Sūtras, appearing perhaps from the first and second century CE onwards, provided the basis for various further philosophical positions. By contrast with the negative formulations of the Mādhyamika, these approaches, variously known as Cittamātra ('mind only'), Yogācāra or Vijñānavāda, emphasized more positive conceptualizations of mind or consciousness as the basis of reality. The *Saṃdhinirmocana Sūtra*, traditionally reckoned as the first Sūtra of this school, described itself as taught at a 'Third Turning of the Wheel of the Dharma', with the 'Hīnayāna' as the first, and the Mādhyamika as the second (see Chapter 3). It was followed by a number of other important Mahāyāna Sūtras presenting similar ideas. Another group of Mahāyāna Sūtras teaching the so-called 'Buddha-nature' or Tathāgatagarbha doctrine, according to which the potential for Buddhahood is present within all beings, is also often classed with the Yogācāra. A series of five texts that were traditionally held to have been revealed to the fourth-century teacher Asaṅga by the *bodhisattva* Maitreya were also important for the development of this school. Mahāyāna scholarship in India developed as a series of combinations and elaborations of these various Mādhyamika and Yogācāra positions.

The study of philosophy in Tibet included both the study of Buddhist philosophical positions and of the teachings for the path to Buddhahood more generally, and was combined with the study of logic, epistemology and formal disputation. While the major Mahāyāna Sūtras were all translated into Tibetan and included in the Kangyur, Tibetan scholars generally worked less from the Sūtras or from their commentaries than from the *śāstras*, independent treatises composed by the great Indian Buddhist scholars. A relatively small number of these were the focus of intellectual work, and numerous further commentaries and independent treatises were in turn written on the basis of these texts. They included:

- The *Abhidharmakośa* of Vasubandhu and the *Abhidharmasamuccaya* of Asaṅga as the basic texts for the Sarvāstivādin Abhidharma.
- The *Mūlamadhyamakakārikā* of Nāgārjuna along with Candrakīrti's commentary, Āryadeva's *Catuḥśataka* and Candrakīrti's own *Madhyamakāvatāra*, which were the main sources for the Mādhyamika teachings.
- The five texts revealed to Asan·ga by Maitreya, particularly the *Mahāyānasūtrālamkāra, Madhyāntavibhāga, Abhisamayālamkāra* and the *Ratnagotravibhaga* (also known as the *Uttaratantra*), along with Asan·ga's own *Mahāyānasam·graha*, which weere the bases for Yogācāra philosophy.
- A further very influential text, Śāntideva's *Bodhicaryāvatāra*, mentioned in Chapter 3, which became a primary source for teachings on the development of *bodhicitta*.
- The works of the two great Buddhist logicians, Dignāga and Dharmakirti, which provided the basis of the curriculum on logic and epistemology.

While virtually all Tibetan monastic traditions gave some place to philosophical study, it was particularly valued by the Sakyapas and later by the Gelukpas. The texts were studied in a variety of ways. In the most widespread Tibetan scholarly tradition, that of the Gelukpas, the philosophical positions within the various Indian *śāstras* were analysed, refined and abstracted to provide a series of five doctrinal positions (*drupta, siddanta* in Sanskrit):

- Vaibhāṣika
- Sautrāntika
- Cittamatrā
- Svātantrika Mādhyamika
- Prāsangika Mādhyamika

While these five positions derived historically from positions actually adopted within various Indian Nikāyas and Mahāyāna schools, they were taught in a relatively abstract philosophical form within the Gelukpa schools. They were presented as a series of formal possibilities, each superseding the one before, and leading to the Prāsangika Mādhyamika, seen as the highest and most perfect of philosophical positions.

A number of the texts that discuss these philosophical positions (sometimes referred to in English as the study of *tenets*) are available in English versions, all deriving from the work of the great Amdo polymath Jamyang Shepa Ngawang Tsondru and his reincarnation Konchog Jigme Ongpo. Within these analyses, each successive school was seen as subtler and closer to the true nature of reality. Thus the Vaibhāṣika and Sautrāntika, positions associated with the Nikāya ('Hīnayāna') school of the Sarvāstivādins, accept the existence of external objects (the *dharmas*, elementary point-moments assumed by the Abhidharma, the basic philosophy of the early schools); the Cittamatrā positions regard the mind-continuum (consciousness) as primary and the apparent world as created by it, while the two Mādhyamika positions (the first itself subdivided into two) provide progressively more subtle mediations between external existence and consciousness, culminating in the Prāsangika Mādhyamika's systematic refusal to make any explicit assertions, relying instead on drawing out the mistaken consequences of its opponent's arguments. The point of the exercise is primarily to develop skill in logical disputation, so that the student becomes able to act as an embodiment of the Prāsangika perspective. This is a form of logical analysis highly valued by the Gelukpa, for whom it counts as a form of meditation, and elements of it are included in the *lam rim* scheme under the heading of *vipaśyanā*.

Non-Gelukpa approaches provide both somewhat different analyses of the various positions, and add further subsequent positions, such as the Shentong version of Mādhyamika discussed in Jamyang Kyentse's text, and the Tantric philosophical positions studied both there and in Mipam's. Gelukpas by contrast tend to argue that the Tantra does not have a philosophical position distinct from that of Prāsangika Mādhyamika.

Other aspects of Indian Buddhist scholarship were also continued both by the Gelukpas and by the other traditions. Thus the Gelukpa monastic curriculum leading to the monastic degree of Geshe Lharampa consisted of five subject areas, each based around the study of one or two Indian *śāstra* texts:

- Logic and epistemology (*pramāṇa*) was studied, mainly on the basis of Dharmakīrti's *Pramāṇavarttika;*
- Maitreya's *Abhisamayālamkāra* and Śāntideva's *Bodhicaryāvatāra* provided the basis of the curriculum for Prajñāpāramitā, the study of the *bodhisattva* path;
- Mādhyamika philosophy was studied on the basis of the works of Nāgārjuna, Āryadeva, Candrakīrti and Śāntarakṣita, particularly Candrakīrti's *Madhyamakāvatāra;*
- Abhidharma was studied on the basis of Asanga's *Abhidharmasamuccaya* and Vasubandhu's *Abhidharmakośa;*
- Monastic discipline (*vinaya*) was studied on the basis of the *Vinayamūlasūtra* of Gunaprabha.

In practice, the textbooks (*yigcha*) used in the Gelukpa schools were not the actual Indian *śāstra* texts but Tibetan works composed on the basis of the interpretations of these works by Tsongkapa and his immediate disciples. The major training institutions around Lhasa used different sets of *yigcha* written by later Gelukpa lamas such as Jamyang Shepa Ngawang Tsondru, whose texts were used at Drepung Gomang and Drepung Deyang colleges, or Panchen Sonam Drakpa, whose texts were used at Ganden Shartse and Drepung Loseling. Gelukpa colleges outside Lhasa generally followed one or more of these yigcha.

Each of these five areas took several years to study, so that the complete study of this curriculum could take up to twenty years. The process might be significantly shortened for reincarnate lamas, who were thought of as having carried over learning from a previous life, and would in any case generally have received extensive tuition from an early age.

The non-Gelukpa traditions developed similar curricula leading to the award of monastic degrees, though these academic curricula were generally less central for their traditions than in the Gelukpa tradition. The Rimé lamas in the late nineteenth century, who were as described in Chapter 2 mainly from non-Gelukpa monasteries in Eastern Tibet, led a reaction against what has often been described as an excessively formalized and scholastic system, and introduced a renewed emphasis on the direct study of the Indian texts in translation. One of the leading Rimé scholars, Kenpo Shenga, wrote annotations for a set of thirteen main Indian *śāstra* texts, and these have been very influential within the non-Gelukpa traditions in recent times.

Other classical fields of Indian learning

So far we have been discussing traditions of study that are linked quite directly in one way or another to the path to Buddhahood. As mentioned at the start of this chapter, these formed only part of the curriculum at the great Indian monastic universities, and other more practical topics including medicine, astrology, literature, and the arts and crafts in general were also studied extensively and made the subject of textual scholarship.

Much of this work too was translated into Tibetan, and the Tengyur contains a large body of material representing many different aspects of Indian Sanskrit scholarship. Thus there are translations of standard works on medicine, on grammar and literary theory, translations of Sanskrit plays, works on astrology, on *kāmaśāstra* (erotics) and so on. Much of this material was picked up by Tibetan scholars and developed into part of the Tibetan scholarly tradition.

Non-Indian aspects of Tibetan knowledge

While the majority of formal Tibetan knowledge came from India, it was developed creatively by the Tibetans over many centuries, and their work is by no means purely derivative. In other areas, the Tibetan contribution is more obviously original. Thus the Tibetans created a substantial historical literature, much of it focusing on the histories of monasteries, lamas, and important secular families. These books were quite varied in nature, including both legendary material and carefully researched historical narratives with developed procedures of critical reflection.

Tibetan society also had a vast body of informal knowledge, some of it explicit in stories, proverbs, craft lore and the like, much of it implicit. This was certainly true of the Tibetans before the coming of Buddhism. Matters such as the knowledge of proverbs, oratorical ability, knowledge of wedding songs and speeches, folk stories and narrations, invocations to local deities, and the like were of great importance among both agricultural and pastoral populations. Much of this material was recorded by native Tibetan scholars in past centuries; much more has been recorded in recent years.

In fact such knowledge appears to have been explicitly recognized and categorized in early texts as *drung de'u bön*, three somewhat obscure terms. The first two might be rendered 'narrations' and 'symbolic languages', following the interpretation of the contemporary lama-scholar Namkhai Norbu Rinpoche. *Bön* in modern times is the term for the Bon religion (see Chapter 11), and it also seems to have been the name of a class of priests in the imperial period, but it could perhaps here be more generally rendered as 'religious knowledge'. It is unclear how much of this lore was written down in the pre-Buddhist period.

What is clear is that Tibetans, particularly in the more practical areas of life, were willing to build eclectically on the basis of knowledge from many sources, including their own practical investigations. This can be seen particularly clearly in the area of medicine, and a discussion of this field now follows as a final example of the complexity and sophistication of Tibetan knowledge.

Figure 5.3 Tibetan medical dispensary, Majnu-ka-tilla, Delhi. Photo by author (1996).

Medicine

Tibetan medicine is a classic example of what can be called a kind of practical eclecticism, as well as illustrating some of the complexities of an apparently Indian Buddhist monopoly over scholarly knowledge. The principal textual reference of the Buddhist medical tradition today is a collection of four texts called the Four Tantras (*Gyüshi*), occasionally the Fourfold Medical Tantra in recognition of the somewhat evident fact that they were compiled in their present form at the same time by one individual, or possibly several individuals working together. Large parts of this text are still memorized by Tibetan doctors as part of training.

The *Gyüshi* has something of the form of a Tantra, in that it takes the form of a verse dialogue between a Buddha (more specifically, a sage emanated by the Buddha of medicine, Bhaiṣajyaguru), and an interlocutor, in which the former expounds the main teaching to the latter in response to a series of questions. The whole dialogue is described, as is also standard for Tantras, as taking place in a visionary realm, the Paradise of Bhaiṣajyaguru. Some Tibetans in fact regard the *Gyüshi* as a divinely-inspired work, a genuine revelation of the Buddha in his manifestation as Bhaiṣajyaguru. Others regard it as the work of one of the most famous of Tibetan doctors, Yuthok the Younger, who lived in the twelfth century.

On closer examination, things are not so simple. For one thing, large parts of the *Gyüshi* are close adaptations of the Tibetan translation of one of the best-known of Indian medical texts, the *Aṣṭāṅgahṛdaya* of Vāgbhaṭa, who lived in around the seventh century. The close relation between *Gyüshi* and *Aṣṭāṅgahṛdaya* was well known to many Tibetan medical authorities in the past and evident to anyone who undertakes a systematic comparison of the relevant chapters. This might lead one to assume that the *Gyüshi* is an Ayurvedic text, and certainly much of it closely reflects the Ayurvedic teachings of Vāgbhaṭa. Other parts, however, very clearly do not derive from Vāgbhaṭa or from Ayurveda. The fourth of the four texts contains important descriptions of diagnosis on the basis of the pulse and on the basis of urine. Neither pulse diagnosis or urine diagnosis formed part of the Ayurveda of Vāgbhaṭa's time, and the likelihood is strong that the pulse diagnosis derived from Chinese medicine, which had been using it for many centuries, and the urine diagnosis from the Greek-derived medical system used among the Arabs and Persians. Other elements of the *Gyüshi*, for example much of the material on spirit-causation of illness, appear to derive from indigenous Tibetan sources. In fact, it is possible that the initial creation of the text took place among Bonpo medical circles. They possess a text, the *Bumshi*, which is verbally very close to the *Gyüshi*, and there are aspects of the text that suggest that the *Gyüshi* may, as the Bonpo themselves claim, have been borrowed and adapted from the *Bumshi*.

The Tibetans' own account of the origin of Tibetan medical knowledge emphasizes the Greco-Persian contribution, since it describes a healing competition in the time of the Tibetan emperor Songtsen Gampo at which Indian, Chinese, and Persian doctors competed. The Persian, whose name was Galenos, an obvious reference to the great Greek doctor Galen, was successful, and the Persian medical tradition was, according to this account, established in Tibet.

One can ask, though, how central the *Gyüshi* really is to medical education. In one sense, it is essential, in that being recognized as a doctor, particularly in the medical colleges in Lhasa and some major monasteries, was dependent on being able to memorize this text, and still to some degree remains so today. In another sense, though, the *Gyüshi* is less central to contemporary medical practice than one might suppose. The medical recipes in the *Gyüshi* are rarely used, having been replaced by the more complicated medical compounds of contemporary practice. It is also evident that knowing the verses alone would not enable one to practise as a doctor. What is at least as significant is the period of apprenticeship that follows on graduation as a scholar who knows the *Gyüshi*. It is in this situation of apprenticeship that the doctor-to-be learns to recognize different diseases as defined by Tibetan medicine and to apply the subtle differentiation and calibration of remedies that are characteristic of the system. It is in the situation of apprenticeship, too, that doctors begin to acquire real ability in the art of pulse diagnosis, which is in fact of major significance within the tradition as practised today.

None of this suggests that medicine is really particularly Buddhist, except in terms of the Buddhist frame story of the *Gyüshi* text, and the not entirely convincing linkage of the three *nyepa* (Skt. *doṣa*) or fundamental disease-causing agents in Ayurveda (approximately equivalent to wind, bile, phlegm) to the three roots of *saṁsāra*, desire, anger and ignorance, an equation which does not occur in Vāgbhaṭa. However, there is an important lineage of Tantric practice, the *Yutog Nyingtig*, which appears to go back to the twelfth century and in which the cult of Bhaiṣajyaguru plays a significant role, and many older doctors in particular undertook this practice as part of their medical training. Tantric ritual practices, including the mantra of Bhaiṣajyaguru and other rituals relating to that deity, are still significant in medical practice.

One might consider one further aspect of medicine here, which is that the Thirteenth Dalai Lama visited India in 1910–12, at the time of an earlier Chinese invasion of Tibet, and is said to have been very impressed by what he saw of the Indian public health system. The principal modern Tibetan medical college, the Mentsikang, was founded in Lhasa at his direction after his return to Tibet in 1912, and in some respects it reflects what he had learned in India, for example about the desirability of population-wide health measures. The director of the Mentsikang, Kyenrab Norbu, was a modernist in many ways, and his institution exerted enormous influence over Tibetan medicine as practised today.

All this is typical of the field of Tibetan knowledge as a whole; Indian influences are mixed with others, which are often less explicit; Buddhism is omnipresent, but its influence may be profound or relatively superficial; indigenous Tibetan understandings are present in various places; and the whole system is often not quite as ancient or traditional as it might look, since Tibetan knowledge continued to develop and innovate over the centuries.

The next chapter deals with another important area in which Buddhist concepts developed a complex relationship with indigenous ideas, that of ethics.

Key points you need to know

- Buddhist knowledge was not dogma in the sense that belief in it was required. However, India was a major source of knowledge for the Tibetans, and knowledge was closely associated with Buddhism and the great educational institutions of Buddhist India – thus there was no sense of an opposition between religion and science, more of a close affinity between them. Much of the curriculum of these institutions was continued and developed further in the great Tibetan monasteries.
- The basic parameters for understanding the structure and nature of the world however were largely derived from India. They included the idea of human life consisting of a continuing series of rebirths, the six kinds of rebirth, and the law of karma linking action in one life with result in future lives, as well as the structure of the earth and the heavens and hells above and beneath it.
- Buddhist philosophy is an important adjunct to Buddhist practice. It was and continues to be taught on the basis of Indian and Tibetan texts as a series of different philosophical positions leading to the insight of *sūnyatā* or 'emptiness', the lack of ultimate reality in any assertions about the nature of the universe. Buddhist philosophy thus tends to relativize systems of knowledge, so that different ways of thinking about the world appear less as logically inconsistent alternatives, and more as provisional and partial attempts to grasp a reality beyond our comprehension.
- Tibetan society in the past was comfortable with a variety of kinds of knowledge about the world from the religious and academic to the folk-loric and legendary, all of which coexisted without direct conflict. Empirical investigation was also common, for example in areas such as geography and medicine. Medicine is also characteristic of much Tibetan practical knowledge in that it is a synthesis of elements taken from many sources, including Indian, Greco-Arabic and Chinese medical traditions, developed in Tibet into a new synthesis adapted to Tibetan needs and resources.
- The Tibetan world was full of meaning. Events of all kinds were seen as significant and meaningful rather than as resulting from coincidence. Signs and connections could be read by those with the relevant skills, and divina-tion and astrology were important.

Discussion questions

1 Compare the relationship between religious and secular knowledge in Tibet with that of mediaeval Europe or of modern science.
2 How did the Tibetans continue and adapt the knowledge of Buddhist India?
3 What are the fundamental ideas of Tibetan Buddhist philosophy?
4 Discuss the relationship between Tibetan medicine and Tibetan Buddhism.

Further reading

Adams, Vincanne, Sienna Craig and Mona Schrempf (eds). *Medicine Between Science and Religion: Explorations on Tibetan Grounds.* Oxford: Berghahn Books, 2010.

Cabezon, José I. and Roger R. Jackson (ed.). *Tibetan Literature: Studies in Genre. (Essays in Honor of Geshe Lhundup Sopa).* Ithaca, New York: Snow Lion, 1996.

Clark, Barry. *The Quintessence Tantras of Tibetan Medicine.* Ithaca, NY: Snow Lion Publications, 1995.

Cornu, Philippe. *Tibetan Astrology.* Boston: Shambhala, 1997.

Dhonden, Yeshi. *Health through Balance: An Introduction to Tibetan Medicine.* Edited and translated by Jeffrey Hopkins. Ithaca, New York: Snow Lion, 1986.

Dreyfus, Georges B. J. *The Sound of Two Hands Clapping: The Education of a Tibetan Buddhist Monk.* Berkeley: University of California Press, 2003.

Gyatso, Desi Sangye. *A Mirror of Beryl: A Historical Introduction to Tibetan Medicine.* Essex: Wisdom Books, 2010.

Gyurme Dorje (trans. and commentary). *Tibetan Elemental Divination Paintings: Illuminated Manuscript from the White Beryl of Sangs-rGyas Rgya-mtsho.* London: John Eskenazi, 2008.

Henning, Edward. *Kālacakra and the Tibetan Calendar.* New York: American Institute of Buddhist Studies, 2007.

Kongtrul, Jamgön. *The Treasury of Knowledge.* Several volumes. Ithaca, NY: Snow Lion, 2003 onwards.

Parfionovitch, Yuri, Fernand Meyer and Gyurme Dorje. *Tibetan Medical Paintings: Illustrations to the Blue Beryl Treatise of Sangye Gyamtso (1653–1705).* London: Serindia, 1992.

Perdue, Daniel E. *Debate in Tibetan Buddhism.* Ithaca, NY, USA: Snow Lion, 1992.

Sakya Pandita Kunga Gyaltshen. *A Clear Differentiation of the Three Codes.* Translated by Jared Douglas Rhoton. Albany, NY: State University of New York Press, 2002.

6 *Ethics and Tibetan Buddhism*

In this chapter

This chapter discusses the questions of ethics and morality in Tibetan societies. Buddhism itself provides a thorough basis for lay morality, but in practice the relationship between this and the everyday morality of Tibetan life is a complex one. The chapter investigates various aspects of this relationship and of the ethical dimensions of the Buddhist path.

Main topics covered

- Introduction
- Bases for Buddhist ethics
- Alternative moral dimensions in Tibetan Buddhist society
- Historical dimensions

Introduction

Chapter 6 deals with ethics in Tibetan Buddhism. The question of ethics in Buddhism is at one level straightforward, in that all Buddhist paths and practices have a strong and explicit ethical dimension. At another level, it is more complicated. The foundation for the lay ethics of Buddhist societies is the inevitable natural law of karma, of action and result, which means, in general terms, that some (good, virtuous) actions are rewarded by positive results in a future life, such as rebirth as a human being in a comfortable and prosperous household, with a healthy body and successful life, and other (bad, non-virtuous) actions are punished by negative results such as rebirth as an animal, a *preta* (hungry ghost) or in hell. By and large, as we will see, the avoidance of non-virtuous actions and the performance of virtuous actions leads to much the same kind of everyday morality found in other ethicized religious traditions. In reality, while we might want to be cautious about equating 'non-virtuous action' with 'sin' in the Christian sense (there is no all-powerful God here to define one's actions as sinful), virtue and non-virtue come quite close to familiar concepts of good and evil found in many religious traditions.

Karma however has its limitations, since no amount of virtuous action by itself will lead to escape from the endless cycle of rebirth, with its associated sufferings, that constitutes *saṃsāra*. An awakened being has gone beyond karma, in that his or her actions, which are no longer driven by attachment (craving, *tṛṣṇā*), no longer attract karmic consequences. Does this mean that a Buddha is free to undertake any action, however damaging its consequences to others?

This problematic conclusion is avoided, in Mahāyāna Buddhism at any rate, by the way in which altruism and compassion are built directly into the structure of both the path to Buddhahood and the universe itself. The only effective motivation for achieving Buddhahood is, as we have already seen, *bodhicitta*, the desire to attain Buddhahood in order to relieve all beings from their suffering. Compassion itself, *karuṇā* (*thukjé* in Tibetan), is a basic attribute of Buddhahood, intrinsic to the Buddha-nature that underlies all beings and phenomena and to the *dharmakāya* that is the very nature of the universe. The path to Buddhahood is certainly intended, at one level, to take the aspirant beyond ordinary concepts of 'good' and 'evil', but it cannot diverge from the fundamental principle of compassion for the sufferings of living beings and action to remedy that suffering.

Thus this generates two levels of morality, an ordinary morality for lay people built around concepts of virtue and non-virtue, and a higher morality for the *bodhisattva* built around compassionate action. The classic Tibetan example of how this might work out is the famous story of the monk Lhalung Pelgi Dorjé who is said to have killed the anti-Buddhist emperor Langdarma, so precipitating the end of the early Tibetan empire. Pelgi Dorjé's action was justified, according to the Buddhist apologia, since it prevented Langdarma from committing yet more evil (i.e. non-virtuous) actions than he had already performed, and in the process creating yet more suffering for living beings. Langdarma's aim of destroying Buddhist institutions would also cut off the possibilities for future Tibetans to access the teachings of the Buddha.

Thus the death of Langdarma can be regarded as a good outcome both for Langdarma and for his intended victims, as well as a necessary action to preserve the future of Buddhism in Tibet. In fact, the monastic ritual dances (*cham*) performed by Tibetan monasteries are routinely described as (among other things) a commemoration of this event. Yet Tibetan Buddhist tradition preserves some ambivalence about the whole episode. For one thing, Pelgi Dorjé had committed murder, thus breaking his monastic vows, and according to Tibetan historical narrative he was regarded as ineligible to pass on the lineage of monastic ordination, despite the extreme shortage of monks at the time (a minimum of five ordained monks are required for a legitimate ordination ceremony). It is also often said by lamas that Pelgi Dorjé still had to undergo the karmic consequences for his act of murder, despite the compassionate motivation that underlay it.

In more practical and real-life contexts, the sense that an awakened being is beyond ordinary good and evil can lead to problematic consequences, in that it can provide an obvious legitimation for exploitation by religious personnel such as reincarnate lamas, who may be regarded (and may regard themselves) as somehow beyond ordinary morality. How far this happened in practice it is difficult to say, though the naïve assumption that the lama can do no wrong undoubtedly causes some of the misunderstandings that take place between Tibetan lamas and their Western disciples. The question of monastic vows (particularly vows of celibacy) and whether a sufficiently advanced practitioner is entitled to break them can be a particularly fraught issue. Some high-status Tibetan lamas have undoubtedly believed that they are so entitled, though the normal situation for non-celibate lamas is that they do not take vows of celibacy, so that the issue does not arise.

In any case, this two-level system of morality underlies the Buddhist system of ethics as it operates in Tibetan society. We might ask, though, how seriously the everyday, karma-based system of ethics is taken by Tibetans, and whether there are in fact other, implicit, systems of morality within Tibetan society. A number of scholars of Tibetan society have argued persuasively that there are.

Certainly there seem to be some problems in assuming too high a level of compliance to Buddhist ethical principles among Tibetans. Some early scholars of Tibetan societies assumed in a rather simplistic way that the Tibetans were good Buddhists, that they literally followed the Buddhist ethical teachings, and so they had become good and ethical people. The Austrian anthropologist Christoph von Fürer-Haimendorf, who worked for many years in London at the School of Oriental and African Studies, and did much important early survey work on so-called tribal populations in India and Nepal, famously argued in this way in his (1964) book *The Sherpas of Nepal: Buddhist Highlanders*. This book, along with the various other works that Fürer-Haimendorf wrote in the early 1960s, provided one of the first detailed ethnographic descriptions of a culturally and ethnically Tibetan population. He claimed that the people of Khumbu in Nepal, the Sherpa community which he studied, were collectively minded, socially engaged and worked together cooperatively in a remarkably positive way. He explained this in terms of their commitment to the well-known Buddhist principles of virtuous action.

A few years later, an American anthropologist, Sherry Ortner (later to become well known for her writings in feminist anthropology) also worked with Sherpas in Nepal. However she described the Sherpas with whom she was working – in the valley of Shorung, some 25 miles to the south of Fürer-Haimendorf's community of Khumbu – as individualistic, living in relatively isolated and separate households, and as appearing to have great difficulty in managing a bare minimum of cooperation. This is a classic situation in anthropology, and one can try to make sense of it in a variety of ways. Fürer-Haimendorf and Ortner were very different people, from different generations and approaches within anthropology. Ortner's fieldwork might well have been better than Fürer-Haimendorf's; she was certainly there for considerably longer. Ortner may have been exaggerating the differences between her account and Fürer-Haimendorf's for rhetorical effect; there is always some mileage in arguing that the previous generation of scholars got it wrong. The Sherpas of Shorung in the 1970s might indeed have behaved rather differently from the Sherpas of Khumbu in the late 1950s; there is some evidence that suggests that this was the case. Khumbu, at a higher altitude, with a harsher climate and a closer village settlement pattern, was perhaps by necessity a more cooperative place.

It makes more sense, however, to start by assuming that Sherpa, and more generally Tibetan, culture, is neither some kind of unreal Buddhist paradise in which everybody always behaves towards everybody else in the sweetest and most enlightened of manners, nor a seething hotbed of primal selfishness in which everyone is out for themselves and the devil take the hindmost. Tibetan culture has been profoundly affected by its engagement with Buddhism, but most Tibetans are fairly ordinary human beings, with ordinary human motivations and desires, and their values are not confined to those prescribed by Buddhism. The Buddhist principles of virtuous action are, after all, meant as a corrective to the way people ordinarily behave. Certainly many Tibetans engage extensively in activities that are culturally normative but clearly problematic from the Buddhist point of view, including gambling, heavy drinking, fighting, feuding (in the case of nomadic pastoralists in particular), hunting and killing animals, and warfare.

There is a kind of opposition between tame and wild in Tibetan culture and society that expresses itself in many different ways. The work of Buddhism historically and mythologically in Tibet has been a work of 'taming' (*dulwa*). Mythologically, this goes back to a well-known story in which Avalokiteśvara, in the form of a monkey-*bodhisattva*, fathered the Tibetan people out of compassion for a wild mountain *sinmo* or female demon. The Tibetan people are said to have inherited qualities from both parents. The six children of this primal couple ran around the Tibetan forests without food to eat until Avalokiteśvara gave them seeds and introduced them to agriculture. Bringing the earth under cultivation in Tibetan is again the same word *dulwa*, taming. They then multiplied in number, generating the six original tribes of the Tibetan people.

A later if somewhat more forceful story of 'taming' or 'subduing' refers to another *sinmo*, to whose resistance was attributed the difficulty faced by the early seventh-century Songtsen Gampo, first ruler of a unified Tibetan empire, in building the Jokang, the Buddhist temple at Lhasa which was meant to house the first Buddhist image of Tibet and which remains today one of the most sacred places of Tibet. The body of this *sinmo* was in some sense the land of Tibet itself, and she was only overcome by the building of a series of twelve temples on her limbs to pin her down and hold her in place.

Figure 6.1 *Laptse* or altar to local gods in a Central Tibetan village near Tsurpu Gompa. Photo by author (1987).

In Chapter 2, we read the episode in which Padmasambhava, himself closely linked to Avalokiteśvara, came to Tibet and tamed (again *dula*) the local and regional deities of Tibet, binding them to the service of the Dharma. Many of these gods were associated with wild animals such as the wild yak (*drong*), wild ass (*kyang*) and wild sheep or argali (*nyen*). *Dulwa* is also the Tibetan name for the Vinaya, the disciplinary code of Buddhist monasticism. But through all of this culturally very admirable and valued process of taming, Tibetans continued to value the wild (*gö*) dimension of Tibetan life, culturally typified by the nomadic population (*drokpa*) with their emphasis on toughness, wildness, warriorship and a certain characteristically Tibetan style of *machismo*. *Wangtang* or power is also a quality valued and respected in Tibetan society. Here it is worth noting that the lama himself, while intimately bound up with the role of taming, is himself, structurally, the tamer, not the tamed, and while many lamas have taken on the role of gentle, mild and compassionate spiritual guides, others have cultivated a much tougher and wilder demeanour and style.

The subject of this chapter, then, is not only what Buddhist ethics is, but how it became part of Tibetan society, and how Tibetans reconcile its demands with the other ethical demands and personal desires and ambitions around which their lives are organized.

Bases for Buddhist ethics

To begin with, though, it is important to have a sense of what Buddhist ethics might consist of. Here, as noted above, there is a significant distinction, though also ideally a harmony, between the ethics of the *bodhisattva*, the aspirant to Buddhahood, and the lay ethics that Buddhist teachings enjoin for everyday lay members of society. We begin with the first.

As we have learned in previous chapters, a key principle of Tibetan Buddhism itself is its orientation towards Buddhahood. Buddhahood is the awakened and enlightened state associated with the historical Buddha but also in some sense accessible to everyone, since it is as it were built into the very nature of the universe. Particularly within the Nyingma and Dzogchen tradition, there is a strong sense that if we see through and cleanse the confusions, defilements and obscurations of our everyday perceptions and understandings, Buddhahood will naturally emerge, and we will act in a spontaneously compassionate manner, both sensing the world and behaving in such a way as to maximize the benefit and reduce the sufferings of our fellow living beings.

Figure 6.2
Chorten – reliquary and symbolic representation of the Buddha – outside Junbesi village, Nepal. Photo by author (1971).

The motivational state towards achieving Buddhahood, *bodhicitta* in Sanskrit, *changchub sem* in Tibetan, is a vitally important part of this process. *Bodhicitta* is associated with the desire – actually more than desire, the urgent need and demand – to free our fellow beings from the suffering in which they are enmeshed because of their everyday, unenlightened condition. It is a state or condition that is cognitive, emotional, and also physiological. As discussed in Chapter 4, it has a strong connection with sexual and procreative energy, which is one reason why sexual imagery and practices form part of the repertoire of Tantric meditation.

There are numerous teachings about how to awaken or arouse *bodhicitta*, many of them derivative from Indian texts such as the *Bodhicaryāvatāra* of Śāntideva, but others developed within Tibet. To have awakened *bodhicitta* within oneself is to be in some sense at least a *bodhisattva*, one of the heroic self-sacrificing beings who are central cultural heroes of Tibetan religion. The Tibetan translation of *bodhisattva* could be translated literally as '*bodhicitta* hero'.

Bodhisattva is a somewhat multivalent term, since it can refer both to someone who is as it were in training to become a Buddha, but it can also refer to beings who are in effect deities such as Avalokiteśvara or Mañjuśrī. Here we are concerned primarily with the first meaning. In this sense a *bodhisattva* is someone who has made a certain amount of progress towards Buddhahood, and specifically who has awakened the central motivation of *bodhicitta* within himself. This sense of *bodhisattva* is closely linked to the *bodhisattva* vows, which all Buddhas are held to have made at some stage in the past, at the point when they entered onto the path that would eventually lead them to Buddhahood. These vows are also however part of contemporary practice. They are the second of the three sets of vows taken by Tibetan Buddhist practitioners, following on the *pratimokṣa* (Vinaya) vows and preceding the Tantric vows taken as part of Tantric initiation. In the present-day context, *bodhicitta* vows are an important preliminary to Tantric practice, and almost all Tibetan Buddhist practices, as described in Chapters 3 and 4, include some kind of a formula of awakening the *bodhicitta* (*semkyé*). In reciting this formula, the participants reiterate their commitment to achieving Buddhahood in order to free all beings from their sufferings.

As all this may suggest that *bodhicitta*, while constantly referenced in Buddhist practices, is associated with a kind of radical aspiration somewhat beyond the immediate abilities of most lay people or even many monastic practitioners. One level down, as it were, from *bodhicitta* itself, are the various training formulae and devices which define the path to Buddhahood, which for most people is aiming towards a goal at some considerable distance in the future. From the time of early formulations such as the eightfold noble path and the three trainings of *śīla*, *samādhi* and *prajñā* – discipline or ethics, meditation or mental cultivation, and wisdom or insight into reality – there has been a clear and explicit ethical code attached to this path, classically expressed in the various sets of precepts and regulations given in the different versions of the Buddhist Vinaya or disciplinary code. This includes regulations for celibate monastics, but also vows for those who are taking on less total levels of commitment – what in Sanskrit are called *upāsaka* and *upāsikā*, *śrāmaṇera* and *śrāmaṇerī*. These are classically translated as male and female lay-follower, and male and female novice, though in Tibetan tradition the first of these (*genyen/genyenma*) is often taken as an initial set of vows on joining a monastic community.

These rules were held to have been taught by the historical Buddha in the course of the initial organization of his own monastic community. They are however not so much divine commands as administrative regulations for a particular way of life, and they are explained in terms of the Buddha's responses to various problems that arose in the life of the early community. At the same time, as in other Buddhist societies, the disciplinary rules are tied into the structure of *karma*, of ideas about actions and their consequences. Taking vows is a very powerful and positive action in karmic terms, and breaking them, or even formally renouncing them, is likely to have negative consequences in future existences. A corollary is that taking them temporarily, even for a day or for a short retreat, is also a very virtuous and karmically positive action. Many lay Tibetans do this regularly in the context of the so-called *nyungné* practice, which consists of temporary fasting and observance of monastic-style discipline, alongside the recitation of appropriate prayers.

Monastic life in Tibet is regulated, as in other Buddhist countries, by these Vinaya rules, and the large teaching monasteries of Central Tibet, in effect monastic universities with in some cases more than ten thousand students, had an internal disciplinary force of particularly tough and aggressive monks who were used to impose order on the occasion of large gatherings. More generally, the state of discipline in Tibetan monasteries doubtless varied, but the ideal of a well-run and disciplined monastery was present and respected. While not all Tibetan lamas or practitioners were necessarily monks, those who had taken monastic vows were expected to take them seriously, and breaking one's vows – usually a question of breaking the vow of celibacy – was regarded as a serious issue.

Since the awakened state of Buddhahood, for Tibetans as for all Buddhists, is by definition beyond and outside the processes of karma and the cycle of continuous rebirth (*saṃsāra*) that those processes keep in operation, there is a kind of paradox or at least tension here. Buddhist discipline has good karmic consequences, but even good karma keeps one bound to the wheel of rebirth, and the ultimate aim is to escape from it or perhaps better to transcend it. The apparent contradiction is resolved in a variety of ways. One common formula is the need to accumulate vast amounts of both wisdom and good or positive karmic activity as an essential precondition to the attainment of Buddhahood. Another common formula is the set of four basic meditations that we met in Chapters 3 and 4: on the rare and precious opportunity offered by human existence, on its impermanence, on the inevitability of the consequences of our actions in future lives, and the sufferings of the saṃsāric world of constant rebirth. In the context of preliminary Buddhist teachings, the implication of all this is that we need above all at least to perform virtuous actions so as to avoid the lower forms of rebirth, as animals, *preta*, or beings suffering in hell, all of which forms of life are accompanied by so much suffering and other difficulties as to make further spiritual progress difficult or impossible.

As this suggests, karma is closely linked in Tibetan thought, both that of religious teachers and of lay people, with death and rebirth and the fate of human beings after death. Death is a special preserve of Buddhist clergy in Tibet as in other Buddhist countries (by contrast, they have relatively little to do with birth, marriage and other life-cycle rituals). Ideally, a competent lama can help to guide the consciousness of the deceased so as to avoid the lower rebirths and attain rebirth in one of the pure paradisial realms such as the Western Paradise (Dewachen) of the Buddha Amitābha, or the Copper-Coloured Mountain (Zangdok Pelri) of Padmasambhava. There are also specific practices studied by many lay people to achieve such forms of rebirth. However the possibility of such a positive outcome does not detract from the importance of virtuous action, in fact virtuous action would seem to increase one's chance of achieving such a fortunate outcome.

This kind of perspective is constantly repeated in Buddhist teachings on occasions such as the regular life-empowerment ceremonies performed by most large monasteries. It is closely related to the Buddhist morality of ordinary lay life. The basic formula here is that of the ten non-virtuous and virtuous actions, forms of behaviour that lead respectively to evil and good consequences (see the box below).

The ten non-virtuous and virtuous actions

The ten non-virtuous actions (Skt. *akuśala*, Tib. *migewa*) are divided into three actions relating to the body, four relating to speech, and three relating to mind.

Physical (Body)

1 Taking life
2 Stealing
3 Sexual misconduct

Verbal (Speech)

4 Lying
5 Abrasive words that cause division
6 Harsh words that condemn others
7 Senseless talk

Mental-emotional (Mind)

8 Covetousness
9 Harmful motivation, ill will

10 Wrong views

The ten virtuous actions (*Skt. kuśala,* Tib. *gewa*) are the opposite of each of these:

Physical (Body)

1 Not taking life
2 Not taking what is not given
3 Avoiding sexual misconduct

Verbal (Speech)

4 Not deceiving
5 Speaking harmoniously, resolving conflicts
6 Avoiding harsh words that condemn others
7 Avoiding senseless talk

Mental-emotional (Mind)

8 Avoiding covetousness, cultivating satisfaction and contentment
9 Avoiding malice, behaving in a helpful and positive manner
10 Avoiding wrong views

This is the level of morality that Fürer-Haimendorf referred to as constituting the everyday morality of Sherpa society. The teachings on the ten non-virtuous and virtuous actions are found in studies of many other Buddhist societies, and form a kind of common property across lay Buddhism in many different societies. This is what anthropologists refer to when they speak of the principle of *merit* in Buddhist societies. 'Merit' here translates Sanskrit *puṇya,* Tibetan *sönam,* and it refers to positive karma – the idea being that one should accumulate as much *sonam* as possible, through the virtuous actions, while avoiding the non-virtuous actions that can lead to bad karmic consequences. Non-virtuous actions are those motivated by the three roots of *saṃsāra* mentioned in Chapters 3 and 5, desire, hatred and delusion (*rāga, dveṣa, moha* in Sanskrit); virtuous actions are those motivated by their opposites (non-attachment, benevolence, understanding). Particularly important for accumulating *sonam* are actions such as becoming ordained as a monk, building temples and religious monuments, making gifts to the clergy and the like.

Figure 6.3 A *maṇi*-wall, a structure with stones bearing mantras, erected on a pass in Sherpa country. Photo by author (1971).

There is no doubt that the ten virtuous actions are often referred to as a basis for lay morality, but, as with other Buddhist societies, we are left with a question of how far they are in practice the basis of everyday lay morality for the Tibetans.

Other moral dimensions in Tibetan Buddhist society

A few years after the publication of Fürer-Haimendorf's book, two articles appeared in a Festschrift for him (Mayer, 1981), by two younger anthropologists who had also worked with Tibetan populations in Nepal, Barbara Aziz and Nancy Levine. Each suggested that there were problems in assuming an absolute dominance of Buddhist values in Tibetan societies. Levine suggested that while the Nyinba people, whom she had studied, overtly subscribed to the kind of karmic moral code sketched above, in practice Nyinba social life had implicit values that often conflicted with this straightforward karmic morality.

To put it in slightly different terms, if Tibetans are concerned about their personal stock of *sonam* – merit or good karma – they are also concerned about how they are scoring on other scales as well, and these other scales are more to do with the present life. They include *lungta*, a term which can be translated as 'good fortune', as well as other matters such as health, personal power (*wangtang*) or status. As Lichter and Epstein put it, 'Much of the ritual carried out by lamas (and to a lesser degree monks) for the Tibetan laity is to do with good fortune and with protection from misfortune within one's present lifetime' (Lichter and Epstein, 1983).

Consider the *lungta* or 'prayer-flags', which are garlanded around Tibetan settlements, hung out at Tibetan New Year, and in smaller versions on coloured paper thrown out as offerings to the local deities. Details vary. Some, as with the example illustrated, give a series of mantras in Sanskrit. In other cases, the requests may be

Figure 6.4 *Lungta* or prayer-flag. Reproduction from blockprint in author's possession.

in Tibetan as well, e.g. 'may life-force (*sok*), bodily health (*lü*), power (*wangtang*), good fortune (*lungta*), life-duration (*tshe*), merit (*sönam*) and prosperity (*paljor*) increase!' In invocations such as this, *sönam* or good karma is treated as simply one more positive quantity that can be increased by ritual action. This does not mean that the Buddhist teachings on the effects of karma are irrelevant in Tibet, but it points to a contextual and situational element in their deployment.

Barbara Aziz's point was similar though argued from a slightly different perspective. She looked at the *ganye* groups, which are networks for mutual aid and support that form an important part of Tibetan social life, and pointed out that the values of supporting your *ganye* friends and associates could well contradict those of karmic morality (Aziz, 1981). She gives an example from when she was about to leave the refugee settlement in the Nepal hills where she had undertaken her initial fieldwork. She mentioned to a *ganye* friend that she was going to give the large and impressive paraffin pressure-lamp that she had used to write by (this was in pre-electricity days) to the local monastery. The friend was outraged: Why don't you give it to someone in the village who really needs it?

What Aziz's example demonstrates is that Buddhism was and is not the only source of a positive moral and ethical code among Tibetans. There are also values attached to community, as distinct from those attached to Buddhism. Sometimes the two can go together. Avoiding conflict and destructive gossip are positive karmic actions and also good for the community. But this is by no means necessarily the case. When Fürer-Haimendorf used Buddhist morality to explain the positive moral character of Khumbu village life, he was arguably blurring together two things that are really rather different in character. Tibetans value good relations within the village community for their own sake, not just because they are taught that they are karmically good for them.

An interesting side-issue here is that while particularly pious women may be regarded in Buddhist terms as *kandroma*, highly evolved spiritual beings (*ḍākini* in Sanskrit), and may be highly valued and respected by the community, the same women are also at some risk of being regarded as witches or sorcerers who unwittingly use their powers to attack other members of the community. There is an idea here perhaps that if you are too committed to the individual pursuit of Buddhism, this might be in some sense at the expense of the community to which you also have obligations.

The point becomes stronger if one looks at some more recent studies of Tibetan Buddhist communities, such as Charles Ramble's *Navel of the Demoness*, which appeared in 2008, and is about yet another culturally Tibetan group in the Nepal highlands.

The demoness (*sinmo*) in question is a variant of the *sinmo* who was nailed to the ground by a series of temples in a well-known Tibetan historical myth, discussed further in Chapter 9. The name of the village Ramble studied, Te, can mean 'navel' in

Tibetan, and it is sometimes explained as being the navel of the *sinmo* in geomantic terms. This rather neatly makes the point that these people see themselves as much on the side of the demoness, who is really the earth-goddess of Tibet, as of Buddhism. In any case, Ramble argues that village morality in Te is really not about Buddhism at all. The hereditary Buddhist lamas, like the hereditary priests of the local deities that the village he studied also had, are effectively people employed by the village to carry out protective activities on its behalf, by mediating with the powerful and dangerous forces of the spiritual world.

As outlined in Chapters 1 and 2, this was very much the mechanism by which Tantric practice and Buddhist monasticism became entrenched within Tibetan communal life back in the ninth to twelfth centuries. Ramble's village is perhaps an extreme example, and it is probably no accident that this is a 'remote' village, and indeed one of a group of villages that went to some lengths in recent generations to secure its remoteness and separateness from regional powers. Nowadays, of course, even Te is part of the modern Nepali state, its remoteness and independence is fast receding into history.

In fact Buddhist practice itself might easily be regarded as somewhat selfish and individualistic, an accusation made after all by Tibetan Buddhist teachers themselves, as by the Mahāyāna more generally, against the so-called 'lesser vehicle' school of the Hīnayāna. This helps perhaps to understand why there is so much stress on altruism in Tibetan Buddhism. It is necessary to counter the possibility that Buddhist practitioners, including the lamas who were providing ritual services for Tibetan villagers and rulers throughout the centuries, might be seen as not altruistic at all, but selfishly concerned with their own salvation. This is not to say that the altruism is not often genuine, or that one should never take it at face value, but rather to point out that Tibetan Buddhism has had to do quite a lot of work over the centuries to persuade the Tibetan people that it was worth their while to devote a very substantial part of their resources to the support of Buddhism.

Ethnographic research on the Himalayan peoples who live on the edges of the Tibetan plateau or in the Southeast Asian highlands is quite interesting in this regard. These communities, for example the Tamang or Gurung in Nepal, or the Lisu, Akha and others in Southeast Asia, have come into contact with Buddhism and many of them have adopted aspects of it, as also in the Nepalese case from Hinduism. However, the values here are much more explicitly local village values to do with the community, with Buddhism and other concerns of major religions drawn on in a secondary way, to a greater or lesser degree. One could look, for example, at Ernestine McHugh's writing about the Gurung, or at David Holmberg's on the Tamang, both Nepalese highland people living close to the Tibetans. In religious terms, anthropologists often speak of such societies as being concerned not with merit but with blessing – meaning access to positive spiritual influences and power in order to achieve positive ends within the present life.

Blessing is a term used in relation to Tibetan Buddhism as well, where it translates the Tibetan *chinlab*, but we should perhaps keep the two usages, anthropological and Tibetan, rather separate – *chinlab* is often, and perhaps primarily and normatively, sought in relation to specifically religious goals. A lama or deity may be requested, 'bless me (*chingi lab*) in order to carry out such and such a practice in order to attain the state of Buddhahood'. The term *chinlab* is also used for the transfer of spiritual power from lama to laity at major Tantric rituals, and as we will see in Chapter 8 this transfer can quite specifically be about this-worldly benefits, such as health, long life and prosperity. The term for these rituals, *wang* or *wangkur*, refers specifically to the transference of power; *wang* is a standard Tibetan term for power, in the secular and political sense as much as the spiritual.

If one takes the words of the lamas in a literal sense, then much of this is a kind of secondary business, an unfortunate requirement to cater to the spiritually immature desires of ordinary people. Passages can be found in the autobiographies of lamas where they lament the need to spend large parts of their time going round giving empowerments to ordinary lay people, while they would much rather be in a remote hermitage getting on with their own spiritual practice. In fact, this is something of a cliché, in such literature, though one can imagine that it may have had more than a grain of truth at times.

One can see though, here again, the nature of a transaction from which both the laity and the lamas are in a sense profiting. On the laity's side, this is because of the valued access that their relationship to the lamas affords to spiritual power. This power can (and is expected to) be utilized for pragmatic as well as spiritual purposes. For the lamas, the exchange provides the basis for the lay support of both Buddhism as a whole, and for that particular lama and monastery. There is a competitive and market-driven side to Tibetan religion, and while connections with monasteries and lamas may be passed down from generation to generation within a family, a charismatic lama can also build up a following quite rapidly on the basis of his reputation and the associated belief that he has particularly effective access to spiritual power. This may work in terms of people who want to dedicate themselves to personal spiritual practice under his guidance, but it can also, and perhaps more commonly, be a question of people who see him as able to perform powerful and effective rituals of value in dealing with their everyday lives.

In this chapter, my emphasis has mainly been on the attitudes of lay people who are not necessarily seriously committed to spiritual practice. They may perhaps become so at a later stage in their lives; it is expected and usual for old people who have brought up their families and retired or withdrawn from active involvement in the social life of the community to devote themselves to spiritual practice. But for most of the population of adult laymen and women in both pre-modern or contemporary Tibetan communities, religion is at the edge rather than the centre of their values and concerns. It may, as Lichter and Epstein (1983) put it, provide a certain ongoing qualification of secular goals, and encourage a certain 'ironic detachment from a happiness that they [know] that they cannot ultimately hold on to'. That does not, however, stop most of them from continuing to try.

What is also important, though, is Barbara Aziz's point, the existence of an alternative value system which is firmly grounded in the community and in people's relationships with one another, and which can in fact be seen as having a certain tension with Buddhism and its own intrinsic morality, however that is phrased.

Historical dimensions

How though did this situation arise? The above account has emphasized the question of ritual services performed for the village community, but it is clear that this is far from the whole story. Certainly it was not where the story started off, since Buddhism was originally introduced into Tibet under the patronage of the early imperial dynasty, not by villagers, and Tibetan rulers throughout the centuries have had a close relationship to Buddhism. What was it that they saw in Buddhism that led them to patronize it?

There are a number of points to consider here. First we can note that if there is a kind of deal in the more recent situation between village and Buddhism, there was also an earlier deal between Tibetan rulers and Buddhist lamas and monasteries. Here again, this is not intended to dismiss the spiritual aspirations of both lamas and lay people. It is important however to be aware of the practical political interests that the lamas and monasteries offered to rulers of that time. In the Indian context, Śaiva and Vaiṣṇava Tantra also became part of the accepted current technology for running a state, for ensuring its prosperity and defending it from its enemies. This is perhaps not such an alien way of thinking about the issue, if one considers the way in which Christian clerics and monasteries were expected to play their own roles in support of mediaeval European states. In the Indian and later the Tibetan case this worked at many different levels, including the performance of major state ritual for the installation of rulers, the ongoing performance of ritual to maintain state power and prosperity and to defend the state, the training and provision of staff for the state administration, because monasteries were also the main agents of education in bureaucratic skills.

Second, the patronage of Buddhism also provided a legitimation and justification of the state. The Tibetan emperors and their successors originally saw themselves as descendants of the mountain gods, as did many of the older aristocratic families. They gradually came to adopt an alternative mode of understanding their origins, as descendants from a branch of the Indian royal family of the Licchavis, within which the historical Buddha himself was held to have been born. Tibetan rulers thus saw themselves on the Indic model of the *dharmarāja*, kings who lived according to justice (*dharma*) and in Buddhist terms also supported and maintain the Buddhist teachings (*dharma*). The Tibetan kings now described themselves as *chögyel*, the Tibetan translation of *dharmarāja*, taking over from the earlier concept of the divine *tsenpo* or emperor. Part of the ideology here is that the success of the territory over which such a king rules was linked to his patronage of Buddhism. A king who supported Buddhism could expect, as various Sūtras maintained, that his country would be prosperous, the weather would be good, the soil fertile, the crops would grow well, and so on.

A third point is the link between Buddhism and trade. This went back a long way, and Buddhist clergy could be expected to be well connected and knowledgeable about what was going on in neighbouring states. Thus they might be useful to rulers in ways other than the purely religious, as sources of information about and connection with the wider world of which the ruler's kingdom might be just a small part. In other words, one of the useful things about Buddhism was its very universality, the fact that it was not just grounded in locality and place, but generalizable.

There is also the role of the Buddhist ethical code in state governance. Rulers could no doubt see the advantage of Buddhist ethical teachings in providing an ethics that was not local but state-wide, and hopefully was conducive to good governance. The local community had an ethical understanding, as we have learned, but it is much more locally and immediately grounded. The *ganye* approach which Aziz (1981) describes for Tibetan village morality was a morality of getting by, mutual support and solidarity, rather than an ideology of obedience to the desires and commands of local rulers and managers. Often, like the 'moral economy of the peasant' celebrated in James C. Scott's (2009) book of that name, it must have been largely devoted to keeping the local rulers off one's backs and doing one's best to help each other avoid their demands and depredations.

With the periodic collapse of state power in Tibet, these more local forms of morality gained in importance. Tibetan villages varied a great deal in how accessible they were to centres of power, and with the shifts and declines of governmental structures, places that were at one stage close to administrative centres might find themselves much more remote a few decades later. Some of our best examples of village-based ethical system, as with Charles Ramble's (2007) book, are of villages at the edges of the Tibetan cultural region, though one can certainly find elements of it in more centralized regions as well. This suggests that it may be useful to see these issues in the context of the historical flow back and forth of centralized power, armies and states, over the Himalayan plateau, and the need for people – particularly ordinary people – to find ways to survive in the face of what must from their point of view have been both dangerous and often difficult to predict. Another, more recent book of James C. Scott's, his *The Art of Not Being Governed* (Scott, 2009), deals with such issues. Much of it is concerned precisely with how people on the edges of state systems cope with their random and unpredictable incursions, and, while his own emphasis is more on highland Southeast Asia, much of what he says seems to have considerable applicability to Tibetan regions. Scott suggests that such people often learn to be relatively adept at identity switching. They become able to work in a variety of different cultural modes, behaving themselves where appropriate as proper members of a centralized state, at other times operating in a much more stateless and self-governing mode. They acquire the necessary skills to produce the appropriate identities and cultural styles so as to be able to carry off these various roles effectively. When things become too difficult, they may seek to escape to remote areas where the local powers cannot get at them, or where it is simply too expensive and too much bother to try to exploit them. This seems to be a very common Tibetan cultural pattern. Many Tibetan groups in the Himalayas, including the Sherpas studied by Fürer-Haimendorf and Ortner, have stories and legends of having migrated to their present remote location to escape from wars or other troubles in Tibet proper. A well-known idea which we have already come across in Chapter 2 is that of the hidden valley or *béyul*, peaceful, often uninhabited, difficult to access, and revealed by a charismatic and visionary lama who leads people there at a time of crisis to take refuge. The former kingdom of Sikkim was said to have originated as such a *béyul*, and there are a number of other such places of refuge along the Himalayas.

If we think of all this in terms of ethics and morality, it suggests, at the least, a certain ambivalence towards the exploitative tendencies of both aristocratic families

Figure 6.5 *Atsara* in Bhutanese *cham* at Kalimpong. Photo by author (2009).

and lamas. One can see elements of this ambivalence in Tibetan popular song and literature, for example in the street songs of Lhasa, often scathing in their denunciation of the corruption of aristocrats and lamas, or in the popular literature of Bhutan. One can see it acted out too in popular ritual. Again Bhutan has some of the best examples, in the role of the *atsara* or ritual clowns in the masked dances, who mediate in a fascinating way between the Buddhist deities and holy men and the Bhutanese lay lookers, or the village festivals of southern Bhutan, some of which have what seems deliberate indulgence in obscenity and sensuality, playing off village values against Buddhism in a way somewhat reminiscent of old-style European carnivals. These are villages that have been part of a Buddhist state for some centuries, but are remote enough to be able to get away with asserting their own values.

To end, though, what was the role of Buddhist ethics and morality within Tibetan Buddhist communities, and how deep did it go into everyday life? While authors such as Fürer-Haimendorf may have exaggerated the extent to which Tibetans lived according to Buddhist morality, it seems unlikely that Buddhist ethical principles did not have a significant effect overall. Even leaving aside specific teachings on lay moral conduct, the idea of the lamas, and to a lesser degree all Buddhist practitioners, as expressions and ideally at least exemplars of the Buddha's compassionate activity on behalf of the Tibetan people and other living beings must surely have had some effect on people's ideas about ethics and morality. As with the moral teachings of other major world religions, no doubt the impact of Buddhism on everyday behaviour varied from place to place and time to time. It is difficult to tell in retrospect how deep it went, how much impact it had, and how far ordinary lay people took up Buddhist ideals in a serious way in their everyday lives, and even when we have legal records or other such documents it is hard to reconstitute the context in which they might have made sense.

In the next chapter, we turn to the considerably smaller section of the Tibetan population who were in one way or another much more seriously committed to living in terms of the Buddhist way of life: the lamas, monks and lay Buddhist practitioners.

Key points you need to know

- Tibetan Buddhism has a strong ethical orientation that manifests in a number of different ways. Lay Buddhist ethics, as in other Buddhist societies, are based on the principles of *karma*, of the inevitable results of positive and negative actions, and summarized in ten kinds of virtuous and non-virtuous action. Beyond this lies the ethics of the path to Buddhahood, which is based on *bodhicitta*, the drive to relieve the sufferings of all beings, but can lead elite practitioners to undertake actions that transcend and may in some cases contradict ordinary morality.

- For ordinary lay Tibetans, Buddhist morality is widely known, but can exist in some tension with the implicit or explicit moral sense of everyday life. Buddhist morality is about taming and control, but Tibetans also value strength, self-assertiveness and personal success. Various Tibetans myths, legends and rituals illustrate these themes.
- The path to Buddhahood is structured through three sets of vows, each of which has a strong ethical dimension. These are the *pratimokṣa* vows, which are similar to the vows taken by Buddhist lay and monastic practitioners in almost all Buddhist societies, the *bodhicitta* vows, and the vows taken as part of Tantric initiation.
- Lamas, monks and lay people are bound together by an implicit contract, in which the support of the laity is exchanged both for the merit that can lead to a better rebirth, but also for the practical aid of Tantric ritual in achieving this-worldly success.

Discussion questions

1 How do Buddhist morality and everyday morality relate to each other in the life of ordinary lay Tibetans?
2 Discuss the various meanings of *bodhicitta*.
3 In what ways does the ethical dimension of Buddhism help to explain how Buddhism became part of Tibetan society?

Further reading

Aziz, Barbara N. 'Jural friends and Buddhist teachers', in Adrian C. Mayer (ed.). *Culture and Morality*. Delhi: Oxford University Press, 1981.

Calkowski, Marcia 'Contesting hierarchy: on gambling as an authoritative resource in Tibetan refugee society', in Charles Ramble and Martin Brauen (eds). *Anthropology of Tibet and the Himalaya*. Zürich: Völkerkundemuseum der Universität Zürich, 1993.

Fürer-Haimendorf, Christoph von. *The Sherpas of Nepal: Buddhist Highlanders*. London: John Murray, 1964.

Holmberg, David H. *Order in Paradox: Myth, Ritual and Exchange among Nepal's Tamang*. Ithaca, NY: Cornell University Press, 1989.

Kammerer, Cornelia and Nicola Tannenbaum (eds). *Merit and Blessing in Mainland Southeast Asia in Comparative Perspective*. New Haven, CT: Yale University Press, 1996.

Kongtrul, Jamgön. *The Treasury of Knowledge*. Several volumes. Ithaca, NY: Snow Lion, 2003 onwards.

Levine, Nancy E. 'Perspectives on love: morality and affect in Nyinba interpersonal relationships', in Adrian C. Mayer (ed.). *Culture and Morality*. Delhi: Oxford University Press, 1981.

Lichter, David and Epstein, Lawrence. 'Irony in Tibetan notions of the good life', in Charles F. Keyes and E. Valentine Daniel (eds). *Karma: An Anthropological Inquiry*. Berkeley: University of California Press, 1983.

Mumford, Stan R. *Himalayan Dialogue: Tibetan Lamas and Gurung Shamans in Nepal*. Madison, WI: University of Wisconsin Press, 1989.

Ngari Paṇchen Pema Wangyi Gyelpo. *Perfect Conduct: Ascertaining the Three Vows*. Wisdom, 1996.

Ramble, Charles. *The Navel of the Demoness: Tibetan Buddhism and Civil Religion in Highland Nepal*. New York and Oxford: Oxford University Press, 2007.

Sakya Pandita Kunga Gyaltshen. *A Clear Differentiation of the Three Codes*. Translated by Jared Douglas Rhoton. Albany, NY: State University of New York Press, 2002.

Scott, James C. *The Moral Economy of the Peasant: Rebellion and Subsistence in Southeast Asia*. New Haven: Yale University Press, 1977.

Scott, James C. *The Art of Not Being Governed: An Anarchist History of Upland Southeast Asia*. New Haven: Yale University Press, 2009.

7 *Lamas and other religious practitioners*

In this chapter

This chapter is concerned with the various religious practitioners who keep Tibetan Buddhism in operation as a functioning religion. Much of the chapter deals with the lamas, the people who provide religious leadership and act as teachers and ritual performers. The term *lama* has quite a wide range of meanings, and there are different ways in which one can become a lama, which are discussed here. The chapter also discusses other celibate and lay religious practitioners, and looks briefly at some of the temples and monastic institutions within which these people operate.

Main topics covered

- Lamas and lay practitioners
- The two propagations of the teachings
- Hereditary lamas
- Visionary lamas
- Reincarnate lamas
- The Gelukpa system of election
- Celibate monastic practitioners (monks and nuns) and non-celibate yogins
- Temples and monastic establishments

Lamas and lay practitioners

This chapter is about Tibetan religious personnel – lamas, lay practitioners, monks, nuns and yogins – and the institutions with which they are associated. The lamas themselves are an obvious starting point and in fact will be the centre of this chapter in many ways. Most people in today's world have heard of the Dalai Lama, but there were and are many thousands of lamas in all Tibetan cultural regions, and they made up quite a varied group.

In fact, while 'lama' is one of the most ubiquitous words in Tibetan Buddhism it is surprisingly hard to arrive at a clear picture of what a lama is. In some older books and travelogues all Tibetan monks and religious practitioners tend to get referred to indiscriminately as 'lamas'. In some Himalayan populations, too, 'Lama' functions as a surname, presumably originating with people from hereditary lama families, of which more later.

These usages are mentioned mainly to point out that they are secondary and marginal. Generally speaking, it would be quite wrong and misleading to refer to all Tibetan monks as lamas. Lamas are very much an elite subgroup within Tibetan religious personnel, and they are not necessarily monks in the sense of having taken vows of celibacy, though many of them are monks and have taken such vows. Having taken celibate vows is not part of the requirements for a lama. This is one of the points where religious leadership in Tibetan Buddhism contrasts most strongly with much of the rest of the Buddhist world, particularly the countries where Theravada Buddhism is practised, where the role of monk or *bhikkhu* is central and unchallenged. At the same time, the dominant Gelukpa tradition places great importance on celibacy in general, and lamas in this tradition normally are monks. Married lamas belong primarily to the other three main orders, particularly the Nyingmapa, and also to the Bon tradition.

In general, a lama:

- may be celibate or non-celibate;
- may be primarily a meditator, scholar, a missionary, or an administrator;
- may or may not be the head of a monastery; and
- may have become a lama in any of a variety of ways, some of which we will look at in more detail in this chapter.

However he (or very occasionally, she) is always, ideally at least, a religious leader and teacher.

When we first come across the term 'lama' in Tibetan history it is used primarily as a translation of the Sanskrit – and general Indian – term 'guru'. Guru can refer in Indian languages to almost any traditional teaching relationship, but in the Tibetan context the meaning is more specialized, and it refers primarily to a spiritual teacher, particularly a Tantric teacher. There are more specialized terms for various Tantric teaching roles, but lama is the most general and most important one. One important term which in some respects contrasts with lama is *geshé*. The original meaning of *geshé* is 'spiritual friend' (Skt. *kalyāṇamitra*; the term is an abbreviation for Tib. *gewé shenyen*), and in this sense it is normally restricted to teachers of non-Tantric teachings. In later centuries it became a label for a monastic degree, particularly in the Gelukpa tradition.

A lama however is normally expected to be a teacher and practitioner of Tantra. The Tibetans saw themselves as continuing a whole series of Tantric teachings from India and Nepal in lineages that ran from teacher (in other words guru or lama) to student. These lineages can still be traced, more or less plausibly, from Indian teachers in the tenth or eleventh centuries via a succession of guru–disciple links down to the present time, and they constitute one of the key components of Tibetan Buddhism and of its various religious institutions. Tibetan religious histories such as Gö Lotsawa's *Blue Annals* or Tāranātha's *Seven Instruction Lineages* are to a significant degree concerned with tracing and validating these lineages in terms of the known historical record.

Here it is worth being aware that lineage and clan descent and household continuity are important components of Tibetan secular society, as of many traditional Asian societies. Tantric initiation lineages, and to a lesser extent other religious quasi-descent systems such as monastic ordination and college membership, play an equally significant role within the religious context. As we will see, there can also be considerable overlap between biological and spiritual descent, as with the families of hereditary lamas who are quite an important part of the Tibetan religious system. The reincarnate lama and *terma* systems, which we will come to later, add another twist to this particular story, since the lineages here are thought of in these cases as being constituted to a significant degree by the same people being reborn in successive generations.

Teachings, in any case, are not just to be practised; they are to be continued, to be passed on to future generations. Transmission and continuity are very critical and important issues. The word 'tantra' literally means thread, as in weaving, so the idea of continuity is already built into the concept. In the Tibetan language, the same word – *gyüd* – or close variants of it also refer to lineage of both biological and spiritual kinds. It is important that clans and households continue from generation to generation, and it is equally, if not more, important that monasteries and monastic units, and the associated lineages of teachings, are passed on from one generation to the next.

Here a key issue is that Tantric Buddhism is a gnostic tradition, in the sense that it is a system of esoteric or secret teachings, and the spiritual teacher has a key role, since he or she – usually he – is the sole point of access to the teachings. This is not only in the technical sense that the teacher has to give the student the formal permission to practise the teachings, but also because the point of the process is to bring about a radical transformation in the students such that they are ultimately capable of realizing or perceiving the truth of the teachings directly and intuitively. This implies that a real teacher has already achieved this direct insight himself. The aim of the tradition, in other words, is not for students to learn the discursive content of the teachings, but for them to become what the teachings are describing.

In this sense the lama's role is more like that of a psychotherapist, or maybe a sports coach or an acting coach, than like that of an academic teacher. It is probably most natural for contemporary Westerners to think of the lama as like a therapist, but this can be a somewhat tricky comparison. The point of Buddhist Tantric practice is not really that the patient is in need of therapy because of individual problems or difficulties. The end point of the process is an essentially social or collective goal. By achieving Buddhahood, the practitioner contributes to the only available collective solution to the universal problem of suffering.

The Buddhist process of awakening, in other words, is only to a limited degree a solution for the *individual* human being. Contemporary Western society is highly individualistic in its values, and our model of psychotherapy is largely based on this individualism. Consequently, we tend to see therapy in terms of self-development, and its aim as being that of improving our individual experience. This is not quite the object of the Buddhist Tantric tradition. While there is certainly stress on the kindness of the lamas in giving the teachings, and on their care for their disciples, individual awakening is tied up with collective awakening. As has already been pointed out several times, the central motivation for the attainment of Buddhahood is the desire to attain it in order to relieve all beings of their sufferings, not to relieve one's own sufferings. A related point is that the unreal and constructed nature of the self-concept is in any case a central issue for the tradition. The unreality of the self is a key issue for Buddhist philosophy, but it is also, and ultimately more importantly, a key issue for Buddhist practice.

This is one of the areas where Western Buddhists can have some difficulty in following what Tibetan teachers are doing, and particularly what they might have been doing in traditional Tibetan societies. A typical Western Dharma centre consists of, let us say, twenty or a hundred people, most or all of whom are there primarily because of what they, as individuals, expect or hope to achieve through the practice. People may think of themselves as more or less 'committed', or as more or less 'advanced' in their practice, but it is rare for people to think of themselves as being there primarily to do the cooking, look after the buildings, or to act as support staff for the small minority of elite practitioners. Everybody wants to do the practice and to see themselves as on the fast road to Buddhahood.

Yet in a traditional Tibetan monastery, many of the people there have a much more secondary role. They may not even be there by personal choice; within the traditional Tibetan political system, it was common for villages in centralized areas to have a tax-obligation of providing a certain number of young men to serve as monks in a nearby monastery. Thus quite a few monks were, effectively, conscripts not volunteers. This had a political and strategic element, since many large monasteries were situated in strategically important locations that governed major trade routes. It also however helps to make the point that religious personnel are supposed to be doing something on behalf of the community, or of society as a whole. This of course is why, or at any rate one of the reasons why, the community might support them.

This individual/collective issue will arise again later, but it is useful to be aware of it at this point, in particular because one of the ways in which the role of lama has extended from that of personal guru is in the direction of leader of a community. In relation to the lama's role as leader of a community, it should be noted that the role of lama is not the same as that of abbot or *kenpo* of a monastery or other religious establishment. It is also worth noting that the Tibetan word *gompa*, while conventionally translated as 'monastery', is considerably wider in its application than the English word might suggest. In particular, it does not necessarily imply a community of celibate monks. In any case, a monastery in the strict sense, or a religious community or establishment in a wider sense, may have several people who would be referred to as lamas, and while the person who is occupying the role of abbot may be one of them, that is essentially a separate role, to do with administration more than spiritual teaching. A lama is not a lama because he is head of a monastery, in other words, although he may be one. Nor is he a lama because he is recognized as head of a community, or even a head of state. If there is a central element to the identity of lama, it is that a lama is a lama because he is believed to be a master and effective performer of Tantric ritual. He is, in other words, someone who is held to have a particular and important set of skills which gives him the ability to influence and control the spirit-world, and so human good and ill fortune, through the exercise of Tantric power.

These are skills that have to be learned, and in most Tibetan traditions, as mentioned in Chapter 4, the primary defining qualification for being a lama is to have done at least one extended Tantric practice retreat of the standard length of three years, three months and three days. During this time the apprentice lama learns to control the inner energies of what in Western terms we might term his or her mind–body complex; in Tibetan terms one would speak of body, speech and mind. The lama also becomes familiar with the process of identification with a Tantric deity. These two things, it should be noted, are more or less equivalent, which comes back to the point above that Buddhahood is not really a matter of developing one's individual potentialities, but of attuning oneself to potentialities that are essentially transpersonal. There are various ways in which one could think about this, but one way to put it is that the lama learns to shape his mind–body complex into that of the deity. This is a question of control over what are thought of as internal flows, that are also closely linked to control over breathing and over the physical body.

This is the milieu of Tantric practice, which in India was in many ways common property between Hindu (more properly Śaiva) and Buddhist practitioners. It was in fact the context out of which modern yoga derived, and the Tibetan equivalent of yoga – *neljor* – is used to refer to these exercises. An important point here, though, is that this is thought of as a highly skilled undertaking. A prospective lama has to put in serious work over a prolonged period of time in order to be able to accomplish it. Also, the skills in question are thought of as important for society as a whole.

So a lama is somebody who has learned how to do something that is of great value to Tibetan society, which is passed on from one person to another in an extended and intimate process of apprenticeship. It is important that it be transmitted from generation to generation, because it is thought necessary, or was thought necessary in traditional Tibetan society, that there be a body of people with the requisite skills around. This is in part because Tibetans valued the quest for Buddhahood for its own sake, as their central cultural achievement, but also, and importantly, because the lama's skills as a Tantric ritualist were seen as important for the ongoing viability of the community. This issue will be discussed further in Chapter 8.

Other meanings of *lama* tend to be in one way or another derivative from this central issue of mastery over Tantric yogic practice and the transmission of that mastery to the next generation. For one thing, teaching in general (including the alphabet, Buddhist philosophy, and so on) was increasingly seen in Tibet on the model of the lama's teaching of Tantric practice. This teaching was placed in a suitable ritual frame, there was a formal transmission of the text, and the teacher was regarded, in effect, as a lama. The more significant developments however concerned the wider social role of the lama. To understand more of how these aspects of the role of the lama developed, it is useful to return to some of the history sketched in Chapter 2.

Figure 7.1 Temple of Tratruk. The initial foundation is attributed to the time of Songtsen Gampo, early seventh century. Photo by author (1987).

The two propagations of the teachings

As described in Chapter 2, the Tibetans took the techniques of Tantric yoga in the first place from India, and in two major waves or periods of propagation of the Buddhist teachings in Tibet. The first (the *ngadar* or 'early spreading' in Tibetan parlance) was during the time of the early emperors (*tsenpo*), and while it is clear that there were several important figures involved, the later tradition increasingly tended to collapse them all into the single primal yogin, Padmasambhava, and his relationship with his Tibetan students, above all his consort Yeshe Tsogyel and his royal disciple, the King Trisong Detsen.

In Chapter 6, the interests of the early emperors in promoting Buddhism as a moral and ethical tradition were discussed. The emperors were doubtless interested, as the later tradition suggests, in Tantra as well. This interest, however, may have been primarily in Tantra as a sort of magical technology to support the power of the state, rather as it seems to have been adopted at around the same time in Cambodia, Java and parts of East Asia. Tantra had a somewhat dubious moral side in the Indian context. Such matters as magic to kill one's enemies, to cause illness, to compel a woman's love, to ensure success in warfare, and the like were quite standard, and the Buddhist and Śaiva Tantras provide detailed instructions on how to do all these things and many others.

Tantra also was in some conflict with monastic celibacy, especially since the sexual practices associated with the higher (Mahāyoga/Anuttarayoga) Tantra classes, such as the Hevajra, Cakrasamvara, Guhyasamāja and Kālacakra Tantras, appear to have been quite important in India, more so than they would become in later Tibetan tradition. These practices were closely connected with the question of control over internal energies that I mentioned earlier. This meant that the most natural context for Tantra was as a tradition of lay practitioners, not as a monastic tradition, although not all Tantra involved sexual practice by any means; much of it could be – and clearly was – performed by celibate monastics.

In its earliest forms, it seems likely that Tantra was about power and its exercise, and it was not particularly interested in conventional morality in its techniques or practices. If anything, Tantric adepts saw themselves as linked to a higher morality, as operating on a plane of action that was beyond the world of ordinary appearances and conventions. Consequently, rulers and powerful people in India and in Tibet might well want access to Tantric techniques themselves, but would not necessarily be enthusiastic about their being spread around too widely. Being a ruler involved keeping as much of a monopoly as possible on the exercise of Tantric power, as of other forms of power and force.

As time went on, and particularly perhaps as the Tantric teachings and practices began to infiltrate into the large Buddhist monastic universities of Northeast India, their Buddhist versions increasingly developed a strong ethical dimension structured around the altruistic motivation of *bodhicitta*, the desire to achieve Buddhahood in order to relieve the sufferings of all beings. There are some interesting questions about how and when this development took place, and I am not sure that we have entirely convincing answers as yet, but certainly most of the Buddhist Tantra that came to Tibet in the eighth century, and which is now classed within the Mahāyoga and Anuttarayoga Tantras, would already have had a fairly strong ethical orientation.

Tantra still retained an antinomian style however, and must have kept a sense of being dangerous and powerful. It appears that the Tibetan emperors maintained tight control over the translation and distribution of Tantric material. While there were translations into Tibetan of many of the Tantric texts available, including some material such as the *Guhyasamāja* which belonged to the potentially antinomian Mahāyoga or Anuttarayoga mode of Tantric practice, not much of this was made public. There were also, of course, translations of the Sūtra texts during the early empire, and a transmission of the Vinaya lineage, with the foundation of the first Tibetan monastery at Samyé. The process of systematizing and codifying the translations also began, with the court-sponsored creation of a standard dictionary of Tibetan equivalents for Sanskrit terms, the *Mahāvyutpatti*.

The collapse of the empire, probably in the 840s, led to something of a dark age, though it is not entirely clear how long it lasted, how dark it was, and whether monasticism as such survived. The later tradition, as given in for example the fourteenth-century *History of Buddhism* by Butön, the distinguished scholar responsible for the codifying of the Kangyur and Tengyur, explained that the lineage of monastic ordination did survive, just about, so there was both an older Vinaya transmission from the early period and a newer and second Vinaya transmission from the later period. It seems clear though that the monastic tradition virtually disappeared, and that Tibetan Buddhism survived primarily as a practice of lay Tantric practitioners. Exactly how this happened cannot be followed in detail, but it would seem that surviving Tantric practitioners gradually transformed their esoteric tradition of magical power into something that was recognized and valued by local Tibetan communities as the best available technology for dealing with the problems of everyday life, such as the defence of the community from dangerous and threatening spirit forces.

Presumably, in doing so, they took over from earlier practitioners who had done similar work. Early writers on Tibetan Buddhism tended to identify these practitioners with the follower of the Tibetan religious tradition of Bon, which claims to go back in Tibet before the introduction of Buddhism (see Chapter 11). What, if anything, village ritualists in the pre-Buddhist period had to do with the traditions that fed into what was later called Bon is actually not at all clear. What little we know about early Bon appears to refer to a court tradition, not a village tradition.

After this rather murky period, which lasted for perhaps around 150 years, the later diffusion (*chidar*) got underway in around the late tenth century. By this time, Buddhism was going into decline in much of India, but was still supported and patronized in a number of the regions that the Tibetans could reach relatively easily, including Nepal, Kashmir, and above all the Pāla empire in Northeast India (present-day Bengal and Bihar), which had strong connections with the Buddhist states of Southeast Asia. By this time, too, the Indian Tantric lineages had developed considerably further. New forms of practice had been introduced, culminating in the famous Kālacakra Tantra tradition, which was perhaps introduced to India in around the year 1000, and the monastic universities were becoming more extensively involved in Tantric practices. North India would come under Muslim rule at the end of the twelfth century, Kashmir somewhat later, leaving the Nepal Valley as the one remaining island of Vajrayāna or Tantric Buddhism accessible to Tibet. Between the late tenth and late twelfth centuries, however, there was a period of nearly 200 years in which there was fairly extensive contact between Tibet and the Buddhist centres of North India.

This later diffusion of Buddhism took place under the patronage of a surviving branch of the imperial dynasty in Purang in Western Tibet, and through their support of a group of Tibetan translators and scholars. The best known and most successful of these scholars was the great translator Rinchen Zangpo (958–1055), who was also responsible according to later tradition for building a large number of monasteries in Western Tibet.

The Western Tibetan kings were also responsible for inviting an important Tantric scholar from the Pāla empire in Northeast India (present-day Bengal and Bihar), Dipaṃkara Śrījñāna or Atiśa (c.980–1054), and he in his turn was closely involved with the re-establishment of a flourishing monastic tradition in Central Tibet. This is what was later known as the Kadampa tradition, and it is also regarded as ancestral by the later Gelukpa monastic order, the largest and most influential of Tibet's Buddhist orders and traditions.

Some of these early monasteries survived into modern times, and it is worth noting that in their original forms at any rate they were still fairly small institutions. The large-scale monasteries of later Tibetan tradition, with hundreds or even thousands of monks, were still far in the future.

The kings and major lay patrons again seem to have seen themselves as primarily interested in Buddhism as an ethical tradition for the laity, and there are a number of indications of their desire to restrict Tantric teachings. Atiśa was a Tantric practitioner, and he and his followers transmitted many important Tantric lineages but, as already mentioned, the Kadampa were based around celibate monasticism, and Atiśa's well-known *Guide to the Stages of the Path to Enlightenment (Bodhipathapradīpa)* makes it clear that monastics should not be engaged in higher Tantric practice. Here it is likely that he was complying with the wishes of his Tibetan lay patrons.

Meanwhile, these state-sponsored journeys were by no means the only contacts between India and Tibet. Tibetans started to travel increasingly to India in search of

Figure 7.2 Atiśa's monastery of Nyetang. Photo by author (1987).

Tantric teachings, while Indian Tantric ritualists and other Buddhist teachers began to see Tibet as a possible destination for patronage and employment.

The push and pull factors here are intriguing. On the Indian side, the religious and political scene was changing, and the situation must have been increasingly inhospitable for Buddhist monastics, particularly of the Mahāyāna persuasion, or for itinerant lay Tantrics. The successor states of the Pāla empire seem to have been more favourable to Hinduism than Buddhism, but they kept up some level of support for Buddhist institutions, and there are signs of Buddhist practice continuing until fairly late in other regions as well, such as Videśa in Central India, and the South. However, there are signs that Buddhism in the Pāla empire was turning increasingly towards the Theravāda state of Arakan in northern Burma by the twelfth century, even before the Muslim conquest and the consequent end of state support for Buddhism in the entire region. Tibet, although doubtless a cold and inhospitable destination in the South Asian imagination, was at least close at hand, and a source of potential patronage.

On the Tibetan side, many of those who went to India or who sought the new Tantric teachings seem to have come from traditional hereditary religious backgrounds, whether Buddhist or Bon. Thus the Sakya lamas claimed to have a hereditary lineage of Tantric practice going back to the early empire, while the famous Kagyüdpa saint and poet Milarepa is said to have come from a family of Bon practitioners. While it is not very clear what 'Bon' might mean at this time, one might guess that these were families who were one way or another in the business of dealing with the spirit world, and who felt the need to acquire what must have seemed like new, superior, more up-to-date and impressive knowledge and techniques. Many of them must have been thinking, initially at least, in terms of setting up a family business, and some, like the Sakya lamas, did so with considerable success.

The Buddhist practices already incorporated a substantial range of techniques for practical, pragmatic ends, such as acquiring health, good fortune and prosperity, or carrying out defensive and destructive magic, and this technology was developed considerably further by the Tibetans themselves. The practices were however by now thoroughly ethicized, and the value system implied by Buddhahood and *bodhicitta* was incorporated into them in all kinds of ways, beginning with the *guruyoga*, the practices developed mainly as far as we can tell within the Sakya tradition according to which the lama is worshipped as a Tantric deity and in effect as a form of the Buddha. (A version of these was described in Chapter 4, as part of the Tantric *ngöndro* practices.) Buddhist values increasingly pervaded the whole enterprise, and Buddhist monasticism also became a growing part of Tantric practice in Tibet.

This second propagation was the origin of what are called by Tibetans the New or *Sarma* Tantric lineages, to distinguish them from the old or *Nyingma* lineages dating from the period of the first propagation. Of a large number of Sarma teachers and lineages, things gradually settled down to a smaller number of significant monastic-based traditions, of whom the most significant in time were to be the Kadampa, whom we have already met, the Kagyüdpa, who claimed to pass on the teachings of a number of Indian *siddhas*, particularly Nāropa, and who were to develop the major innovation of the reincarnate lama system, and the Sakyas, whose principal source was a teaching lineage traced back to Virūpa and centring on the Hevajra Tantra.

Over time, a series of different models of organization and continuity developed among these traditions. The need to regulate the affairs of monastic institutions seems to have been felt at quite an early stage and the practice developed of the writing of charters (*chayik*), which gave a set of rules and regulations according to which the establishment should operate. Procedures also developed to maintain the leadership of the institution.

The oldest models are the most straightforward. One was that of the election or selection of some member of the community to act as its head, generally by mutual agreement. This was the system employed by the Kadampa, but it is rather poorly adapted, at least in this basic form, to long-term continuity. The other mode is that of hereditary succession. On this system, a lama was succeeded on his death by his son or another close relative.

Hereditary lamas

The Sakya lama family of Kon can serve as a case in point of the hereditary lama pattern, though a very eminent one, particularly in the modern period. This family claimed to originate in an old aristocratic family from the imperial period, with a version of the standard myth of descent from the mountain gods. An early member had been a minister to the emperor Trisong Detsen and a student of Padmasambhava; another had been one of the first seven Tibetan monks. The family's principal religious 'property' until the eleventh century was a version of one of the main Buddhist Tantric lineages to have been introduced at the time of Padmasambhava, the practice of Vajrakilaya (*Phurba* in Tibetan), perhaps originating in Indian rituals of house and temple foundation but developed in its Buddhist Tantric version into the Tantric cult of a fierce deity related to such other fierce Tantric deities as Hayagṛva or Vajrapāṇi. This ancient Phurba practice remains a key element in the Sakya family's reputation for magical power, which has continued down to modern times.

In the eleventh century, a member of this family, Kon Konchog Gyelpo, became the student of a Tibetan teacher and translator, Drokmi Lotsawa, who had been to India and acquired a set of teachings associated with one of the legendary Indian *siddhas*, Virūpa. These teachings focused on one of the later Tantric deities, Hevajra. Konchog Gyelpo founded a small monastery, which became known as *Sakya* (literally, 'pale earth'), at a place where Atiśa was said to have prophesied that many emanations of the great Bodhisattvas Avalokiteśvara, Mañjuśrī and Vajrapāṇi would arise in the future. He and his descendants developed the core of practices and teachings they had received from Drokmi Lotsawa into a comprehensive training system, the Lamdré, which incorporated both Sūtra and Tantra components and leading to the mastery of the Hevajra Tantra practices. The Sakyas gradually became an extremely powerful family, with the headship of the family continuing to be passed down in a hereditary manner until the present day. Traditionally, some sons would become monastic practitioners, and others would continue the hereditary lineage. The Kon family gradually developed a substantial monastic community and also a significant scholarly tradition. A thirteenth-century member of the family, Sakya Paṇḍita, as has already been mentioned in previous chapters, became a renowned scholar, learning Sanskrit and being able to debate with Indian scholars on their own terms, and was the first Tibetan to claim the Indian title of *paṇḍita*, or learned scholar. Sakya Pandita and his successors built up connections with the Mongol invaders of Tibet, so successfully that they became in effect the rulers of Tibet under the Mongols for a century or so. They built a second, much larger, monastery at Sakya, one of the great monuments of Tibetan religious architecture, and their influence gradually spread around the entire Tibetan plateau, with two further monastic orders, Ngorpa and Tselpa, branching off from the original Sakya order.

Sakya Pandita's writing is not only scholarly but often highly polemical. His best known work in this style is the famous *Domsum Rabye* or 'Analysis of the Three Vows'. This is a treatment of the three sets of vows, the Pratimokṣa (Vinaya) Vows which the Tibetans have in common with all Buddhist monastic traditions, the *Bodhicitta* Vows and the Tantric Vows taken at the time of Tantric initiation. It is also, however, a powerful polemical statement intended to demonstrate that the Sakya version of Tantric Buddhism is the only authentic and valid tradition.

The Sakyas are unusual in that their main branch has retained the hereditary model of succession despite becoming a major centre for celibate monasticism. Most of the other large monastic traditions progressively moved from hereditary succession to a different model, that of succession by reincarnation, the *tulku* system. We will come to this shortly, but it is important to appreciate that while the other large monastic traditions have adopted the *tulku* system, there are still many small and middle range hereditary lama families, primarily though not only in the Nyingmapa tradition. Another important example of a major monastic centre that remains based on a hereditary lineage is also Nyingmapa, the monastery of Mindrolling, founded in 1646. Like Sakya, this is associated with a hereditary lama family claiming ancient aristocratic status and divine descent.

The *tulku* or reincarnation system has gradually taken over in almost all other major monasteries. However the idea of a hereditary lineage of religious practitioners has by no means disappeared from the Tibetan scene, and to be the son of a high status lama gives a lama, at least, a major advantage in trying to establish his own reputation. In recent times, one can look at the children of such major married lamas as Śākya Śrī or Dudjom Rinpoche. Both had substantial families, including sons, grandsons, and in Śākya Śrī's case by now a third and fourth generation of descendants, many of whom became significant lamas in their own right. The term *dunggyüd* refers to the idea of a spiritual ability passed down in the lineage, and it parallels ideas of hereditary transmission of ability in other areas – such as medical expertise – and for that matter also of the hereditary transmission of low status in the case of the low-caste group found in many Tibetan communities.

At a somewhat more humble level again, there are the many *ngakpa* lamas, lay *yogins*, *serkyimpa* and *gomchen* who are ordinary villagers or pastoralists who also have some Tantric training and ability. In many of the more remote parts of Tibetan cultural regions, the ritual life of the community is or was carried out by lamas of this kind, often working under the direction of a more eminent local hereditary lama, and gathering regularly to perform rituals in the local temple. Versions of this pattern have been described in some detail for Dolpo in Nepal, for example, for Rebkong in Northeast Tibet, where lamas of this kind have coexisted for some centuries with a number of monastic communities, and in parts of Bhutan.

While hereditary status, training in a distinguished monastery, and other such formal attributes can be quite important as bases for reputation, these relatively humble practitioners may also come to be recognized as having genuine spiritual power. In fact, there is something of a standard Tibetan trope of a humble lay yogin who manifests miraculous signs at his death, revealing that he was all along a highly realized being. Another common image is of the rough, even uncouth lama who acts in unconventional and even apparently immoral ways, but is again in reality a highly developed spiritual practitioner, who can look at somebody and directly intuit their inner consciousness. As these images suggest, having the name of a High Lama is not the only thing that counts in relation to reputation as a spiritual practitioner. Being an elegant lama seated on a high throne in a wealthy monastery does not necessarily mean that one is universally respected. There is an anti-hierarchical potential within the whole Tantric milieu, since what really matters is one's ability and realization, not who one is in terms of family or formal status in a hierarchy. By and large Tibetans behave with great respect towards lamas who have distinguished titles and important positions, but there is always a possibility that the picture can be subverted, and even reversed. This is most often true with the forms of Buddhist practice associated with the Nyingmapa tradition, the tradition that claims to go back to Padmasambhava and the imperial times, and its system of visionary revelations, and this is worth a brief description before coming to the reincarnate lamas.

Visionary lamas (tertön)

We have already come across the idea of lamas as emanations of deities, with Atiśa's prophecy regarding the Sakya lamas as emanations of three *bodhisattvas*. This prediction was taken fairly seriously by the Sakyas; Sakya Paṇḍita in particular is depicted iconographically, like some other great scholarly lamas of later years such as Tsongkhapa, with the sword and book which are the attributes of the Bodhisattva of Wisdom, Mañjuśrī (Jambeyang).

This is an idea that already had some Indian predecessors, and it seems to have been part of a range of developing idioms for conceptualizing lamas and their powers and connections in Tibet in the eleventh centuries onwards.

A second such idiom, developing at around the time, and apparently in parallel among both Nyingma and Bonpo traditions, was that of the 'discovered text' (*terma*) and the visionary lama (*tertön*). The Nyingmapa (and even more the Bonpo) had something of a problem at this period. While there were lineages of Tantric lineage transmission, the so-called *kama* lineages, such as the Sakya Vajrakīlaya lineage mentioned above, that claimed to go back to the early teachings of Padmasambhava and his collaborators in the ninth century, these lineages were few and far between. It was relatively easy for the growing 'New Tantra' traditions, with their direct and recent connections with Indian teachers, and their impressive collections of authenticated Indian texts, to cast aspersions on the validity and authenticity of the Nyingmapa traditions. The Nyingma Tantric material, dating from an earlier stage of Indian

Buddhism, did not have practices that could compete with some of the new practices introduced in the New Tantra period, for example the Sakya *guruyoga* traditions, or the long-life practices of White Tārā brought in by Atiśa and transmitted among the Kadampa lineages.

The *terma* system provided an answer. The first *terma* (the word can be translated 'treasure' in the sense of a hidden text or object which has been rediscovered), may literally have been what they were claimed to be, old texts hidden at the time of the collapse of the early Tibetan empire and rediscovered at a later point. In time, though, the *terma* tradition developed into something rather different. For one thing, *terma* were increasingly not primarily physical objects. Even where there was a physical object, it might be no more than a few lines of cryptic script, which stimulated the visionary abilities of the *tertön* lama to recover the entire body of teachings at

Figure 7.3 Image of the *tertön* Dudjom Lingpa with two other lamas. Zangdok Pelri Monastery, Kalimpong. Photo by author (2007).

which they hinted. At the same time, a theory of the *tertön* lama developed according to which these lamas were former disciples of Padmasambhava who had received the teachings in question from him while they were physically in his presence. The teachings had been buried in their consciousness-continuum, so that they could be rediscovered in a future age when people had need of them, perhaps as a result of the *tertön*'s encountering the stimulus of the external terma. Thus, rather like the *bodhisattva*-emanation status of the Sakya lamas, the *tertön* idiom allowed lamas to be seen as more than ordinary human beings, and as rebirths of mythical figures from the past. In this it was like other idioms developing at this period such as that which identified high-status lamas with one or another of a list of future Buddhas of the Bhadrakalpa.

Although there are one or two exceptions, *tertön* were hardly ever celibate monastics. In fact they are generally thought of as needing the right female partner, and the right circumstances, to be able to reveal their *terma*. They are figures of Tantric power much more than of the disciplined monastic life. There is much more that could be said about *terma* and *tertön*, and the reader is referred to specialist publications such as those of Tulku Thondup and Andreas Doctor. A related concept, mentioned in Chapters 2 and 6, is of *béyul*, 'hidden valleys', which were generally discovered and opened by *tertön* in their role as visionary and charismatic lamas, and which provided places of refuge in times of conflict or political oppression.

Perhaps the key thing about the *terma/tertön* idiom is that it provided for an injection of new material into the ongoing Nyingmapa tradition, and allowed for a continuous creativity and innovation which gave the Nyingmapa a very different character from the Sarma traditions. In time the *terma* lineages would greatly outnumber the *kama* lineages which were supposed to have been handed down directly from the early lamas. *Terma* lineages are also often valued for their freshness and vitality. A *terma* lineage may be only two or three generations old, and this is seen not in terms of its modernity, but in terms of its energy and vitality, its closeness to the living source of Buddhahood. *Terma* traditions could also be developed into systems of great depth and complexity, as with the *Longchen Nyingtik* system of Jigmé Lingpa, which was a major stimulus for the Rimé lamas in the nineteenth and early twentieth century, and so brought about extensive changes in the Sakyapa and Kagyüdpa traditions as well as the Nyingmapa.

Reincarnate lamas

The last major idiom through which the identity of lamas was understood is both the most remarkable, in many ways, and also the best known outside Tibet, at least in the person of its most famous example, the current Dalai Lama. This is the process of recognizing the reincarnation of a deceased lama, and training the child to take over the position and in a sense also the identity of the former lama,

Figure 7.4 Trulshik Rinpoche. Photo by author (1971).

including his property and political position. What is less widely appreciated is that by modern times there were many hundreds, probably thousands, of these reincarnating lamas throughout the whole region in which Tibetan Buddhism had become established.

The idiom of rebirth again builds on ideas that seem to have been current in India of Tantric gurus being rebirths of previous gurus, and also on a specific Sarma Tantra practice which was part of the 'property' passed through the original Kagyüd lineage and claimed to go back to the Indian guru Nāropa. This is a set of teachings on controlling and directing one's consciousness at the time of death, so as to be able to take rebirth deliberately and with full awareness as the child of suitable parents. It forms part of the so-called 'Six Practices of Nāropa'. Lamas of this tradition, in other words, were supposed to be able to control their rebirths, and it was among various Kagyüd suborders that the idea of recognizing the rebirth of a lama and installing him as his successor first evolved.

The first of these rebirth-lineages began with Dusum Kyenpa (1110–1193), one of the students of Gampopa, himself a disciple of the famous poet and yogin Milarepa, who had acquired the Six Practices and the other Kagyüdpa teachings from the great translator Marpa. Gampopa was a significant turning point in the lineage, which until that point had been yogic rather than monastic. Gampopa had trained in the monastic and scholarly tradition of the Kadampas before coming to Milarepa, and his major disciples, Dusum Kyenpa included, all founded what were in time to become significant monastic and scholarly centres.

Dusum Kyenpa himself was not succeeded on his death by a recognized rebirth. However Karma Pakshi (1203–1283), a lama who was born some ten years after Dusum Kyenpa's death, was retrospectively identified as the rebirth of Dusum Kyenpa. The first real use of the rebirth approach to identify a lama's successor occurred at Karma Pakshi's death in 1283. He is said to have predicted where his rebirth would be found, and this lama, Rangjung Dorje (1284–1339) was thus the first full instance of the *tulku* pattern. He was retrospectively designated the Third Gyalwa Karmapa, with Dusum Kyenpa now regarded as the Second; further reincarnations have continued down to the present day (see table in Appendix 1).

The most famous of all these reincarnation-sequences is of course that of the Dalai Lamas, which began with Gedündrup, a disciple of Tsongkapa in the fifteenth century (see Appendix). The Dalai Lamas were regarded as emanations of the deity Avalokiteśvara, as were the head lamas of the Karma Kagyüd and Drukpa Kagyüd, and their palace at Lhasa was named the Potala after the mountain-residence of the deity.

The *tulku* pattern really took off in the sixteenth and seventeenth centuries, at which time most major monasteries began to recognize *tulkus*, normally rebirths of the monastery's founder. A consistent procedure developed. Often the deceased lama might make some predictive remarks about his intention before his death (the Gyalwa Karmapas generally left a letter containing a prediction). Leading lamas of the tradition would perform divination, search parties would be sent out to look for

Figure 7.5 The Potala in Lhasa. Photo by author (1987).

suitable children, and likely children tested by giving them objects that belonged to the deceased lama mixed with other objects, and by having someone who knew the previous lama well as part of the search party, whom the child could be expected to recognize.

How much of this, in any given case, is literal reality, and how much convenient fiction is unclear. Tibetan lamas themselves can be very open about the politics involved in recognizing rebirths, and about children being 'recognized' as *tulkus* for political convenience or other reasons. It was clearly in the monastery's interest to present a clear, cut and dried, case for the validity of the rebirth, whether or not all went quite as planned.

The *tulku* system solves a number of problems rather neatly. As celibate monasticism became increasingly prevalent, the hereditary principle became problematic,

Figure 7.6
Young *tulku* with the abbot of Drepung Loseling Monastery, Bodh Gaya. Photo by Ruth Rickard (1994).

since a celibate lama should of course not have children of his own. Rebirth provides a way to get around the problem of celibacy. Since the lama is in theory the same person as his predecessor, his right to continue in his role is difficult to challenge, and the rebirth of a famous and distinguished lama gets off to a head start in establishing his own credentials, especially since he is likely to receive specialized training from an early age. The whole somewhat theatrical process of recognition is also, at least if it comes off properly, an impressive demonstration that the lamas have the advanced yogic powers that they are supposed to have. Having a number of such lamas also adds greatly to the prestige and status of a monastic institution.

The system does not always work perfectly however, in part because it rapidly became caught up with the politics of powerful and wealthy families within which most *tulku* were found. Often, there were two or three plausible candidates, and if each was supported by powerful political interests, reaching a decision could be difficult or impossible. A major problem of this kind blew up over the recognition of the rebirth to Pema Karpo (1527–1592), one of the greatest scholars of the Kagyüd tradition and the fourth in the Gyalwang Drukchen series of reincarnations. The Gyalwang Drukchens are an important incarnation lineage, like the Gyalwa Karmapas the head of a major division of the Kagyüdpa tradition, and with extensive material property and spiritual status. There were two major contenders to be Pema Karpo's successor, both with substantial political support. After a prolonged struggle, one contender (Pagsam Wangpo, 1593–1653) was enthroned at the Drukpa's main monastery at Ralung, but the other (Shabdrung Ngawang Namgyel, 1594–1651) fled to Bhutan and established himself among the Drukpas there. He became the first head of a monastic state in Bhutan paralleling that of the Dalai Lamas at Lhasa, which achieved dominance in Central Tibet at around the same time under the leadership of the Fifth Dalai Lama. The controversy over the recognition of Pema Karpo's successor led to a split in the Drukpa tradition that has continued into modern times, and also contributed to a long series of conflicts between Central Tibet and Bhutan.

The problem recurred in Bhutan in the next generation, when there were three contenders to succeed the Shabdrung Rinpoche, and so to become the next Bhutanese head of state. The following war was brought to an end by a mediated agreement according to which the three contenders were *all* recognized, one as the rebirth of the Shabdrung's body (*ku*), one of his speech (*sung*) and one of his mind (*tuk*). The mind emanation (*tuktul*), as the most senior, was recognized as the political head of Bhutan. The body incarnation died young, but the mind and speech emanations continued to reincarnate separately down to the twentieth century, when the first king of Bhutan, a Bhutanese local ruler who had taken over control of the country with British support, forbade any further rebirths of the *tuktul* line. This was incidentally not entirely successful. Two subsequent *tuktul* came to sticky and almost certainly unnatural ends, but further rebirths have continued to be recognized. The same is true of other high-profile cases in which attempts have been made by political authorities to bring a rebirth lineage to an end.

One can continue with further examples of this kind, including the two high profile recent cases, that of the Sixteenth Gyalwa Karmapa (1924–1981), the oldest of all the rebirth lines, which has led to a major split within the Karmapa order, and that of the rebirths of the Tenth Panchen Lama, the second highest Gelukpa rebirth (1938–1989), which is in dispute between the Chinese authorities and the Tibetan government-in-exile at Dharamsala. For all these problems, the tulku system has become a routine and well-established feature of Tibetan religion.

In practice, one often finds combinations of these various principles of recognition of lamas within a single monastery and family. An example is the Ripa Ladrang, a medium-sized monastic tradition originally based in the region of Pakshö in Eastern Tibet. The principal monastery of the Ripa tradition was founded by Pema Deje Rolpa, the son of a *ngakpa* lama from a Kagyüd background, in the late eighteenth century. It developed both a series of hereditary heads of the tradition, who were the lineal descendants of the founder, and a series of recognized rebirths, which were also found in the same family. The family left Central Tibet in 1959 and eventually settled at the Tibetan refugee settlement at Chandragiri in Orissa. The abbot of the monastery, Andzin Rinpoche, was recognized as a rebirth of the founder, Pema Deje

Figure 7.7 Namka Rinpoche (left) and Andzin Rinpoche (right) in their shrine-room at Chandragiri, Orissa. Photo by author (1990).

Rolpa, and shared leadership of the community with his close relative Namka Drimé Rinpoche, who was the head of the family lineage and a noted *tertön* lama. Namka Drimé Rinpoche's son, Gyetul Jigmé Rinpoche, had been recognized as the *tulku* of a monastery in Pemakö where the family stayed on its way out of Tibet. The Ripa Labrang have now also established a Dharma centre in the USA, and Namka Drimé Rinpoche and his son, Gyetul Jigmé Rinpoche, regularly travel there to give teachings and Tantric empowerments.

The Ripa Labrang illustrates several other factors that are typical of Tibetan Buddhism, particularly in areas such as this, which were on the edges of the area of control of the Lhasa state and dominated by non-Gelukpa traditions. One is the pattern of marriages in the family, which were mainly with other medium- to high-status hereditary lama families and wealthy merchant families. Another is the mixture of Kagyüd and Nyingma traditions; the original founder was Kagyüd, but a marriage in the next generation brought in Nyingma teachings of the Taktsam tradition, and another marriage made a connection with the Drukpa Kagyüd/Rimé tradition of another high-status hereditary lama, Śākya Śrī.

The Gelukpa system of election

It is worth though mentioning the remarkable elaboration of the selection principle developed in the Gelukpa system, since this controlled the appointment of what was formally the highest monastic position in the entire Gelukpa order, the Ganden Tripa or successor to the throne of Tsongkapa at Ganden monastery. This procedure has been described in detail by Alex Berzin, from whom I summarize here. It should be noted that the Ganden Tripa rather than the Dalai Lama was the official head of the Gelukpa tradition, although the Dalai Lama became by far the most important single lama within this tradition.

This system worked as follows. Monks who had earned one of the two *geshé* degrees (*lharampa* or *tsokrampa*) in Ganden, Sera or Drepung, the principal Gelukpa monastic universities in the Lhasa region, were eligible to enter one of the two elite Tantric colleges at Lhasa (Gyumé and Gyutö). After intensive study and examination on Tantra they could be awarded a further degree, the *geshé ngakrampa*, which meant that they were officially recognized as experts on both Sūtra and Tantra teachings. Only *geshé ngakrampa* were eligible to be appointed as *gekö* or disciplinarians (proctors) of the Tantric colleges. The *lama umdzé* or junior abbot of each of these colleges is appointed from among former *gekö* of the respective college, and subsequently serves as *kenpo* or abbot. When the headship of one of the two Ganden colleges (Shartsé and Changtsé) became vacant, the senior retired abbot of the appropriate Tantric college (Gyutö for Shartsé, Gyumé for Changtsé) took over. These two college heads then alternated in becoming Ganden Tripa or head of the entire Geluk order.

Figure 7.8 Assembly of monks at Tango Gompa, Bhutan. Photo by author (2010).

In theory, given this system, it was not necessary for the Ganden Tripa to be a reincarnate lama or *tulku*, but in practice the people appointed to these senior ranks in recent years have virtually all been *tulku*, which illustrates how the prestige of the reincarnation system has come to dominate the entire leadership of Tibetan Buddhist monasticism.

Celibate monastic practitioners (monks and nuns)

We turn now to look at the celibate practitioners within Tibetan Buddhism. These are people who have taken on the various stages of celibate ordination (novices, monks, nuns) provided by the Buddhist Vinaya or disciplinary code, in the same way as men and women do within the Buddhist traditions of Southeast Asia and East Asia, and with only minor differences in disciplinary code.

In fact, many of the lamas discussed above were and are celibate practitioners who have also taken on these vows. As we have seen, however, it is not necessary to be a celibate monk to be a lama, and, equally, the vast majority of celibate practitioners in Tibet were not lamas, but occupied more junior positions within the monastic system.

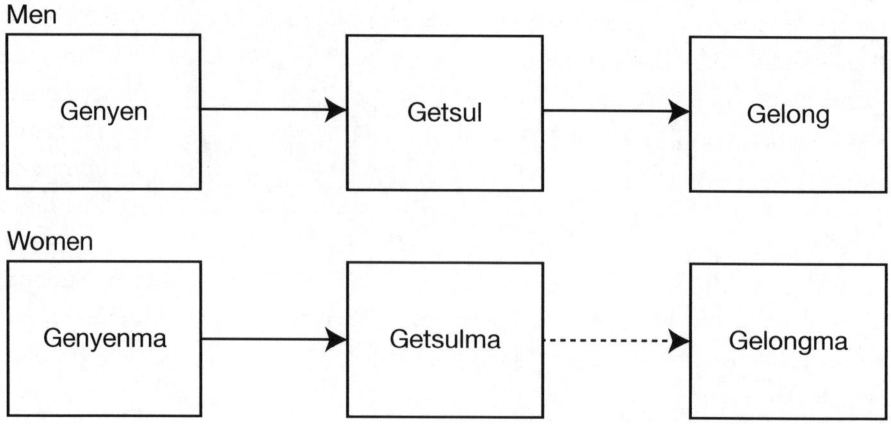

Figure 7.9 Stages of ordination.

The diagram presents the successive stages of ordination through which male and female Tibetans might go in the course of a monastic career. Thus the three male grades, with their conventional English translations, are

genyen (= Skt. *upāsaka*), '(male) lay follower'
getsul (= Skt. *śramaṇera*) '(male) novice'
gelong (= Skt. *bhikṣu*) '(fully-ordained) monk'

and the corresponding three female grades are

genyenma (= Skt. *upāsikā*), '(female) lay follower'
getsulma (= Skt. *śramaṇerī*) '(female) novice'
gelongma (= Skt. *bhikṣunī*) '(fully-ordained) nun'

In fact, the standard English translations, lay-follower, novice and (fully-ordained) monk or nun, are somewhat misleading. They may have been appropriate for some periods of Indian society, and may be appropriate today for the Theravādin traditions of Southeast Asia, but they do not work well for the Tibetan terms in pre-modern or contemporary practice. Thus *getsul* vows might be taken by laymen, especially on a temporary basis, but they were and are also regularly taken at entry to a monastic community, in conjunction with the ceremony known as *rabjung*, a term which literally refers to renunciation of lay life. Also, while many male monastics in Theravādin countries take *bhikṣu* ordination while in their twenties, Tibetan male monastics may not proceed to *gelong* ordination until fairly late in life, if at all. However, the vows and commitments corresponding to each stage, which derive from the Vinaya, the Buddhist disciplinary code, are essentially the same as those for the corresponding Sanskrit grades.

As for the female stages of ordination, these again correspond to the three successive sets of vows in the Vinaya, culminating in the *bhikṣuni* (*gelongma*) ordination, the female equivalent to the role of *bhikṣu*. However, as is also the case in the Theravāda Buddhist societies of Southeast Asia and Sri Lanka, the *bhikṣuni* (*gelongma*) ordination does not exist as a practical possibility, although there have been attempts to reintroduce it in recent years. This issue, and the problematic status of nuns more generally, is discussed further in Chapter 10.

Tibetan men and women become monastic practitioners, and Tibetans support monasteries, for a variety of reasons. On the whole, a personal desire for Enlightenment may be only one of the factors involved, and not necessarily the major one. We have already met the idea of conscript monks, and we have also encountered the idea that the monastery is doing a job on behalf of the community. From this point of view, being a monk might be less an individualistic career choice, as it might be in contemporary Western society, and more something that was taken on out of duty to one's family and community, and on behalf of them as much as oneself.

Families in various parts of Tibet had a tradition of putting one of their sons into the local monastery, though the extent to which this happened seems to have been somewhat exaggerated in older books on Tibet. These often speak of one in three of the male population being monks, but as far as can be established the proportion of monks even in the more centralized parts of Tibet in pre-modern times was probably around 10 to 12 per cent at most. Here monks refers to people who were wearing robes, observing vows of celibacy, and living in monastic communities; only a proportion in pre-modern Tibet would normally have taken full monastic ordination. The proportion of nuns in relation to the total female population was much lower, maybe 2 to 3 per cent, although it is hard to be sure because many nuns seem to have spent much of their time at home, assisting with family chores. The question of women as religious practitioners will be discussed further in Chapter 10.

Theoretically, once one has taken monastic vows, one should keep them. In practice, in pre-modern Tibetan societies, the relationship between monastic and lay life was often relatively fluid. People broke vows of celibacy because of attraction to someone of the opposite sex, and might leave the monastery as a consequence. This was not a positive thing to do, but it was common and relatively well accepted. Since ex-monks would often have acquired a significant amount of education, were relatively literate, and so on, they had skills that might be useful in lay society.

It was also not uncommon for men to return their vows for family reasons, for example because a brother who was head of the household had died. In this case, the monk might formally return his vows, come home, and take over as head of the household and as husband of the wife or wives of the joint family. Tibetan families were often polyandrous, with several brothers married to the same wife or wives, so there was in any case a sense that the woman was married to the brothers as a group. As mentioned earlier in this chapter, the continuity of the household was very important, and ideally it was to be achieved by the continuity of the male lineage. Thus if there were no sons, and there was a brother available who was a monk, it might be seen as his duty to the household to leave the monastic life and return home so as to father a son that might take over, or at least a daughter who might marry a husband who would take over as head of the household. Here again there is the notion we encountered in Chapter 6 that people's responsibility is to the collective, to the community, not just to themselves. Being a monk is a good thing, and it is good for society that there are monks, but the continuation of society itself can often be seen as a higher value than that of being a monk. This could of course lead to situations of conflict, since the brother who is a monk may be unwilling to come home, and so on.

There might also be economic reasons for a boy or young man to become a monk in one of the larger, state-supported monasteries, since for a family that had limited economic resources this would mean one less mouth to feed. This was less likely to be a factor for women, since female monastic institutions were generally smaller and had less financial support. As mentioned earlier, female religious might remain within the household, and might also move fairly easily between household and a monastic institution. There is a considerable pragmatism in Tibetan society with relation to the decisions which are made in relation to monastic careers as in other matters.

In the post-1959 period, refugee monasteries in India and Nepal became in effect orphanages for large numbers of children who had lost parents or whose parents did not have the resources to support and educate them. In some areas, this is still the case, with monasteries relying on children from poor families of Tibetan or Himalayan Buddhist backgrounds to keep their numbers up. In the contemporary situation in Chinese-controlled Tibet, becoming a monk is also, potentially at least, a political choice, which can be closely linked to the assertion of Tibetan nationalism as well as to Tibetan religion.

Thus the monastic population of Tibet was quite varied. At the top end, as one might say, are the highly trained scholar-monks of the large monasteries that maintained a strong academic tradition, and the equally highly trained elite ritual practitioners of large high-status monasteries that specialized in ritual. There were other specialisms, such as artistic work, since a large monastery needs skilled craftsmen of various kinds, as well as guards, monastic police and the like. Many monks acquired basic skills in reading and ritual performance but remained practitioners at a fairly humble level. The number of people who were able to perform advanced Tantric ritual at more than a superficial level was probably relatively small in most monasteries. Even a tradition like that of the Drukpa Kagyüd, whose identity is closely linked to the yogic tradition of Milarepa, had only a small elite group of monk-yogins.

Lay yogins and other non-monastic practitioners

In fact, most yogins were probably not monks in the sense of being permanent members of a large monastic establishment, though they might take vows of celibacy for some or all of their careers. This is not so much because of the conflict between monastic vows and Tantric sexual practice, although that can be an element, because the tradition of performing Tantric practice without a physical sexual component has now become very well-established and is in fact normative. However, serious yogic practice is scarcely compatible with the routine life of a busy monastery, and committed yogic practitioners might be more likely to be found attached to a respected Tantric lama on a temporary basis, or travelling on their own and making a living through offering ritual services to the communities where they are staying.

Figure 7.10
Thubten Repa, a lay yogic practitioner at Chandragiri, Orissa. Photo by author (1989).

Tibetan lay people might often regard an accomplished lay yogin as likely to be a more effective ritual practitioner than a monk, in part because he would be likely to have had more opportunity to acquire the relevant experience.

In some parts of Tibet, it is quite common for many laymen, and occasionally some lay women as well, to have received some Tantric training and to participate in rituals in local temples. Rebkong in Northeast Tibet (Amdo) has lay temples of this kind in which *ngakpa* and *ngakma* (male and female Tantric ritualists) from the Nyingmpa tradition gather for regular rituals. Similar practitioners in West-Central Tibet (Dingri) are called *serkyim*; in Bhutan the term *gomchen* is used. Several of the Tibetan highland communities in Nepal have similar communities. The degree of guidance from local lamas varies across these communities, though where there is a respected lama in the community from the Nyingma tradition he generally acts as a leader and spiritual guide. It seems likely that these traditions of lay practice grew up in remote areas and at times when there were few if any local monasteries. Since nowhere is really remote today, and the exodus of lamas from Tibet after the Chinese takeover resulted in many of them settling and starting communities in many of these areas, there has been a shift to celibate monasticism in several of them, though the older pattern of lay practice still mostly persists to some degree.

Monasticism and non-monastic practice in Tibetan societies

Generally speaking in Tibetan societies, monasticism is valued, but it is not seen as the only appropriate mode of Buddhist practice. Similarly, in Tibetan monasteries, discipline is important but full monastic vows are not necessarily central in the way that they are in Thailand or Burma, where *bhikṣu* status was something of a *sine qua non*. One can perhaps exaggerate the difference here, since these societies too had traditions of forest monks in isolated hermitages developing magical power, where the focus was more on meditation than on formal monastic status, and they also had quasi-Tantric traditions of magical power such as the Burmese *weikza*. Normatively, though, Theravādin societies emphasized the monastic role to a much greater extent than in Tibet, where the leading religious roles, those of the lamas, are not necessarily occupied by celibate monk.

If one looks for an explanation of why this is so, and why being a monk is less central for Tibetan Buddhism than in Theravāda Buddhism, then at one level one can look at doctrinal issues. Thus the importance of the *bodhisattva* ideal in Mahāyāna Buddhism might be seen to undermine the monastic role, while the importance of Tantric power, with its complex and ambivalent relationship to celibate monasticism, might also be seen to encourage forms of leadership that do not involve celibacy. However this does not really answer the question of why these forms of Buddhism came to predominate in Tibet. After all, Tantra was a significant part of Southeast Asian and Sri Lankan Buddhism at one time. Elements of it survive, in the form of esoteric sects and groups, and quasi-Tantric forms of meditation. However, they have become marginalized, whereas in Tibet they are much more central. It seems that this can be understood to a considerable degree at least in terms of the relatively weak and decentralized nature of the Tibetan state. Tantric and quasi-Tantric practices were routinely criticized by state religious authorities in Southeast Asian countries, and often actively suppressed by the state. While there were attempts to restrict them in Tibet, particularly in the early empire and in the tenth and eleventh centuries, these were ultimately unsuccessful. It seems likely that the lack of effective centralized power in much of Tibet, and the existence at most times of many areas where practitioners of officially-disapproved forms of Buddhism could find refuge and support, were important factors.

There are limits however to how much can be explained by a purely sociological argument. Tantric Buddhism survives in Nepal and Bali, and Tantric Hinduism remained a key part of Indian states for many centuries. The social context is nevertheless clearly relevant and significant. In the South Asian pattern, and in Southeast Asia too, in the period when there were Tantric states in Southeast Asia, Tantra seems to have been mainly a preserve of ruling elites and generally to have had a slightly shady and problematic edge to it. Tantric practitioners exercised magical power on behalf of the state. Ruling elites were expected to have access to power, and were in a sense entitled to use it, but there was always a certain amount of moral uncertainty about it. This meant that over time the role of Tantra was vulnerable to critique, and the colleges of Tantric practitioners were always at risk of finding themselves unemployed. Kashmir would be a classic example, where one finds the Hindu rulers who patronized Tantra, such as Harsha (ruled 1089–1111), being replaced by anti-Tantric kings, and ridiculed by later historians and satirists. Excessive involvement in Tantric power, in other words, might be an effective argument for a change of regime. Similarly the Burmese king Anawrahta (Aniruddha) (ruled approximately 1044–1077) is traditionally supposed to have converted Burma from the questionable, Tantric, magical, superstitious Buddhism of the so-called Ari monks to proper pure Theravāda. In this case, Anawrahta's work seems to have been less complete than later historians have claimed, with the 'purification' of the Buddhist Saṅgha (in other words, the abolition of Mahāyāna and Tantric practices) in fact being a gradual process over a longer period, and never entirely complete, but the general point remains.

Such a move in any case needs at least two factors to be successful, a regime that sees some advantage in 'purification', and a situation in which it is able to enforce it. In fact, we can see attempts at the same kind of move in Tibet at around the same time, when the king of the then quite important Western Tibetan state of Guge, Yeshe Ö (d.1024) proclaiming a number of edicts against the alleged misuse of Tantra. These moves were part of the background for the move to celibate monasticism in Tibet, but they never succeeded in preventing Tantric practice, even lay Tantric practice, presumably because the region where their writ ran was so limited in comparison to Tibet as a whole.

Nevertheless, there is a gradual move throughout Tibetan history, continuing in the modern period, towards large-scale celibate monasticism combined with reincarnate-lama leadership. Even high-status lineages of hereditary lamas like the Sakya and Mindrolling families, or more recently the descendants of Śākya Śrī or Dudjom Rinpoche, seem increasingly to be drawn towards this pattern. It remains to be seen whether this will continue within the contemporary environment. A significant factor here is likely to be the spread of Tibetan Buddhism to the West and to other regions where monasticism is a marginal and problematic mode of practice, and one which society is by and large unwilling to support.

Temples and monastic establishments

As we have seen, there were a variety of different ways in which lamas passed on their status, power and charisma to their successors. One could describe all this in Weberian terms as a process of the 'routinization of charisma' by which the personal authority of a charismatic leader gradually becomes transformed over time into the institutional authority of his or her successors. For Max Weber this was an inevitable process, and one can certainly see a movement in this direction throughout Tibetan history. However, the Tibetan system has only gone a certain distance in this direction. There are large monasteries that have existed for many hundreds of years, with a highly sophisticated mode of reproducing their leadership, either by descent, or by reincarnation (the *tulku* system). We can see how these great monasteries developed over time, how *tulku* were recognized mainly within high-status families and how the appointment system became highly politicized. But there was also a much more open and fluid aspect to Tibetan religion, which can be seen most clearly with the *tertön* or visionary lamas, and with the small *gompa* run mostly by lay practitioners under the leadership of a local hereditary lama. The difference corresponded to some degree to that between the different regions of Tibet, those which were more centralized and more under the control of big families or monasteries, and those which were more marginal and self-governing. While some parts of the Tibetan plateau, such as those along the major trade routes that went through the most populous region of Central Tibet, were always pretty close to centres of power, and others generally marginal, some regions shifted back and forth depending on the historical situation. Thus parts of northern Nepal were at times more integrated and centralized, at other times less so.

What this meant in terms of monasteries and religious centres was that at any given time in Tibetan history after the fourteenth or fifteenth century one might find large monasteries with hundreds of celibate monks, in some areas, while in other areas they might be more or less absent. The specific areas might well shift however over time. One can see this in the area Charles Ramble describes in *Navel of the Demoness*, where there had been a quite substantial Sakya monastic presence in the recent past linked to the rulers of the small state of Lo Möntang (Mustang), to the north.

In this case the decline of monasticism was linked to the decline of political power by the Lo Möntang kings. Elsewhere the reasons for its growth or decline might be economic rather than political. Thus it has been argued plausibly that the growth of Nyingma monasticism in the Sherpa regions of eastern Nepal was linked to the introduction of the potato in the mid-nineteenth century, which enabled the production of an agricultural surplus in what had been a fairly marginal area with the traditional Tibetan high-altitude crop, barley. This meant that some people got wealthier, but also that they put their wealth into sponsoring monasteries. These were initially small branch monasteries of the larger Nyingma monastic centres north of the Himalayan ranges in Tibet itself. The suppression of the Tibetan monasteries in the 1960s meant that these became more significant centres, and also led to the building of a relatively large monastery in Sherpa country headed by Trulshik Rinpoche, a refugee lama from one of the traditional sources of Sherpa monasticism, Rongphu monastery in southern Tibet.

As mentioned earlier, the Tibetan word *gompa* refers to a variety of different kinds of religious establishment, and the English word monastery can be somewhat misleading. Tibetan monks follow the Buddhist Vinaya code as do monastic practitioners in other Buddhist societies, but not all *gompa* are communities of celibate monks. Generally speaking non-monastic Tantric practitioners will wear the white and red *ngagpa* shawl (*zenta*) and white skirt (*shantap*) and wear their hair long and wound up on their head. But even where people are wearing monastic robes this does not necessarily mean that they are monks. In some traditions, such as that of the Bhutanese *gomchen*, it is normal for people to wear monastic robes for ritual contexts. We might sketch quickly a number of different types of *gompas*, and see them in relation to the four main divisions of the monastic orders, Nyingmapa, Sakyapa, Kagyüdpa and Gelukpa.

Within these traditions we can find many different types of monasteries, as indicated below.

1 Small communities of lay practitioners attached to a temple and a lama

Here the lama will probably be from a hereditary background, and the lay practitioners will live in their own houses most of the time, though they may stay in the *gompa* for periodic retreats. An institution of this kind would normally belong to the Nyingma tradition but it could also have connections with some of the non-celibate lineages in the Kagyüd and Sakya traditions. It would not be Gelukpa, since they have a stronger emphasis on celibate monasticism as an essential aspect of Buddhist institutional practice.

Figure 7.11 Kardang Gompa, Lahul, India – temple, *chortens*, house. Photo by author (1989).

2 Small communities of celibate monastics attached to a temple and a lama

Here there may be houses attached to households within the village or villages that support the monastery, where those members of the family who are permanently or temporarily observing vows may live. Many small monasteries are supported by local villages and are closely integrated with them. If there is a hereditary or celibate lama, he will normally have a household (*labrang*) within the monastery, possibly integrated with the main temple. A monastery of this kind might have thirty to a hundred celibate monks and one or two reincarnating lamas. In some cases, outside the Gelukpa tradition, there might be both a hereditary and a reincarnating lineage, and there might also be celibate and non-celibate practitioners.

3 Medium to large communities of celibate monastics

Such communities might have extensive land holdings of their own and substantial buildings, often with several reincarnate lamas, each with his own financially-independent *labrang*, and accommodation for hundreds of monks. These medium to large communities may have separate attached hermitages or retreat centres. Monasteries of this kind are also common in trading centres in pastoral areas.

Figure 7.12 Lamayuru Gompa, Ladakh. Photo by Ruth Rickard (2011).

Figure 7.13 Part of Labrang Gompa, Amdo. Photo by author (2010).

4 Large teaching monasteries

These teaching monasteries included the big Gelukpa establishments in Central Tibet and in Northeast Tibet (Amdo) and large teaching monasteries in the other traditions. The largest of these were the Gelukpa monastic universities such as Sera, Ganden, Drepung, Tashilhunpo, Kumbum and Labrang. These institutions each had a number of distinct teaching colleges, as well as residential hostels for monks from different regions. Thus Sera monastery, one of the three big monasteries near Lhasa, had over 6000 monks at its height in the first half of the twentieth century, and occupied about 28 acres (11 hectares). It had three major colleges, Je Tratsang and Me Tratsang, which trained monks over a 20-year period for the scholastic *geshé* degree, and the Ngakpa Tratsang that provided advanced training in Tantric ritual. There were 33 hostels (*kamtsang*) for students from different parts of Tibet, a large assembly hall, a number of smaller temples, and a variety of small retreat houses or hermitages linked to the main monastic complex. Each of the colleges also had its own temples. A variety of reincarnate lamas were associated with the monastery and its colleges, and had separate households within the complex. In Northeast Tibet (Amdo) colleges for Kālacakra study and for medical study are also common.

This variety of institutions arose from the variety of environments and political units that was sketched in Chapter 1. Marginal areas tended to have small non-celibate *gompas* and small monasteries, while villages in more centralized areas tend to have medium-sized monasteries. Large monasteries are generally in politically significant locations, linked to centres of state power or control over major trade routes.

Key points you need to know

- In most Buddhist countries the key leadership role is that of the fully-ordained Buddhist monk or *bhikkhu* (*gelong* in Tibetan). While there are many ordained monks in Tibet, the main religious leaders are the lamas.
- While many lamas are monks, most monks are not lamas, and many lamas are not monks, particularly in the non-Gelukpa traditions. The two roles overlap, but they are quite distinct from each other. Lamas vary from local village-level lamas to the heads of major religious traditions such as the Sakya Tridzin or Gyalwa Karmapa. They are all however teachers (the word is used to translate Sanskrit *guru*) and above all they are all masters of Tantric ritual. Training in Tantra is passed from lama to student, and the role of the lama is central in this transmission.

- Lamas are also often administrators of substantial estates, and people of great authority in Tibetan society. They may also have direct political power, as with the Dalai Lamas in Tibet and the Shabdrung Rinpoche in Bhutan.
- As this social and political role of the lama suggests, Buddhism in Tibet is a collective project as much as an individual one, with its goal the welfare and collective improvement of the community as much as individual attainment of Buddhahood.
- As lamas acquired estates and followings, the question of succession became increasingly significant. Various modes of succession developed, including hereditary succession, the recognition of *tertön* or visionary lamas (in the Nyingma and Bon traditions), the recognition of reincarnate lamas, and other systems of selection and succession.
- Other significant religious roles are that of male and female ordained celibate practitioners (monks, nuns, male and female novices), and yogic practitioners, who usually did not take vows of celibacy.
- Tibetan religious communities (*gompa*) also varied considerably from small village temples to sizeable monastic towns or cities containing many constituent temples, colleges and lama households. The variety of religious roles and communities can be connected with the lack of strong centralized authority through much of Tibetan history.

Discussion questions

1. What is the difference between a lama and a monk? Why did Tibet develop different kinds of religious leadership from those found in most other Buddhist societies?
2. Discuss the development of hereditary and reincarnate lamas in Tibetan society. How do their social and religious roles make sense within the specific character of Tibetan society?
3. Why might a Tibetan become a monk or a lay yogin?

Further reading

Aris, Michael. *Bhutan: The Early History of a Himalayan Kingdom.* Warminster: Aris and Phillips, 1979.

Aziz, Barbara N. *Tibetan Frontier Families: Reflections of Three Generations from D'ing-ri.* New Delhi: Vikas, 1978.

Barron, Richard. *The Autobiography of Jamgön Kongtrul: A Gem of Many Colours.* Ithaca, NY & Boulder, CO: Snow Lion Publications, 2003.

Chang, Garma C.C. (trans.). *The Hundred Thousand Songs of Milarepa*. 2 vols. Boulder, CO and London: Shambhala, 1977.

Dudjom Rinpoche, H.H. *The Nyingma School of Tibetan Buddhism: Its Fundamentals and History*. Translated and edited by Gyurme Dorje and Matthew Kapstein. 2 vols. Boston, MA: Wisdom Publications, 1991.

Doctor, Andreas. *Tibetan Treasure Literature: Revelation, Tradition and Accomplishment in Visionary Buddhism*. Ithaca, NY: Snow Lion, 2005.

Gyaltsen, Sakyapa Sonam. *The Clear Mirror: A Traditional Account of Tibet's Golden Age*. Translated by McComas Taylor and Lama Choedak Yuthok. Ithaca, NY: Snow Lion, 1996.

Gyatso, Janet. *Apparitions of the Self: The Secret Autobiographies of a Tibetan Visionary*. Princeton, NJ: Princeton University Press, 1998.

Hookham, Shenpen. 'In search of the Guru', in John Snelling (ed.), *Sharpham Miscellany: Essays in Spirituality and Ecology*. Totnes: The Sharpham Trust, 1992.

Könchog Gyaltsen, Khenpo (trans.). *The Great Kagyü Masters: The Golden Lineage Treasury*. Edited by Victoria Huckenpahler. Ithaca, NY: Snow Lion, 1990.

Kunga Rinpoche, Lama and Brian Cutillo (trans.). *Drinking the Mountain Stream: Further Stories and Songs of Milarepa, Yogin, Poet and Teacher of Tibet*. New York: Lotsawa, 1978.

Kunsang, Erik Pema (trans.). *The Lotus-Born: The Life Story of Padmasambhava*. Boston and London: Shambhala, 1993.

Lhalungpa, Lobsang P. (trans.). *The Life of Milarepa: A New Translation from the Tibetan*. Boston: Shambhala, 1977; New York: Arkana, 1984.

Nalanda Translation Committee. *The Rain of Wisdom*. Boulder, CO and London: Shambhala, 1980.

Obermiller, E. *History of Buddhism (Chos-ḥbyung by Bu-ston)*. 2 vols. Heidelberg: Otto Harrassowitz, Leipzig, 1932–33.

Ricard, Matthieu (trans.). *The Life of Shabkar: The Autobiography of a Tibetan Yogin*. State University of New York Press, 1994.

Roerich, George N. *The Blue Annals*. 2nd edn. Delhi: Motilal Banarsidass, 1976.

Smith, E. Gene. *Among Tibetan Texts: History and Literature of the Himalayan Plateau*. Boston: Wisdom Publications, 2001.

Snellgrove, David L. *Four Lamas of Dolpo*. 2 vols. Oxford: Bruno Cassirer, 1967.

Sørensen, Per K. *Tibetan Buddhist Historiography: The Mirror Illuminating the Royal Genealogies*. Wiesbaden: Harrassowitz Verlag, 1994.

Stearns, Cyrus. *Luminous Lives: The Story of the Early Masters of the Lam 'Bras Tradition in Tibet*, Boston: Wisdom Publications, 2001.

Taranatha, Jonang. *The Seven Instruction Lineages*. Translated and edited by David Templeman. Dharamsala: Library of Tibetan Works and Archives, 2002.

Thondup Rinpoche, Tulku. *Hidden Teachings of Tibet: An Explanation of the Terma Tradition of the Nyingma School of Buddhism*. London: Wisdom, 1986.

Tulku Urgyen Rinpoche. *Blazing Splendor: The Memoirs of Tulku Urgyen Rinpoche as told to Erik Pema Kunsang and Marcia Binder Schmidt*. Hong Kong: Rangjung Yeshe, 2005.

8 *Tibetan Buddhism as practical religion*

In this chapter

This chapter deals with Tibetan Buddhism as practical religion. What is meant here by practical religion is primarily the ritual management of power to protect the community and to maintain the health and prosperity of its members. The chapter explores the way in which Tibetans see Tantric power as important, and examines some of the ways in which it is used for the benefit of the community.

Main topics covered

- Practical religion in Indian Buddhism
- Practical religion in Tibet
- Lamas, monks and monasteries as fields of karma
- Death rituals – 'Tibetan Book of the Dead'
- Maintenance of good relations with local gods and spirits; protection against malevolent spirits
- Rituals for prosperity, success and good fortune
- Rituals for health and long life
- Divination and diagnosis
- Tibetan ritual: pragmatic, karma-oriented and Bodhic dimensions

Introduction

It has already been suggested several times in this book that what I am calling here 'practical religion' is core business for Tibetan Buddhism. In fact, it was a central part of what most pre-modern religions were concerned with, although the tendency of Western scholars to view religion with vision shaped by the Reformation and the dominance of a Protestant perspective means that it is often given less importance than it should be. Tibetan Buddhism, though, presents itself primarily as a path to liberation and Buddhahood, not as a way of solving the this-worldly problems of its followers. How are these two important aspects of the religion reconciled?

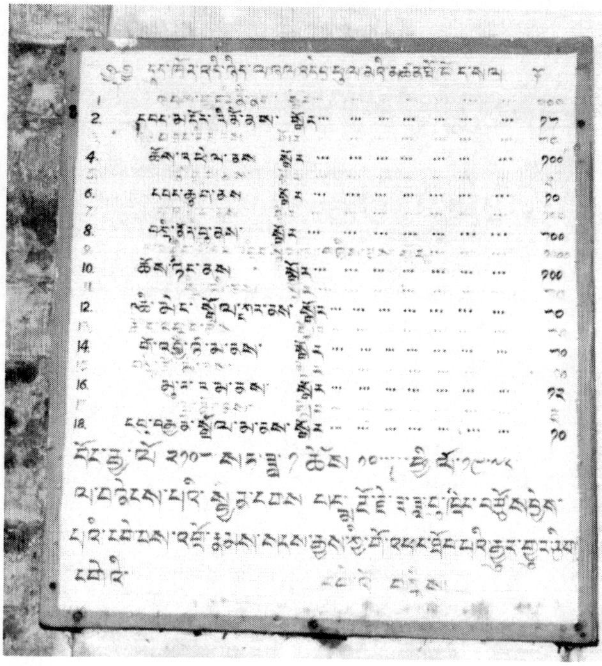

Figure 8.1
Cost (in Indian rupees) for different ritual services. Nyingmapa monastery, Rewalsar, India. Photo by author (1989).

Practical religion in Indian Buddhism

To start with, we look at some of the background in Indian Buddhism, since Buddhism in India also had a strong practical component back to its early days. This has recently been argued at some length by Robert DeCaroli. He points out in his book *Haunting the Buddha* that the early Buddhist monks developed expertise in dealing with the spirit-world, and particularly with death and the spirits of the dead, and suggests that this was one of the reasons why they were valued by the secular world of their time. The use of specific chants (*paritta*) for protection against various dangers is already mentioned in early Sūtras, and is routine in modern Theravāda countries such as Sri Lanka, Thailand and Burma. The use of amulets consecrated by monks believed to have advanced powers, of protective tattoos of Buddhist formulae, and the like, is also widespread. However, for the most part there is a pragmatic division of labour in Theravādin countries today between religion of local gods and the Buddha. Prosperity, success, good health and protection in everyday life is the business of the local gods, not of Buddha, although the role of Buddha as an ultimate source of power means that in practice the lines can be blurred at times.

Tibetan Buddhism derives, however, as we have seen, from Indian Tantric (Vajrayāna) Buddhism, and here the use of Buddhist Tantric power for this-worldly purposes had already developed much further. The likelihood is that the Tantrics in India were initially private operators, rather than members of monastic establishments, and that they attracted patronage from local rulers and powerful men to a significant degree because they provided access to power. While the central purpose of the Vajrayāna, at any rate the so-called Anuttarayoga Tantras, is Enlightenment, the acquisition of powers to affect the everyday world is at the least an important by-product of Tantric practice. Thus Buddhist Tantric practice can be described in terms of the attainment of the various *siddhi* (Tibetan *ngödrup*) or Tantric accomplishments. The word is closely related to the term *siddha* (Tibetan *druptop*), meaning one who has attained something, that is some kind of power; this is an ordinary word for a Tantric practitioner. Another related term is *sādhanā* (Tib. *druptap*), meaning a set procedure for spiritual practice.

Enlightenment was itself described as the supreme and ultimate *siddhi*, but there are many others, the so-called 'ordinary' *siddhis*, and it is these we are concerned with here. One of the most important was the power over life, the ability to live indefinitely and/or control the time of one's death, a theme that was taken up and developed in Tibet as described later in this chapter. There were various other classifications of pragmatic, practical, this-worldly ritual activity. The best-known version for the Buddhist Tantras lists four kinds of activity:

- Peaceful or pacifying
- Increasing or bringing about prosperity
- Dominating or bringing under control
- Destroying.

For more details of what kinds of activities Buddhist Tantric ritualists might have been engaged in, one can look at the mantra-chapters – one could perhaps equally translate these as 'spell-books' – in many of the Tantras. Thus the second chapter, the *Mantrapaṭalam*, of the main Hevajra Tantra text, begins by listing a whole series of mantras and then gives a number of detailed descriptions of rituals. These include rituals to control the weather, to destroy one's enemies and to attack their gods, to subdue a young woman, and to find lost wealth. Specific mantras are also given to repel various dangerous wild animals. Further practical rituals along similar lines are specified in the commentaries, where one can learn how to paralyse an enemy, how to cause two people to quarrel, entice or subdue a man or woman, or cause somebody to die. All this may not be quite what one expects to find in a highly-regarded Buddhist text, most of which, it should be added, is quite explicitly directed towards the attainment of Buddhahood. Other Vajrayāna texts contain similar material, including also rituals for healing wounds and illnesses, and rituals for counteracting the effects of poisons. Presumably all these rituals are included because performing rituals such as these was, quite simply, part of how a Tantric practitioner of the time earned his or her living. There is a kind of matter-of-factness about these books of spells, and they cover very much the kinds of ritual which one might suppose that a Tantric magician of the time might be asked to perform by his or her employer: controlling the weather, finding lost property, healing, love magic, dealing with enemies.

Practical religion in Tibet

If we turn to look at what happened when this material moved to Tibet, one could imagine the early emperors being interested in the large-scale military magic. By the tenth and eleventh centuries, however, when most of this material was being transmitted to Tibet, there would have been relatively few people who would have had the resources and the interest to sponsor a large-scale ritual to stop enemy armies in their tracks. The rulers of Guge, nevertheless, may well have had the possible political utility of Tantric practice in mind as well as the more altruistic motivations attributed to them by the later historical tradition. As for destructive magic, there are many stories about its employment in the Tibetan histories; probably the most familiar to non-Tibetan readers would be the narrative (in the biography of Milarepa) of Milarepa's employment of destructive magic as a young man in order to take revenge on some of his relatives. It seems likely though that it was more positive forms of ritual practice that enabled the lamas to establish themselves as important to Tibetan village communities: rituals to control the weather (protection against hail remains an important specialism of Tibetan lamas), to protect people, animals, houses and crops, against malevolent supernaturals, to heal illness, to bring about prosperity and good fortune. Guiding the consciousness of the deceased at death also became a Tibetan specialization at a relatively early stage. This was not merely a matter of the welfare of the deceased, but also of ensuring that the ghost of the dead person did not stay around and cause problems for the living. In the following sections, we examine some of the major areas of practical religion in Tibet in some more detail.

Lamas, monks and monasteries as fields of karma

We begin though with perhaps the most straightforward and conventional of relationships between Buddhist personnel and lay communities, one that is shared with all parts of the Buddhist world. Monks, monasteries and lamas are recipients of offerings, and these offerings are part of a transaction, in which the giver gains through performing a virtuous action, and so acquiring *sonam*, 'merit' that will in its turn have good karmic consequences. In the common Buddhist expression, the monastic community is a 'field of karma' in which one can sow one's offerings. Tibetan monks do not go on food-collecting rounds as do some Theravādin monks, but the idea of monks and lamas as suitable recipients for offerings is well ingrained in Tibetan thought. Most monasteries have standard arrangements by which one can offer food for the monks for one or more meals, an offering that is expected to have positive effects for one's own life and prosperity as well as being a karmic action with a reward in a future life. Monks and nuns may also be sponsored to perform rituals such as the *nyungné* fasting practice on behalf of the donor, an essentially non-Tantric practice aimed specifically at purification and the acquisition of good karma. These practices may be done because of a general feeling that donors would like to improve their karmic status or, perhaps, demonstrate their wealth and generosity to other members of the community, but they may also be a response to a divination (*mo*) saying that this would be a desirable thing to do (see below), or to a predicted bad astrological period or other difficult time.

More extensive acts of generosity may include paying for the building or renovating of temples, or the building of Buddhist ritual constructions such as *stūpa* (Tib. *chorten*) or *maṇi*-walls. Often these are sited at geomantically significant posts, such as river confluences, with a secondary aim of ensuring a positive flow of spiritual influences through the landscape (see Figure 8.2). There is some overlap here with activities performed by lay people to bring about good fortune, such as the erection of *lungta* ('prayer-flags'), pieces of cloth in the colours of the five elements block-printed with mantra and ritual diagrams, or the scattering of smaller *lungta* printed on small pieces of coloured paper. Erecting *lungta* too may be a response to divination or astrological predictions, and be a way to influence future events to benefit one or avert possible misfortune. *Lungta* are usually put up by lay people, but the technology of mantra and printing was for Tibetans a Buddhist technology associated with the monasteries.

Figure 8.2 Three *chorten* at the river confluence at Chudzom, Bhutan. Photo by author (2009).

Death rituals – 'Tibetan Book of the Dead'

Another classic area where monks in virtually all Buddhist countries have played an important role is that of rituals at the time of death. As noted above, this appears to go back to the early days of Buddhism in India.

The specific Tibetan versions are oriented around the 49-day interval between death and rebirth taught within the Mahāyāna texts accepted by the Tibetans. This 'intermediate period' (*antarābhava, bardo* in Tibetan) is the focus of one of the 'Six Yogas of Nāropa' practices that the Kagyüdpa claimed to have derived from their Indian Tantric teachers. The ability of the Gyalwa Karmapa lamas to control their rebirths, thus initiating the practice of recognizing *tulku* (Chapter 7) is associated with this practice. These practices were further developed in *terma* traditions from the fourteenth century onwards into liturgical procedures by which a lama could guide the consciousness of a dying person through the experience of the intermediate state. These are the *Bardo Tödröl* ('Liberation through Hearing in the Intermediate State') texts published in the 1920s in Kazi Dawa Samdup's translation as the 'Tibetan Book of the Dead', and they have become perhaps the best known of all Tibetan Buddhist texts and teachings outside Tibet.

In practice, Tibetan rituals at death are quite varied, and do not necessarily involve the recitation of the *Bardo Tödröl*. Lamas and monks nevertheless almost always play a central role in managing the process of death and subsequent rituals. Related Tantric practices (*powa*) are however now quite widely taught to lay people, who can use them as a preparation for death and, if possible, as a meditation to practise at the time of dying.

Maintenance of good relations with local gods and spirits; protection against malevolent spirits

In the following sections, we move on to areas less characteristic for Buddhist clergy in other Buddhist societies. The various local gods and spirits have been mentioned in previous chapters. Keeping on good terms with them, in particular with the 'owners' of the immediate locality and region (*sadak, shipdak, yullha*), generally gods of local mountains and lakes, was an important issue for pre-modern Tibetan societies, and remains important for Tibetan communities today, since the gods can easily be offended or upset and can cause misfortunes and problems of many kinds.

Both lay people and Buddhist ritual specialists are involved in keeping up these good relations, but the approach and techniques are significantly different. Lay people characteristically maintain good relationships with local gods by making regular offerings, both daily or less frequently on behalf of the household, or on one or more annual occasions on behalf of the village community. The standard form of lay offering (*sang, sangchö*) consists of a fire of scented wood (usually juniper) in which

Figure 8.3 Offerings to local deities, Yarlung Valley. Photo by author (1987).

yoghurt, butter, sugar and other 'pure' offerings are made. These are accompanied by verses of offering to the deities, which may involve more or less reference to specifically Buddhist material. The village rituals may be performed in a village temple, or at offering-cairns and other constructions (*laptsé*) above the village, often way up on the mountainside. Often the villagers will circle round the village fields, carrying Buddhist sacra such as the volumes of the Large *Prajñāpāramitā Sūtra*, and stopping at each *laptsé* to make offerings.

Sang can be performed on many occasions. Houses will often have small ovens for burning *sang* offerings on the roof or in the courtyard; at the other extreme, there are very large *sang* ovens in front of the Jokang in Lhasa, and visitors to the shrine buy *sang* offerings to burn there.

While many *sang* offering verses are quite short, there are much more elaborate versions of the practice which have been created by lamas and which incorporate elements of Tantric practice, such as the widely-used *Riwo Sangchö* practice devised by Lhatsün Namka Jigmé (1597–1653), the *tertön*-lama who 'revealed' the hidden land of Sikkim in the seventeenth century. The basic approach in lay performance of *sang* ritual however is that offerings are made to the local gods from a position of relative inferiority, and their assistance is politely requested.

The relationship between the lamas and the local gods is different, since it is grounded in the 'taming' of these gods by Padmasambhava and other lamas following in his tradition. When Padmasambhava subdued these deities, they swore oaths to

Figure 8.4 *Sang* offering in front of Jokang, Lhasa. Photo by author (1987).

Figure 8.5 *Sang* offering substances on sale near Jokang, Lhasa. Photo by author (1991).

protect the Buddhist teachings and yielded up the mantra formulae which constituted their heart-essence and through which they could be controlled. It is the lamas' consequent ability to *compel*, rather than simply to request, the assistance and good behaviour of the local gods that underlies monastic ritual to these gods. This power is effected through the Tantric guardian deities, transformed versions of the great Tantric *yidam* and so ultimately of the Buddha himself, whose identity the lamas can take on. This process is at the centre of much monastic ritual, and while the lamas make offerings to the local gods and spirits, they do so from a position of superiority, and the assumption is that, if the ritual is performed effectively, then the local spirits have no choice but to comply. The expertise of the lama who is performing or directing the ritual is key to the enterprise, however. This is why Tibetans are concerned, particularly on important occasions, to have a lama in charge who is known to be an effective Tantric ritual performer.

As with the *powa* practices, simplified versions of these Tantric practices are available for lay people. The box below gives a short prayer of this kind, along with three levels of interpretation of the prayer as given by the well-known twentieth-century lama Dudjom Rinpoche.

The Prayer for the Removal of All Obstacles (*Barché Kunsel*)

This is a short and very widely used prayer to Guru Rinpoche (Padmasambhava) from the Nyingmapa tradition, deriving from a *terma* or 'revealed' practice of the nineteenth-century *tertön* lama Chokgyur Lingpa.

> Buddha of the three times, Precious Guru,
> Master of all *siddhis*, Lord of Great Bliss,
> Remover of all obstacles (*barché*), Forceful Tamer of Demons,
> I pray to you and ask you for blessing (*chinlab*).
> Bless me to pacify outer, inner and secret obstacles and
> May my intention be spontaneously accomplished.

The following summarizes a short text by the late Dudjom Rinpoche which interprets these verses at three different levels:

> At the outer level, the first two and half lines refer to Buddha, Dharma and Saṅgha. At the inner level, they refer to the Three Roots, Guru, the *yidam* deities, and the *ḍākinis* and *dharmapālas*. At the secret level, they refer to the Three Kāyas, Dharmakāya, Sambhogakāya and Nirmāṇakāya. Guru Rinpoche is the complete embodiment of all these aspects, and so

> spontaneously tames the four terrifying demons, liberates beings and relieves their sufferings, and liberates obscurations and habitual patterns of consciousness into non-dual space and awareness.
>
> We pray to him externally, with intense devotion, internally acknowledging our own body, speech and mind as Guru Rinpoche's body, speech and mind, and at the secret level by maintaining a state of uncontrived self-awareness.
>
> In asking for his blessings, we are asking him to bless our body, speech and mind to accomplish the *vajra* body, speech and mind. The outer obstacles which we ask him to remove are the sixteen great fears, which include disease, wild animals, and poverty as well as pride, desire, envy and anger; the inner obstacles are the four great demons or *māra* (ego-clinging, attachment, self-deception and death), while the secret obstacles are the defilements of the five poisons, desire, hatred, ignorance, pride and envy. All of these are obstacles to our attainment of liberation and Buddhahood.

The intention whose accomplishment we ask for at the temporal level consists of the conditions conducive to the attainment of Buddhahood, a long life with good health and other positive qualities in this and future lives, but at the ultimate level it is the direct realization of the natural state of being, which is itself Buddhahood.

The lesser malevolent spirits are also subject to Tantric power, though since many of these lesser spirits are thought of as a somewhat unruly entourage to the major local gods, who are released by the latter if they are displeased with an individual or community, then keeping on good terms with the local gods normally means that they too will be kept under control. A key ritual sequence in most regular monastic ritual is the *dokpa* or 'turning back' of misfortune and negative influences.

Another important role in relation to the local gods is that of spirit-medium (*lhawa, pawo, kandroma*). The basic idiom of Tibetan spirit-mediumship is much as in many other societies in that the deity is thought of as 'taking over' the medium and speaking through him or her. The *lhawa* provide a way for people to find out whether a particular problem or illness is the result of offending one of the local deities, and if so what ritual action would be appropriate. *Lhawa* may also receive offerings on behalf of the spirits and give orders in their name, as in the *laru* festivals in Rebkong in Amdo. Historically, it seems that most *lhawa* were male, but increasingly these days they are women (often called *kandroma,* the Tibetan translation of *ḍākinī*).

Although the term 'spirit-medium' has been used here, Tibetan *lhawa* and similar practitioners, as with many such specialists, particularly in the Himalayas, do not fit neatly onto either side of the dichotomy sometimes drawn by Western scholars between 'shamans' and 'spirit-mediums', and they are frequently also referred to by Western scholars and authors as 'shamans'. While they act as media through which local deities and spirits communicate, they also often perform healing rituals in their own right, sucking out illness from the patient's body, or summoning back lost soul-substance or vital energy (*la*). This latter idiom, in which illness is seen as the result of the loss of some kind of bodily energy or vitality to an offended or malevolent spirit, is a very widely distributed mode of explanation for illness globally. In the Tibetan context, it links up with the general understanding of spirit-causation of illness. There is a strong ecological dimension here, focused on the need to respect the local spirit world and stay on good terms with it as a way of maintaining success, prosperity and good fortune as well as good health. The practice of village-level shamans of this kind tends to be under the overall supervision of local lamas and monasteries, which are usually responsible for identifying and recognizing upcoming spirit-mediums and helping them to develop their abilities. The costumes worn by spirit-mediums incorporate specifically Tantric Buddhist elements, such as the five-Buddha (*rig-nga*) headdress, and the invocations used to induce possession also have Buddhist elements.

A similar role to that of the *lhawa*, at a somewhat higher social level, is taken by the monastic spirit-mediums for the guardian deity (*sungma, chökyong*). These specialists, also generally referred to in Tibetan as *sungma* or *chökyong*, occasionally as *kuten* (support for the deity), are generally called oracle-priests in Western accounts. The best known of them is the principal state oracle of the Dalai Lama's government, often known as Nechung for the small monastery near Drepung where he resided until the Chinese occupation. This oracle, now at Dharamsala and consulted regularly by the Tibetan government-in-exile, is the voice of the important Tibetan protective deity Pehar, a deity who is held to be in origin a Tibetan regional deity but to be at an advanced stage on the path to Buddhahood. A number of other major monasteries have such spirit-mediums.

The role of the monastery or village temple in maintaining defences against hostile supernatural forces is acted out in the ritual dances (*cham*) which are performed, usually at least once annually by most monasteries of any size. While, as mentioned in Chapter 6, these are often associated with the killing of the anti-Buddhist emperor Langdarma by the monk Lhalung Pelgyi Dorjé, itself a kind of metaphorical statement of the overcoming of the forces of evil, they are really an acting out of the Tantric rituals of destruction of malevolent spirits, in which the deities of the *maṇḍala* are physically performed by masked dancers. As such they are related to other Tantric dance forms in Nepal, India, Sri Lanka and Indonesia. In pre-modern Tibet, these must have been very impressive spectacles, in which the Buddhist Tantric powers were brought to life before the eyes of the lay community. They usually form part of an extended sequence of rituals that also includes some kind of *tsewang* (long-life empowerment) or other ritual conveying healing and blessing to the lay community.

Figure 8.6 *Cham* ritual dance, Namdrolling, Bylakuppe, South India. Photo by Ruth Rickard (1991).

Rituals for prosperity, success and good fortune

Another major issue is providing for prosperity and good fortune. This is one function of maintaining good relations with local gods, performing *lungta* rituals and *sang* offerings, but it can also be approached directly through the Tantric practice of deities of success and good fortune. The best known of these are the various forms of Jambhala. Jambhala is also known as Vaiśravana. In this form, he is one of the Four Great Deva Kings, and so is represented with his jewel-producing mongoose in the entrance halls of many Tibetan temples. Rituals to Jambhala may be performed on behalf of the community or commissioned by individuals.

Another procedure to bring about prosperity and positive effects is the 'treasure vase' (*terbum*). These are vases filled with ritually-prepared ingredients, consecrated and placed within the earth so as to encourage positive influences. The idea is somewhat related to that of Chinese *fengshui*, and in fact there is a Tibetan tradition of siting places in relation to the landscape (*saché*) with considerable similarity to *fengshui*. Ritual objects such as *terbum*, or constructions such as *chorten* (*stūpa*), are part of this general mode of thought of ensuring positive flows of influence from the environment. A special class of *terbum*, the *norbum* or 'wealth vases', are specifically designed to attract wealth and prosperity. A number of monastic centres now make these commercially, and they can be ordered over the Internet. Such vases can also be made for other positive purposes. One of the major international Tibetan Buddhist organizations, Siddhartha's Intent, which is directed by Dzongsar Khyentse Rinpoche, has been engaged since 1991 in installing some six thousand treasure vases around the world in order to promote world peace.

Rituals for health and long life

An introduction to Tibetan medicine was given in Chapter 5. Tibetan medicine has some relationship with Buddhism, as many lamas were doctors, and some were also scholars in medical knowledge, and the medical texts have a strong Buddhist flavour and may be carried out in connection with Buddhist practice, particularly that relating to the Medicine Buddha (Menla). Tibetan medicines, which are mostly prepared from herbal and mineral ingredients, generally receive some kind of Buddhist consecration, which is thought to contribute to their efficacy. Essentially, though, Tibetan medicine is a medical system rather than a spiritual one.

Lamas are involved in the question of health in other ways as well, however. A particularly important aspect of Tibetan Tantric practice is concerned with the attainment of long life. There are numerous lineages and deities of this kind, although the three main long-life deities are generally given as White Tārā (Drolkar), Amitāyus (Tsepakmé) and Uṣṇiṣavijāya (Namgyelma) (see Figure 8.7). Of these, the rituals of White Tārā and Uṣṇiṣavijāya derive from India. Those of White Tārā centre on enclosing and protecting the life-energy of the individual; those of Uṣṇiṣavijāya provide blessing for long life and success. White Tārā is particularly associated with Atiśa, the Indian teacher who came to Tibet in the early eleventh century and whose students founded the Kadampa tradition.

Figure 8.7 Three long-life deities (White Tārā, Amitāyus, Uṣṇiṣavijāya). Gangteng Monastery, Pobjika, Bhutan. Photo by author (2009).

The Amitāyus practices by contrast seem to be mainly Tibetan in origin. While Amitāyus was a significant figure in the Indian context, he was identified closely with Amitābha, and the main emphasis was on rebirth in Amitābha's Western Paradise. In Tibet, while the connection with Amitābha never disappeared, Amitāyus seems to have developed a distinctive identity to do with the attainment of the *siddhi* of control over life and the attainment of immortality, itself one of the classic Indian *siddhis*. The first Amitāyus texts of this kind were *terma* texts discovered by the twelfth-century *tertön* Nyangrel Nyima Özer (1124–1192). He is one of the earliest important Buddhist *tertön* and was responsible for a *terma* biography of Padmasambhava in which Padmasambhava is described as having attained the *siddhi* of immortality, along with his Indian consort Mandāravā, through the practice of the deity Amitāyus, who appeared to them and conveyed the blessing of immortal life to them. Nyangrel Nyima Özer also provided a ritual text by which the practitioner could identify with Padmasambhava and Mandāravā, and invoke the blessing of Amitāyus. The practice involves a sequence in which the deteriorated life force is summoned back into a vase containing the life-giving elixir. This *tseguk* or 'life-recalling' sequence has strong shamanic overtones, and it became a central element of subsequent Amitāyus practices, eventually also being incorporated into White Tārā practices as well.

These *tsedrup* or '[immortal] life-realization' rituals are complex Tantric practices, and might be performed either in a retreat dedicated to long-life practice or as part of a longer retreat involving a variety of different practices. The questions arise both of where the whole focus on the *siddhi* of immortality comes from, and how the immortality that is attained might be understood. While the precise technique seems a Tibetan innovation, the emphasis on cultivation of immortality (not just of longevity), along with some aspects of the methods employed, is very reminiscent of Chinese 'inner alchemy' and *yangsheng* practices, and on the various Śaiva (Nāth) yoga practices, possibly derivative in part from these Chinese traditions, which became prominent in India in the eighth to tenth centuries. The pursuit of immortality itself seems to fit rather poorly into a Buddhist tradition that emphasizes the unreality of the self that is attempting to attain immortality, though the great Buddhist saint Nāgārjuna is said to have attained it. It is possible to argue that the true achievement of immortality is precisely the realization of the unreality of the finite mortal self. In practice, however, *tsedrup* are thought of not so much as conveying immortality as strengthening the life forces so that one's health is improved and one lives longer.

As mentioned above, the regular monastic festivals held in most major monasteries on one or more occasions each year generally also include a long-life empowerment (*tsewang*) or other empowerment intended to convey blessings of health and long life to the recipients. These use much the same techniques as the *tsedrup*, except that here the practice is being done on behalf of the community as a whole, and the life energies which are summoned back into the nectars and pills are distributed to the lay population. In fact healing and the maintenance of good health is a major concern of

Tibetan Buddhist practice, and the longevity rituals are a key part of this. One could say that they are a key component of the contract between Tibetan villages and their communities of Buddhist practitioners. Thus the large monastic festivals contain a sequence of 'receiving blessings', in which lay people line up to receive empowered pills and liquids and be touched on the head by various sacred objects by the leading lama or lamas of the community. These processes are often seen by the laity primarily in terms of long-life blessings.

Longevity practice is the most elaborate and complex of a whole series of ways in which lamas use Buddhist Tantric procedures in relation to medicine and healing. The generic idea here is that of the conveyance of power and blessing (*wang, chinlab*). These generally involve the 'charging up' or empowering of liquids and pills. The pills, as here, contain health-promoting substances in a generic sense but they are not really medicinal, since the focus here is on the conveyance of blessing and power.

For the most part, the *tsewang* are occasions for conveying health and long life to whoever comes along for a particular monastery festival or other event where the empowerment is given. There are however some exceptions. Thus *tsewang* are sometimes given nowadays in cases of serious illness or injury, sometimes in the hospital context. A variety of healing mantras can also be employed directly for healing, and in fact there are texts that go through the various disease categories in the *Gyüshi*, the main Tibetan medical text, providing appropriate mantras in each case.

Lamas and monasteries also act as providers of various other healing substances which are used more directly by lay people themselves for healing. These include blessed water, empowered medicinal pills and other substances, grains empowered by possessed oracle-priests, pieces of clothing from the clothes of revered lamas, and so on. This provision of healing substances by lamas has received relatively little attention in studies of Tibetan healing, but it is actually quite common and important within Tibetan communities today.

Divination and diagnosis

A final important topic for this chapter is that of divination (*mo*). Divination and astrology are key issues for the whole area of practical religion, since they help to generate both the sense of danger to be averted and a sense of control over it. We have already had some discussion of astrology, which can itself be considered as a form of divination, in Chapter 5, and of the spirit-mediums, who again have a role in divination, earlier in this chapter. Astrology, at least in its Tibetan form, is more technical than ritual, while spirit-mediumship works through the direct voice of a local deity.

Other forms of divination are more related to the world of Tantric practice, and involve the invocation of appropriate Tantric deities. There are both lay practitioners and also lama-practitioners, and the pair of photographs in Figure 8.8 depicts a lay diviner using one of the most common methods, counting off beads on a rosary. She

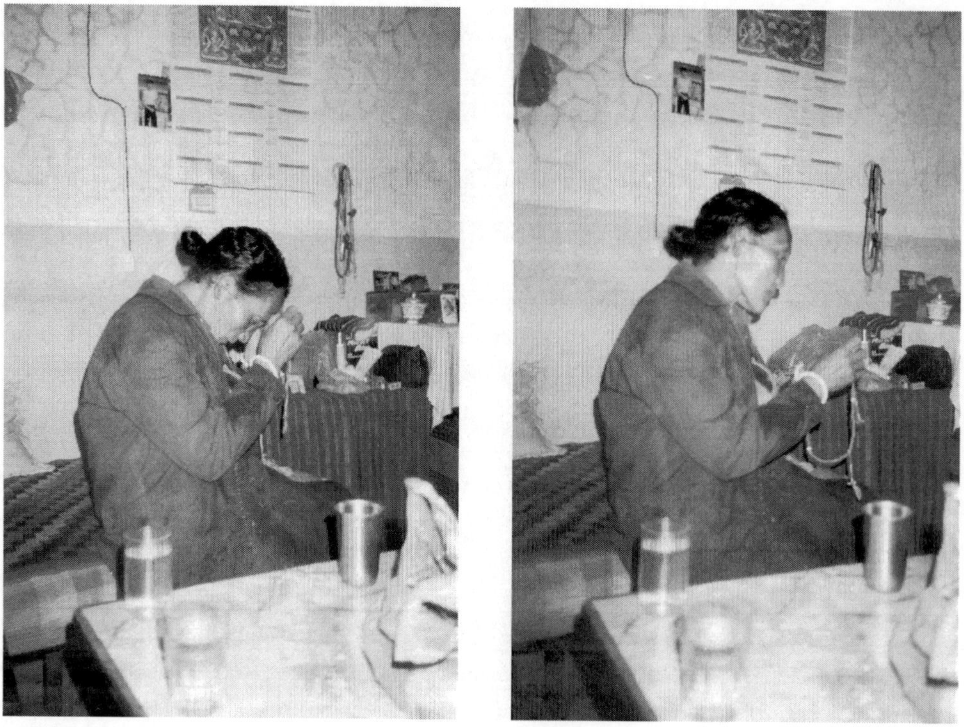

Figure 8.8 Ama Anga in Dalhousie. Photos by Linda Connor (1996).

is thought of as a holy and pious woman, and her ability to do *mo* (divination) is in part a reflection of this. As in other areas where there are both lay and specialist forms of practice, however, there is a sense that the whole business of divination is under the lama's general supervision. When Tibetans feel in need of a really accurate and convincing divination, they will go to an important lama who is known for his divinatory ability, rather than to a village lay diviner.

Lamas use a variety of techniques. A common one involves looking for images in a metal mirror, a practice (*prasena* in Skt., *tra* in Tibetan) that is often carried out in the context of a ritual to the goddess Dorjé Yudronma. Other more exotic methods include throwing dice, throwing knotted cords (*jutik*), and manipulating divinatory arrows (*damo*), a practice associated with the Tibetan epic hero Ling Gesar.

The point of *mo* or divination is not so much to predict the future as to find out what is the best course of action in particular circumstances. It is perhaps useful to compare divination to the question of diagnosis in both Tibetan and in Western medicine. They are perhaps more similar than might appear at first sight.

The Tibetan term that is translated as diagnosis is *chépa*, meaning distinction, differentiation, or analysis, and it is distinct from *mo*. Diagnosis or *chépa* is finding out the correct category in which to put the situation. The most important Tibetan diagnostic techniques are examination of the pulse, and examination of urine. Pulse diagnosis, as

Figure 8.9 Namka Drimé Rinpoche performing Gesar arrow divination. Photo by author (1990).

in Chinese and Indian traditional medicine, involves reading several different 'pulses' on the two wrists of the patients, each of which refers to different organs or regions within the body. The pulse can also indicate various kinds of disturbance of the three *nyépa*, the so-called 'humours', fundamental causal agents of illness in Tibetan medical tradition. Similar indications can be read from the colour, smell and appearance of the urine. All this enables the *amchi* or Tibetan doctor to place the patient's problem into a particular category, and so to prescribe an appropriate remedy.

The categories used by the *amchi* are not Western medical categories, and in some cases, for instance, go well beyond the boundaries of biomedicine. They include, for example, the activity of malevolent spirits. The connection between pulse and diagnostic category is also often difficult to trace in Western terms, but we at least have the possibility of a physiological linkage between pulse or urine on the one hand and organic disorder on the other. Here I leave aside such arcane matters as reading the pulse of one person on behalf of an absent family member, or using the pulse to predict the outcome of a military engagement in which the person whose pulse is being read will be engaged. These forms of pulse reading, while included in the *Gyüshi*, are rarely (if ever) practised today.

On the face of it, then, there is a distinction between *mo* and Tibetan medical diagnosis, and one might want to make a somewhat stronger distinction again between *mo* and Western (biomedical) diagnosis. It is nevertheless useful to see *mo* and medical diagnosis within the same general frame. Certainly, for contemporary Tibetans, both can be part of how people make decisions about treatment. People will often consult a lama for a *mo* in relation to serious medical issues. For example, during research I was involved in some years ago in a small Tibetan community in Dalhousie in northern India, Tibetans would routinely consult a diviner about whether a child should be born at home or in hospital, and if so which hospital. (Given the state of local medical facilities, the choice was a serious one.)

Mo can clearly take on awareness of wider social and cultural issues. For example, the Dalhousie lama gave a childbirth *mo* that suggested that a newly-arrived couple who spoke neither Hindi or English should go to the Tibetan biomedical hospital in Dharamsala (some fifty miles away by road) and should use a Tibetan taxi driver. Medical diagnosis too can be something of a compromise between cultural issues and the doctor's medical understanding.

If one looks at Western medical diagnosis in these terms, one can also see it less as the series of objective scientific judgements driven by empirical tests claimed for contemporary 'evidence-based' medicine, and more as a process of guesswork about possible outcomes as a result of particular choices. Even if one can be sure that the patient has pneumonia, not all cases of pneumonia have the same outcome, and the factors that might lead one way or another are difficult to quantify. There may also, within a medical system such as the UK National Health Service, where state-provided facilities are rationed in accordance with the nature of the patient's condition, be implications in making one or another diagnosis for the treatment that the patient receives. A contemporary Western biomedical practitioner might be more or less explicit about admitting such factors, and would be unlikely to consult a pack of tarot cards or copy of the *I Ching* to assist in the decision, but a comparison of this kind may help to render Tibetan divination less exotic and more comprehensible as a way of making important decisions in one's life. A comparison with consulting a Western financial adviser might be even closer, but I will leave readers to pursue such reflections themselves.

Tibetan ritual: pragmatic, karma-oriented and Bodhic dimensions

The material presented in this chapter has served to make the importance of the whole area of practical religion in Tibetan Buddhism very evident. One can speak of a 'pragmatic' aspect or dimension to Tibetan religion, which exists alongside though in close relationship to what could be called the 'Bodhic' aspect, which is oriented directly towards the attainment of Buddhahood. Those practices concerned primarily with improving one's karmic status and so one's prospects of a positive rebirth can perhaps be considered as constituting a third, intermediate, karma-oriented aspect or dimension.

It is worth adding that rituals and practices for pragmatic purposes are almost always justified and explained, to some degree at least, in terms of higher spiritual ends. The acquisition of health, long life and prosperity gives people the ability to commit themselves and their resources to serious Buddhist practice, while for the lama offering services of this kind is a way of attracting disciples who may then be encouraged to take on more spiritually-oriented teachings. There is little doubt that they are also valued by the recipients in this-worldly terms, and that this may be the primary reason for undertaking them. The nature of Tibetan Buddhist ritual and practice, growing as it does out of tradition which is based around the idea of esoteric knowledge and of secret, inner and higher teachings of all kinds, helps to avoid any overt contradiction. Tibetan practices regularly keep open multiple levels of meaning, and often allow the participants to undertake them for immediate practical benefit, for long-term personal spiritual benefit, or as part of the path to an attainment of Buddhahood so as to relieve the suffering of all beings, who are ultimately no different, and not separate, from oneself.

Key points you need to know

- A central issue for Tibetan Buddhists is the ritual management of Tantric power to protect the community and to maintain the health and prosperity of its members. This practical focus is something that Tibetan Buddhism shares with most pre-modern religions, and Tibetan Buddhism has retained it more than many other Buddhist traditions that have been more influenced by European, and specifically Protestant Christian, notions of religion.
- Historically, too, Tibetan Buddhism, with its heritage from Tantric Buddhism in India, has been more concerned with questions of everyday life than Buddhism in countries such as Sri Lanka or Thailand, where these were mostly the domain of parallel religious cults of this-worldly spirits and deities carried out by lay priests.
- As in other Buddhist countries, making offerings to Buddhist clergy (which in Tibet includes lamas as well as monks and nuns) is a primary way for lay people to gain merit or 'good karma' that will have positive effects in future lives. Lay people also regularly seek the assistance of Buddhist clergy at the time of death and for funerary rituals. Practices for guiding the consciousness of the dying person, including among others the rituals related to the so-called 'Tibetan Book of the Dead', are of considerable importance.

- Buddhist clergy are also primarily responsible for maintaining good relationships with the local spirits and deities. The role of clergy here differs from that of lay people; lay people make offerings to local gods and seek their protection, while lamas are expected to control the local gods and ensure their obedience through Buddhist Tantric power. Their ability to do this goes back to the original 'taming' of the local gods by Guru Padmasambhava.
- As with other Tibetan Buddhist rituals, however, these processes of 'taming' can be understood at a number of levels (usually classified as 'outer', 'inner' and 'secret').
- Lay shamanic specialists, such as the *lhawa* or spirit-mediums, provide a channel for communication with local deities, and also perform some ritual services, including the recovery of lost soul or spirit-essence (*la*). These specialists are generally trained under the supervision of lamas and are thought of as subject to their authority.
- Monastic festivals, including ritual dances (*cham*) and long-life empowerments (*tsewang*) are an important occasion for demonstrating and representing the ongoing exchanges between community and clergy. These and other rituals are concerned with the defence of the community against supernatural harm and the maintenance of the health, welfare and prosperity of its members. Long-life rituals include a more sophisticated version of the recovery of lost soul or spirit-essence (*la*) that is also performed by lay specialists.
- Divination is a major concern of Tibetan Buddhists and can be carried out by lamas as well as by lay diviners. It is concerned not so much with prediction as with deciding the best course of action in a particular situation.
- Tibetan Buddhist practices can be thought of as concerned with a variety of levels or spheres: pragmatic (this-worldly), karma-oriented (concerned with future lives), and Bodhic (concerned with the attainment of Buddhahood). All of these are important to Tibetans, and Tibetan religious practices can often be understood and practised at more than one, or all three, of these levels.

Discussion questions

1. How does Tibetan Buddhism combine the provision of practical solutions to everyday life problems with the maintenance of its orientation towards the attainment of Buddhahood and the liberation of all beings from suffering? Consider how these different aspects might be more significant for different people or at different times in their lives.
2. What do the lamas and monasteries offer to the lay population of Tibet?
3. Does divination make sense in the contemporary world?

Further reading

Beyer, Stephan. *The Cult of Tara: Magic and Ritual in Tibet*. Berkeley: University of California Press, 1973.

Blezer, Henk. *Kar gliṅ Źi khro: A Tantric Buddhist Concept*. Leiden: Research School CNWS, 1997.

Cabezón, José Ignacio (ed.). *Tibetan Ritual*. Oxford: Oxford University Press, 2010.

Cuevas, Bryan J. *The Hidden History of the Tibetan Book of the Dead*. New York: Oxford University Press.

DeCaroli, Robert D. *Haunting the Buddha: Indian Popular Religions and the Formation of Buddhism*. New York: Oxford University Press, 2004.

Dickman, Mike. *Treasure-Trove of Protections and Blessings: The Seven Chapter Prayer of Orgyen Rinpoche*. Brooklyn, NY: Cool Grove Press, 2004 [contains full translation of Dudjom's commentary on the *Barchad Kunsel*].

Dorje, Gyurme. *The Tibetan Book of the Dead: First Complete Translation*. Harmondsworth, UK: Penguin Classics, 2007.

Gouin, Margaret E. *Tibetan Rituals of Death: Buddhist Funerary Practices*. London: Routledge, 2010.

Karmay, Samten G. *The Arrow and the Spindle: Studies in History, Myths, Rituals and Beliefs in Tibet*. Vols 1 and 2. Kathmandu: Mandala Book Point, 1998 and 2005

Kohn, Richard J. *Lord of the Dance: The Mani Rimdu Festival in Tibet and Nepal*. Albany, NJ: State University of NY Press, 2000.

Lhalungpa, Lobsang P. *The Life of Milarepa*. A new translation. London: Paladin Books, 1979.

Lopez, Donald S., Jr. (ed.). *Religions of Tibet in Practice*. Princeton, NJ: Princeton University Press, 1997. (Princeton readings in religions series. Other translations can be found in other volumes in this series, including *Buddhism in Practice*, 1995 (ed. Donald S. Lopez) and *Tantra in Practice*, 2000 (ed. David Gordon White).)

Ortner, Sherry B. *Sherpas Through Their Rituals*. Cambridge: Cambridge University Press, 1978.

Ramble, Charles. *The Navel of the Demoness: Tibetan Buddhism and Civil Religion in Highland Nepal*. Oxford: Oxford University Press, 2007.

Woolf, Marsha and Karen Blanc. *The Rainmaker: The Story of Venerable Ngagpa Yeshe Dorje Rinpoche*. Boston: Sigo Press, 1994.

9 *Tibetan Buddhism and Tibetan identity*

In this chapter

This chapter is about Tibetan Buddhism's relation to questions of place and identity. The Tibetan sense of place has already come up in previous chapters, in relation to ideas of local gods, the taming of the land, and so on. Here, Tibetan ideas of place and identity will be dealt with more systematically. We will also look at how they contribute to Tibetan senses of identity, in relation to each other and to the surrounding world.

Main topics covered

- Tibetan identity
- Local and regional identity: local gods, lineages, clans, households
- Local and regional identity: Buddhist saints and pilgrimage sites
- Regional and national identity: Buddhism as a unifying factor
- The stories of Ling Gesar

Introduction

An initial question in relation to Tibetan identity might be, how far were Tibetans conscious of themselves as 'Tibetans'? The answer, for pre-modern times, is probably only to a limited degree. Much of the Tibetan sense of place is quite locally grounded, so that people were more likely to think of themselves in terms of local or regional identities than in terms of Tibet as a whole. While Tibetan regions have had a common written language, and a generally shared set of cultural items, for many centuries, there is also much local variation. The spoken language varies considerably and the major dialects are not immediately mutually intelligible.

There is of course a Tibetan name for Tibet as a whole, *Böd*, the root from which terms in other languages such as Bhotia and Tibet derive, but for people in many parts of Tibet this term referred primarily to Central Tibet (Ü-Tsang). In many areas things were much more local. People identified much more strongly with the traditional kingdoms, regions, and petty states: Pagshöd, Derge, Shigatse or Lhodrak. On the edges of the Tibetan cultural region to the south, east and northeast there were communities with mixed and complex ethnicity, including peoples such as the Gurung and Tamang to the south in Nepal; Yi, Naxi, and Mosuo to the southeast in Yunnan, the people of the Gyelrong area in the east, and Mongols and Turkic-derived groups (*Hor*), as well as the various Tu or Monguor people, in the northeast. People living in these areas might identify more with the wider community than with specific ethnicity, especially as Tibetan Buddhism provided a substantial shared cultural heritage across these ethnic boundaries.

Tibetan nationalism in any strong sense is a recent creation, as with nationalisms in most parts of the world. Nationalisms in the modern sense got going in nineteenth-century Europe, and gradually spread elsewhere, mainly to begin with in urban populations. In the Tibetan case, the growth of a Tibetan national consciousness can first be seen in the writings of the radical Gelukpa monk, scholar and political activist, Gendün Chöpel (1903–51). It was Gendün Chöpel who first popularized the idea of a 'Greater Tibet' or *Böd chenpo*. It is probably significant that Gendün Chöpel lived in Rebkong, an particularly ethnically complex area of Amdo (Northeast Tibet), which had also been subjected to bloodthirsty campaigns by Chinese Muslim (Hui) warlords of Qinghai, including the notorious Ma Bufang, in the early twentieth century. The villages in the Rebkong region also had a mythology of descent from the army of Songtsen Gampo back in the seventh century and from survivors of other later campaigns.

There were, however, shared and integrative factors across the entire Tibetan cultural region, including Tibetan Buddhism itself.

Buddhism in Tibetan is *nangpé sangyepé chö* – the Buddhist dharma of the insiders – where *nang* means 'inside'. *Nangpa*, 'insider', unqualified, often means 'Tibetan', though there are of course other people who are Buddhist as well, including the Mongolians who belong to the same tradition of Buddhism as the Tibetans. The opposition between 'outside' and 'inside', *chi* and *nang*, is significant in Tibetan culture and society, linking among other things to the importance of the household, and of belonging to a household (again, being a *nangpa* or 'insider') and so being part of a Tibetan community. It is also often developed in Buddhist contexts into a threefold division (*chi nang sang*, outer, inner and secret, with 'secret' frequently meaning Tantric). Buddhist practices are often classified using this 'outer, inner, secret' structure, and interpretations of a particular practice may also be classified as 'outer, inner and secret'.

Another significant usage of this division is in relation to *namtar* or biographical texts (including hagiographies and autobiographies). *Namtar* literally implies an account of the individual's progress towards liberation, and this is the proper focus of such a Tibetan biographical account, although in practice many other kinds of events and concerns may be included. *Namtar* are often classified as 'outer', 'inner' and 'secret', where 'outer' refers to external events, 'inner' to teachings received and other formal events in one's spiritual life, and 'secret' to the progress to Buddhahood via Tantric practice, revelations from deities and the like. This concept of *namtar* also gives a sense of some of the concerns that might be part of a normative sense of identity in Tibetan culture.

The sense of Buddhism as being 'our religion', in some sense a special Tibetan inheritance, is taken up in a classic nineteenth-century Buddhist treatise, the *Kunsang Lamé Shellung*, with the idea that now that India has been taken over by non-Buddhists, Tibet has taken over its role as a 'central country' where Buddhism is protected. However, while all this encourages a sense of Buddhism as something shared by Tibetans, 'insider' is not that strong a category here, given the missionary aspects of Buddhism in Mongolia, Yunnan and elsewhere. Tibetan Buddhism has always been a missionary religion to a significant degree, both in terms of its overall ideology and in terms of the activities of individual lamas to build up their followings by expanding into new territories, and today's 'outsiders' are potentially at least tomorrow's 'insiders'.

Local and regional identity: local gods, lineages, clans, households

When we turn to look at the sense of place in a more local sense, however, Buddhism can enter into the issue much more directly. The Tibetan landscape is in part mapped and understood in specifically Buddhist terms, as having numerous places within it where Buddhist power can be accessed in some way, and which are generally associated with great lamas and practitioners of the past. However, not all Tibetan ideas of place and identity are necessarily Buddhist, and we need to spend some time looking at some of those that are not primarily Buddhist in order to understand how they and the more Buddhist conceptions relate and are interwoven in practice.

It should be made clear that we do not have a clear and straightforward story here. Reconstructing early Tibetan ideas about place, deity and identity is much like reconstructing similar issues in early mediaeval Britain or Ireland. There are fragments of history, fragments of myth, by no means all consistent with each other, and written down for the most part hundreds of years after the events they refer to, or claim to refer to. Also, whereas in Western Europe there is a reasonably clear archaeological record, Tibetan archaeology is in a much more basic state, so the archaeological record cannot so easily be used as a background into which the cultural fragments might be fitted. However, there is enough to suggest, at least, various ideas around which early Tibetan concepts of place and spirit seem to cohere.

The local gods have already been mentioned several times in this book. Various elements in early Tibetan material and in Tibetan folklore suggest a close link between people and the spirit world in earlier times. These include the *la* concept, mentioned in Chapter 8 in the context of healing. The *la* was there described as a kind of separable soul. There is more to be said about the *la*, though many of the ideas about it seem to have been more significant, and meaningful in a different way, in the earlier material. Thus the *la* in the Tibetan epic poems associated with the heroic figure Ling Gesar (see later) often has an external residence. This may be a turquoise, worn by the person, but can also be some separate object. This allows for a person to be attacked and weakened by destroying the external residence of his or her *la*, a common theme in the epic.

There is also the practice, still prevalent in parts of Tibet, of a *la*-tree being planted at the birth of a child. Communities too have *la*-lakes and *la*-mountains. If the level of the water in the lake is low, that can mean trouble for the community. The lake can also be a means of divination, because of its links to the people with whose *la* it is connected. This is the case, for example, with the Lame Latso lake in Central Tibet, where lamas traditionally go for visions to help them discover rebirths of the Dalai Lama and other high lamas. Damage to the lake could threaten the community. This has been a theme in relation to recent Chinese government plans to use significant Tibetan holy lakes for hydroelectric power schemes.

Figure 9.1 *Lungta* by sacred lake in Sikkim. Photo by Ruth Rickard (2011).

It is significant that lakes and mountains also have indwelling deities (*lha*). The relationship between *lha* and *la* appears close, especially in the early textual material such as the Dunhuang texts, and the words are also sometimes spelled alike, although not normally in modern Tibetan. Another area where there appears to be an overlap between *lha* and *la* concepts is that of the *gowé lha*, a set of five protective gods associated with each person. Lists vary but they typically include the god of the region (*yül lha*), the god of the father or lineage, god of the mother or home, and warrior god (*drabla*). They are sometimes thought of as residing in parts of the body, and also as responsible for the general good fortune of the individual. While this set of gods is still invoked in contexts such as wedding speeches, and there are some ritual texts for it, it seems fairly residual in recent centuries. It nevertheless points to the close relationship between the concepts of *la* and *lha*, particularly when it is remembered that these deities are generally mountain or lake gods. The claims by the Tibetan emperors and old aristocratic families of descent from the mountain gods also suggests some feeling of overlap, if not an original identity, between these concepts. So perhaps does the basic Tibetan purificatory practice of *sangchö*, in which offerings of scented smoke to the local deities is seen as bringing about purification and restoring the proper order of things.

One possible reading of all this material, as I suggested some years ago, is that the earlier relationship was something like that in much Aboriginal Australian cosmology. In other words, people, at any rate in earlier times, felt a strong connection, verging on partial identity, with locality, and they felt that they were in a sense

Figure 9.2 The mountain deity of Yarlha Shampo, Central Tibet. This was the ancestral mountain god of the Yarlung dynasty of Tibetan emperors. Photo by author (1987).

out there in the physical landscape as well as within their material bodies, that they were in a sense projections or children of the powers of the landscape. Thus *sangchö* was in a sense purifying both landscape and oneself at the same time, and bringing individual and land back into proper relationship.

Tibetan ideas of clan and lineage, and of the household, have already been mentioned, but some further discussion is required. The clan and lineage component to Tibetan society today is strongest among the nomadic pastoralists (*drokpa*). In agricultural areas, the basis of the social structure is more the ongoing continuity of the household through time than that of the clan. In the terms explored in some of the late work of the French anthropologist Claude Lévi-Strauss, Tibetan agricultural societies could be described as house-based. 'House' here has the sense of an ongoing household based around elements of descent but primarily concerned with the continuity of property. Lévi-Strauss regarded house-based societies as a 'hybrid, transitional form between kin-based and class-based social orders'. In the European and Japanese cases that are most familiar, these are mostly aristocratic households, but this is not necessarily the case. In Tibet, house organization can be found in relation to the Tibetan nobility, but also a more egalitarian style of house organization exists

Figure 9.3 House in Central Tibet. Photo by Ruth Rickard (2006).

at the village level. This is a pattern that seems to spread over into the Southeast Asian highlands. It may be significant that house-based village organization is a way of running things without the need for much direct state involvement.

Thus in Tibetan society one belongs to a village through belonging to a house that is part of that village. The major houses of the village are generally regarded as equal in status, with ritual and administrative duties rotating around them on a regular basis, though there are often also other houses of lesser or marginal status, generally thought of as having arrived later than the founders of the main houses. However, houses are also tied up to kinship groups, since a household is ideally linked to a particular lineage, which is also linked to the worship of specific lineage deities. We will have more about this aspect of kinship in a little while, but variants of the key Tibetan term for lineage (*rü, rüpa*) are found throughout Tibet. *Rü* literally means 'bone' and the idea here is that the bones come from the father, the flesh from the mother. *Papün* – literally 'father-brother' – is another term for patrilineal groups. In some regions, such as Ladakh (where the pronunciation is *paspun*), these groups gather together for worship of lineage deities and on other occasions.

There is a feeling here that some kind of power, ability, and intrinsic nature is passed down the lineage. Thus a good doctor (*amchi*) should come from a lineage of *amchi*, and Tantric ability is passed down through lama lineages. Many of the older lama lineages were also significant aristocratic lineages. Similarly *low* status is also passed down through lineage, with communities of blacksmiths and other low status groups being regarded as intrinsically lower in nature. This is not quite the Indian caste system, but it has some similarities with it, particularly in the way in which status differentiation is signalled through the refusal of high-status people to share a drinking vessel with low-status people. So we have here a stratified society with continuity, and religious obligations, such as sponsoring and arranging major village festivals, rotating around the major households of the village.

There are some wider frameworks of ideas surrounding the clans and lineages. We have already met the idea of the six original Tibetan clans (in some other accounts they are four) descending from Avalokiteśvara, in the form of the monkey-*bodhisattva*, and the rock-demoness. The story tells how the monkey-*bodhisattva* retreated to the isolated regions of Tibet in order to meditate. A local demoness became enamoured of him, and he gave in to her demands for sex when she threatened suicide. The Tibetans inherit their religious nature from the father's side, and their rough and aggressive character from the mother's side. It is hard to know for certain whether the monkey and rock demoness predate the Buddhist story, though it scarcely sounds like something that would have been made up as part of a myth of Avalokiteśvara.

In fact there are both non-Buddhist and Buddhist versions of these narratives. The non-Buddhist ones tend to start with one or more cosmic eggs, possibly an Indian theme, which break open, hatching out ancestral deity figures. We will see a version of such a cosmology in Chapter 11.

Local and regional identity: Buddhist saints and pilgrimage sites

The story of the monkey-*bodhisattva* is probably an example of how clan and lineage chronicles gradually acquired Buddhist elements. Another important Buddhist theme that entered fairly early on into Tibetan senses of their history has already been mentioned, the story of Padmasambhava's epic process through the land of Tibet, in which he subdued and tamed the mountain deities at a sequence of name places, has already been mentioned. There are also many cave sites in Tibet and the Himalayas where Padmasambhava is said to have meditated, as well as other sites associated with the religious activities of other famous saints and high lamas. This provides an alternative mode of sacralizing to the old mountain-god narratives. Major pilgrimage sites such as the sacred mountains of Kailash (Gangri Tise in Tibetan) or Tsari have also been connected with sets of Tantric sacred sites such as the twenty-four sites of the Cakrasamvara Tantra. The original locations of these places cannot all be clearly identified, but they seem to have all been in South Asia (Bangladesh, North India and Pakistan). A series of duplicate sites were identified within Tibet, where they were accessible for Tibetan pilgrims.

The resultant network of associations that can be built up can be seen in an area like Lahul. This small region, Tibetan Buddhist by religion though only partly Tibetan linguistically, is now located in India, immediately north of the Kulu Valley

Figure 9.4 Cave associated with the female saint Machik Labdrön , near Taktsang, Paro, Bhutan. Photo by author (2009).

in Himachal Pradesh. It has an old-style mountain god (Gephan) with a myth linking him to other local gods, but is nowadays regarded as a land specially associated with the *ḍākinis*, and is centred on a holy mountain from the Cakrasamvara cycle (Drilburi). The location was sacralized through a famous early Drukpa Kagyüdpa lama, Gödtsangpa. It renewed its links to the Drukpa in more recent times when two local men went to study with a distinguished Drukpa Kagyüdpa lama, Śākya Śrī, in Eastern Tibet, returning to become lamas of local monasteries. In the 1960s Apo Rinpoche, one of Śākya Śrī's grandsons, settled in the area after leaving Tibet as a refugee. He built a monastery near Manali in the Kulu Valley and also took over Kardang Gompa in Lahul proper. His son, Se Rinpoche, is the senior lama at both monasteries today.

Regional and national identity: Buddhism as a unifying factor

The stories of the early Tibetan emperors (*tsenpo*) also act as something of a unifying mythos. This term *tsenpo*, which is not the normal Tibetan word for king (*gyelpo*), is applied only to these early rulers, many of whom also have the syllable *tsen* in their name (e.g. Song-*tsen* Gampo, Trisong De-*tsen*). *Tsen* is also the name of a powerful class of gods. Some years ago, Chris Beckwith suggested that the term 'emperor' was a better English translation, and certainly the last few members of the series both ruled over substantial multi-ethnic empires in their own right and dealt with the Chinese emperors on terms of equality.

There are numerous versions of the legends of the Tibetan *tsenpo*, with considerable inconsistencies between them, and difficulties in making a clear and coherent narrative out of them. These stories were assembled many years ago by the Scandinavian Tibetanist Erik Haarh. There are thirty or so named *tsenpo*, depending on which version of the list one uses, between the first, Nyatri Tsenpo, and Songtsen Gampo, the relatively historical founder of the Tibetan empire in the early seventh century. The first *tsenpo*, Nyatri Tsenpo, is sometimes described as being of divine origin, but there are also versions of the story in which he is a member of the Licchavi dynasty to which Śākyamuni Buddha belonged. The Licchavi were in fact a branch of the 'Lunar Dynasty' of eastern India, which supplied most of the Jain Tīrthaṅkaras (the Jaina equivalents to the Buddhas) and many famous Hindu figures, including the deity Rāma. At any rate, Nyatri Tsenpo is described as being chosen by the local rulers, heads of the various local clans or ruling families, to be their king. All this is still very much in the realm of myth and legend.

The first seven kings are called the 'seven heavenly kings' and are said to have been connected to the heavens by a cord. Rather than dying, they ascended to heaven by means of the cord when their sons were old enough to take over. The eighth king, Drigum, was responsible for the breaking of this connection with the divine, by instigating a battle with the clan-heads in which he was killed and the cord cut, and subsequent kings were buried in massive tomb-mounds. Many of these tombs survive, although the tombs were all raided and little is left of the contents.

By the seventh century, our accounts of the dynasty are clearly historical. The major figure of the early seventh century, Songtsen Gampo, carved out a substantial empire, including almost the whole of the region where Tibetans now live, and established his capital at Lhasa. Among other things he defeated Ligmincha, king of the rather shadowy but also presumably historical neighbouring state of Shangshung, and incorporated Shangshung into his empire. Shangshung is a particularly significant region for the origins of the Bon religion, the pre-Buddhist religion that is discussed in Chapter 11.

Tibetan historical accounts say that contacts with Buddhism began several kings before Songtsen Gampo, when a casket containing the text of a Buddhist Sūtra magically descended on the then king's palace. Songtsen Gampo is also regarded as an Avalokiteśvara manifestation and a patron of Buddhism. His two principal wives were from Nepal and China, and are described as being responsible for the first substantial introduction of Buddhism to Tibet. Both brought Buddha images that were placed in temples in Lhasa. The local gods of Tibet resisted the construction of the main temple, at the site which is now known as the Jokang, and on the advice of the Chinese queen who was skilled in *fengshui*, a series of twelve temples were built to nail down the land of Tibet, conceived of as a demoness lying on her back. They consisted of four *runon* or 'district controlling' temples on the shoulders and

Figure 9.5 Tomb of an early Tibetan king, Yarlung Valley. Photo by author (1987).

hips, four *tadul* or 'border taming' temples on the elbows and knees, and four *yangdul* ('further taming') temples on the hands and feet. Tratruk Gompa (Figure 7.1) was originally one of these temples.

While some of the temples undoubtedly go back to the early empire (seventh to ninth centuries CE), these accounts derive from much later *terma* sources. It is clear nevertheless from inscriptions of the royal period that Songtsen Gampo was regarded as being responsible for the introduction of Buddhism into Tibet.

In fact it seems likely that while there was some state patronage for Buddhism at the time of Songtsen Gampo, court ritual remained as a whole non-Buddhist. The next major step was in the late eighth century, at the time of Emperor Trisong Detsen, when the first Tibetan monastery was formed. There is more legend and story here, involving the building of the first Tibetan monastery (Samye) under the direction of the Indian abbot Śāntarakṣita, more resistance from the local spirits and also from non-Buddhist ministers at court, and the invitation of the Tantric guru Padmasambhava from India. This was the occasion for the previously-mentioned 'taming' of the Tibetan landscape in the form of the heroic journey of Padmasambhava, encountering the deities in each place and requiring them to submit to the power of the Buddha Dharma. The imperial dynasty's control over Tibet collapsed a couple of generations later, though a number of local rulers and aristocratic families continued to claim descent from the imperial family.

What is clear in the following period is that descent from the early imperial dynasty was a meaningful issue, and that it provided one of a number of possible centres of focus for the construction of authority in the subsequent years. However, though the dynasty and the early empire were often referred to, they never really provided the basis for creating an effective new Tibetan state. The nearest that the Tibetans came to this was the identification of the Dalai Lamas as rebirths of Songtsen Gampo.

This was however some way ahead when Buddhism first entered Tibet. What is striking is the kind of break with past conceptions of identity that was created by the arrival of Buddhism. Unlike Japan, where local gods were reinterpreted as versions of Buddhist Tantric deities, the idiom in Tibet was that the local gods were lesser beings, and were retained in a subordinate position. Buddhist preaching concentrated on a simple theme: the gods cannot help you in the next life – only the Buddhist priests can help ensure a successful rebirth. One text that survives in quite a few versions is a 'Story of the Cycle of Birth and Death' found in nine Dunhuang manuscripts. It describes the death of one of the gods, following which the deity's son, who is the central character in the story, travels in search of a spiritual teacher who can restore his father to life. Eventually he meets the Buddha, who tells him that nobody can escape the action of karma, and that only the Buddhist teachings and virtuous action are of any use in the face of death. These can help one to avoid the lower rebirths. Other Dunhuang texts have a similar message: only the teaching of the Buddha is powerful enough to protect one from birth and death.

These texts also present Buddhists as powerful magic-workers. It was clearly not enough to claim special jurisdiction in the area of birth and death. The Buddhists had to be able to compete successfully in relation to everyday this-worldly ritual too. We have seen something in the previous chapters of how they did this. This is of course a key element in relation to the Padmasambhava narrative, and Padmasambhava became as it were the primal shaman from whom derived the ability of later lamas to control the forces of the Tibetan environment.

The classic presentation of the new position came with one of the most important of *terma* or visionary texts, the *Mani Kabum*, held to have been discovered in several sections between the eleventh and twelfth centuries. In it, Songtsen Gampo is presented as an emanation of the *bodhisattva* Avalokiteśvara, and his two wives (the Chinese and Nepalese princesses) as the goddesses Tārā and Bhṛkuṭī. This is the first text as far as we know to do this, and also the first to present Avalokiteśvara as the monkey-ancestor of the Tibetan people and indeed as specially linked to the Tibetan people. This is the connection that was eventually transformed into the idea of the Dalai Lamas as emanations of Avalokiteśvara, and so as the personal representative of the protective role of the deity of compassion. The *Mani Kabum* also includes ritual texts centring on Avalokiteśvara and teaching his famous six-syllable mantra, *oṃ maṇi padme hūṃ*.

The Stories of Ling Gesar

The stories of the epic hero, Ling Gesar, seem to represent an intermediate stage between the narratives of the mountain gods and the Buddhist-inspired stories of Avalokiteśvara and the early kings. While known throughout Tibet, they are most significant today in East and Northeast Tibet (Kham and Amdo) and in Ladakh in the far west. They are performed unaccompanied as a sequence of spoken narratives and songs for the principal characters, with a complete episode taking one or more days to recite. There are around eight or ten central episodes, but there are also many additional episodes – so many that there have been attempts to claim the epic as the longest in the world. Performances may be read from manuscripts, block-prints or modern printed versions, but the most prestigious singers, the *babdrung*, are inspired bards who are thought of as seeing the story directly through a kind of shamanic vision.

The epic appears to consist of a variety of early narrative elements that have been reshaped into the form of epic ballads and stories. The name Gesar ultimately appears to derive from Caesar, through a number of intermediary steps. Ling Gesar however is a fully Tibetan character and is now identified in East Tibet at any rate with a Tibetan ruler of the tenth or eleventh century. Gesar nevertheless retains the epithet *masang*, a term for a phase of not-quite-human beings in early Tibetan history. In Eastern Tibet, the events of the story are said to have taken place in that region.

Figure 9.6 Painting of Ling Gesar in possession of Namka Drimé Rinpoche, Chandragiri, Orissa. Photo by author (1990).

Kings of Ling claimed descent from Gesar's half-brother, and numerous other aristocratic families claim to go back to the warriors who were Gesar's companions.

The Gesar stories have been influenced by Buddhism, and Gesar himself is described as a Buddhist lama and a regent or agent of Padmasambhava and Avalokiteśvara. The legend is very widely spread throughout Tibet, and sites associated with Gesar are found throughout Tibetan regions from the far west to the Himalayas to the east (Kham). Very divergent places claim to be the site of Gesar's birth, and locations throughout the Tibetan region are associated with events from the story, much like the way in which locations throughout Britain are associated with Arthur and Merlin. Figure 9.7 shows a rock in the Kulu Valley that is identified locally as the wife of the demon king of the North, Lutsen, a significant character in one of the core episodes of the epic, turned into stone by Gesar. Nearby marks on the hills were made by Gesar's horse, while a Hindu temple further down the valley is identified as the *stūpa* beneath which Lutsen himself was buried.

Figure 9.7 Rock in Kulu Valley, identified with the demoness in the Gesar story. Photo by author (1992).

The epic was also adopted in Mongolia, where it is one of several major epic narratives. In Tibet, it is really the only extant epic story, except to the extent that stories of religious heroes such as Padmasambhava, Milarepa or Tönpa Shenrab constitute an alternative. However these narratives are not performed in epic style, and are much more explicitly Buddhist (or in the case of Tönpa Shenrab, Bonpo) in tone and content.

Gesar himself is a divine emanation, and is counselled by the mountain goddess Manene. There is a lot of intriguing detail here, especially in relation to Gesar's wars with surrounding peoples, and I have written about all this at some length elsewhere. Gesar, though described as a *gyelpo* or king, is the ruler of an alliance of pastoralist tribes much more than the king of a centralized state. In the later episodes of the epic, he defeats the rulers of various surrounding peoples – Bhutanese (Mönpa), Mongolians, Kashmiris, and so on – but rather than these people being taken over as part of his kingdom, they become allies who assist him in future campaigns. He is far less thoroughly incorporated into Buddhism than the other great prototype of Tibetan kingship, Songtsen Gampo. Gesar is a creative trickster figure as much as a lama, and he seems to represent an alternative Tibetan identity, one less incorporated into the state, perhaps, for all that he himself is a king and link to the origin of a dynasty of kings. The parallel status of Gesar and Songtsen Gampo is illustrated in Tibetan wedding rituals, which are characteristically modelled on one or the other.

Conclusion

This chapter has shown the local and partial nature of these various pre-modern narratives of identity, nationality and the state. What one sees are fragments of models and ideas that are combined in different ways in different Tibetan communities, pastoralist and agriculturalist, centralized and stateless. What is noticeable throughout is the way in which Tibetan Buddhism has become interwoven in many ways with the sense of being Tibetan and, to a degree at least, though the Avalokiteśvara narratives and their adoption by the Fifth Dalai Lama and the Gelukpa state, become identified with a kind of Tibetan proto-nationalist story. In more recent times, one can see the Thirteenth Dalai Lama's attempts to create a relatively unified state, and the emergence with Gendün Chöpel and a few others of a sense of Tibetan national identity, in the 1920s. But it was really Chinese policy towards Tibet, initially in the form of the Qinghai warlords of the early twentieth century, and then of the Chinese People's Republic, that created a true Tibetan nationalism, by drastically changing the rules of engagement between China and Tibet. No previous Chinese state had attempted to impose control over people's day-to-day existence in Tibet, either within the Lhasa state or in the Tibetan regions of Qinghai, Sichuan, Gansu and Yunnan where more than half the Tibetan population of the People's Republic now lives.

Gesar has been picked up both as a religious and a political figure in recent years, by Tibetan lamas and by elements among the political resistance to Chinese rule. Avalokiteśvara had the leading role, however, with the assumption by the Fourteenth Dalai Lama in the late twentieth century of a largely successful role as leader of the Tibetan people. Thus the narratives of the *Maṇi Kabum* and other Tibetan histories eventually provided the basis for the genuine Tibetan nationalism that has been brought into being by the resistance to Chinese rule.

The next chapter, Chapter 10, deals with issues relating to gender and Tibetan Buddhism.

Key points you need to know

- Tibetan identity was mostly regional or local until recent times. Nationalism, as elsewhere in the world, was largely a modern invention. However, Tibetan regions as a whole had a common written language, a largely shared religion and many shared cultural items.
- Local and regional identity was linked with cults of local and household deities, and local sacred places. The *la* or spirit-essence was thought of as connected with the surrounding environment. Aristocratic families often claimed descent from local mountain gods. *Sang*-offerings to the local gods

remain an important part of Tibetan religion, often carried out in a style strongly influenced by Buddhism.

- Households are an important building block of Tibetan communities and the continuation of households through time is a significant value. Lineage or family descent is also important, especially among the nomadic pastoralist communities.
- Many important pilgrimage sites throughout Tibet and the Himalayas are linked to important Tibet-wide figures of history and legend, including Guru Padmasambhava and the epic hero Ling Gesar.
- Tibetan nationalism began to develop in the 1920s, but has become a significant force mainly in resistance to Chinese rule from the 1950s onwards.

Discussion questions

1 How significant was 'Tibet' for Tibetan identity in pre-modern times? How significant was 'Buddhism'?
2 Discuss how ideas about local gods and spirits linked Tibetans to their environment.
3 How did Tibetan nationalism develop in modern times?

Further reading

Bernbaum, Edwin. *The Way to Shambhala*. Garden City, NY: Anchor Press, 1980.

Blondeau, Anne-Marie (ed.). *Tibetan Mountain Deities, their Cults and Representations*. Vienna: Verlag der Österreichischen Akademie der Wissenschaften, 1998.

Blondeau, Anne-Marie and Ernst Steinkellner (eds). *Reflections of the Mountain: Essays on the History and Social Meaning of the Mountain Cult in Tibet and the Himalaya*. Vienna: Verlag der Österreichischen Akademie der Wissenschaften, 1996.

Buffetrille, Katia and Hildegard Diemberger (eds). *Territory and Identity in Tibet and the Himalayas*. Leiden: Brill, 2002.

Buffetrille, Katia. *Pèlerins, Lamas et Visionnaires: Sources Orales et Écrites sur les Pèlerinages Tibétains*. Vienna: Arbeitskreis für Tibetische und Buddhistische Studien, Universität Wien, 2000.

Carsten, Janet and Stephen Hugh-Jones (eds). *About the House: Lévi-Strauss and Beyond*. New York and Cambridge: Cambridge University Press, 1995.

David-Neel, Alexandra and Lama Yongden. *The Superhuman Life of Gesar of Ling the Legendary Tibetan Hero, as Sung by the Bards of his Country*. London: Rider & Co, 1933.

Diemberger, H. 'Montagnes sacrées, os des ancêstres, sang maternel – le corps humain dans une communauté tibétaine du Nepal (les Khumbo)' in M. Godelier and M. Panoff (eds). *La Production du Corps*. Paris: Èditions des Archives Contemporaines, 1998.

Dowman, Keith. *The Power-Places of Central Tibet. The Pilgrim's Guide*. London: Routledge and Kegan Paul, 1988.

Ferrari, Alfonsa. *Mk'yen Brtse's Guide to the Holy Places of Central Tibet*. Rome: IsMEO, 1958.

Gardner, Alexander. 'The twenty-five great sites of Khams: a narrative map of an imperiled place', in Wim van Spengen and Lama Jabb (eds), *Studies in the History of Eastern Tibet*. Halle: International Institute for Tibetan and Buddhist Studies. 2009.

Gutschow, Niels, Axel Michaels and Charles Ramble (eds). *Sacred Landscape in the Himalaya*. Vienna: Verlag der Österreichischen Akademie der Wissenschaften, 2003.

Haarh, Erik. *The Yarlung Dynasty*. Copenhagen: G.E.C. Gad's Forlag, 1969.

Huber, Toni. *The Cult of Pure Crystal Mountain: Popular Pilgrimage and Visionary Landscape in Southeast Tibet*. New York and Oxford: Oxford University Press, 1999.

Huber, Toni (ed.). *Sacred Spaces and Powerful Places in Tibetan Culture*. Dharamsala: Library of Tibetan Works and Archives, 1999.

Kapstein, Matthew. 'Remarks on the *Maṇi bKa'-'bum* and the cult of Avalokiteśvara in Tibet', in Steven D. Goodman and Ronald M. Davidson (eds). *Tibetan Buddhism: Reason and Revelation*. Albany, NY: State University of NY Press, 1992.

Karmay, Samten G. *The Arrow and the Spindle: Studies in History, Myths, Rituals and Beliefs in Tibet, Volume 1*. Kathmandu: Mandala Book Point, 1998.

Macdonald, Alexander W. (ed.). *Mandala and Landscape*. Reprinted Delhi: D.K. Printworld, 2007.

McKay, Alex (ed.). *Pilgrimage in Tibet*. Richmond, Surrey: Curzon, 1998.

Sagant, Philippe, 'With head held high: the house, ritual and politics in East Nepal.' *Kailash*, Vol. 12, pp. 161–222.

Samuel, Geoffrey, 'Ge-sar of gLing: the origins and meanings of the East Tibetan epic', in Geoffrey Samuel, *Tantric Revisionings: New Understandings of Tibetan Buddhism and Indian Religion*, Delhi: Motilal Banarsidass, 2005.

Stein, R.A. *L'Épopée Tibétaine de Gesar dans sa Version Lamaïque de Ling*. Paris: Presses Universitaires de France, 1956.

Wylie, Turrell V. *The Geography of Tibet according to the 'Dzam-gLing-rGyas-bShad*. Rome, IsMEO, 1962.

Zangpo, Ngawang. *Sacred Ground: Jamgon Kongtrul on 'Pilgrimage and Sacred Geography'*. Ithaca, NY & Boulder, CO: Snow Lion Publications, 2001.

10 *Tibetan Buddhism, women and gender*

In this chapter

The main focus of this chapter is on women in Tibetan society and women in Tibetan Buddhism, though we will also be looking briefly at the construction of masculinity in Tibetan society and in Tibetan Buddhism, since the gender roles of women and men in Tibetan society as elsewhere form a total picture and cannot be considered in isolation from each other.

Main topics covered

- Gender in Tibetan society
- Women's religious roles within Indian Buddhism
- Women religious roles within Tibetan Buddhism
  - Women as lay patrons
  - Women as monastics
  - Women as yogic practitioners
  - Women as Tantric consorts (*sangyum, kandroma*)
  - Women as hereditary lamas

Introduction

The growth of the women's movement in the 1970s and 1980s meant that most academic disciplines and fields of study found themselves called on in some way to respond, and to realize that the place of women in their area of study had been largely omitted, marginalized or taken for granted. This had an impact on studies of Tibetan Buddhism as well, and it was reinforced by the concerns of the first generation of Western women to become involved in Tibetan Buddhism as nuns and as lay practitioners. The rethinking of Tibetan studies, and of Tibetan Buddhist studies, has been slow and still far from complete. It is not easy to reach a balanced assessment of the situation, one that neither inappropriately imposes Western individualist values on a society working on very different assumptions, nor glosses over real elements of inequality and exploitation.

Unfortunately, we do not yet have the solid base of ethnographic research on women, gender relations and gender values in the wider Tibetan society that we have, for example, for Indian or Southeast Asian societies. Tibetan studies have tended to be dominated by Buddhist studies, and Buddhism is unquestionably largely dominated by male practitioners, so that issues relating to women tend to be marginalized. Tibetan society outside the monasteries has received much less attention.

Barbara Aziz pointed to this issue back in the late 1970s, and wrote the first major study of Tibetan society to give a serious place to women in 1978 (*Tibetan Frontier Families*). However there have been only a handful more studies since, and while they are valuable, they provide more a series of snapshots than a comprehensive picture. They include, among others, Nancy Levine's study of polyandry in northern Nepal, Christine Daniels' work on women at the refugee community of Bodhnath in Nepal, Joanne Watkins' book on the Nyeshangte women in northern Nepal, research on nuns in Ladakh and Nepal by Kim Gutschow, Anna Grimshaw and Yolanda van Ede, and Charlene Makley's writings on nuns at Labrang in Amdo, and on wider gender relations in contemporary Amdo.

To this we can add a number of studies of exemplary Buddhist women, providing descriptions of the relatively small number of women who became distinguished teachers and lamas. There are also autobiographical accounts by a few contemporary Tibetan women, mostly from privileged backgrounds, and attempts by feminist Buddhist thinkers such as Rita Gross and Anne Klein to describe and promote the more gender-positive aspects of Tibetan Buddhism. All of this literature is useful, but it is often not very revealing about the lives of more ordinary women, inside and outside Buddhist monasteries.

There are two main themes that emerge from this literature. The first is generally positive. Tibetan women are more equal to men in social terms than women in much of South Asia (India, Pakistan, Bangladesh) or traditional East Asia (China). They are free to move around as they wish, have a considerable degree of personal and financial autonomy, and are often openly part of decision-making processes within the household. In all these respects, Tibetan society's closest parallels in the wider region are probably in Southeast Asia (Thailand, Burma, Malaysia, Java, the Philippines). There are however some questions and limitations in relation to this relatively gender-positive picture, and we will examine them later.

The second theme, though, concerns women in Buddhism, and here the picture is less positive. Although there are plenty of aspects of Tibetan Buddhism that might support equality for male and female practitioners, women, for the most part, have been treated as second-class citizens within religious contexts. Female monastics (nuns) in particular were often treated badly, looked down upon, treated as domestic servants and given little material support by Tibetan society as a whole. The role of female Tantric practitioner offered more options for an autonomous spiritual career, but could also include problematic elements of exploitation. The situation for female monastics has improved in recent years in some respects and is continuing to improve, but there is still a long way to go before Tibetan Buddhism could be considered a genuinely gender-equal tradition. We look at these two sets of issues in turn.

Gender in Tibetan society

Let us start then with women in Tibetan lay society. A number of early observers (for example, Bea Miller) pointed to women's relative equality in Tibet in comparison with the Hindu and Muslim societies of South Asia, and for that matter the Buddhist and Confucian societies of East Asia. Indians and Chinese in the late nineteenth and early twentieth century seem regularly to have been shocked at the degree of autonomy which Tibetan women enjoyed, their freedom in public, their ability to enter into open argument with their menfolk, the relative lack of strongly-defined sex roles, and the like. In these respects they seem more like the women of Southeast Asian societies than those of South or East Asia. This does not, by the way, seem to have a great deal to do with Buddhism, since although many of the Southeast Asian societies in question (Thailand or Burma, for example) are Buddhist, others are Muslim (Malaysia or Java) or Christian (the Philippines).

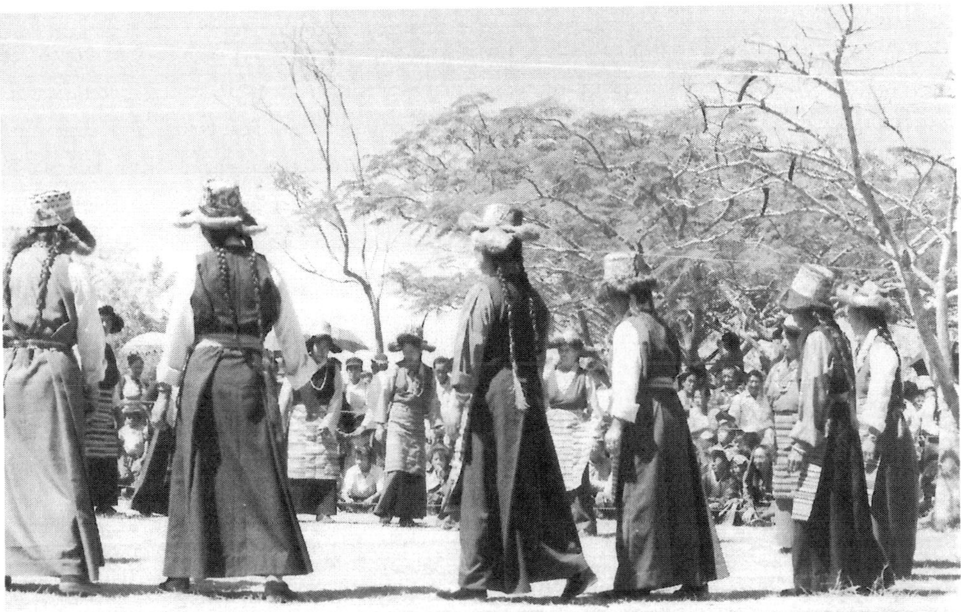

Figure 10.1 Tibetan women dancing at Losar (Tibetan New Year), Bylakuppe, South India. Photo by Ruth Rickard (1991).

These observations about the relative equality of women in Tibetan society are not meaningless, but they need to be put into context. One element here is the low population density of Tibetan society, the relatively small size of households, and the significance of long-distance travel for trade. Tibetan men or women were probably much more frequently called on to manage on their own than most men or women in South or East Asia, and the relative lack of strongly-defined sex roles probably has to be seen at least in part in relation to this situation.

More recent studies, beginning with Barbara Aziz's work in the 1970s, have pointed to the degree of systematic inequality between men and women that exists in Tibetan society. There appear to be regional variations here, and variations between pastoral and agricultural communities. The situation of women in pastoral communities in the Northeast of Tibet (Amdo) seems particularly difficult, though it is possible that some at least of this situation is an effect of modernity and Chinese control. In the contemporary situation, men's traditional work has become increasingly irrelevant, and the skills that gave their lives some sense of meaning and accomplishment are no longer of much value. Young men can easily see themselves on the fringes of Chinese society, rather than at the centre of the old nomadic culture. Motorbikes do not entirely substitute for horses and for the traditional skills of nomadic life. Women's domestic work however still needs doing, and this unbalanced situation has intensified inequalities that may have been less significant in the pre-modern period.

Here it is worth giving some thought to the question of masculinity and how it is understood in Tibet. The contrast between 'wild' and 'tame' dimensions of Tibetan society was mentioned in Chapter 6, and one can see a clear opposition between the aggressively assertive male personality associated particularly with men in Kham and Amdo, and the 'tamed' role of the monk. As in other Buddhist societies, where similar conflicts can be found, this leaves somewhat up in the air both what the 'ideal' male personality might be, and also what might be an appropriate relationship between men and women.

One aspect of an answer can be found in the human life-cycle. Generally speaking, most young men and young women are not expected to be deeply religious in their orientation. As in many societies, it is usual for men and women to move towards religion later in life, after they have raised a family and when their children are ready to take over their roles as heads of households. This ideal is also built into domestic practices, since it is quite common for older couples to move out of the main house into a smaller dwelling, where they can focus on religious pursuits. Also, while young men are often expected to be tough and assertive, middle aged and older men are valued if they can mediate quarrels and settle disputes. This is a key function of oratory in Tibetan society. As we saw in Chapter 6, for younger people to be too involved in religion can even be seen as problematic, because of the value attached to the continuance of lay society and of the household. Young people who feel the motivation to become deeply involved in Buddhist practice, whether as monastics or as full-time lay yogic practitioners, are likely to run into opposition from their families, as many of the life stories of Buddhist practitioners in the past and in recent times bear witness.

Here we can recall that the classic story of the historical Buddha's life describes him as abandoning his royal life and responsibilities to go off to the wilderness, despite his father's attempts to keep him enclosed within the domestic world of the palace. The tension between engagement in secular life and ascetic withdrawal runs through all Buddhist societies in one way or another.

Another element that has a bearing on the construction of a specific Buddhist style of masculinity in Tibetan society, however, as contrasted with other Buddhist societies, is the powerful key cultural role of the non-celibate Tantric lama, as symbolized by such figures as Padmasambhava and the epic hero Ling Gesar. Both have strong elements of aggressive masculinity. Padmasambhava is very much a figure of Tantric power, exploited directly against the spirit world and on behalf of the Tibetan people. He is not a warrior in the literal sense of being engaged in physical combat with other human beings, but he is most certainly a figure of dominating power. His regent or representative Ling Gesar is definitely a warrior as well as a lama. He is regularly described in the epic stories as going off into retreat between campaigns; in terms of British mythology, he combines the roles of King Arthur, the war-leader, and Merlin, the wise sage and magician.

More generally, Tantric practice offers opportunities for the redirection and transmutation of anger and aggression, as for other emotions, rather than asking for them simply to be suppressed, and Tantric ritual, as we have seen, can be directed outwards in a dominating and even destructive mode. Thus there is at the very least a cultural model for a mode of masculinity that expresses Buddhist spirituality in forceful outwards activity.

We can ask where all this leave Tibetan women in everyday life. Despite Tibetan women's participation in public life, there are clearly constraints on them that do not apply in the same way to men. If women in South Asia have to be constantly concerned about *izzat*, about honour and the possibility of losing it, Tibetan women everywhere have to concerned about *ngotsa* or shame. The effect is an internalized set of rules about how one can behave which may not be immediately obvious to the casual observer, and an obligation familiar to many women in Asian societies to guard their behaviour so as to preserve the community's moral reputation.

How these various elements work out appears to vary considerably between Tibetan communities in the contemporary world. Joanne Watkins' description of the self-confident and assertive lay women of Nyeshang in Nepal, with their effective roles as traders in the outside world, and recognized authority and status within the family, might be at one end of the contemporary situation; even women religious practitioners (*jomo*, nuns) seem to receive substantial support from what is in fact a quite wealthy trading community with international connections. At the other extreme, perhaps, are the women of Labrang in Amdo described by Charlene Makley, trapped at the point of conflict between a collapsing pastoralist society and a Han Chinese dominance that defines their menfolk as inferior and marginal members of an ethnic minority. Women's behaviour and scope of action here can be quite narrowly circumscribed, if as noted above, the boundaries are not necessarily apparent to outsiders. The nuns at Labrang were particularly badly off, and Makley gives a harrowing description of how many of them earn a bare minimum income for survival through performing *nyungné* ceremonies in which they, in effect, have to starve themselves so as to accumulate merit for their sponsors.

All this aside, women in lay life are not confined to the household, are able to speak openly and assertively in front of men both at home and in public, and have an effective public role in many areas. It is when we turn to the area of religion that things become more complicated, as the references to nuns above already suggest. In fact, while a substantial proportion of Tibetan women enter the monastic life, they are not technically able to become fully-ordained nuns (*bhikṣūni* – Tibetan *gelongma*), and their status is in many respects lower than that of male celibates.

Women's religious roles within Indian Buddhism

To make sense of this situation it is useful to begin with the role of women in classical Indian Buddhism. As noted in Chapter 7, Buddhist order (Saṅgha) has three main grades for men and three main grades for women. These grades are distinguished by successive sets of vows or commitments, which are passed on in ordination ceremonies that claim to go back to the time of the historical Buddha. However, while the male and female grades are, on the face of it at least, parallel to each other, offering identical routes for men and women, in reality the *gelongma* ordination (Skt. *bhikṣuni*) has not been available for Tibetan women, since this ordination lineage, although existing in India and transmitted to East Asia, was never effectively established in Tibet. Thus the parity between male and female ordination is more apparent than real.

The Theravādin equivalent to the *gelongma* ordination, the *bhikkhuni*, does not exist either in contemporary Theravādin countries, although there have been recent attempts to revive it. As this might suggest, the question of female monastics is a vexed one within the Buddhist tradition. The classic story of how the Buddha Śākyamuni instituted this order describes how he was extremely reluctant to do so. He is said to have agreed only when his favourite disciple Ānanda pleaded on behalf of Mahāprajāpatī, his mother's sister and his own foster-mother, who brought him up after the death of his mother shortly after his birth. Mahāprajāpatī had previously asked three times on her own behalf and been refused three times. The Buddha is described as finally agreeing, after admitting to Ānanda that women would be capable of realizing the various stages of the Buddhist path were they allowed to enter the homeless life of the wandering Buddhist ascetic. He is said to have imposed, however, a whole series of extra restrictions on women who become *bhikṣunī*, the eight 'strict rules' or *garudharmā*, in addition to those observed by male *bhikṣu*. These rules make them explicitly subordinate to the male *bhikṣu* in a variety of ways. The Buddha is also described as predicting that the institution of the *bhikṣunī* order will have dire consequences for the Buddhist Saṅgha as a whole.

This strange episode has provoked considerable reflection by scholars and by contemporary Buddhist women, including an interesting article by Reiko Ohnuma that examines the theme of the Buddha's obligation to his mother and foster-mother. With its ritual repetition of the threefold request, and Ānanda's strategem to circumvent its refusal, the traditional story seems unlikely to be a literal historical account. What the story clearly does do is to depict a tension in the early order between those who approved of female monastic practitioners and those who did not. Over time, the latter party appears increasingly to have gained the upper hand. Evidence suggests that fully-ordained nuns were common in early Buddhist India and of high status, but they became increasingly less so as time went on.

In an article some years ago on the attitudes to women as practitioners in Buddhist texts, the American Buddhist scholar Alan Sponberg distinguishes four main outlooks. In the first (which he calls 'soteriological inclusiveness') the path to *nirvāṇa* or Buddhahood is open to all, and is the same for both men and women. Sponberg sees this as the 'original' message of the Buddha, and given the apparent openness of the early ascetic orders as a whole to women, this may well have been the attitude at the earliest stages of the tradition.

However, Sponberg suggests, this original openness was rapidly compromised as Buddhism became an accepted institution within Indian society. At the point when the Vinaya codes were formulated, the attitude had already shifted to what he calls 'institutional androcentrism'. There was scope for women to pursue a monastic career, but within accepted social standards of male authority and female subordination. This is what we see represented in the stories of the Buddha, Ānanda and Mahāprajāpatī. The texts of Indian Buddhism, with a few notable exceptions, were also mostly written by male monastics. These were men who had committed themselves, or been committed, to a life of monastic celibacy, and who tended to regard women primarily in terms of the threat to their monastic career. Women thus appear in the texts as seductresses and temptresses who can lead the male monastic to break his vows and draw him back into the secular world. Sponberg labels this 'ascetic misogyny'. Finally, in the Mahāyāna and Vajrayāna ('Tantric') texts, we find an assertion of the need to overcome the duality between male and female, with both male and female identities seen as partial and incomplete modes of being which need to be transcended for the achievement of Buddhahood. This fourth attitude ('soteriological androgyny' in Sponberg's terms) is most clearly visible in late Indian and Tibetan Tantric Buddhism. Thus the subtle body practices are premised on the existence of both male and female polarities within all men and women; both polarities are necessary, both genders contain both, and neither alone is sufficient for the attainment of Buddhahood.

Sponberg's categories are perhaps a little over-schematic, but they help to make the point that the Buddhist tradition is far from speaking with a single voice on questions of gender. This ambivalence has remained until modern times, and we can see elements of all four attitudes in Tibet. They also help us to see attitudes as shifting over time, in relation to the gender attitudes of the wider society. Thus the increasing militarization of Indian society throughout the first millennium, especially after the breakup of the Gupta and Vākāṭaka states in the early sixth century, appears to have led to an increasing emphasis on masculine aggression and warriorship, and to progressively more restrictive roles for women. This development never went as far in Southeast Asia or Tibet, but it helps to explain why the flourishing female monastic tradition apparent in sources such as the donors' inscriptions at early Indian Buddhist sites became increasingly marginalized. It also helps explain why the *bhikṣūni* ordination dropped out in much of the Buddhist world, surviving only in East Asia where female monasticism had become part of a rather different set of social structures. In fact, if traditional historical accounts are to be believed, the male

Figure 10.2 Women carrying Buddhist books on their backs as part of a village festival, Yarlung valley, Central Tibet. Photo by author (1987).

monastic (*bhikṣu*) ordination also nearly disappeared at various points, both in Sri Lanka and in Thailand, to be revived by major state-supported projects to reintroduce it from regions where it had survived.

Nevertheless, Indian Buddhism introduced a variety of new roles for women to Tibetan societies, and they have been taken up, as in other areas of Tibetan Buddhism, in ways that made sense for the wider society as well as for individuals trying to make some personal sense of their own lives and spiritual careers.

Women's religious roles within Tibetan Buddhism

Women as lay patrons and supporters

We begin with women as lay patrons and supporters of Buddhism. Since Tibetan monks do not go around village communities collecting food on a daily basis, like many monks in Southeast Asia, the traditional Southeast Asian role of laywomen as offering food to monks does not work in the same way. Women however have an important role as patrons of Buddhist lamas and monasteries and can often be found providing food and other practical assistance at major monastic rituals, on behalf of their households or the wider community. Since Tibetan women, like women in most Southeast Asian countries, often have an independent income as traders and businesswomen, they may also be sponsors of rituals in their own right. For women to be lay patrons of Buddhism is certainly seen as culturally acceptable and appropriate, but it does not necessarily or normally involve the women being given access to teachings in their own right, except as part of the audience for the general teachings presented by lamas to the laity at monastic festivals and the like.

Women as monastics

Many women have undertaken monastic careers in Tibetan society, although far fewer than men. At a rough estimate, some 2 per cent of women in the early twentieth century were monastics, compared to around 12 per cent of the male population, although this figure may understate the number of unmarried women wearing monastic-style robes and spending much of their time at home rather than in the monasteries. It is also clear that nuns have been less respected than monks, and were regularly the object of derogatory comments and generalized prejudice. There is a whole body of folklore on the theme of the sexual desires of nuns, and often a default assumption that they became nuns because they could not find a suitable husband. All this seems very much out of line with the reality of nuns' lives as it appears in recent studies. It is nevertheless clear that nuns often in practice ended up as domestic servants either in their own homes or in the monasteries, and that as in Southeast Asian

Figure 10.3 Tibetan nuns at Kālacakra empowerment, Sarnath, India. Photo by Ruth Rickard (1991).

Buddhist countries they have had to struggle in recent years for any kind of serious recognition, or for access to Buddhist teachings at more than an elementary level. A key element here, as in Southeast Asia, appears to be a strong sense that while it is appropriate for men to pursue a religious career, woman's 'natural' role in life is that of wife and mother.

There have been a number of declarations in recent years by important lamas, including His Holiness the Dalai Lama, about the need to change the situation and to give nuns higher recognition. Much of this is doubtless a response to the impact of Western thought and Western values, and especially of Western women interested in Buddhism (the Sakyadhītā organization, which is international, not just Western, has been particularly significant here). Whatever the reasons, there are signs of change, and there are now nunneries where the women get the kind of instruction previously mostly reserved for men. There is still a reluctance by many Tibetans, both men and women, to treat Tibetan nuns on a par with monks, and lay support for women's monastic institutions remains at a low level. Both institutions and individual nuns find it difficult to attract significant levels of lay support, and maintaining adequate food and housing is often a major issue. This has also been a problem for Western women who have taken up Tibetan monastic ordination, with the exception of a few high-profile women teachers who have managed to establish successful Dharma centres and monastic institutions in the West.

In these circumstances, the question of *bhikṣūni* ordination (*gelongma* in Tibetan) has tended to be a secondary one. The existence of an ongoing *bhikṣūni* ordination lineage in several East Asian countries (including Taiwan, Hong Kong, Korea and Vietnam) has meant that there is a possibility for women who have received *getsulma* vows in the Tibetan tradition to proceed to *bhikṣūni* vows from one of the East Asian lineages, and perhaps eventually to reintroduce the *gelongma* ordination into Tibetan practice. The East Asian lineages belong to the Dharmaguptaka Vinaya, however, not to the Mūlasarvāstivāda Vinaya followed by the Tibetans, which has meant that it has been difficult to get agreement among all Tibetan religious leaders as to whether this should be done and if so in what way. At an International Congress on Buddhist Women's Role in the Sangha held in Germany in July 2007, H.H. the Dalai Lama, who has supported the reintroduction of *gelongma* ordination himself since 1987, reiterated his support and suggested that women could begin to practise certain monastic ceremonies in preparation for ordination, but that the actual reintroduction of the lineage would have to await consensus among the main Tibetan religious traditions. As far as I am aware, this was still the situation as this book went to press in 2012.

In the meantime, a number of Western women ordained as nuns (i.e. *getsulma*) in the Tibetan tradition, mostly from Karma Kagyüd, Drukpa Kagyüd and Gelukpa backgrounds have received East Asian *bhikṣunī* ordinations and subsequently adopted the *gelongma* title. The first of these was an Englishwoman, Karma Khechog Palmo (Freda Bedi, 1911–1977), who was ordained as a nun by the Sixteenth Gyalwa Karmapa in 1963, and subsequently received the *bhikṣunī* ordination from the Chinese tradition in Hong Kong in 1972; others followed in subsequent years.

It is unclear at this stage how much interest there is among Tibetan female monastics in taking up the option of *gelongma* ordination, but there are indications that at least some Tibetan *getsulma* would take up the option if it became formally established within Tibetan monastic lineages. At present, the issue of ordination seems to be seen by most Tibetan nuns as secondary both to the question of serious spiritual practice and to practical issues of material survival, but the situation could change significantly in the next few years.

Women as yogic practitioners

This is a context that occurs primarily among Northern (Tibetan and Mongolian) Buddhists, and which in some respects at least allows for more gender equality. Yoga, as explained in previous chapters, implies Tantra. Indian and Tibetan Buddhist teachings on Tantra, which fit into Sponberg's category of 'soteriological androgyny', imply that women are appropriate and in some respects necessary participants in the

Tantric context. Tantric root vows commit male practitioners to respect for women. The attainment of Enlightenment implies the bringing together within the central channel of the body of both male and female sexual substances (white and red *bindu*), and both are thought of as present in both genders, so there is no physiological reason why women should not be involved in these practices. In addition, literal performance of the Tantric sexual practices by men involves the participation of women, but that is a somewhat different issue that will be discussed further on.

Female practitioners are unusual though not unknown in contemporary Indian Tantric contexts. Attitudes to them vary, though as in the Buddhist context there seems a strong feeling that religious asceticism is not an appropriate path for women. The strongest evidence for equality perhaps comes from the Baul and related traditions of West Bengal and Bangladesh, where male and female yogic practitioners for the most part live together in stable marriages. Elsewhere, there are occasional female *sādhus* who have succeeded in attaining a degree of acceptance and recognition within the ascetic community. In much of the Indian Tantric scene however women seem to be regarded as at best a necessary accessory for male access to Tantric power.

Whether this was true in earlier times is a contested issue. Some years ago, in a book called *Passionate Enlightenment*, Miranda Shaw argued that in early Tantric contexts women dominated as teachers and practitioners, but that the evidence for this dominance has been distorted or lost because of the lack of interest in preserving it among the male clerics who increasingly took over as masters of the tradition.

There may well have been some degree of rewriting by later male scholars so as to minimize the female contribution. Women practitioners appear to have had a significant presence in non-monastic Tantric circles in India in the ninth and twelfth centuries. At least one Tibetan lineage, the Shangpa Kagyüdpa, a kind of parallel transmission to the main Kagyüdpa lineages revived by the Rimé lama Jamgön Kongtrül, specifically traces itself back to female Indian practitioners, claiming its origins in the teachings of Nāropa's sister or consort Niguma. Stories about a number of other female practitioners have been preserved, along with some texts authored by them. Shaw's claims have however generally been regarded as exaggerated, and other evidence about this period suggests that it was a time when women's role in religion was on the whole on the decline.

At any rate, it appears that the Tantric Buddhism passed on from India to Tibet gave only a somewhat conditional and limited role to women. However there have been a series of important women Tantric practitioners in Tibet, going back to semi-legendary figures such as Yeshe Tsogyal through a number of relatively well-known historical teachers and practitioners over the centuries, mainly in the Nyingma tradition. In the area of yogic practice, there may be some restrictions on what are thought of as suitable methods for women, and women may initially have considerable difficulty in being accepted as a practitioner, but determined women have often been able to find lamas who will accept them as serious practitioners and provide them with Tantric teachings.

Yeshe Tsogyal, who as consort and scribe to Padmasambhava had a crucial and central role in the transmission of the *terma* traditions is a major precedent. Another, in the New Tantra traditions, is Machik Labdrön (1055–1149), who was a disciple of the Indian male teacher known in Tibetan as Padampa Sangyé and was herself the originator of a major yogic practice (*chöd*). Her practices were systematized and institutionalized by male lamas, notably the Third Karmapa in the early fourteenth century, but they remain important for all the main yogic traditions. Other important women teachers included the female *tertön* Jomo Menmo (1248–1283), and Jetsün Migyur Paldrön (1699–1769), daughter of the distinguished *tertön* Terdak Lingpa and a critical figure in the development of Mindrolling, one of the six major Nyingmapa teaching centres. There were undoubtedly many lesser-known female yogic practitioners throughout the centuries. It is likely that some at least of them, like Ayu Khandro (1839–1952) whose life story has been passed down by Namkhai Norbu Rinpoche, had significant local reputations as teachers and holy women. Perhaps the best-known woman teacher in the first half of the twentieth century was Jetsunma Shugseb Rinpoché (1865–1951), a woman master whose early life was a long struggle to receive teaching and be taken seriously as a practitioner, but who eventually founded a monastery near Lhasa, was recognized as a great practitioner and widely respected by lamas and lay people. Another famous woman lama of the early twentieth century was Sera Khandro (1899–1952), the consort of one of the sons of the *tertön* Dudjom Lingpa, but also a significant *tertön* and teacher in her own right.

Women as Tantric consorts (*sangyum, kandroma*)

The role of women as yogic practitioners, as in Sera Khandro's case, can also include being a Tantric consort to a male lama. This is a context in which women have an indispensable place, at any rate for the literal performance of the sexual practices, and where they are at least in theory supposed to receive considerable respect; this is in fact required by the vows taken at Tantric initiation. In practice, being a Tantric consort can mean any of a variety of different things. As mentioned in Chapter 4, this is a complex and sensitive area, particularly given the differences between traditional Tibetan and contemporary Western understandings.

In Tibet, at any rate from the rise of dominance of the Gelukpa order with its emphasis on monasticism, most Tantric practice, whether carried out by celibate monastics or by lay yogic practitioners, does not involve physical sexual activity. The sexual yogas are still practised, however, and in some cases this has given women, as consorts (*sangyum, kandroma*) of high lamas, the opportunity to gain access to the highest levels of the Tibetan Buddhist tradition and to move into leadership positions within Tibetan Buddhist society. This was the case for example with Kandro Orgyen Tsomo, the consort of the Fifteenth Karmapa, Kakyab Dorjé. In this case, as quite often, the initial justification for the lama's taking a consort was for health reasons; the sexual practices can assist with the extension of life, a tradition that goes back at least to the Kālacakra Tantra. Kandro Orgyen Tsomo became a recognized teacher in her own right, however, known as the 'Great Dakini of Tsurpu' and living for many years after the Fifteenth Karmapa's death in 1922.

Women as hereditary lamas

These various pathways, especially that of yogic practice, have led to a number of women through the centuries being recognized as significant Tantric lamas in their own right. Another pathway that has provided access to teachings is that of being born into a hereditary lama family, and several fairly high-profile women lamas have emerged from hereditary lama backgrounds in recent years. The public role of these teachers is no doubt in part motivated by the large number of Western and other non-Tibetan women practitioners of Tibetan Buddhism. Buddhism's relatively gender-equal image has been part of its attraction to many women who come from Western religious backgrounds which themselves offer limited roles for women. Thus leading Tibetan lamas have undoubtedly felt some pressure, as with the *bhikṣunī* issue, to provide a positive response. Three of the most prominent of these female lamas are described briefly here.

Jetsun Kushok Chimé Luding Rinpoche (b.1938) was born into the hereditary lama family of Sakya as the elder sister of the current (Forty-first) Sakya Tridzin or head of the Sakya tradition. She received much of the same training as her brother, including the *lamdré*, the central body of Sūtra and Tantra teachings of the Sakyas, which is based on the Hevajra Tantra. She left Tibet in 1959 and eventually settled with her husband in Vancouver. At the Sakya Tridzin's request, she begain to teach in public in the 1980s.

Mindrolling Jetsün Tsering Paldrön (also known as Khandro Rinpoche) was born in India in 1967 as daughter of Mindrolling Trichen, the then head of the Mindrolling tradition, mentioned above as one of the major Nyingma traditions. When she was two years old, she was recognized by the Sixteenth Karmapa as the reincarnation of his predecessor the Fifteenth Karmapa's consort, the 'Great Dakini of Tsurpu', and consequently received the Karma Kagyüd as well as Mindrolling teachings. She established a retreat centre in India for both Tibetan nuns and Western practitioners, and is now a well-known teacher both in India and in the West.

Kandro Trinley Chodon was born in the late 1960s as the daughter of Apo Rinpoche, the grandson of the east Tibetan Rimé lama Śākya Śrī. Apo Rinpoche was mentioned in Chapter 9 as settling in Manali in the Kulu Valley in North India after leaving Tibet in 1959. His daughter received a thorough training along with her three brothers, all of whom were recognized as *tulku*. She was married in 1998 to Jigmé Ngawang Namgyel (1955–2003), the claimant to the title of Shabdrung Rinpoche (the former head of state of Bhutan). Jigmé Ngawang Namgyel had been brought up under Indian police protection near Manali and was eventually installed as head of Pedong Gompa, near Kalimpong in Northeast India. Unfortunately, he died not long after his move to Pedong. Following her husband's early death, Kandro Trinley Chodon has emerged as a teacher in her own right, and has begun to establish a series of centres in India and the West.

Conclusion

Overall, the picture for women in Tibetan Buddhism has been problematic and in some respects still is, as with the situation of many women who are living as nuns with little support for the lay community. There are however changes taking place in many directions, in part as a result of the increasingly close contacts between Tibetan Buddhists and Buddhist women in the rest of the world. At least some of the senior male leadership of Tibetan Buddhism has clearly accepted the need for change and is actively promoting it, and there are indications of Tibetan Buddhist women themselves taking an increasingly active and open role. The situation is likely to be considerably different in a few years' time.

Chapter 11 deals with the Bon religion of Tibet.

Key points you need to know

- Tibetan women are more equal to men in social terms than women in much of South Asia (India, Pakistan, Bangladesh) or traditional East Asia (China). They are free to move around as they wish, have a considerable degree of personal and financial autonomy, and are often openly part of decision-making processes within the household.
- Women within Tibetan Buddhism were treated as inferior in many ways, and the situation here is only slowly improving.
- Women are nevertheless involved in Tibetan Buddhism in many capacities, both as lay patrons and as religious practitioners in their own right.
- Tantric Buddhism in theory allows for a significant role for women both as practitioners in their own right and as Tantric consorts. The increasing dominance of Tibet by male celibate monasticism has meant that women have found it difficult to access the teachings, but a significant minority have become practitioners, particularly in the Nyingmapa and Kagyüdpa traditions. Women from high-status hereditary lama families have been especially well-placed to receive teachings on the same basis as men.

- In recent years, in part as a result of the involvement of Western women in Tibetan Buddhist practice, there has been increasing pressure for discrimination against women within Tibetan Buddhism to be ended and women to be given equal access to Buddhist teachings.

Discussion questions

1 Discuss the apparent contradiction between the relatively strong position of women in Tibetan society, and their much weaker position in Tibetan religion.
2 In what ways has Tantric Buddhism provided possibilities for women to pursue a religious career not open within other Buddhist traditions?
3 Discuss recent changes in the position of women in Tibetan Buddhism.

Further reading

Allione, Tsultrim (ed.). *Women of Wisdom*. London: Routledge and Kegan Paul, 1984.

Aziz, Barbara N. *Tibetan Frontier Families: Reflections of Three Generations from D'ing-ri*. New Delhi: Vikas, 1978.

Aziz, Barbara N. 'Women in Tibetan society and Tibetology', in H. Uebach and J. L. Panglung (eds), *Tibetan Studies*, vol. 2. Munich: Bayrische Akademie der Wissenschaften, 1988.

Cabezón, José Ignacio (ed.). *Buddhism, Sexuality, and Gender*. Albany, NY: State University of New York, 1992.

Campbell, June. *Traveller in Space: In Search of Female Identity in Tibetan Buddhism*. London: Athlone, 1996.

Daniels, Christine. 'Defilement and purification: Tibetan Buddhist pilgrims at Bodhnath, Nepal'. Unpublished D.Phil Thesis, University of Oxford, 1994.

Diemberger, Hildegard. *When a Woman Becomes a Religious Dynasty: The Samding Dorje Phagmo of Tibet*. New York: Columbia University Press, 2007.

Ede, Yolanda van. *House of Birds: A Historical Ethnography of a Tibetan Buddhist Nunnery in Nepal*. University of Amsterdam, Faculteit der Maatschappij- en Gedragswetenschappen, 1999.

Edou, Jérôme. *Machig Labdrön and the Foundations of Chöd*. Ithaca, NY: Snow Lion, 1995.

Grimshaw, Anna. *Servants of the Buddha: Winter in a Himalayan Convent*. Cleveland, Ohio: Pilgrim Press, 1992.

Gross, Rita M. *Buddhism After Patriarchy: A Feminist History, Analysis, and Reconstruction of Buddhism*. Albany, NY: State University of New York Press, 1993.

Gutschow, Kim. *Being a Buddhist Nun: The Struggle for Enlightenment in the Himalayas*. Boston: Harvard University Press, 2004.

Gyatso, Janet and Hanna Havnevik (eds). *Women in Tibet: Past and Present*. New York:

Columbia University Press; London: Hurst & Company, 2005.
Harding, Sarah (ed. and trans.). *Machik's Complete Explanation: Clarifying the Meaning of Chöd*. Ithaca, NY: Snow Lion Publications, 2003.
Havnevik, Hanna. *Tibetan Buddhist Nuns: History, Cultural Norms and Social Reality*. Oslo: Universitetsforlaget, 1990.
Klein, Anne C. *Meeting the Great Bliss Queen: Buddhists, Feminists, and the Art of the Self*. Boston: Beacon Press, 1994.
Levine, Nancy E. *The Dynamics of Polyandry: Kinship, Domesticity, and Population on the Tibetan Border*. Chicago: University of Chicago Press, 1988.
Makley, Charlene. 'The body of a nun: nunhood and gender in contemporary Amdo' in Janet Gyatso and Hanna Havnevik (eds), *Women of Tibet: Past and Present*. New York: Columbia University Press, 2005.
Makley, Charlene E. *The Violence of Liberation: Gender and Tibetan Buddhist Revival in Post-Mao China*. Berkeley and Los Angeles: University of California Press, 2007.
Ohnuma, Reiko. 'Debt to the Mother: a neglected aspect of the founding of the Buddhist nuns' order', *Journal of the American Academy of Religion*, Vol. 74, pp. 861–901, 2006.
Schaeffer, Kurtis. *Himalayan Hermitess: The Life of a Tibetan Buddhist Nun*. Oxford: Oxford University Press, 2004.
Watkins, Joanne C. *Spirited Women: Gender, Religion and Cultural Identity in the Nepal Himalaya*. New York: Columbia University Press, 1996.
Willis, Janice D. (ed). *Feminine Ground: Essays on Women and Tibet*. Ithaca, NY: Snow Lion, 1989.

11 The Bon religion of Tibet

Pre-Buddhist survival or variant form of Buddhism?

In this chapter

Chapter 11 deals with the various religious forms which are referred to in Tibetan as Bon (pronounced bön). The most important of these, and the main subject of the chapter, is as discussed in Chapter 2 essentially a variant of Tibetan Buddhism. It developed in the tenth and eleventh centuries, and has close resemblances to Nyingmapa Buddhism in particular. This Bon religion claims however to have pre-Buddhist origins and probably preserves at least some genuinely ancient features. The term 'Bon' is also used to refer both to a class of priests or ritualists in the early Empire, and to a variety of popular religious practices relating to local gods and spirits in the modern period.

Main topics covered

- Yungdrung Bon
- Bonpo narratives and teachings
- Bonpo history and the relationship with Buddhism
- The history of Bon studies
- Modern developments

Introduction

At first glance, the scene shown in Figure 11.1 could be in any Tibetan Buddhist monastery. Readers who are familiar with Buddhist iconography, however, might be puzzled by some details, such as the identity of the main cult-figure in the temple. In fact, he is one of a number of standard iconographical forms of Tönpa Shenrab, the central Buddha figure of the Bon religion of Tibet. Specifically, he is a form called Nampar Gyalwa, or the All-Victorious, representing Shenrab radiating white light to vanquish evil spirits. He bears some resemblance to one of the commonest forms of Padmasambhava, that known as Nangsid Silnon. Like the Nangsid Silnon form of

Figure 11.1 Temple at Bongya Monastery, Rebkong. Photo by author (2010).

Padmasambhava, Nampar Gyalwa is an image of a guru figure exercising power over the world of everyday existence.

Figure 11.2 shows Tönpa Shenrab in one of his other common forms. He is not holding a *dorjé* (Sanskrit: *vajra*), the standard Tantric Buddhist ritual sceptre, in his hand, but a *yungdrung* or swastika-sceptre. The young monks in the monastery are followers of a religion known as Yungdrung Bon. *Yungdrung*, the Tibetan name of the swastika symbol, also has the meaning 'eternal, enduring', somewhat like *vajra* in Buddhist Sanskrit.

Yungdrung Bon

Shenrab is regarded by contemporary Bonpo followers as being an enlightened Buddha, and indeed as having attained Buddhahood several hundred years before the historical Buddha, in a country to the west of Tibet, the realm of Ölmo Lungring, a region also sometimes described as Tasi, which is the Tibetan word for Iranian populations (it is a variant of the word 'Tajik'). Some Bonpo sources in fact regard Śākyamuni as a later manifestation of Tönpa Shenrab, which provides a natural explanation within the Bonpo frame of thought for the similarity between Bonpo and Buddhist teachings. More will be said later about the Bonpo understanding of their own history. The most normal context, though, in which Bon is encountered today

Figure 11.2
Tönpa Shenrab. Bongya Monastery, Rebkong. Photo by author (2010).

is as a tradition of monastic and lay religious practice with close resemblances to that of Buddhism, distributed through many parts of Tibet, Nepal and the Tibetan diaspora, and altogether representing perhaps 5 to 10 per cent of the total population of Tibet.

It is also important in understanding the situation of the Bonpo in India today to know that they have been, and have understood themselves to be, a marginalized group in relation to the Tibetan refugee community as a whole. While they were eventually recognized in 1979 as a valid Tibetan religious tradition by the Office of the Dalai Lama at Dharamsala, on the same footing as the four Buddhist traditions, this followed on twenty years in which they were largely ignored by the refugee administration, received none of the substantial funding which was channelled through the Dalai Lama's Office, and were often neglected or treated dismissively by the Dharamsala administration and by the majority of Tibetan Buddhists among the refugees.

Bon has been variously described as the pre-Buddhist religion of Tibet and as Tibet's indigenous religion, though as mentioned above the Bonpos themselves see their religion as having originated outside Tibet and as having been introduced to Tibet long before the advent of Buddhism. While the relationship between Buddhism and Bon has often been antagonistic, the two religions have influenced each other extensively, and the practice of the Bon religion of today closely resembles that of Tibetan Buddhism. Thus, while there are differences today between the Bon religious tradition and the various Buddhist religious traditions, there are many similarities and common features.

Bonpo teachings resemble the teachings of the various religious traditions of Tibetan Buddhism, particularly those of the Nyingma, although they have also developed a philosophical and debating tradition modelled on that of the Gelukpa. Bonpo lamas and monks have the same social and religious role as Buddhist lamas and monks. Bonpo deities and rituals resemble and in many cases are used for the same purposes as Buddhist deities and rituals, though the names and detailed iconography are usually different.

Thus the benevolent female deity here, Chamma, closely resembles the Buddhist deity Drölma (Tārā), while other Bonpo deities closely resemble Avalokiteśvara, Mañjūśrī or Bhaiṣajyaguru.

Figure 11.3a
Chamma. Tsiwu Gompa, Qinghai. Photo by author (2010).

Figure 11.3b
A modern Nepali image of the corresponding Buddhist deity, Tārā. Photo by author.

We have already met the deity Phurba under his Sanskrit name Vajrakilaya. Both the Nyingmapa and the Sakya possess Phurba lineages claiming to go back to the early imperial period; for the Nyingmas this is one of the important set of eight *kagyé* deities associated with Padmasambhava and his contemporaries, while for the Bonpo it is one of the set of five fierce Sékar deities. Phurba is one of the principal deities of the Bon tradition, existing in both peaceful and wrathful forms, but particularly associated with ritual to destroy obstacles and hostile forces in a forceful manner. The most important lineage is a *terma* lineage that is said to have been revealed by the Bon *tertön* Kutse Da-ö in the early eleventh century.

Many Bon texts are also verbally close to Buddhist texts, suggesting a considerable amount of borrowing between the two traditions in the tenth and eleventh centuries. While it has generally been assumed that this borrowing proceeds from Buddhist to Bonpo, and this seems to have been the case for the Phurba practice, some of it may well have been in the opposite direction. Thus it is quite possible that the main

Figure 11.4
Phurba. Triten Norbutse, Kathmandu. Photo by author (2006).

Buddhist medical text, the *Gyüshi* or 'Four Medical Tantras', was borrowed, as the Bonpo claim, from the closely similar Bon text, the *Bumshi*.

Indeed the word *bon* itself has much the same meaning for the Bonpo as the word *chö* (*dharma*, teaching) has for the Buddhists. For both Bon and Buddhism, the ultimate aim of the teachings is the attainment of the state of Enlightenment represented by the concept of *sangyé* – the Tibetan word that translates the Sanskrit word Buddha.

Bonpo narratives and teachings

At the same time, while both the Tibetan Bon religion and Tibetan Buddhism have continuities with the pre-Buddhist period in Tibet, these are arguably stronger and more open on the Bon side. These links give the Bon tradition much of its distinctive character. Thus Bon texts include quite a lot of apparently early mythological material.

An example is the narrative of the origins of the universe, the *Sipé Dzöp'ug*, a text attributed to Shenrab and included in the Bonpo Kangyur. This narrative involves the creation of two eggs, a light egg and a dark egg, through the activity of a creator god, Trigyel Kugpa, also known as Shenlha Ökar. From the egg of light emerged a white man with turquoise hair, Sangpo Bumtri, the lord of the world of existence. From the oceans arose a turquoise blue woman, Chucham Gyalmo, also known as Satrig Ersang. These two gave birth to wild animals and birds, and then to nine brothers and nine sisters. These brothers and sisters are deities and also the ancestors of various further deities and of human beings.

The eldest of the sisters, Sipé Gyalmo or 'Queen of Creation', is an important Tantric deity. She resembles the Buddhist deity Palden Lhamo, who may well be modelled in part on her. She and her younger sisters feature in one of the principal monastic ritual dances (*cham*) of the Bonpo tradition. The black egg likewise gave birth to a man of darkness, who created a female consort out of his shadow, and these two and their descendants are the origin of the demons of the Bonpo universe.

Shenlha Ödkar and Sanpo Bumtri are now regarded as two of the three aspects of Shenrab, with Shenlha Ödkar as a kind of *dharmakāya* figure, but this whole mythology sounds decidedly pre-Buddhist, and in some form probably goes back to pre-Buddhist origins.

The Bon material tends to be rather more explicit than Tibetan Buddhist literature about the practical and everyday side of the religion, with less of a tendency to subsume everything underneath purely Dharmic motivations. Thus Bon versions of the classifications of the teachings are more inclusive of the 'practical' elements; compare these Nine Ways or *tekpa gu* of Bon (taken from Snellgrove's *Nine Ways of Bon* and shown in the box) with the well known Nine Yānas or Ways (also *tekpa gu*) of the Nyingma tradition (discussed in Chapter 4).

Figure 11.5
Sipé Gyalmo. Triten Norbutse, Kathmandu. Photo by author (2006).

The Nine Vehicles According to a Bon text (the *Sijid*)

'Bon of Cause'

1 *Chashen tekpa* (Way of Prediction) – Divination, prediction, rituals for good fortune, medical diagnosis and treatment
2 *Nangshen tekpa* (Way of the Apparent World) – Rituals to local gods and spirits
3 *Trulshen tekpa* (Way of Illusion) – Destructive rituals
4 *Sidshen tekpa* (Way of Existence) – Funerary rituals for guiding consciousness in afterlife period

'Bon of Effect'

5 *Genyen tekpa* (Way of the Lay Follower) – Lay morality, ten virtuous and non-virtuous actions, etc.
6 *Dangsong tekpa* (Way of the Ascetic) – Teachings for celibate monastics
7 *Akar tekpa* (Way of the White A, Way of Pure Sound) – Tantric teachings
8 *Yeshen tekpa* (Way of the Primeval Shen) – More advanced Tantric teachings
9 *Lamé tekpa* (Supreme Way) – Dzogchen teachings

In this scheme, the Bon teachings are divided into four sets of teachings of the 'Bon of Cause', essentially practical rituals aimed at everyday, *saṃsāric* purposes (including funerary rituals and the guiding of the consciousness in the after-death stage), and five levels of the 'Bon of Effect', covering the Bonpo version of the Buddhist path, and corresponding to the nine stages of the Nyingmapa path. For the Nyingmapas, as for the Sarmapa schools, the this-worldly practices are treated as secondary and ancillary, although in reality of great importance. The Bonpo, at any rate in this classificatory scheme, include them on the same level as the teachings aimed directly at liberation and Buddhahood.

Bonpo history and the relationship with Buddhism

The Bon version of their own history is more or less as follows: Tönpa Shenrab is said to have visited Tibet in his lifetime and to have brought some, though not all, of the teachings of Bon to the Tibetans at that time. Bonpo sources give a variety of dates for Tönpa Shenrab; one date for his birth would correspond to 1917 BCE. According to Bonpo histories, such as the 'Treasury of Good Sayings' (*Lekshé Dzö*) translated by Samten Karmay, many of these teachings were subsequently lost to the Tibetans in the course of two persecutions, one at the time of Drigum, the perhaps mostly mythical early ruler of Central Tibet in whose time the sky-cord was cut, and another at the time of Trisong Detsen, the late eighth-century Tibetan emperor who patronized the Buddhists and was associated with the great Buddhist lama Padmasambhava. The relationship between Padmasambhava himself and Bon is rather complex. In Buddhist tradition, one of Padmasambhava's twenty-five close disciples is a lama called Drenpa Namka. In Bonpo tradition, this lama is described as a Bon lama and is sometimes also described as Padmasambhava's father. Thus Drenpa Namka rather than Padmasambhava becomes the key figure for the exercise of Tantric power over the spirits and deities of Tibet.

At the time of the second persecution, the Bonpo teachings were said to have been hidden in the form of texts translated from the language of Shangshung, a kingdom in present-day Western Tibet that had remained a stronghold of Bon until it was conquered by the pro-Buddhist kings of Central Tibet. Western historians have generally placed this conquest in the time of the early emperor Songtsen Gampo (early seventh century), while Bonpo historians make it somewhat later, at the time of Trisong Detsen himself. These texts were gradually rediscovered from the tenth century onwards by a series of *tertön* or 'treasure-revealer' lamas of whom the most famous was Shenchen Luga, who may have lived in the early eleventh century. Thus almost all Bonpo teaching lineages today go back to these various *terma* texts. Only a few exceptions are believed to have been passed directly from teacher to student from the early times down to the present. The most important of these is the Shangshung Nyengyüd lineage of Dzogchen teachings, which is supposed to have been transmitted from Shangshung and to have been continued in Tibet.

The texts as we have them today are in Tibetan, though there are enough fragments of Shangshung language to make it clear that it was a real language, and closely related to existing languages in the Kinnaur region of the western Himalayas. There is little doubt that there was a historical Shangshung kingdom in what is now Western Tibet, and that it was incorporated into the Central Tibetan empire in the seventh or eighth century. We do not however have any real full-length texts in the Shangshung language, and many of the fragments in Bon texts give the impression of being artificially constructed by people without real knowledge of the language.

As discussed in Chapter 2 and elsewhere, the ideas of earlier Buddhas and of rediscovered texts are found throughout Indian Buddhism as well as in Tibet. While what could be called the mainstream of Tibetan Buddhism attributes the Buddhist teachings in their present form to the historical Buddha Śākyamuni, like all other Buddhists it holds that he (i.e. Śākyamuni) was only the most recent of a long series of Buddhas throughout the history of the world who have taught the Dharma. For the mainstream Buddhists too, Śākyamuni is a kind of earthly projection of the cosmic principle of Buddhahood (the Dharmakāya or cosmic 'body' of the Buddha), which is a transpersonal reality innate within the very nature of human being. Thus the Bonpo view of Tönpa Shenrab as a Buddha, and of Śākyamuni as a later manifestation of the same being or principle, is not particularly incompatible with this mainstream, or indeed with much of later Indian Buddhism.

As for hidden texts, we have already seen that mainstream Tibetan Buddhists, particularly in the Nyingma tradition, also believe that numerous texts and teachings were concealed in the time of Padmasambhava and discovered by Buddhist *tertön* or 'text-discoverers'. Thus the Nyingma tradition today, like the Bonpo, consists both of lineages of teachings (*kama*) held to be transmitted directly from teacher to student from early times, and 'rediscovered' or *terma* teachings, with the latter being much the most common. There have been relatively close relations at some periods of history between Bonpo and Nyingma, and at least one major early text-discoverer was regarded as having revealed both Bonpo and Nyingma teachings. Two major sets of practices, those of the Tantric deity Phurba and of the 'Great Perfection' or Dzogchen, form part of both Bonpo and Nyingma teachings, although the actual teaching lineages within the two religions are distinct. Bonpo lamas also took part in the nineteenth-century Rimé religious movement among the non-Gelukpa traditions in Eastern Tibet. Jamgön Kongtrül, one of the central figures of the Rimé approach, was himself originally from a Bon background, and the important twentieth-century Bon lama from Eastern Tibet, Shardza Tashi Gyaltsen (1859–1933), also had Rimé connections.

On the whole, though, the relationship between mainstream Buddhists and Bonpo has been characterized by suspicion, conflict and at times outright persecution of Bon by pro-Buddhist rulers. The standard mainstream Buddhist perspective on Bon would agree that it is a pre-Buddhist religious tradition, but see it as non-Buddhist (*mutekpa*, 'heretical') and indeed anti-Buddhist. One of the defining tropes of the mainstream Buddhist history of early Tibet is the recurrent attempts of pro-Bon ministers and members of the royal family to prevent the establishment of Buddhism in Tibet. These attempts, in the Buddhist account that is, culminated in the reign of the evil pro-Bon king Langdarma, whose assassination by the Buddhist monk Lhalung Pelgi Dorje brought the early Tibetan empire to an end.

Langdarma was again probably historical in some form, but there is no real evidence for his being a Bonpo supporter, and indeed it seems unlikely that there was anything existing in Tibet at that time with much resemblance to Yungdrung Bon as we know it today. However, present-day Bonpo are heirs to a history of distrust and at times active persecution on behalf of Buddhists, and this history is still very much alive among contemporary Tibetan Buddhists.

The history of Bon studies

The mainstream Buddhist view of Bon has also contributed to Western stereotypes and misunderstandings of the Bon religion. Thus early Western scholars regarded Bon variously as shamanistic, animistic, preoccupied with magic and sorcery, and involving deliberate inversions of Buddhist ritual. They considered the Bonpo history of their religion to be almost entirely fictional, and assumed that virtually all of the Bon scriptures were plagiarized from Buddhist scriptures. In fact, with the exception of two early translations by Laufer and Francke that attracted little attention, there was very little research on Bon until the 1960s. Bon studies in the West moved past these mainstream Buddhist stereotypes in the 1960s, when David Snellgrove, professor of Tibetan Studies at SOAS, visited a number of Bon monasteries in northern Nepal, and subsequently arranged for several Bon scholars to come to the West. One of these, Samten Karmay, became a major contributor to Western academic writing on Bon in his own right. Snellgrove, Karmay, and the Norwegian Tibetanist Per Kvaerne between them, in collaboration with leading Bon religious scholars in exile and in Tibet, put Bon studies on an entirely new footing over the next twenty or so years, based on both a serious study of the Bon texts and field research among contemporary Bon populations. They have been followed by a younger generation of Bon scholars, among them Dan Martin, Henk Blezer and Charles Ramble, again mostly working through a mixture of textual and field data.

A further set of studies in the 1980s onwards looked at references to the term *bon* and the related term *shen* in the early texts, including the important body of early Tibetan material found at the oasis town of Dunhuang, which was under Tibetan occupation for a period in the eighth and ninth centuries. This led to an understanding that *bon* in these early texts did not appear to refer to a religion, but rather to a class of priests active during and after the imperial period.

All this has greatly increased our understanding of Bon as a religion, but a number of questions still remain unresolved. Perhaps the most intriguing is the existence of a whole series of village-level priests and ritual officiants throughout the Himalayas who are referred to as *bon, lhabon* or some other variant of these names. The priests are often lay people who take on the role on an occasional or part-time basis. They have little or nothing to do with the developed religious tradition of Yungdrung Bon, although the ritual texts and invocations that they employ occasionally refer to deities and mythological themes also found in Yungdrung Bon. They are often associated with animal sacrifice, which is not a practice in Yungdrung Bon, though in most cases the sacrifices are described as something that took place in the past, rather than today. In other areas of southern Tibet, similar kinds of priests are referred to by other names, such as *aya*.

These various *bon* and *aya* priests are not in any kind of conflict or competition with Buddhism; the relationship is rather a complementary one, as with the Khumbo people where the Buddhist lama uses one side of the altar while the *lhabon* (locally pronounced *lhawen*) uses the other. While scholars have often assumed that the supposed early Bon religion was in some sense 'shamanic', in the sense of involving ecstatic states in which practitioners enter the spirit world, there is nothing especially 'shamanic' about any of these practitioners. One exception here is a class of ritual specialists among the Tamang population in Nepal. These are referred to as *bombo*, a variant of *bonpo*, and are shamans who employ ecstatic states and have a mythology of competition with the lamas. In general, though, the village-level *bon* priests simply make invocations and offerings to deities as part of calendrical and other rituals.

It is unclear whether the term *bon* for these various priests goes back to the earlier presence of a more developed *bon* priesthood, or whether the term has simply been applied in more modern times to a variety of priests of local deities in regions on the edge of the main Tibetan cultural region. They undoubtedly add, however, to the confused image of Bon among contemporary Tibetan Buddhists. The issue of animal sacrifice in particular has led to a distinction between a 'black Bon' (*bon nag*) that involves animal sacrifice, and a 'white Bon' (*bon kar*) that rejects it, that seems to have little if anything to do with the way in which Yungdrung Bon practitioners understand their identity.

The origins of Yungdrung Bon itself however seem to be fairly clear, and to have much in common with the origins of the Nyingmapa tradition of Tibetan Buddhism. In the tenth and eleventh centuries, it seems likely that there was a substantial population of hereditary ritual practitioners in Tibet, continuing both elements of Tibetan Tantric practice and elements of earlier court and village-level ritual. The renewed contact with Tibetan Buddhism in the early eleventh century placed these groups of practitioners in a difficult position. Their fragmentary ritual repertoire was bound to appear limited and inadequate in the face of the sophisticated new techniques being introduced from India, along with the full panoply of Indian Buddhist philosophy and scholarly knowledge. The *terma* concept, itself quite compatible with Indian Buddhist ideas of concealed and revealed texts, provided a way to build up a repertoire of practices and texts that was competitive with the new Sarma traditions, while claiming continuity in a respected past. The Yungdrung Bon and Nyingmapa traditions, originating in similar circles, adopted different approaches. While the people who created or rediscovered Yungdrung Bon looked back to Tibet's pre-Buddhist heritage, claiming that Tibet already had, in effect, a Buddhism of its own rooted in a Buddha-figure before Śākyamuni, the early Nyingmapa sought rather to ground their religious tradition in the charismatic figure of Padmasambhava and the Buddhism of the early empire.

After contact was re-established with Buddhist teachers and institutions in India in the late tenth century, new more normative Buddhist institutions grew up, increasingly based around celibate monasticism. These institutions generally accepted the Nyingmapa as Buddhists, if criticizing them at times for supposed deviations from authentic Indian tradition. The Yungdrung Bon followers seem to have been seen as non-Buddhist and lumped together with village sacrificial rituals and other non-standard practices as remnants of pre-Buddhist Tibetan religion and of the forces that opposed the initial growth of Buddhism in Tibet.

How much real continuity existed between either Yungdrung Bon or Nyingmapa and the time of the early empire is hard to trace in detail, and the question of how much credence to give to Bonpo accounts of their early history will doubtless remain unresolved for the foreseeable future. It seems likely however that the competing but in many ways parallel and closely linked religious traditions of Yungdrung Bon and Nyingmapa originated in some such historical sequence as that sketched above.

Modern developments

Bon monasteries and religious institutions suffered much the same fate as Buddhist monasteries during the 'Cultural Revolution' in China. Like the Buddhist institutions, they were allowed to rebuild from the 1980s onwards under strict supervision by the Chinese authorities.

A substantial number of Bonpo refugees left Tibet at the time of the Chinese take-over, and the major Yungdrung Bon teaching centres of Menri and Yundrungling were reformed at Dehra Dun in India. There are a number of other Yungdrung Bon monasteries and religious centres in Nepal, Europe and North America.

The Bonpo have continued to suffer from discrimination by other Tibetans in the refugee context. The Fourteenth Dalai Lama, as head of the Tibetan government-in-exile however, took steps from the late 1970s onwards to improve the situation of the Bonpo. He spoke out against discrimination, arranged for the inclusion of Yungdrung Bon representatives in the Dharamsala administration and in the Tibetan assembly, and himself visited Menri in 1978 and took part in Yungdrung Bon ceremonies, declaring Bon a fifth school of Tibetan Buddhism, and emphasizing the importance of preservation of the Bon spiritual tradition. While there was opposition to these moves among conservative lamas, the general level of respect for Bonpos and the Bon tradition among Tibetans as a whole has undoubtedly risen considerably. A growing Western interest in the Bon tradition has also helped to raise the status of Bon. Thus Yungdrung Bon has increasingly moved beyond the negative stereotyping of the past into genuine acceptance as a valid spiritual tradition on a par with other Tibetan Buddhist traditions. While it contains certain unique features, its commonalities with the Buddhist traditions are strong and real, and make its acceptance as a fifth school of Tibetan Buddhism fully appropriate.

The last chapter of the book, Chapter 12, returns to Tibetan Buddhism as a whole, and discusses its situation in the contemporary world.

Key points you need to know

- The term Bon has been used to describe several different aspects of Tibetan religion that are only loosely connected with each other, if at all. The main subject of this chapter, Yungdrung Bon, is essentially a variant of Tibetan Buddhism that developed in the tenth and eleventh centuries, with close resemblances to Nyingmapa Buddhism in particular. It claims to have pre-Buddhist origins and probably preserves at least some genuinely ancient features.
- The followers of the Bon tradition, perhaps 5 to 10 per cent of the Tibetan population, were traditionally discriminated against by Tibetan Buddhists, but have now been recognized by the Fourteenth Dalai Lama as a fifth major tradition of Tibetan Buddhism.
- Yungdrung Bon traces its origins to Tönpa Shenrab (Shenrab Mibo), believed to have been a Buddha who achieved Buddhahood many hundred years before the historical Buddha Śākyamuni, in a country to the west of Tibet known as Ölmo Lungring, perhaps corresponding to parts of present-day Iran or Central Asia.
- Tönpa Shenrab is said to have visited Central Tibet, but his teachings are claimed to have been passed down through the kingdom of Shangshung in what is now Western Tibet. Most were lost during periods of persecution, so that with few exceptions the Yungdrung Bon practice lineages today derive from *terma* revelations.
- Bonpo deities and rituals resemble and in many cases are used for the same purposes as Buddhist deities and rituals, though the names and detailed iconography are usually different.

- Bon mythology, such as the Bon account of the creation of the world, may preserve genuine early Tibetan material.
- The term *bon* is also used to refer to a class of priests during the early Tibetan empire, and to a variety of village-level religious practitioners found along the Himalayas and elsewhere in Tibetan regions, who seem mainly concerned with invocations to local deities.

Discussion questions

1 Discuss the various meanings of the term *bon*, and the ways in which the term came to be attached to such various religious practices.
2 What does Yungdrung Bon have in common with Nyingmapa Buddhism? In what ways does it differ?
3 What aspects of Bon may go back to early Tibetan religion?

Further reading

Chaoul, Alejandro. *Chöd Practice in the Bön Tradition*. Ithaca, NY: Snow Lion, 2009.

Hanna, Span. 'Vast as the Sky: The *terma* tradition in modern Tibet', in Elisabeth A. Stutchbury, Hamish Gregor and Geoffrey Samuel (eds), *Tantra and Popular Religion in Tibet*. New Delhi: International Academy of Indian Culture and Aditya Prakashan, 1996.

Karmay, Samten G. *The Treasury of Good Sayings: A Tibetan History of Bon*. London: Oxford University Press, 1972.

Karmay, Samten G. *The Great Perfection: A Philosophical and Meditative Teaching of Tibetan Buddhism*. Leiden: Brill, 1988.

Karmay, Samten G. *The Arrow and the Spindle: Studies in History, Myths, Rituals and Beliefs in Tibet*, Vols 1 and 2. Kathmandu: Mandala Book Point, 1998 and 2005.

Karmay, Samten G. and Yasuhiko Nagano. *A Survey of Bonpo Monasteries and Temples in Tibet and the Himalaya*. Osaka: National Museum of Ethnology, 2003.

Karmay, Samten G. and Jeff Watt (eds). *Bon: The Magic Word. The Indigenous Religion of Tibet*. New York: Rubin Museum of Art; London: Philip Wilson, 2007.

Klein, Anne and Tenzin Wangyal Rinpoche, Geshe. *Unbounded Wholeness: Bon, Dzogchen, and the Logic of the Nonconceptual*. Oxford and New York: Oxford University Press, 2006.

Kvaerne, Per. *The Bon Religion of Tibet: The Iconography of a Living Tradition*. London: Serindia Publications, 1995.

Martin, Dan. *Unearthing Bon Treasures: Life and Contested Legacy of a Tibetan Scripture Revealer, with a General Bibliography of Bon*. Leiden, Boston and Köln: Brill, 2001.

Norbu, Namkhai. *Drung, Deu and Bön: Narrations, Symbolic Languages and the Bön Tradition in Ancient Tibet*. Dharamasala: Library of Tibetan Works and Archives, 1991.

Orofino, Giacomella. *Sacred Tibetan Teachings on Death and Liberation*. Bridport, Dorset: Prism, 1990.

Reynolds, John Myrdhin. *The Oral Tradition from Zhang-Zhung*. Kathmandu: Vajra Publications, 2005.

Shardza Tashi Gyaltsen. *Heart Drops of Dharmakaya: Dzogchen Practice of the Bon Tradition*. Translation and Commentary by Lopon Tenzin Namdak. Ithaca, NY: Snow Lion Publications, 1993.

Snellgrove, David L. *Himalayan Pilgrimage*. Oxford: Bruno Cassirer, 1961.

Snellgrove, David L. *The Nine Ways of Bon: Excerpts from gZi brjid*. London: Oxford University Press, 1967.

Wangyal, Tenzin. *Wonders of the Natural Mind: The Essence of Dzogchen in the Native Bon Tradition of Tibet*. Barrytown, NY: Station Hill, 1993.

12 *Tibetan Buddhism today and tomorrow*

In this chapter

This chapter provides a brief description of the contemporary state of Tibetan Buddhism.

Main topics covered

- Tibetan Buddhism in the People's Republic of China
- Tibetan Buddhism in the Himalayas and the Tibetan Diaspora
- Tibetan Buddhism in Mongolia, Buryatia, Tuva and Kalmykia
- Tibetan Buddhism as a global religion
- Conclusion: Tibetan Buddhism in a new environment

Introduction

As the preceding chapters have indicated, Tibetan Buddhism has proved a versatile and adaptable religion, and it exists today in a variety of different social, cultural and ecological contexts, both within Chinese-controlled Tibet, among culturally Tibetan regions in the Himalayas, and among the Tibetan diaspora.

In Chinese-controlled Tibet, Tibetan Buddhists have lived through a difficult period, which is still far from over. The massive destruction of Buddhist monasteries and temples during the Cultural Revolution, accompanied by the forced disrobing of monks and religious leaders, many of whom were imprisoned for long periods, tortured or killed, ended some thirty years ago, but the damage done at that time cannot easily be reversed, particularly since the tolerance of the government of the People's Republic of China towards religious expressions of any kind, particularly when linked to claims of cultural and political autonomy, remains limited. The departure into exile in and around 1959 of much of the senior leadership of Tibetan Buddhism, along with many tens of thousands of ordinary monks and lay people, also had a major impact. The continuity of teaching of Tibetan Buddhism, particularly at the higher levels of practice, was largely broken in Tibet itself, though it continued elsewhere, and its re-establishment is a slow and challenging process.

Tibetan Buddhism has adapted, however, with some effectiveness to its difficult new situation. It is worth noting that Tibetan Buddhism has always also had a missionary and outward-going orientation, based in part in the need of lamas and monasteries to gather disciples and acquire new sources of support. This manifested throughout Tibetan history as a gradual expansion into the border areas to the south, east and northeast of Tibet, as well as in the progressive conversion of most of the Mongol population to Tibetan Buddhism from the thirteenth century onwards. The Manchu emperors of China were also strong supporters of Tibetan Buddhism. They were identified by the Tibetans as emanations of the deity Mañjūśrī, and while this was probably more of a polite fiction than a piece of serious theological doctrine, it nevertheless points to the close linkages with the Manchu regime. This regime built many Tibetan Buddhist temples, including a splendid series at their summer resort of Jehol in Chengde as well as the Yonghegong in Beijing, and also acted as patrons for the publication of the Kangyur and Tengyur in Beijing. Tibetan lamas also gathered many followers among the Han Chinese in the 1920s and 1930s. This interest in Tibetan Buddhism among both the Han Chinese and other Chinese minority populations such as the Mongols and Manchus is long-established and increasingly reviving in recent years as part of the general religious revival within contemporary China.

Over the last half-century, since the massive Tibetan diaspora which began in and just before 1959, what was already a varied tradition divided over a range of ecological niches has become much more varied, much more scattered and increasingly globalized. Tibetan Buddhism is now very well established as a religious tradition in many parts of the world, among both its traditional population of Tibetans, Mongolians and nearby peoples, but also among many other world populations.

Tibetan Buddhism in the People's Republic of China

Perhaps inevitably, Tibetan Buddhism in the People's Republic has taken on elements of opposition both to Chinese rule and to Chinese cultural hegemony. Monks and nuns have been in the forefront of protests against oppressive aspects of Chinese rule, while the Dalai Lama, as the pre-eminent Tibetan lama, former head of the Lhasa state and (until recently) head of the government-in-exile became a central symbol of Tibetan freedom. For the Chinese state, the powerful and largely autonomous role of Tibetan lamas and monastic corporations was from the beginning both barely comprehensible and clearly incompatible with their vision of the relation between state and religion. The government of the People's Republic has seen religion either as a rival source of power to be suppressed or as, at best, an arm of state policy, to be kept under strict control. In this it continues in many ways a long-standing orientation of

Figure 12.1 Square in front of the Jokang, Lhasa. Photo by the author (1987).

Figure 12.2 Reconstruction at Samye Monastery, Central Tibet. Photo by author (1987).

the Chinese state, prevailing through much of the history of the Chinese empire, from which Tibetans were protected by their remoteness and lack of effective inclusion.

After the period of outright suppression of Buddhism, including destruction of Buddhist institutions during the Cultural Revolution, and the partial relaxation in the 1980s, the PRC government resumed a policy of maintaining strict control both over Tibetan Buddhist institutions and their leaders, and over ordinary monks, nuns and lay Buddhists. Tight quotas have been imposed on the number of monks and nuns at monastic institutions, and their activities kept under close supervision. Both monks and nuns have nevertheless been at the forefront of demonstrations against Chinese rule, and imprisonment and torture remain a routine experience.

The most senior Gelukpa reincarnate lama remaining in Tibet, the Tenth Panchen Lama, Chökyi Gyaltsen (1938–89) was appointed as chairman of the Preparatory Committee for the Tibet Autonomous Region in 1959 after the Dalai Lama's flight to India, in effect taking over as figurehead of the Chinese administration of Tibet. The Tenth Panchen Lama turned out to be less supportive of Chinese policies in Tibet than the Chinese government might have wished, however. After he protested about the treatment of the Tibetan people, he was stripped of his official positions in 1964, publicly humiliated and imprisoned. He was released in 1977 but kept under house arrest in Beijing until 1982, when he was declared rehabilitated and allowed again to take on some political offices. He died in 1989, shortly after delivering a significant speech criticizing Chinese policy in Tibet. The identity of his reincarnation became a source of dispute between the Chinese government and the Tibetan government-in-exile, and the candidate chosen by the Dalai Lama is at present still in Chinese custody (see Appendix).

Within this generally oppressive context, the visionary and creative dimension of Tibetan Buddhism has re-emerged, leading to the arising of new *tertön* and the development of new *terma* appropriate to the political situation. The most significant of these so far was the late Kenpo Jigphun (Jigme Phuntsok, 1933–2004), who built up a substantial religious movement based in Golok in Northeast Tibet, which has for many centuries been a particularly 'wild' area of primarily pastoralist population, centred on the great holy mountain of Amnye Machen and particularly resistant to incorporation into centralized rule.

The Dalai Lama's own role throughout has been to work towards negotiation with the Chinese state and, especially after the end of the armed resistance movement (Chushi Gangdruk) in 1974, to discourage armed revolt. Pragmatically, he has aimed at the attainment of as much Tibetan cultural and administrative autonomy as possible within a Chinese state. Unfortunately, the Chinese leadership so far has been unwilling to make many concessions, and has resorted to violent suppression of opposition to Chinese rule and to demonizing the Dalai Lama and the resistance as 'splittists' or worse. Elements of a more moderate approach have appeared at times, but renewed protests during the Olympic year of 2008 again led to the forceful imposition of police and military rule.

In relation to Tibetan Buddhists within China itself, and to the future of the Tibetans as an autonomous culture, it is hard to guess what is ahead politically. The most hopeful future would seem to be one in which growing democratization in China as a whole opens up a space for pragmatic accommodation between Tibetans in China and the other populations in the Chinese People's Republic. Despite the difficult experiences of the past fifty or sixty years, all hope is perhaps not lost for a movement of this kind. The increasing interest and sympathy among Han Chinese for Tibetan Buddhism should also lead in time to greater levels of understanding among the Chinese leadership regarding the true nature of the situation in Tibet.

On the Tibetan side, it is also important to note that many of the protests of 2008 had more to do with civil rights, the imposition of resettlement programmes, and other pragmatic issues than with independence as such. The Tibetan nationalist agenda and the desire for genuine independence is real, but in some ways it is more important for the diaspora than within Tibet. Much of the population in Tibet proper is primarily concerned with the everyday issues of living together with Han Chinese and other ethnic groups as part of the Chinese state. Also, the Chinese state investment in Tibet, and the development of tourism, has had good as well as bad effects, and an important aspect of the Chinese religious revival has been a growing Han Chinese interest in Tibetan Buddhism. Thus there are factors that might lead in time to a situation of mutual accommodation between the Chinese state and the Tibetans. However, there are clearly many things that could go wrong with this relatively optimistic scenario.

Figure 12.3 Namdrolling Monastery, South India. Photo by Ruth Rickard.

Tibetan Buddhism in the Himalayas and the Tibetan diaspora

Meanwhile, Tibetan religion and culture are being continued in a variety of forms, all of them transformed substantially, in regions outside the People's Republic of China. Some of these regions are parts of South Asia that were traditionally Tibetan in culture. These include Ladakh, Lahul and Spiti, Sikkim, the Darjeeling Hills and parts of Arunachal Pradesh in India, parts of Northern Nepal, and the independent state of Bhutan. The Kathmandu Valley, which has now become a major centre for the non-Gelukpa traditions, has also had a long-standing Tibetan presence and close cultural links with Tibet. Many religious communities and monasteries, however, have been established in areas of Tibetan refugee settlement such as Dharamsala and the agricultural settlements in South India which did not have any significant previous presence of Tibetan culture or religion. Others are located among the worldwide Tibetan diaspora, which now includes substantial communities in Switzerland, the USA, Canada and other countries around the world. Thus, Tibetan monasteries and religious institutions have become part of the cultural underpinning of the Tibetan diaspora.

The Dalai Lama, as the former head of the Lhasa state, senior lama of the Gelukpa order and the most respected of all reincarnate lamas, became by necessity the national leader of the Tibetan people and head of the government-in-exile located at Dharamsala in Northern India. He has worked over many years to create a structure of democratic institutions for the Tibetan community in exile, and in May 2011 officially devolved his political role as head of the government-in-exile to an elected leadership.

His headship of the exile community has also been marked by sustained efforts to unify the community against a variety of divisive issues and tendencies. These have involved both regional and religious differences. The Lhasa administration was closely identified with the Gelukpa school and with Central Tibet. The Dharamsala government-in-exile began as a continuation of the Lhasa government, dominated by former Lhasa officials and Gelukpa lamas, and was initially distrusted by many senior religious figures of other traditions, as well as by lay Tibetan refugees from areas that had not traditionally been within the Lhasa state. The Dharamsala administration under the Dalai Lama has nevertheless managed, over time, to create a relatively inclusive and democratic structure that has received broad support across the Tibetan communities in exile. Senior figures from the three non-Gelukpa Buddhist schools and from the Bonpo have been included in the religious administration, and relations between the different lamas and schools are now on the whole very positive. This is a considerable achievement, since the relations between these groups were often competitive and conflict-ridden in Tibet before 1959, and mutual distrust was initially widespread. The Dalai Lama's government at Dharamsala has also continued under difficult circumstances to argue for a negotiated settlement rather than armed struggle with China.

There have nevertheless been a series of major disputes within the exile community. Apart from ongoing questioning of the appropriateness of the Dalai Lama's non-violent approach to the Chinese occupation of Tibet, these have included the conflict over the recognition of the rebirth of the Sixteenth Karmapa, who died in 1981 (see Appendix), and also the conflict regarding the Shugden deity, which reached its peak in the mid-1990s. The cult of this deity is associated with conservative elements in the Gelukpa tradition who are hostile to alliances with other religious schools. It was promoted in the early twentieth century by the prominent Gelukpa lama Pawongka Rinpoche (1874–1941). Pawongka Rinpoche's students and disciples included the regent Taktra Rinpoche, who headed the Lhasa government from 1941 to 1950, and one of the Dalai Lama's own tutors, Trijang Rinpoche (1900–1981), as well as many other senior Gelukpa lamas.

The Dalai Lama, evidently motivated at least in part by the need to avoid identification with a deity so closely associated with Gelukpa supremacy and Gelukpa suppression of other traditions, began to distance himself from the Shugden cult in the 1980s, eventually asking all the major Gelukpa monasteries to cease practising the cult in public. A number of senior Gelukpa figures, including the former *geshé* Kelsang Gyatso, who directed a large network of 'New Kadampa' Buddhist centres in the UK, Europe and North America, refused to accept this demand and to varying degrees rejected the Dalai Lama's authority. The controversy was a source of major tension within the exile community, particularly in India, throughout the 1990s, but appears to have died down somewhat in recent years.

Tibetan Buddhism in Mongolia, Buryatia, Tuva and Kalmykia

As mentioned in earlier chapters, Tibetan Buddhism spread among a number of non-Tibetan peoples in the course of Tibetan history, including the Mongolian populations of the Mongolian People's Republic, the Chinese People's Republic, and the former Soviet Union (in Buryatia and Kalmykia), as well as neighbouring Turkic groups such as the people of Tuva. While religion in these areas is largely outside the remit of this book, the presence of the Dalai Lama and other senior refugee lamas outside Tibet has led to increased contact with many of these regions, so that Tibetan Buddhism in these countries, which had gone through periods of suppression in the course of the twentieth century under Chinese and Soviet regimes, as well as in independent Mongolia, has undergone a considerable revival in recent years.

Tibetan Buddhism as a global religion

The presence of many senior refugee Tibetan lamas in Nepal and India after 1959, along with the increasing numbers of young Westerners travelling to these regions, has led increasingly to lamas being invited to Western countries, both on teaching visits and to establish permanent centres. The first Tibetan monasteries in the West

Figure 12.4 Gompa founded by Namkhai Norbu Rinpoche at Merigar in Tuscany, Italy. Photo by Helen Williams (2011).

were established in Europe and North America in the late 1960s and helped to fuel a growing global interest in Tibetan Buddhism. While some of these, such as the community at Rikon in Switzerland, were established primarily to serve the refugee population, most were and are supported primarily by the many new non-Tibetan followers of Tibetan Buddhist lamas. By now, there are many hundreds of Tibetan lamas from all schools of Tibetan Buddhism, including the Bonpo, resident in the West or regularly visiting Western countries, with numerous teaching and retreat centres and 'Dharma groups' in most major Western countries. A similar network of lamas and centres has grown up among the Chinese communities of Taiwan, Hong Kong, Singapore and Malaysia.

This story too lies mostly outside the scope of this book, but it is worth at least referring to here. The encounter between Tibetan Buddhism and the West has often been creative, but the growth of genuine mutual understanding has been a relatively slow process. Many of the early teachers, such as Chögyam Trungpa, Tarthang Tulku or Chögyal Namkhai Norbu, reshaped traditional practices in often quite radical ways for their Western students. The whole question of translating Buddhist teachings into accessible English and other Western languages itself raises many problems, for reasons that should be clear to the reader of this book. Much of the specialized vocabulary of the Tibetan teachings does not translate directly into modern European languages, with words such as 'mind', 'self' and 'consciousness' being particularly treacherous. It has been tempting to translate Buddhism into the language of psychology and psychotherapy, but this is often misleading since it can easily lead to Buddhism being read in primarily individual terms. The development of transpersonal schools of psychology in the West, in part under Buddhist influence, has provided some assistance here, as has the by now quite extensive engagement of Western scholars on Buddhist philosophical material, usually in conjunction with Tibetan lamas.

Over time, substantial numbers of Western and Asian students have become more deeply engaged with the Tibetan Buddhist tradition, often undertaking extensive retreats, including the traditional three years, three months and three days retreat. They have learned to read, speak and translate Tibetan, and increasingly are being authorized to act as lamas and teachers by their Tibetan gurus. There has been a general move towards the establishment of more traditional modes of Tibetan practice in the West and in these other new regions for Tibetan religious activity, but also a complex and often fascinating process of mutual learning between Tibetan lamas and their non-Tibetan followers. Given the uncertain situation in Tibet itself and among the diaspora in India and Nepal, this new global community of Tibetan Buddhist practitioners is likely to be an increasingly significant part of the overall Tibetan Buddhist scene. It is difficult to predict though exactly what that will mean for the ongoing nature of the Tibetan Buddhist tradition.

The Dalai Lama himself has become a spiritual leader on a global scale, and has undertaken numerous teaching tours around the world, as well as a long series of Kālacakra and other empowerments, through which many Westerners and other non-Tibetans have been drawn to some extent into the *maṇḍala* of Tibetan Tantric practice. In part, this has doubtless been motivated by the need to build up support for the Tibetan cause around the world, but it has also helped to establish a genuine global presence for elements of Tibetan religion. Thus a religion which was in the 1950s little known to the outside world except through superficial stereotypes and misrepresentations has gradually become a vital part of global religion, and touched the lives of many millions of people.

Conclusion: Tibetan Buddhism in a new environment

This book has stressed the importance of environment and of context, and of seeing Tibetan Buddhism as a way of living within a particular space, physically, climatically, and in terms of the political and economic environment within which its institutions took shape and established themselves. That environment is now dramatically different, both within and outside the People's Republic of China. Both Buddhist lamas and ordinary Tibetans have had to learn to live within complex new, often multinational or transnational, environments and networks. Yet Tibetan Buddhism, despite the traumatic nature of much of the last half-century, has become firmly established in a variety of contexts and situations around the world, and is a significant part of global spiritual and religious life. Its success so far suggests that, at the very least, there is a good chance of Tibetan religion in its various forms continuing to be a significant and growing part of global culture and society for many years to come.

Key points you need to know

- Tibetan Buddhism is a versatile and adaptable religion, and despite the traumas of the Cultural Revolution and the difficulties of Chinese rule more generally, it remains alive within Chinese-controlled Tibet and is finding new followers throughout the world.
- Within Chinese-controlled Tibet, the period of liberalization in the 1980s has been followed by continuing attempts to subordinate Tibetan Buddhism to state policy and intermittent suppression where these attempts have failed.
- Elsewhere, Buddhist teaching and practice traditions have continued and flourished among culturally Tibetan populations in the Himalayas, among the Tibetan diaspora, and increasingly among non-Tibetan populations around the world. Tibetan Buddhism has also undergone a revival among traditionally Buddhist populations in independent Mongolia and in Mongolian regions of Russia and China.
- Tibetan Buddhism is taking on new forms as it becomes an increasingly global religion and adapts to new languages and to peoples from very different cultural backgrounds to that of Tibet. The long-term consequences of this transformation are difficult to foresee, but the religion as a whole is establishing itself effectively on a global scale, and increasingly entering into dialogue with Western modes of thinking and knowledge.

Discussion questions

1. Discuss the possibilities for Tibetan Buddhism as a global religion.
2. What aspects of Tibetan Buddhism are proving attractive to its new global following?
3. Which aspects are less acceptable?

Further reading

Blondeau, Anne-Marie and Katia Buffetrille. *Authenticating Tibet: Answers to China's 100 Questions*. Berkeley, Los Angeles and London: University of California Press, 2008.

Butterfield, Stephen T. *The Double Mirror: A Skeptical Journey into Buddhist Tantra*. Berkeley, CA: North Atlantic Books, 1994.

Dalai Lama, Fourteenth. *My Land and My People*. New York: Warner Books, 1998.

Dodin, Thierry and Heinz Räther. *Imagining Tibet: Perceptions, Projections and Fantasies*. Boston: Wisdom Publications, 2001.

Dreyfus, Georges. 'Proto-nationalism in Tibet', in Per Kvaerne (ed.), *Tibetan Studies: Proceedings of the 6th Seminar of the International Association for Tibetan Studies*, vol. 1. Oslo: Institute for Comparative Research in Human Culture, 1994.

Dreyfus, Georges. 'Tibetan religious nationalism: Western fantasy or empowering vision?' in P. Christiaan Klieger (ed.), *Tibet, Self and the Tibetan Diaspora: Voices of Difference: Proceedings of the 9th Seminar of the International Association for Tibetan Studies*, Leiden 2000. Leiden: Brill, 2002.

Fields, Rick. *How the Swans Came to the Lake: A Narrative History of Buddhism in America*. Boston: Shambhala, 1992.

Goldstein, Melvyn C. and Matthew T. Kapstein (eds). *Buddhism in Contemporary Tibet: Religious Revival and Cultural Identity*. Berkeley: University of California Press, 1998.

Kapstein, Matthew (ed.). *Buddhism Between Tibet and China*. Boston: Wisdom Publications, 2009.

Klieger, P. Christiaan. *Tibetan Nationalism*. Berkeley, CA: Folklore Institute, 1992.

Korom, Frank J. (ed.). *Constructing Tibetan Culture: Contemporary Perspectives*. Quebec: World Heritage Press, 1997.

Trungpa, Chögyam. *Cutting Through Spiritual Materialism*. Boston: Shambhala, 1987.

Mackenzie, Vicki. *Reborn in the West: The Reincarnation Masters*. London: Bloomsbury, 1995.

Norbu, Dawa. *Red Star over Tibet*. London: Collins, 1974.

Norbu, Namkhai. *The Crystal and the Way of Light: Sūtra, Tantra and Dzogchen*. New York and London: Routledge and Kegan Paul, 1986.

Stoddard, Heather. *Le Mendiant de l'Amdo*. Paris: Société d'Ethnographie, 1986.

Tuttle, Gray. *Tibetan Buddhists in the Making of Modern China*. New York: Columbia University Press, 2005.

Yeshe, Lama. *Introduction to Tantra: A Vision of Totality*. Boston: Wisdom Publications, 1987.

Appendix
Some important lamas

Altogether the number of lamas must run into many thousands, and even the number of recognized reincarnate lama titles is probably around a thousand, so it is hardly possible to list more than a small selection here. I have chosen to give some basic details of some of the most important reincarnation lineages and heads of major orders, along with details of some other well-known lamas active today or in the recent past, since this may help people encountering Tibetan Buddhist traditions to locate who and what they are dealing with. There are also by now a significant number of Westerners who have been trained as Tibetan lamas, though I have not listed any of these below.

GELUKPA

Dalai Lamas

The Dalai Lama reincarnation goes back to Gedundrüp, one of the younger disciples of Tsongkapa, founding figure of the Gelukpa tradition, and founder of the monastery of Tashilhunpo. They were also recognized as emanations of Avalokiteśvara. The current rebirth is the Foureenth.

Table A.1 Dalai Lamas

1	Gedun Drupa (1391–1474)	8	Jamphel Gyatso (1758–1804)
2	Gedun Gyatso (1475–1542)	9	Lungtok Gyatso (1805–1815)
3	Sonam Gyatso (1543–1588)	10	Tsultrim Gyatso (1816–1837)
4	Yonten Gyatso (1589–1617)	11	Khedrup Gyatso (1838–1856)
5	Lobsang Gyatso (1617–1682)	12	Trinley Gyatso (1856–1875)
6	Tsangyang Gyatso (1682–1706)	13	Thupten Gyatso (1876–1933)
7	Kelsang Gyatso (1708–1757)	14	Tenzin Gyatso (b.1935)

The Dalai Lamas were originally the senior reincarnate lamas at Drepung monastery. The third member of the series, Sonam Gyatso, was patronized by the Mongol chieftain Altan Khan, who gave him the title 'Dalai Lama', associated with all subsequent members of the series. The Fifth became ruler of most of Tibet with the assistance of Gushri Khan, and his personal household at Drepung, the Ganden Podrang, became the Tibetan government at Lhasa. The territory over which the Dalai Lamas had authority corresponded roughly to the present-day Tibet Autonomous Region, although numerous other lama and aristocratic families within this region, such as the Panchen Lamas, had high degrees of autonomy.

The Thirteenth Dalai Lama attempted to modernize Tibet in the 1920s and 1930s but much of his work was reversed after his death. The Fourteenth Dalai Lama took power in 1950, but the deteriorating political situation following the Chinese takeover led to his flight to India in 1959. Here he became the head of the Tibetan Government-in-exile and de facto political as well as religious leader of the Tibetan people. He retired from his political role in May 2011.

Panchen Lamas

The Panchen Lama lineage began with Panchen Lobsang Chöki Gyantsen, the tutor of the Fifth Dalai Lama. The reincarnation lineage was subsequently traced back to Kedrubje, senior disciple of Tsongkapa, leading to two different numberings, based on whether Khedrupje or Panchen Lobsang Chöki Gyantsen was counted as the first Panchen Lama. The Panchen Lamas' head monastery was at Tashilhunpo, near Central Tibet's second major regional capital Shigatse. They possessed very extensive monastic estates in West-Central Tibet. The lamas of this series were regarded as emanations of the Buddha Amitābha.

Table A.2 Panchen Lamas

	1	Khedrupje	1385–1438
	2	Sönam Choklang	1438–1505
	3	Ensapa Lobsang Döndrup	1505–1568
1	4	Lobsang Chöki Gyantsen	1570–1662
2	5	Lobsang Yeshe	1663–1737
3	6	Lobsang Panden Yeshe	1738–1780
4	7	Panden Tenpai Nyima	1782–1853
5	8	Tenpai Wangchuk	1855–1882
6	9	Tubten Chöki Nyima	1883–1937
7	10	Lobsang Trinley Lhündrub Chökyi Gyantsen	1938–1989
8	11	Gendün Chöki Nyima [Tibetan government-in-exile candidate]	1989–
8	11	Gyantsen Norbu [Chinese government candidate]	1990–

The Sixth (or Ninth) Panchen, Tubten Chöki Nyima, fled to China as a result of the Thirteenth Dalai Lama's attempts to impose tax liabilities on the Panchen Lama's estate. The Seventh (Tenth), Lobsang Trinley Lhündrub Chökyi Gyantsen, was born in China, and became formal head of the Tibet Autonomous Region for some years after the Fourteenth Dalai Lama's flight to India. He was subjected to re-education during and after the Cultural Revolution, but it seems clear however that he remained a Tibetan nationalist and worked to protect Tibet and its people as far as he was able. The identity of his successor is contested, with one candidate recognized by the Dalai Lama and the Tibetan government-in-exile, and a rival candidate recognized by Chinese authorities. The Tibetan government-in-exile's candidate remains under confinement in China.

Jetsundampa Hutuqtu

Table A.3 Jetsundampa Hutuqtu or Bogdo Gegen

0	1575–1634	Tāranātha Kunga Nyingpo (other previous rebirths also recognized, including the Indian Mahāsiddha Kṛṣṇācārin)
1	1635–1723	Yeshe Dorje (Lobsang Tenpé Gyantsen)
2	1724–57	Lobsang Tenpé Drönmé
3	1758–73	Yeshé Tenpé Nyima
4	1775–1813	Lobsang Tupten Wangchuk
5	1815–40	Lobsang Tsultrim Jigmé
6	1843–48	Lobsang Panden Tenpa
7	1850–68	Ngawang Chöying Wangchuk Trinlé Gyatso
8	1871–1924	Ngawang Lobsang Chöki Nyima Tendzin Wangchuk
9	1932–	Jampal Namdrol Chokye Gyaltsen

The Jetsundampa Hutuqtu or Bogdo Gegen were based in Urga (now Ulan Bator) and were the senior lamas in Outer Mongolia (later the Mongolian People's Republic). The First Jetsundampa Hutuqtu, known in Mongolia as Zanabazar (the Mongolian version of his Sanskrit name, Jñānavajra) came from a Mongolian princely family, and was recognized by the Fifth Dalai Lama as the rebirth of the Jonangpa lama Tāranātha, thus effectively completing the suppression of the Jonangpa tradition in Central Tibet. Zanabazar was a noted sculptor, many of whose works have been preserved. The Eighth Jetsundampa was briefly head of state of independent Mongolia from 1911 until his death in 1924, at which time the Mongolian government prohibited the finding of a rebirth. The Ninth was said to have been recognized by the Tibetan regent Reting Rinpoche and to have lived in secret for many years; his identity was made public by the Fourteenth Dalai Lama in 1991. The names and identifications up to the Eighth are taken from Gene Smith's *Among Tibetan Texts*.

Changkya Rinpoche (Jangjia Khutukhtu)

Table A.4 Changkya Rinpoche (Jangjia Khutukhtu)

			Recognized previous rebirths include Marpa Choki Lodrö and Tsangnyön Heruka
1		d.1641	Khyenrap Dragppa Özer
2	1	1642–1714	Ngawang Lobsang Chöden
3	2	1717–1786	Rolpé Dorjé (Yeshé Tenpé Drönmé)
4	3	1787–1846	Yeshé Tenpé Gyantsen
5	4	1849–1875	Yeshe Tenpé Nyima
6	5	1878–1888	Lobsang Yeshé Tenpé Gyatso
7	6	1871? –90?	Lobsang Pelden Tenpe Dronme
8	7	1891–957	Chöying Yeshe Dorje

The most important lama of this series was the Second (often called the Third), Changkya Rolpai Dorje, who was preceptor to the Qianlong emperor of China, and chief representative of Tibetan Buddhism at the Qing court. He and his successors, mostly based in Beijing, were the senior Tibetan lamas in China proper and Inner Mongolia. The Seventh (or Eighth) Changcha accompanied the Nationalist government to Taiwan in 1949 and died there in 1957. There appears to be a Chinese-endorsed rebirth in the Chinese People's Republic.

The names and identifications here are taken from Gene Smith's *Among Tibetan Texts*.

Jamyang Shepa Tulkus

Table A.5 Jamyang Shepa Tulkus

1	1648–1722	Ngawang Tsöndrü
2	1728–1791(?)	Konchok Jigmé Wangpo
3	1796(?)–1855	Losel Jigme Gyatso (Lobsang Yignyen Tupten Gyatso)
4	1856–	Kelsang Tubten Wangchuk
5	1915–1947	Losang Jamyang Yeshé Tenpé Gyeltsen
6	1948–	Lobsang Jigme Thubten Chökyi Nyima

The first Jamyang Shepa was a leading Gelukpa scholar of his day, author of monastery textbooks still used at Drepung and elsewhere, and the founder of the monastery of Labrang Tashi Khyil in Amdo (Gansu) in 1710. His successors were the senior lamas of this large monastic university. The Sixth was enthroned in 1952, but did not receive a traditional religious education, disrobed and married, and lives as a layman in China.

Gelukpa lamas today

The Dalai Lama is of course internationally by far the best known of all contemporary Tibetan lamas, and his frequent visits to Western and other global destinations to give Buddhist teachings and perform major rituals such as the Kālacakra empowerments have given Tibetan Buddhism much of its present international profile. Many other Gelukpa lamas have been active in the West. One of the first was the Kalmyk Mongolian lama Geshe Wangyal (c.1901–1983) who established a Buddhist monastery in New Jersey in 1958. He taught many early Western students, some of whom went on to become scholars and teachers in their own right. Another distinguished early Gelukpa lama in the West was Geshe Rabten (1920–86), who in 1974 became abbot of the first Tibetan monastery in the West, at Rikon in Switzerland, and again had a number of Western students. A much younger lama, Thubten Zopa Rinpoche (b.1946), along with his teacher Lama Thubten Yeshe (1935–1984), founded a monastic centre at Kopan in the Kathmandu valley, Nepal, in 1969, which developed into a global network, the Foundation for the Preservation of the Mahayana Tradition (FPMT). Another of the largest Western Buddhist organizations, the New Kadampa Tradition, broke away from the FPMT under the leadership of Geshe Kelsang Gyatso, but later became involved in conflict with the Dalai Lama and the majority of the Gelukpa tradition over its endorsement of the controversial Shugden deity.

Kagyüdpa

Two of the main sub-traditions of the Marpa Kagyüdpa, the Karmapa and Drukpa, are discussed here. There are several smaller traditions, such as the Drikung and Taklung Kagyü, as well as the parallel tradition of the Shangpa Kagyü, which does not have monasteries of its own but has been continued by lamas of other traditions such as Jonang Tāranātha and more recently Kalu Rinpoche.

Karma Kagyüdpa

The head lamas of the Karma Kagyüdpa, the Gyalwa Karmapas were the first recognized reincarnate lama lineage (see Chapter 7), with their principal monastery at Tsurpu in Central Tibet. Many of the series were important religious leaders, and like the Dalai Lamas and the head lamas of the Drukpa order they were recognized as emanations of the *bodhisattva* Avalokiteśvara. The Fifteenth Gyalwa Karmapa, Kakyab Dorjé, was deeply involved in the Rimé movement. The Sixteenth, who left Tibet in 1959 and settled in Sikkim, was recognized by the Dharamsala administration as the official head of the Kagyüdpa Order. Other senior Karma Kagyü reincarnate lamas include the Shamarpa and Situ Rinpoche. The recognition of the

Table A.6 Gyalwa Karmapas

1	1110–1193	Düsum Khyenpa
2	1204–1283	Karma Pakshi
3	1284–1339	Rangjung Dorjé
4	1340–1383	Rolpai Dorjé
5	1384–1415	Deshin Shekpa
6	1416–1453	Tongwa Dönden
7	1454–1506	Chödrak Gyatso
8	1507–1554	Mikyö Dorje
9	1556–1603	Wangchuk Dorje
10	1604–1674	Chöying Dorje
11	1676–1702	Yeshe Dorje
12	1703–1732	Changchub Dorje
13	1733–1797	Dudul Dorje
14	1798–1868	Thekchok Dorjé
15	1871–1922	Kakyab Dorjé
16	1924–1981	Rangjung Rikpé Dorjé
17a	1985–	Orgyen Trinlé Dorjé [candidate supported by Dalai Lama and Situ Rinpoché]
17b	1983–	Trinlé Tayé Dorjé [candidate supported by Shamarpa]

Seventeenth has been in dispute since 1992, with one candidate supported by the Dalai Lama and Situ Rinpoche, the other by the Shamarpa. The dispute is still not fully resolved though majority support is for Orgyen Trinlé Dorjé, who has become an increasingly prominent religious leader within the Tibetan diaspora.

The Karma Kagyüdpa tradition is particularly well established in the West. Chögyam Trungpa Rinpoche (1940–1987) was one of the first Tibetan lamas to study and teach in the West. In 1967, he founded a meditation centre in Scotland, Samyê-Ling (now directed by Akong Rinpoche), and went on to found several centres in the United States and Canada. These are now directed by Trungpa's son, Sakyong Mipham Rinpoche.

The Sixteenth Gyalwa Karmapa also visited Europe and the United States, as did the senior Karma Kagyü lama Kalu Rinpoche (1905–1989), whose disciples founded a number of Dharma centres around the world.

Drukpa Kagyüdpa

The Gyalwang Drukpa or Drukchen are the head lamas of the Drukpa Kagyüdpa. Their seat was initially at Ralung in Central Tibet, later at Sangngak Chöling in Southern Tibet. The lineage of this reincarnation series is traced back to Tsangpa

Table A.7 Gyalwang Drukchen

1	1161–1211	Tsangpa Gyare Yeshe Dorje
Gap of 217 years before rebirth recognized		
2	1428–1476	Kunga Paljor
3	1478–1513	Jamyang Chodrak
4	1527–1592	Kunkhyen Pema Karpo
5	1593–1653	Pagsam Wangpo
6	1654–1717	Mipam Wangpo
7	1718–1766	Trinlé Shingta
8	1768–1822	Künzik Chökyi Nyima
9	1823–1883	Migyur Wangyel
10	1884–1930	Mipam Chökyi Wangpo
11	1931–1960	Tendin Khyenrap Gelek Wangpo
12	1963–	Jigmé Pema Wangchen

Gyare Yeshe Dorje, but the sequence of reincarnate lamas appears to have been established in the fifteenth century, replacing an earlier hereditary succession. In the sixteenth century, there was a major dispute over the recognition of successor to the great scholar Drukchen Pema Karpo. The dispute was never resolved. One candidate took over at the Druk monastery of Ralung in Tibet, and is generally known today as the Drukchen or Gyalwang Drukpa; the other, who came from the hereditary lineage of Ralung, became official head of the Bhutanese state, and is known as the Shabdrung Rinpoche.

The Shabdrung Ngawang Namgyel died in 1651, but his death was concealed by the ruling regents until around 1705. A subsequent civil war over rival candidates was resolved by introducing the concept of multiple reincarnations of the Shabdrung's body, speech and mind, with the mind-emanations taking over the Shabdrung's political role. Power was actually exercised by a series of regents. In 1907, Bhutan became a hereditary kingship with British support; the Seventh Shabdrung died in

Table A.8 Shabdrung Rinpoche

1	1594–1651	Shabdrung Ngawang Namgyel
2	1724–1761	Jigmé Drakpa I (First *tugtrul* or mind-emanation)
3	1762–1788	Chöki Gyaltsen
4	1791–1830	Jigmé Drakpa II
5	1831–1861	Jigmé Norbu
6	1862–1904	Jigmé Chogyel
7	1905–1931	Jigmé Dorje

1933, and the Bhutanese state has not officially recognized any subsequent reincarnations, although there have been a number of unofficial rebirths.

The Gyalwang Drukchen lineage has continued to the present day. The current Gyalwang Drukchen is based in Darjeeling in India, and has been active in teaching in the West, as have other senior Drukpa lamas. The monastery of Tashijong in India, founded by the Eighth Khamtrul Rinpoche Dongyud Nyima (1931–1980), formerly of Kampagar monastery in Kham, is another major centre, and is particularly noted for its active yogic tradition.

Sakya

The head lamas of Sakya continue to belong to the Kön family, the most important remaining hereditary lama lineage in Tibet. This family, which like some other old aristocratic families has a legend of descent from the mountain gods, claims to have included ministers of the early Tibetan emperors. After the foundation of the monastery of Sakya in 1073, succession was initially from celibate lama to the son of a married brother; in more recent times, the Sakya Tridzin or head lama of Sakya has generally been married. In accordance with a prophecy attributed to Atiśa, members of the family are held to be emanations of Avalokiteśvara, Vajrapāṇi or (mostly) Mañjūśrī.

The Kön lineage split in the eighteenth century into two sub-lineages, the Drolma Podrang and Puntsok Podrang, with the position of Sakya Tridzin alternating between the two. The current Sakya Tridzin, (Ngawang Kunga Tekchen Palbar Sampel Wangi Gyalpo (born 1945) belongs to the Dolma Podrang, and has lived in India since 1959. The current head of the Puntsok Podrang is Jigdal Dagchen Sakya Rinpoche (b.1929), and has resided in the USA since 1960. These and other Sakya lamas, including lamas from the related Ngorpa and Tselpa traditions, also now have a substantial global following.

Nyingmapa

The Nyingmapa tradition has generally been less structured and hierarchical than the Gelukpa, Kagyüdpa or Sakyapas. A series of major teaching monasteries emerged from the seventeemth century onwards, each of them associated with specific sets of teachings. Dorje Drak and Mindrol Ling are both situated in Central Tibet; Dorje Drak was founded in around 1610, Mindrol Ling in 1676. The remaining four, Dzogchen (1685), Shechen (c.1734), Katok (1656, on the site of an earlier monastery of the same name) and Palyul (1665) are in Eastern Tibet. These mostly have reincarnate lamas, though the head lamas of Mindrol Ling, like those of Sakya, belong to an old hereditary lineage.

A central role in the development of the Nyingma tradition has been taken by the revelations of the *tertön* lamas. Some of the more important figures are Nyang-rel Nyima Özer (1124–1192), revealer of the Sanglingma biography of Guru Padmasambhava and the Kagye Deshek Dupa teachings; Guru Chöwang (1212–1270), revealer of the Lama Sangdu, Rigdzin Godemchen (1337–1408), discoverer of the Changter ('Northern Treasure') tradition; Dorje Lingpa (1346–1405), and Pema Lingpa (1445/50–1521). These are sometimes known as the Five Tertön kings, although lists vary. Important later *tertön* include Karma Lingpa, who discovered the Shitro teachings, which formed the basis of the so-called 'Tibetan Book of the Dead', Jatson Nyingpo (1585–1656), discoverer of the Konchok Chindü teachings, Mingyur Dorje (1645–1667), revealer of the Namchö ('Sky Dharma') teachings, and Terdak Lingpa (1646–1714), discoverer of the Lhoter ('Southern Treasure') tradition, who was closely associated with the Fifth Dalai Lama, himself a *tertön* who revealed a number of Nyingma teachings.

Jigmé Lingpa (1729–98) revealed the Longchen Nyingtik, a series of Dzogchen teachings that was influential on the Rimé movement (see below); another *tertön*, Chokgyur Lingpa (1829–70), was an important member of the initial group of Rimé lamas. His revelations, along with those of his near contemporary Dudjom Lingpa (1835–1904), Dudjom Lingpa's rebirth Dudjom Rinpoche (1904–1987), and other lamas of the nineteenth and twentieth centuries, are sometimes referred to as constituting the *tersar* or 'New Terma'.

A number of Tibetan lamas from Nyingma and Dzogchen backgrounds have been active in the West. Many of these derive from the tradition of Dudjom Rinpoche (1904–87), who himself had many Western students and spent some of his later years at a centre in the Dordogne in France. Another major focus of teaching among diaspora and Westerners has been Ugyen Tulku (1920–96) in Kathmandu. Other internationally active Nyingma lamas include Namkhai Norbu Rinpoche (b.1938), the late Chime Rigdzin Rinpoche (1922–2002) and Chagdud Tulku (1930–2002), and Sogyal Rinpoche (b.1947). The official head of the Nyingma tradition is now Trulshig Rinpoche (b.1923), whose principal monastery is in the Sherpa region of Nepal.

Rimé

The Rimé ('non-sectarian') movement began in Eastern Tibet (Derge state) in the mid-nineteenth century among lamas of the Kagyüdpa, Nyingmapa and Sakya traditions, as well as some Bon lamas. The extent to which it makes sense to speak of a 'movement' remains contested, but the term remains useful as a way of labelling the influential work of an important group of Eastern Tibetan lamas and their followers. While the primary association of these lamas remained with their traditions of origin, their work of collecting, systematizing and transmitting a very wide range of teaching lineages and traditions, which were then passed on by their students and followers, created what became in effect the major counterweight to the much more unified and scholastic approach of the Gelukpa lamas.

The three principal figures of the first generation of Rimé teachers were Jamyang Khyentsé Ongpo (1820–1892), Jamgön Kongtrul (1813–1899) and Chokgyur Lingpa (1829–70). These lamas have all had multiple rebirths, many of whom have played leading roles in Tibetan Buddhism in the twentieth century. These include the Shechen Kongtrul rebirth, Pema Drimé Legkpé Lodro (1901?–1960), Dzongsar Khyentse Jamyang Chöki Lodrö (1896–1959), and Dilgo Khyentse Rabsel Dawa (1910–1991).

Many of the Nyingma, Kagyü and Sakya lamas who have been or are currently active in the West come in part from Rimé backgrounds; this was true for example of lamas such as Kalu Rinpoche and Chögyam Trungpa. The current Dzongsar Khyentse (b.1961), who is the grandson of Dudjom Rinpoche, has a substantial global following, and has also made films (*The Cup, Travellers and Magicians*) under the name Khyentse Norbu.

Yungdrung Bon

As with the Nyingmapa, the Yungdrung Bon tradition was carried mainly by hereditary lay lamas, in this case belonging to six main lineages, some of them still active today. The main Yungdrung Bon teaching monasteries in Tibet were Menri, founded in 1405 by Nyammey Sherab Gyeltsen (1356–1416), and the nearby Yundrungling, dating from 1836.

The Yungdrung tradition, like that of the Nyingmapa, derives much of its teaching from *terma* sources. The first major Bon *tertön* was Shenchen Luga (996–1035); if his traditional dates are correct, he may have predated any of the Buddhist *tertön*. There are many further *tertön*, including the nineteenth-century Dechen Lingpa (1833–70), associated with the 'New Bon' (*bonsar*) tradition, and some Buddhist *tertön*, including Gödemchen and Dorje Lingpa, are said also to have uncovered Bon *terma*. As with the Nyingmapas the practice of finding *terma* still continues.

Menri was re-established in exile in India in 1967, and is directed by the Thirty-third Menri Tridzin, Lungtok Tenpai Nyima (b.1929), with the assistance of Lopon Tenzin Namdak (b.1926); a second traditional teaching centre, headed by Lopon Tenzin Namdak, is at Triten Norbutse near Kathmandu in Nepal. There is also an active Yungdrung Bon organization in the United States under the direction of Tenzin Wangyal Rinpoche (b.c.1960).

Further reading

Smith, Gene E. *Among Tibetan Texts: History and Literature of the Himalayan Plateau.* Boston: Wisdom Publications, 2001.

Glossary

aché lhamo [Tib. a che lha mo] traditional musical plays presenting stories from Buddhist legends.
amban Chinese imperial officials stationed at Lhasa and in Eastern Tibet.
amchi [Tib. a mchi, e mchi] traditional Tibetan doctor.
Amdo [Tib. a mdo] one of the four provinces of Tibet, situated in the northeast.
Anuttarayoga Tantra [Skt.] class of Buddhist Tantric practices.
asura 'demigods' one of the Six Realms of Rebirth; divine beings continually at war with the **deva**.
Atiśa (Dipaṃkara Śrījñāna, ?980–1054) Bengali Buddhist teacher, active in Tibet in the eleventh century.
Avalokiteśvara [Skt.] ***bodhisattva***-deity who represents the compassion of the **Buddha**; see also **Chenresik**.
babdrung [Tib. 'babs sgrung] 'inspired' Gesar bard.
barché [Tib. bar chad] obstacle (generally meaning obstruction by spirits, also inner obstacles to spiritual progress).
Barché Kunsel [Tib. bar chad kun sel] prayer to remove **barché**.
Bardo Tödröl [Tib. bar do thos sgrol] 'Tibetan Book of the Dead'.
béyül [Tib. sbas yul] 'hidden valley'; concealed land, discovered by a **tertön,** to enable people to take refuge for political disturbance or for spiritual purposes. Several Himalayan valleys are regarded as *béyül*.
Bhairava [Skt.] fierce form of **Śiva** associated closely with Tantric traditions.
bhikṣu [Skt.] fully-ordained Buddhist monk, corresponding to Tibetan **gelong.**
bhikṣuni [Skt.] fully-ordained Buddhist nun, corresponding to Tibetan **gelongma**.
bindu [Skt.] internal 'drop', corresponding to **bodhicitta**, manipulated during Tantric inner **yoga** practices.
Bod [Tib. bod] Tibetan name for Tibet; often used to mean primarily Central Tibet.
Bod chenpo [Tib. bod chen po] 'Greater Tibet'; term introduced by Gedün Chopel to cover all areas of traditional Tibetan culture and influence.
bodhi [Skt.] see **Buddhahood.**
bodhicitta [Skt.] 'thought of Enlightenment'; intense desire to attain **Buddhahood** in order to relieve all beings from suffering, the motive force for the attainment of

Buddhahood; in Tantric physiology, male and female sexual fluids as the physical aspect of this motivational force.

bodhisattva [Skt.] person who has made an irreversible vow to attain **Buddhahood**; deity who manifests aspects of **Buddha**-activity.

bombo [Tamang = Tib. bon po] shamanic priests among the Tamang people of Nepal.

Bon [Tib. Bon] term used to describe various pre- and non-Buddhist traditions in Tibet, including the contemporary monastic tradition of **Yungdrung Bon**; **bon** in **Yungdrung Bon** is also a term equivalent to **chö** in Buddhism.

Bonpo [Tib. bon po] follower of the **Bon** tradition.

Buddha [Skt.] term used to describe person or being who has attained state of awakening (**bodhi** or **Buddhahood**), including the historical Buddha Śākyamuni; deity expressing or manifesting aspect of Buddhahood.

Buddhahood state of awakening or Enlightenment (**bodhi**); the central goal of the Buddhist tradition.

Buddhist Tantra see **Vajrayāna**.

Bumshi [Tib. 'bum gzhi] main medical text of the **Bonpo** medical tradition; textually close to the **Gyüshi**, the main text of the mainstream Buddhist Tibetan medical tradition.

Butön Rinchendrub [Tib. Bu ston rin chen grub] Important early scholar of the Shalupa tradition, responsible for the editing of the standard canonical collections of translated Buddhist texts, the **Kangyur** and **Tengyur**.

cakra [Skt.] 'circle' or 'wheel'; in Tantric physiology, the meeting points of the **nāḍī**, the subtle channels along which **prāṇa** circulates.

Cakrasamvara [Skt.] name of important cycle of Buddhist Tantric practices and of its principal deity.

Caryā Tantra [Skt.] class of Buddhist Tantric practices.

chakgya [Tib. phyag rgya = Skt. mudrā] literally 'seal'; a multivalent term referring to ritual hand gestures, also to a real or visualized female consort in Tantric ritual.

cham [Tib. 'chams] Buddhist and **Bonpo** ritual dances, performed as part of monastic ritual or in public as part of monastic festivals.

changchub [Tib. byang chub] Tibetan equivalent to **Buddhahood; bodhi**.

changchub sem [Tib. byang chub sems] Tibetan equivalent to **bodhicitta**.

changchub sempa [Tib. byang chub sems dpa'] Tibetan equivalent to **bodhisattva**.

Chenresik [Tib. spyan ras gzigs] Tibetan name of the Indian bodhisattva **Avalokiteśvara**, believed to have played a guiding role throughout Tibetan history and to have manifested on various occasions in human form, most recently as the **Dalai Lamas**.

chépa [Tib. dpyad pa] diagnosis (in medicine); distinction, differentiation, analysis.

chi [Tib. phyi] outside, later.

chi nang sang [Tib. phyi nang gsang] outer, inner and secret.

chidar [Tib. phyi dar, spyi dar] 'later' or 'general' diffusion of the Buddhist teachings to Tibet from the late tenth to thirteenth centuries, resulting in the New Tantra (**Sarma**) traditions.

chinlab [Tib. byin rlabs] 'blessing' or 'spiritual power' received from a deity or lama.

chö [Tib. chos = Skt. dharma] multivalent term referring to Buddhist religious teachings, underlying nature of the universe (as revealed by these teachings), and to a constituent element of the universe in early Buddhist philosophy.

chöd [Tib. gcod] class of Tibetan practices involving visualization of offering one's body to deities and spirits, accompanied by singing and musical instruments.

Chokgyur Lingpa [Tib. mchog 'gyur gling pa] nineteenth **Nyingmapa** lama associated with the '**Rimé movement**'; later reincarnations of this lama.

chöku [Tib. chos sku] Tibetan equivalent to **dharmakāya**.

chökyong [Tib. chos skyong] deity, generally of Indian or Tibetan origin, who acts as protector of the Buddhist teachings.

chorten [Tib. mchod rten = Skt. *stūpa*] container for holy relics, also acting as symbolic representation of the **dharmakāya**; may be a large outdoors construction, there are also smaller versions inside temples, often containing relics of lamas.

Chucham Gyalmo [Tib. Chu-lcam rgyal-mo] a **Bonpo** goddess.

Cittamātra [Skt.] 'mind-only' teachings, emphasizing the primary role of consciousness in creating phenomenal reality; also known as **Vijñānavāda** or **Yogācāra**.

ḍākiṇī [Skt.] female deities associated with **Tantra**; the Tibetan term (**kandroma**) is used as a term of respect for spiritually-evolved women, also for female spirit-mediums and Tantric consorts of lamas.

daknang [Tib. dag snang] 'pure vision'; term used to describe visionary teachings received by lamas.

Dalai Lamas [Tib. tā la'i bla ma] important series of reincarnate lamas; highest-ranking rebirth series of the **Gelukpa** order, and political rulers of much of Tibet between the seventeenth and the twentieth centuries.

Damngag Dzöd [Tib. gdams ngag mdzod] collection of methods and instructions for practice, compiled in the nineteenth century under the direction of **Jamgön Kongtrul**.

damtsik sempa [Tib. dam tshig sems dpa'] the deity as created 'internally' by the practitioner, to be merged with the **yeshe sempa**.

Derge [Tib. sde dge] small kingdom in Eastern Tibet with traditional affiliations to the **Sakyapa**.

deva [Skt.] generic term for 'god'; also, one of the Six Realms of Rebirth.

Dewachen [Tib. bde ba can = Skt. Sukhāvatī] the eastern paradise presided over by the Buddha Amitābha

Dharamsala Small town in Northern India; residence of the Fourteenth **Dalai Lama** and location of the Tibetan government-in-exile.

dharma [Skt.] term with several overlapping meanings, including Buddhist teachings; fundamental laws of the universe; elements of reality.

dharmakāya [Skt.] '*dharma* body'; one of the three 'bodies' or aspects of manifestation of the **Buddha**; corresponds to the ultimate meaning of Buddha-nature.

Dharmarāja [Skt.] king ruling according to the **Dharma**, king who supports the Dharma

dhyāna [Skt.] meditative absorption; one of the **Six Pāramitā**.

dokpa [Tib. bzlog pa] ritual to avert evil influences or destructive spirits.

Dolpopa Sherab Gyantsen [Tib. dol po pa shes rab rgyal mtshan] important early lama of the **Jonangpa** tradition.

dorjé tegpa [Tib. rdo rje theg pa] Tibetan equivalent to **Vajrayāna**.

drangsong [Tib. drang srong] Tibetan translation for Skt. *ṛṣi* (sage); for **Bonpo**, equivalent to **gelong** (fully-ordained monk).

Drenpa Namka [Tib. dran pa nam mkha'] early **Bonpo** lama.

Drepung [Tib. 'bras spungs] large monastic establishment near Lhasa, consisting of a number of colleges, hostels, hermitages, etc.

Dri River [Tib. 'bri chu] Tibetan name for Yangtse River.

Drigum [Tib. gri gum] legendary early king of Tibet in whose time the 'sky-cord' linking the kings with heaven was broken.

Drikung Kagyüd [Tib. 'bri gung bka' brgyud] sub-division of **Kagyüdpa** tradition.

drokpa [Tib. 'brog pa] pastoralists, Tibetans living a nomadic, pastoralist lifestyle based around herds of yak, cattle and other animals.

Drölma [Tib. sgrol ma] Buddhist goddess, equivalent to Skt. **Tārā**; represents the compassionate action of the **Buddha** to save beings from danger and suffering.

drong [Tib. 'brong] wild yak.

Druk Ralung [Tib. 'Brug Rwa lung] monastery in Central Tibet.

Drukpa Kagyüdpa [Tib. 'Brug pa bka brgyud pa] subdivision of **Kagyüdpa** tradition, originally based at the monastery of Druk Ralung in Central Tibet.

drupta [Tib. grub mtha'] philosophical position or framework; equivalent to Sanskrit **siddhānta**.

Druptap Küntü [Tib. sgrub thabs kun btus] collection of **Sarmapa** texts for ritual practice, compiled in the nineteenth century under the direction of **Loter Wangpo**.

druptop [Tib. grub thob] Tantric practitioner, equivalent to Skt. **siddha**.

Dunhuang texts large cache of texts in Tibetan, Chinese and other languages discovered in caves near the Chinese oasis town of Dunhuang, under Tibetan control for parts of the eighth and nineth centuries and a centre of Tibetan cultural activity for some centuries later. The Dunhuang texts are an important source for early Tibetan religion, culture and history.

Düsum Kyenpa [Tib. dus gsum mkhyen pa] founding lama of **Karma Kagyüdpa**; first lama of the **Gyalwa Karmapa** series of rebirths.

Dza Petrül [Tib. rdza dPal sprul] nineteenth-century lama, author of the ***Kunsang Lamé Shellung***.

Dzamling Gyéshé [Tib. 'dzam gling rgyas bshad] early nineteenth-century Tibetan book presenting a desription of the world (including the countries of Europe).

Dzogchen [Tib. rdzogs chen] 'Great Perfection' teachings; the highest level of teachings in both **Nyingmapa** and **Bon** traditions.

fengshui Chinese techniques for locating and constructing buildings, tombs, etc, so as to maximize their positive spiritual effect.

Four Great Deva Kings set of four **yakṣa** deities associated with the four directions, important in most Buddhist traditions as protectors of the Buddhist teachings and of Buddhist practitioners, and frequently painted at the entrance to Tibetan monasteries.

Ganden [Tib. dga' ldan] large monastic establishment near Lhasa, consisting of a number of colleges, hostels, hermitages, etc.

Ganden Podrang [Tib. dga' ldan pho brang] Dalai Lama's government; originally the name of his personal household at **Drepung**.

Gedündrup [Tib. dge 'dun grub] disciple of Tsongkapa; retrospectively identified as first of the **Dalai Lama** rebirth series.

geko [Tib. dge skos] monk responsible for discipline in monastic community.

gelong [Tib. dge slong] fully-ordained Buddhist monk, corresponding to Skt. **bhikṣu**; highest grade of monastic ordination for men.

gelongma [Tib. dge slong ma] corresponding to Skt. **bhikṣunī**, fully-ordained nun, highest grade of monastic ordination for women.

Gelukpa [Tib. dge lugs pa] one of the **Sarma** ('New') traditions of Tibetan Buddhist practice, dating back to the fourteenth and fifteenth centuries.

genyen [Tib. dge bsnyen = Skt. *upāsaka*] (male) lay follower, ordination taken in Tibet both by laymen and as an initial monastic ordination for men.

genyenma [Tib. dge bsnyen ma = Skt. *upāsīkā*] (female) lay follower, ordination taken in Tibet both by laywomen and as an initial monastic ordination for women.

geshé [Tib. dge bshes = Skt. *kalyāṇamitra*] spiritual teacher or advisor; title of monastic degrees awarded by public examination, especially in the **Gelukpa** tradition.

getsul [Tib. dge tshul = Skt. *śramaṇera*] (male) novice, grade of monastic ordination for men.

getsulma [Tib. dge tshul ma = Skt. *śramaṇerī*) (female) novice, grade of monastic ordination for women.

gomchen [Tib. sgom chen] title for lay religious practitioners in Bhutan.

gompa [Tib. dgon pa] monastery, hermitage, religious centre (not necessarily of celibate monks).

gowé lha [Tib. 'go ba'i lha] set of five deities who look after the fortune of an individual.

Guhyagarbha [Skt.] name of important cycle of Buddhist Tantric practices.

Guhyasamāja [Skt.] name of important cycle of Buddhist Tantric practices and of its principal deity.

guru [Skt.] teacher, especially of **Tantra**.

Guru Rinpoche [Tib. gu ru rin po che] Tibetan name of **Padmasambhava**.

Gushri Khan Mongolian chieftain and political ally of the Fifth **Dalai Lama**.

Gyalwa Karmapa [Tib. rGyal ba Karma pa] title of head lamas of **Karma Kagyüdpa**.

Gyantse [Tib. rgyal rtse] town in West-Central Tibet.

gyelpo [Tib. rgyal po] king.

gyüd [Tib. rgyud] Tantra; Tib. brgyud] lineage, tradition.

Gyüshi [Tib. rgyud bzhi] 'Four Tantras' or 'Fourfold Tantra', name of the principal medical text in the Tibetan medical tradition.

Hevajra [Skt.] name of important cycle of Buddhist Tantric practices and of its principal deity.

Hīnayāna [Skt.] term for the first and lowest of the three 'vehicles' that define the Buddhist path in Tibetan tradition; corresponds in a general sense to the teachings of the **Theravādin** tradition.

iṣṭadevatā [Skt.] deity that serves as focus for personal devotion and spiritual practice, corresponds to Tib. **yidam**.

izzat [Hindi, Urdu, etc.] honour of person/family.

Jainism Indian religion originating in similar early ascetic traditions to Buddhism. Jainas today form a distinct religious group within India.

Jambeyang [Tib. 'Jam dpal dbyangs] Tibetan equivalent for **Mañjuśrī**, *bodhisattva* of wisdom.

Jamgön Kongtrul [Tib. 'jam mgon kong sprul] nineteenth-century **Kagyüdpa** lama associated with the '**Rimé movement**'; later reincarnations of this lama.

Jampa [Tib. byams pa] Tibetan equivalent for **Maitreya**.

Jamyang Khyentsé [Tib. 'jam dbyangs mkhyen brtse] nineteenth-century **Sakyapa** lama associated with the '**Rimé movement**'; later reincarnations of this lama.

Jigmé Lingpa [Tib. 'Jigs med gling pa] **Nyingmapa** lama and **tertön** of late eighteenth century; important influence on the **Rimé** lamas.

jñānasattva [Skt.] equivalent to **yeshesempa**.

jomo [Tib. jo mo] title for nun or other woman of high spiritual attainment.

Jonangpa [Tib. Jo nang pa] One of the Sarma ('New') traditions of Tibetan Buddhist practice, dating back to the eleventh and twelfth centuries. Suppressed in Central Tibet by **Gelukpa** in the seventeenth-century, but survived elsewhere. Known for its endorsement of the **shentong** approach, particularly in relation to **Kālacakra**.

Kadampa [Tib. bka' gdams pa] One of the **Sarma** ('New') traditions of Tibetan Buddhist practice, dating back to the eleventh and twelfth centuries; its teaching traditions were absorbed into later schools, particularly the **Gelukpa**

kagyé [Tib. bka brgyad] eight **Nyingmapa** ritual cycles said to have been passed down from the imperial period.

Kagyüdpa [Tib. bka' brgyud pa] one of the **Sarma** ('New') traditions of Tibetan Buddhist practice, dating back to the eleventh and twelfth centuries.

Kālacakra [Skt.] name of important cycle of Buddhist Tantric practices and of its principal deity.

kama [Tib. bka' ma] teachings believed to have been transmitted by **Padmasambhava** and passed down from lama to disciple to modern times; form a significant part of teachings for the **Nyingmapa**.

Kanam Depa [Tib. ?ka nam sde pa] Traditional ruler of small kingdom of **Powo** in Southern Tibet.

kandroma [Tib. mkha' 'gro ma = Skt. ḍākinī] dangerous female spirit; woman of high spiritual attainment; Tantric consort of high lama; female spirit-medium.

Kangyur [Tib. bka' 'gyur] Tibetan collection of works attributed to the **Buddha**.

karma [Skt.] action; used in English to refer to connection between action and result, especially in a future life.

Karma Kagyüdpa [Tib. karma bka' brgyud pa] Major sub-order of **Kagyüdpa**.

Karma Pakshi [Tib. karma pakṣi] lama of **Karma Kagyüdpa** tradition; second lama of the **Gyalwa Karmapa** series of rebirths.

karuṇā [Skt.] compassion.

kenpo [Tib. mkhan po] abbot, administrative head of a monastery or other religious centre.

Kham [Tib. khams] one of the four provinces of Tibet, situated in the east.

korwa [Tib. 'khor ba] literally, 'circling'; Tibetan equivalent to **saṃsāra**.

Kriyā Tantra [Skt.] class of Buddhist Tantric practices.

ku sung tuk [Tib. sku gsung thugs] body speech and mind; traditional Tibetan division of the entire human mind–body complex.

Kumbum [Tib. sku 'bum] major **Gelukpa** monastery in Northeast Tibet, close to the modern Chinese city of Xining; birthplace of **Tsongkapa**.

kundzob denpa [Tib. kun rdzob bden pa] relative or conventional truth; equivalent to Skt. **saṃvṛti-satya**.

Kunsang Lamé Shellung [Tib. Kun bzang bla ma'i zhal lung] classic commentary to the ***Longchen Nyingtik*** **ngöndro** practices by the nineteenth-century lama Dza Peltrül.

kusum [Tib. sku gsum] equivalent to Skt. **trikāya**.

kuten [Tib. sku rten] 'support'; oracle priest (as 'support' for the deity which possesses him or her).

Kutse Da-ö [Tib. Khu tshe zla 'od] name of a **Bonpo tertön**.

kyabdro [Tib. skyabs 'gro] going for refuge to the **Buddha**, **Dharma** and **Saṅgha**.

la [Tib. bla] vitality, power, separable soul-substance.

labrang or **ladrang** [Tib. bla brang] household (economic unit) associated with a lama.

Labrang [Tib. bla brang; C Xiahe] town in Northeast Tibet which grew up next to the monastery of **Labrang Tashikyil**.

Labrang Tashikyil [Tib. bla brang bkra shis 'khyil] major Gelukpa monastery in Northeast Tibet.

lam rim [Tib. lam rim] 'gradual path' or 'stages of the path'; systematic arrangement of **Sūtra** teachings in the Gelukpa tradition; other traditions have similar sets of teachings.

lama [Tib. bla ma] Tantric guru and ritual officiant; teacher; senior religious practitioner.

Lamdre [Tib. lam 'bras] system of teachings in the **Sakyapa** tradition, based on the ***Hevajra Tantra*** and said to derive from the mahāsiddha Virūpa.

Lamé Latso [Tib. bla ma'i bla mtsho] lake in Central Tibet where lamas traditionally go for visions of rebirths of the **Dalai Lama** and other high lamas.

laptsé [Tib. la btsas] cairn for worship of local gods.

lari [Tib. bla ri] mountain connected with the spiritual welfare of a particular region, family or person.

laru [Tib. klu rol] festivals for local spirits in Rebkong and nearby areas of Amdo (Qinghai), involving dances for men and women and possession of spirit-mediums

latso [Tib. bla mtsho] lake connected with the spiritual welfare of a particular region, family or person.

Lekshé Dzö [Tib. legs bshad mdzod] 'Treasury of Good Sayings', **Bonpo** historical text.

lha [Tib. lha] god (general term, corresponding to Skt. *deva*).

Lhakang [Tib. lha khang] temple.

lhaktong [Tib. lhag mthong] Tibetan equivalent to **vipaśyanā**.

lhawa [Tib. lha pa] spirit-medium, person through whom a god communicates while in state of possession.

Ling Gesar [Tib. gLing Ge sar] Tibetan epic hero.

longchödku [Tib. longs spyod sku] Tibetan equivalent to **saṃbhogakāya**.

Longchen Nyingtik **teachings** [Tib. klong chen snying thig] important series of **terma** revelations by **Jigmé Lingpa**, associated with visions of **Longchen Rabjampa**.

Longchen Rabjampa [Tib. klong chen rab 'byams pa] important fourteenth-century lama and scholar of the **Nyingmapa** tradition.

Loter Wangpo [Tib. ngor pa dpon slob blo gter dbang po] disciple of **Jamyang Khyentsé** and compiler of the ***Druptap Kuntü***.

lu [Tib. klu] spirit associated with lakes and rivers; equated to Indian **nāga**.

lung [Tib. rlung] Tibetan equivalent to Sanskrit **prāṇa** (also equivalent to **vāta**).

lungta [Tib. rlung rta] pieces of cloth or paper printed with mantras and religious emblems, usually in the colours of the five elements, tied on strings or thrown as offerings to local gods in order to secure good fortune and avert obstacles.

Ma Namka [Tib. ma nam mkha' dang mnyams pa'i ...] name of Tibetan refuge formula.

Mādhyamika [Skt.] School of Buddhist teachings which gives primacy to insight into the voidness or emptiness of phenomena.

Mahākāla [Skt.] Buddhist Tantric deity related to **Bhairava**.

Mahāmudrā [Skt.] term for direct experience of reality in **Anuttarayoga Tantra**; the goal of the Buddhist **siddhas**.

Mahāyāna [Skt.] term for the second of the three 'vehicles' that define the Buddhist path in Tibetan tradition.

Mahāyoga [Skt.] class of **Tantras**.

Maitreya [Skt.] Buddhist deity, who will eventually become the next **Buddha** of this world and age.

maṇḍala [Skt.] (1) geometrical array of deities visualized, imagined or represented in two or three dimensions; (2) physical offering, usually of rice, often mixed with precious stones, on a special offering plate, representing the entire universe of traditional Buddhist cosmology with Mount Meru at its centre.

Mani Kabum [Tib. ma ni bka' 'bum] **terma** text narrating the history of Avalokiteśvara, his manifestation as Songtsen Gampo and his association with Tibet.

Mañjuśrī [Skt.] Bodhisattva-deity who represents the wisdom (**prajñā**) of the Buddha.

mantra [Skt.] ritual formula, generally employed in the invocation of a Tantric deity.

māra [Skt.] demonic spirit.

Marpa [Tib. Mar pa] Tibetan lama, said to have visited India and studied with **Nāropa**.

Milarepa [Tib. Mi la ras pa] Tibetan lama and writer of spiritual songs, studied with **Marpa**. His disciples founded the various **Kagyüdpa** lineages.

Menla [Tib. sman bla = Skt. Bhaiṣajyaguru] **Buddha** of medicine and healing.

mo [Tib. mo] divination.

mudrā [Skt.] see **chakgya**.

nāḍī [Skt.] channel, river; in Tantric physiology, the subtle channels within the human body along which **prāṇa** circulates.

nāga [Skt.] Indian water-spirit, in Tibet equated with **lu**.

namshé [Tib. rnam shes] 'consciousness'; equivalent to Skt. **vijñāna**. Includes the subtle 'consciousness' that continues from one rebirth to the next.

namtar [Tib. rnam thar] biography or autobiography, usually of a lama, structured in terms of the subject's spiritual progress.

nang [Tib. nang] inside.

nangpa [Tib. nang pa] insider.

nangpé sangyepé chö [Tib. nang pa'i sangs rgyas pa'i chos] 'the Buddhist **dharma** of the insiders'; Buddhism

Nāropa [Skt.] Indian **siddha** regarded as ancestral by the **Kagyüdpa** tradition. His 'Six Teachings' or 'Six Doctrines' [Tib. nā ro chos drug] are an important set of Completion Stage practices passed down particularly within the **Kagyüdpa** and **Gelukpa**.

neljor [Tib. rnal 'byor] Tibetan term for **yoga**, generic term for forms of spiritual practice involving techniques of mind–body cultivation.

neljorma [Tib. rnal 'byor ma] female practitioner of **yoga**; female deities associated with Tantric practice [= Skt. **yogini**].

ngadar [Tib. snga dar] 'early diffusion' of the Buddhist teachings to Tibet at the time of the early Tibetan empire (seventh to ninth century CE)

ngagpa [Tib. sngags pa] Tantric ritual specialist.

Ngari [Tib. mnga' ris] One of the four provinces of Tibet, situated in the west.

ngöndro [Tib. sngon 'gro] preliminary practices, non-Tantric or Tantric.

Ngorpa [Tib. ngor pa] subdivision of **Sakya** tradition.

ngotsha [Tib. sgo tsha] shame, embarrassment.

ngowa [Tib. sngo ba] dedication of merit, expression that the result of one's virtuous actions should have a particular effect.

Nikāya ordination traditions of early Buddhism; traditionally eighteen in number, and associated with distinct doctrinal positions.

Nikāya Buddhism term often now used for the early Buddhist teachings classified by the Tibetans as 'Hīnayāna'. The **Theravāda** tradition claims to represent the Buddhism of this period.

nirmāṇakāya [Skt.] 'emanation body'; one of the three 'bodies' or aspects of manifestation of the **Buddha**; see **trulku**.

nirvāṇa [Skt.] state of extinction of craving and so relief from sufferings of **saṃsāra**; the ultimate goal of the **Hīnayāna** teachings, but regarded in the **Mahāyāna** as an intermediate goal to be superseded by the attainment of **Buddhahood** (**bodhi**).

norbum [Tib. nor 'bum] vase filled with precious substances and consecrated in special ritual to increase wealth and prosperity.

nyangendé [Tib. mya ngan 'das] Tibetan equivalent for **nirvāṇa**.

nyépa [Tib. nyes pa = Skt. doṣa] the three main causes of illness in Tibetan medicine (**lung, tipa, peken**).

Nyingma [Tib. rnying ma] Literally, 'old'; here referring to the Nyingma school or **Nyingmapa**.

Nyingmapa [Tib. rnying ma pa] a tradition of Tibetan Buddhism that traces its origins back to the 'early diffusion' (**ngadar**) of the Buddhist teachings to Tibet at the time of the early empire (seventh to ninth century CE) and particularly to the activity of the Indian teacher **Padmasambhava**.

Nyingmé Gyudbum [Tib. rnying ma'i rgyud 'bum] collection of Tantric scriptures from the **Nyingma** tradition.

nyungné [Tib. smyung gnas] fasting ritual carried out by lay people or monastics, at full moon or for longer periods; may be done on behalf of someone else to gain merit for that person.

Olmo Lungring [Tib. 'ol mo lung ring] name of valley to west of Tibet; legendary home of **Tönpa Shenrab** and place of origin of **Yungdrung Bon**, situated in **Tazik**.

Padmasambhava [Skt.] primal lama of **Nyingmapa** tradition; a probably semi-legendary Tantric master who is said to have visited Tibet towards end of early empire, in late eighth century. In Tibetan usually referred to as **Guru Pema Jungné** or **Guru Rinpoche**.

Palden Lhamo [Tib. dPal ldan lha mo] Buddhist goddess; protector of Lhasa and the **Dalai Lamas**.

Panchen Lama [Tib. paṇ chen bla ma] second most senior reincarnate lama of the **Gelukpa** tradition; his residence was at **Tashilhunpo**.

Panchen Rinpoche [Tib. paṇ chen rin po che] see **Panchen Lama**.

Papün [Tib. pha spun] patrilineage, group defined by male descent, literally 'father-brother'.

Pāramitā; see **Six Pāramitā**.

paritta [Pali] Buddhist Sūtra recited for protection in **Theravāda** countries.

pawo [Tib. dpa' bo] spirit-medium, person through whom god communicates while in state of possession.

Pema Jungné [Tib. padma 'byung gnas] Tibetan name of **Padmasambhava**.

Phurba [Tib. phur ba] Buddhist Tantric deity important for **Nyingmapa** and **Sakyapa**, equivalent to Skt. **Vajrakilaya**; related **Bon** deity.

powa [Tib. 'pho ba] practices for transfer of consciousness to higher realm at death.

Powo [Tib. spo bo] small kingdom in Southern Tibet.

prajñā [Skt.] wisdom of the **Buddha**; insight into the nature of reality. One of the **Three Trainings**. Also one of the **Six Pāramitā**.

prāṇa [Skt.] breath; in Tantric physiology, the subtle breath that circulates through the **nāḍī** and **cakra** of the subtle body.

pratītyasamūtpada [Skt.] dependent origination, Buddhist principle of phenomena arising in mutual dependence; equivalent to Tib. **tendel**.

preta [Skt.] 'hungry ghosts'; beings are born into the *preta* realm as a result of greed in a former life.

rabjung [Tib. rab 'byung] renunciation of worldly life; ceremony on entering monastic life.

rangtong [Tib. rang stong] 'empty of own-nature'; Tibetan philosophical approach which stresses emptiness, and contrasts with **shentong**.

Ratna Lingpa [Tib. ratna gling pa] fifteenth-century lama; compiler and editor of the ***Nyingmé Gyudbum***.

reincarnate lamas lamas identified as rebirths of a previous lama and generally appointed to the position and status of the previous identity. See ***trulku***.

religious tradition this relatively neutral term has been generally used in the book rather than sect, school or order, since none of these is fully appropriate in the Tibetan context.

rig-nga [Tib. rigs lnga] literally 'Five Families [of Buddhas]', headdress with images or symbols of the Five **Buddhas** worn by spirit mediums and others.

rimé [Tib. ris med] impartial, unbiased, eclectic; term used as a description of the approach of a group of important late nineteenth century lamas in Eastern Tibet, sometimes described by Western scholars as the **Rimé Movement**.

Rinchen Terdzöd [Tib. rin chen gter mdzod] collection of **terma** teachings, compiled in the nineteenth century under the direction of **Jamgön Kongtrul**.

Rinchen Zangpo [Tib. rin chen bzang po] early lama and translator (958–1055).

rongpa [Tib. rong pa] valley people, farmers, agriculturalists.

rü [Tib. rus] patrilineage, group defined by male descent, literally 'bone.'

rüpa [Tib. rus pa] patrilineage, group defined by male descent.

saché [Tib. sa dpyad] siting of buildings in relation to landscape so as to maximize positive influences

sadak [Tib. sa bdag] local god.

sādhanā [Skt.] religious practice, in Tantric Buddhism generally a practice for the invocation of a particular Tantric deity.

sādhu [Skt.] Indian ascetic practitioner.

Śaiva, Śaivite religion, **Śaivism** Indian religious traditions centring on the worship of the god **Śiva**.

Sakya [Tib. sa skya] Literally, 'grey earth'; name of the location of the founding monastery of the **Sakyapa** tradition. (NB The word 'Sakya' is *not* related to Śākya, the name of the historical Buddha's clan.)

Sakya Paṇḍita [Tib. Sa skya paṇḍita] important early scholar of the **Sakyapa** tradition.

Śākyamuni [Skt.] epithet used to refer to the historical **Buddha**, who probably lived in the fifth century BCE. Also known as Gautama or Siddhartha.

Sakyapa [Tib. sa skya pa] one of the **Sarma** ('New') traditions of Tibetan Buddhist practice, dating back to the eleventh and twelfth centuries.

samādhi [Skt.] meditation as a part of the Buddhist path. One of the **Three Trainings**.

śamatha [Skt.] meditation to develop **dhyāna**.

samayasattva [Skt.] see Tibetan **damtsik sempa**.

sambhogakāya [Skt.] 'enjoyment body'; one of the three 'bodies' or aspects of manifestation of the **Buddha**; corresponds to the plane of manifestation of Tantric deities.

saṃsāra [Skt.] phenomenal reality; everyday life characterized as an unending series of rebirths.

saṃvṛti-satya [Skt.] relative or conventional truth.

Samyé [Tib. bsam yas] First Tibetan monastery, founded in Central Tibet in the late eighth century CE.
sang [Tib. bsangs] smoke-offering of scented herbs and woods to local gods.
sangchö [Tib. bsangs mchod] **sang**-offering ritual.
Saṅgha [Skt.] Buddhist community, including monastic and lay members.
Sangpo Bumtri [Tib. Sangs-po 'Bum-khri] **Bonpo** deity.
sangyé [Tib. sangs rgyas] Tibetan equivalent to **buddha**.
sangyum [Tib. gsang yum] 'secret/esoteric mother'; Tantric consort of a male **yogin** or married lama.
Sarma [Tib. gsar ma] Literally 'new', here referring to the Sarma or 'New' schools of Tibetan Buddhist practice, traditions that trace their origins back to the 'later transmission' of the Buddhist teachings to Tibet in the tenth to thirteenth centuries CE. The most important Sarma schools are the **Kagyüdpa**, **Sakyapa** and **Gelukpa**.
Sarmapa [Tib. gsar ma pa] follower of one of the **Sarma** traditions.
Sarvāstivādin One of the ordination lineages (**Nikāya**) of early Buddhism; set of teachings associated with this lineage.
Satrig Ersang [Tib. Sa-trig Er-sangs] **Bonpo** goddess.
Sékar [Tib. gsas mkhar] set of five fierce **Bonpo** deities.
semchen [Tsems can] 'sentient beings', beings that have consciousness.
semkyé [Tib. (byang chub) sems bskyed] practices for arousing **bodhicitta**.
semtsampa [Tib. sems tsam pa] 'mind-only' or **Cittamātra** teachings.
Sera [Tib. se ra] large monastic establishment near Lhasa, consisting of a number of colleges, hostels, hermitages, etc.
Shakya Tubpa [Śākya thub pa] Tibetan equivalent for **Śākyamuni**, name of the historical **Buddha**.
Shalupa [Tib. zha lu pa] one of the **Sarma** ('New') traditions of Tibetan Buddhist practice, dating back to the eleventh and twelfth centuries; its teaching traditions were absorbed into later schools, particularly the **Gelukpa**.
Shangshung [Tib. zhang zhung] kingdom to west of the early Tibetan empire which was incorporated into the Tibetan empire in around 650 CE; the kings of Shangshung were said to have been supporters of the **Bon** religion, and many **Yungdrung Bon** teachings are claimed to be translations from **terma** texts in the Shangshung language.
Shangshung Nyengyüd [Tib. zhang zhung snyan rgyud] **Bon Dzogchen** traditions held to have been transmitted, initially orally, from **Shangshung**.
Shardza Tashi Gyaltsen [Tib. Shar rdza bkra shis rgyal mtshan] twentieth-century **Bon** lama.
shedra [Tib. bshad grwa] college for Buddhist study, generally forming part of a monastery.
shen [Tib. gshen] priest of pre-Buddhist court religion.
Shenchen Luga [Tib. gShen chen kLu dga'] important early **Bonpo tertön**.
Shenlha Ökar [Tib. gShen lha 'Od dkar] **Bonpo** creator god.
Shenrab Mibo [Tib. gshen rab mi bo] founding figure of the **Bonpo** religious tradition; regarded as a **buddha**. Also known as **Tönpa Shenrab**.

shentong [Tib. gzhan stong] 'empty of other-nature'; Tibetan philosophical position closely connected with yogic circles and **Kālacakra** practice; revived in the nineteenth century, an important influence on some **Rimé** lamas.

sherap [Tib. shes rab] wisdom of the Buddha; insight into the nature of reality; equivalent to Skt. **prajñā**.

Shigatse [Tib. gzhis dkar rtse] town in West-Central Tibet.

shiné [Tib. zhi gnas] Tibetan equivalent to **śamatha**.

shingpa [Tib. zhing pa] farmers, agriculturalists.

shipdak [Tib. gzhi bdag] local deity.

siddha [Skt.] term for Tantric practitioner in **Śaivite** or **Vajrayāna** tradition; the Tibetan form (**druptop**) is also used as a title by Tibetan lamas and practitioners.

siddhānta [Skt.] philosophical position or framework.

siddhi [Skt.] power obtained through Tantric practice.

śīla [Skt.] discipline and morality as a part of the Buddhist path. One of the **Three Trainings**.

Sipé Dzöp'ug [Tib. srid pa'i mdzod phug] **Bonpo** narrative of origins of universe.

Sipé Gyalmo [Tib. Srid pa'i rgyal mo)] Bonpo goddess.

Śiva [Skt.] important Indian ('Hindu') deity, significant for the development of Tantric traditions in India.

Six Pāramitā or 'perfections' **dāna** (generosity), **śīla** (discipline, self-control), **kṣānti** (patience), **vīrya** (energy, perseverance), **dhyāna** (meditative concentration), **prajñā** (wisdom).

Six Realms of Rebirth **deva**, **asura**, humans, animals, **preta**, hell-beings.

sonam [Tib. bsod nams] 'merit' or good **karma**.

Songtsen Gampo [Tib. Srong btsan sgam po] important early Tibetan emperor (early seventh century).

śramaṇera see **getsul**.

śramaṇerī see **getsulma**.

stūpa see **chorten**.

subtle body: subtle structure of the body, comprised of channels and **chakra**, through which the **lung** (Skt. **prāṇa**) circulates.

sungbum [Tib. gsung 'bum] term for the collected writings of a lama.

sungma [Tib. srung ma] guardian deity.

śūnyatā [T] 'emptiness' or voidness; teaching of the ultimate lack of independent existence of phenomenal reality.

Sūtra [Skt.] text regarded as presenting the teachings of the **Buddha Śākyamuni**; also class of such texts, kinds of practice associated with such texts.

Taklung Kagyüd [Tib. stag lung bka' brgyud] sub-division of **Kagyüdpa** tradition.

Tantra [Skt.] text regarded as presenting the teachings of the Buddha **Śākyamuni**, generally in visionary form; also class of such texts, kinds of practice associated with such texts; **Śaiva**, **Vaiṣṇava** and **Jaina** texts including similar practices.

tap [Tib. thabs] means, method, Tibetan equivalent to **upāya(-kauśalya)**.

Tārā [Skt.] Buddhist goddess; represents the compassionate action of the Buddha to save beings from danger and suffering.

Tashilhunpo [Tib. bkra shis lhun po] large monastery near **Shigatse**; seat of the **Panchen Lamas**.

Tazik [Tib. stag gzigs] term for regions to west of Tibet, possibly referring to Iranian-speaking peoples but not clearly locatable. Area from which the **Yungdrung Bon** teachings are held to originate (see also **Olmo Lungring**).

tendrel [Tib. rten 'brel] Tibetan translation of **pratītyasamūtpada**; has additional meanings of karmic connection, omen, sign of positive future event.

Tengyur [Tib. bstan 'gyur] Tibetan collection of Buddhist works translated from Sanskrit and other Buddhist languages, including commentaries on Buddhist scriptures.

terbum [Tib. gter 'bum] 'treasure-vase', vase filled with precious substances and consecrated in Tantric ritual in order to generate positive and auspicious influences.

terma [Tib. gter ma] 'concealed' or 'treasure' teachings believed to have been transmitted by **Padmasambhava** during his visit to Tibet, hidden and rediscovered in material or spiritual form by his reborn disciples; form a major part of teachings for the **Nyingmapa**.

tertön [Tib. gter ston] lama who discovers or reveals **terma** teachings; **tertön** are believed to be rebirths of disciples of **Padmasambhava**.

theology Western scholars have traditionally referred to the systematic scholarly elaboration of Buddhist thought as 'philosophy', on the grounds that while there are obvious parallels to theology in other religious traditions, Buddhists were not primarily concerned with understanding the existence and nature of deity. Recently some Western scholars have suggested that the term 'theology' should be used. I have gone for 'philosophy' in this book, as the more familiar usage.

Theravāda, Theravādin Buddhist tradition today found mainly in Southeast Asia and Sri Lanka, claiming to represent original teachings of the **Buddha**.

Three Trainings or **Triple Training** discipline (**śīla**), meditation (**samādhi**) and wisdom or insight into reality (**prajñā**).

tiklé [Tib. thig le] Tibetan equivalent to **bindu**.

tongpanyid [Tib. stong pa nyid] Tibetan equivalent for **śūnyatā**.

Tönpa Shenrab [Tib. ston pa gshen rab] founding figure of the **Bonpo** religious tradition; regarded as a **Buddha**. Also known as **Shenrab Mibo**.

torma [Tib. gtor ma] cake made of barley-flour and butter, coloured and often with elaborate decorations, offered to deities in Tantric rituals.

tradition see **religious tradition**.

Trigyel Kugpa [Tib. Khri-rgyal khug-pa] **Bonpo** creator god, also known as **Shenlha Ökar**.

trikāya [Skt.] 'three bodies' or aspects of manifestation of the **Buddha**; see **dharmakāya, nirmāṇakāya** and **sambhogakāya**.

Trisong Detsen [Tib. Khri srong lde'u btsan] important early Tibetan emperor (late eighth century).

trulkor [Tib. 'phrul 'khor, 'khrul 'khor] physical exercises performed as part of yogic practice, with the aim of improving control over **tsalung**.

trulku [Tib. sprul sku] 'emanation body', Tibetan equivalent to **nirmāṇakāya**; one of the three 'bodies' or aspects of manifestation of the **Buddha**. Some lamas are described as *trulku*, which implies that they are human manifestations of Tantric deities, and also in most cases that they are recognized rebirths of a previous lama ('**reincarnate lamas**').

tsalung [Tib. rtsa rlung] see **subtle body**.

tsam [Tib. mtshams] meditation retreat.

tsampa [Tib. rtsam pa] barley-flour, basic Tibetan foodstuff.

Tsang [Tib. gtsang] Western part of **Ü-Tsang**; its principal urban centres are at **Shigatse** and **Gyantse**.

tsawé lama [Tib. rtsa ba'i bla ma] 'root lama', one's principal guru or spiritual teacher.

tsedrup [Tib. tshe sgrub] ritual for attainment of long life.

tseguk [Tib. tshe 'gugs] ritual for recovery of lost life-force.

Tselpa [Tib. tshal pa] subdivision of **Sakya** tradition.

tsen [Tib. btsan] dangerous supernatural being.

tsenpo [Tib. btsan po] emperor; title of the rulers of the early Tibetan empire (referred to by Chinese as Tubo) which was based initially in the Yarlung Valley, later at Lhasa.

tsewang [Tib. tshe dbang] 'life-empowerment', ritual for conveying long life to others.

tsokshing [Tib. tshogs shing, tshogs zhing] 'refuge field' or 'refuge tree'; visualization of Buddhist deities, generally centred on one's lama or **yidam**, before which one takes refuge.

Tsongkapa [Tib. tsong kha pa] founding lama of the **Gelukpa** tradition.

tukjé [Tib. thugs rje = Skt. **karuṇā**] compassion.

tuktrul [Tib. thugs sprul] emanation of mind or consciousness of lama.

Ü [Tib. dbus] eastern part of **Ü-Tsang**; its principal urban centre is at Lhasa.

Ü-Tsang [Tib. dbus gtsang] one of the four provinces of Tibet, situated in the centre of Tibet.

umapa [Tib. dbu ma pa] Tibetan equivalent for **Mādhyamika** teachings.

upāsaka see **genyen**.

upāsikā see **genyenma**.

upāya [Skt.] 'means' often used for **upāya-kauśalya**.

upāya-kauśalya [Skt.] 'skill in means [for attaining Buddhahood and exercising the powers of the Buddha]', an important concept in Tibetan Buddhism.

Vaiṣṇava [Skt.] Indian religious traditions centring on the worship of the god **Viṣṇu**.

Vajrabhairava [Skt.] Buddhist Tantric deity related to **Bhairava**.

Vajradhara [Skt.] Tantric form of the **Buddha**.

Vajrakilaya [Skt.] Buddhist Tantric deity important for **Nyingmapa** and **Sakyapa**. Equivalent to Tibetan **Phurba**.

Vajrapaṇi [Skt.] Buddhist Tantric deity, originally a **yakṣa** protector of the **Buddha**, later an important Tantric deity similar to **Bhairava**.

Vajrasattva [Skt.] Buddhist Tantric deity, particularly associated with purificatory practices.

Vajrayāna [Skt.] Sanskrit term for Tantric practices employed as part of the Buddhist path; the third of the three 'vehicles' that define the Buddhist path in Tibetan tradition.

vijñāna [Skt.] 'consciousness'; equivalent to Tib. **namshé**.

Vijñānavāda [Skt.] 'mind-only' teachings, emphasizing the primary role of consciousness in creating phenomenal reality; also known as **Cittamātra** or **Yogācāra**.

vinaya [Skt.] monastic disciplinary code.

vipaśyanā [Skt.] meditation to develop **prajñā**.

Viṣṇu [Skt.] important Brahmanical (Hindu) deity.

wang [Tib. dbang] power, empowerment, empowerment ritual.

Wangchuk Dorje [Tib. dbang phyug rdo rje] Karma Kagyüdpa lama (1556–1603); Ninth of the **Gyalwa Karmapa** rebirth series.

weikza [Burmese] persons with occult power.

yakṣa [Skt.] class of Indian deities, including the **Four Great Deva Kings**.

yeshe sempa [Tib. ye shes sems dpa'] the **yidam** or Tantric deity as an 'external' reality, summoned in Tantric ritual to merge with the inner invocation of the **damtsik sempa**.

Yeshe Tsogyal [Tib. Ye shes mtsho rgyal] Tibetan princess, female consort of **Padmasambhava**, believed to have written down the **terma** teachings.

yoga [Skt.] generic term for forms of spiritual practice involving techniques of mind–body cultivation.

Yoga Tantra [Skt.] class of Buddhist Tantric practices.

Yogācāra [Skt.] 'mind-only' teachings, emphasizing the primary role of consciousness in creating phenomenal reality; also known as **Vijñānavāda** or **Cittamātra**.

yidam [Tib. yi dam] deity that serves as focus for personal devotion and spiritual practice; equivalent to Skt. **iṣṭ adevatā**.

yogin [Skt.] person who practises (Tantric) yoga.

yoginī [Skt.] female practitioner of yoga; female deities associated with **Śiva** in **Śaiva Tantra** and also occurring in Tibetan Buddhism (see **neljorma**).

yül lha [Tib. yul lha] local god.

yungdrung [Tib. g.yung drung] swastika symbol used by **Yungdrung Bon** and **Buddhists**.

Zangdok Pelri [Tib. zangs mdog dpal ri] 'Glorious Copper-Coloured Mountain', the paradise presided over by **Guru Rinpoche** (**Padmasambhava**).

Index

Note: An asterisk after the number indicates a glossary entry. Numbers in italics indicate illustrations.